STRUCTURAL, HISTORICAL, AND COMPARATIVE PERSPECTIVES

SOCIOLOGICAL STUDIES OF CHILDREN AND YOUTH

Series Editor: David A. Kinney (from 1999)

Series Editors: David A. Kinney and Katherine Brown Rosier (from 2004)

Recent Volumes:

SOCIOLOGICAL STUDIES OF CHILDREN AND YOUTH
VOLUME 12

STRUCTURAL, HISTORICAL, AND COMPARATIVE PERSPECTIVES

GUEST EDITOR

JENS QVORTRUP

*Department of Sociology and Political Science,
Norwegian University of Science and Technology,
Trondheim, Norway*

SERIES EDITORS

KATHERINE BROWN ROSIER
DAVID A. KINNEY

*Department of Sociology, Central Michigan University,
Michigan, USA*

United Kingdom – North America – Japan
India – Malaysia – China

Emerald Group Publishing Limited
Howard House, Wagon Lane, Bingley BD16 1WA, UK

Copyright © 2009 Emerald Group Publishing Limited

Reprints and permission service
Contact: booksandseries@emeraldinsight.com

British Library Cataloguing in Publication Data
A catalogue record for this book is available from the British Library

ISBN: 978-1-78441-322-4
ISSN: 1537-4661 (Series)

Printed and bound by CPI Group (UK) Ltd, Croydon, CR0 4YY

Awarded in recognition of
Emerald's production
department's adherence to
quality systems and processes
when preparing scholarly
journals for print

INVESTOR IN PEOPLE

I am grateful to the series editors, Katherine Brown Rosier and David A. Kinney, for their invitation to me to act as a guest editor, and I thank them for their unfailing support and patience.

CONTENTS

LIST OF CONTRIBUTORS

Maria Carmen Belloni	Dipartimento di Scienze Sociali, University of Torino, Torino, Italy
Victoria L. Blanchard	Department of Sociology, University of Albany, SUNY, Albany, NY, USA
Luigi Campiglio	Institute of Political Economy, Catholic University of Milano, Milano, Italy
Paul Close	Centre for Higher Education Research and Information (CHERI), The Open University, London, UK
Nancy A. Denton	Department of Sociology, University of Albany, SUNY, Albany, NY, USA
Richard H. de Lone[†]	Carnegie Council of Children (1972–1979) and at his death at Public/Private Ventures in Philadelphia, USA
Donald J. Hernandez	Department of Sociology, Hunter College, City University of New York, New York, NY, USA
An-Magritt Jensen	Department of Sociology and Political Science, Norwegian University of Science and Technology (NTNU), Trondheim, Norway
Vegard Johansen	Eastern Norway Research Institute, Hamar, Norway
Madeleine Leonard	School of Sociology, Social Policy and Social Work, Queen's University, Belfast, Northern Ireland, UK
Suzanne Macartney	U.S. Census Bureau, Washington, DC, USA

Thomas Olk   Faculty of Philosophy III – Educational
                            Sciences, Martin-Luther-University,
                            Halle-Wittenberg, Germany

Jens Qvortrup   Department of Sociology and Political
                            Science, Norwegian University of Science
                            and Technology (NTNU), Trondheim,
                            Norway

Giovanni B. Sgritta   Department of Demography, University
                            'La Sapienza', Rome, Italy

Alison M. S. Watson   Department of International Relations,
                            University of St Andrews, Fife,
                            Scotland, UK

EDITORIAL BOARD

MACRO-SOCIOLOGICAL STUDIES OF CHILDHOOD: A PROLOGUE TO A GUEST ISSUE

Thirty years ago, Richard H. de Lone wrote a remarkable book that appears to have sunk into oblivion. The context and aim of this volume is a good opportunity for reviving the book because it represents an excellent application of a macro-sociological perspective. Its main thesis is that it is children, who are the bearers of the American dream, and that it is they who shall rescue the nation from inequalities. Over and over again throughout US history, the recipe has been investments in education in the hope that these measures eventually will solve inherent tensions between economic rationality (market capitalism producing inequalities) and political aims (favouring equality). In other words, de Lone argues, rather than approaching structural problems with positive bearings on childhood here and now, children are expected to have their individual lot improved in the hope that equality appears in the next generation. In this sense, children are instrumentalised for solving deep-seated tensions in society. This is the wrong order, as de Lone suggests it in the book's concluding chapter: Instead of trying to reduce inequality by helping children, we may be able to help children by reducing inequality (de Lone, 1979, p. 178).

By reprinting chapter 1 from de Lone, the attention is also turned to the full text of his book, which deliberately and successfully brought childhood into a much broader context than one was used to at the time. He forcefully claimed that an analysis of childhood cannot stop at the family level, not even at the level of neighbourhood or local community; indeed, a serious account requires that we come to terms full scale with influences from economy, politics and ideology.

de Lone could not at the time of writing have an idea of an incipient break through a few years later of a 'new paradigm of childhood', a 'new sociology of childhood' or – as it is now more often called – 'social studies of childhood' (Qvortrup, Corsaro, & Honig, 2009a). This innovation was understood as a supplement to psychological child development research with a claim to understand childhood as a social phenomenon. Social studies of childhood, in the wake of fervent research activities in the new field, soon came to face fruitful controversies about its self-understanding; should we talk about sociology of children or sociology of childhood; how should we balance agency and structure in our analyses; is childhood mainly to be seen as a small-scale phenomenon or are children and childhood interesting also for and as a part of the larger social fabric and so on? (About this development, see Qvortrup, Corsaro, & Honig, 2009b).

A significant statement by US psychologist James Garbarino is helpful in delimiting what macro-sociological studies of childhood could be, while contending that in our modern era, to be a child is

> to be shielded from the direct demands of economic, political and sexual forces ... childhood is a time to maximize the particularistic and to minimize the universalistic, a definition that should be heeded by educators, politicians, and parents alike. (Garbarino, 1986, p. 120)

In a sense, I do not want to polemicize against the message, because at one level it is one we can all sympathise with. At the same time, the expressed standpoint may harbour risks that run counter to its intention. Despite all good wishes for children, they are not necessarily well served by being contained, confined, controlled and protected in a particularistic world. One may raise at least two questions: Is it true that children live in a particularistic world and do we have a chance to prevent them from it? and will children who have stayed in such a world be well equipped to enter the universalistic world that awaits them after childhood?

We – and this 'we' definitely includes children – currently live in a world that holds many challenges and dangers; it is not by chance that the notion of risk society has gained currency in recent decades (Beck, 1986). The financial crisis and economic recession, which now befall us, apparently expose even the rich world to threats that it has not for decades experienced at the societal level. The question worth asking is to which extent the threats are impacting children and if childhood is more or less exposed to their perils than other generational categories? We must count on adults' will and ability to protect children from the gravest hazards, but we are hardly able to keep children apart from the world at large. It might even be a disservice to them to nurture an illusion that 'children are a people who live in a foreign country', as a Swedish singer has it in a famous ballad.

Children in the poor world have always been and remain particularly heavily influenced by large economic and societal forces, because the state is too weak to protect them; not least will global economic calamities strike children as a flood and predictably take a toll comparable to the worst tsunamis, and we are probably well advised to be prepared for the adversities – be they small or disastrous. Finally, as Zelizer has pointed out, there is nothing morally wrong in analytically connecting the world of children with that of economics as were they 'hostile worlds' (Zelizer, 2005a, 2005b).

It is the aim of this volume to contribute to a broad structural, historical and comparative understanding of childhood – to a macro-sociological understanding, one may suggest for want of a better expression, knowing that the borderline to 'micro' is somewhat wishy-washy. The idea is obviously not to establish a dissension among scholars who share a commitment to 'social studies of childhood'; nor is the idea to suggest a rank order of practices in the field at large. At the same time, there is the guest editor's (uncorroborated) observation that macro-perspectives on childhood are rather under-represented (why this is so is another matter). I would not mind, on this background, to stimulate an intellectual debate about the position of childhood in society, and in such a debate, there is likely to be on my side a personal preference for a 'macro' line of thinking.

The contributions to the volume speak for themselves and I shall not make an effort to summarise their contents in any detail. Instead I shall seek to thematise some approaches represented in the chapters.

The structure/agency line is classical and still fruitful, although not in an antagonistic sense. Most chapters in this volume are likely to be classified as assuming a structural perspective, but half of them, tentatively, contain an agency perspective as well – sometimes with children as actors, sometimes with adults in that role. The latter invites to discussions about what provides us with the better explanation of how society and childhood develop? What bring them in motion and what are the prime movers? Prejudice has it that a materialist line sits well with a structural approach, while idealism and personal activities belong to each other, yet the pairing is not always that straightforward (see the chapter by Qvortrup, this volume).

Thomas Olk is taking up this epistemological theme almost confrontationally, while asking in the heading: Do Ideas Matter? I shall let readers judge about his answer to this very interesting question in his chapter about policies concerning children and families in Germany and Norway. Are certain structures pressing towards particular solutions as answers to more or less similar requirements? Are we talking about the primacy of economics or the primacy of politics? Some may suggest such a question to be mere hairsplitting, but it is of course interesting to explore the limits of each model. There is no doubt that in all modern countries, there will be a need among working parents for day care (a structural condition), but it is also obvious that not all systems respond equally fast, depending on other or additional causes (cultural, religious, etc.). The choice of Germany and Norway shows that there is no automatism in countries' reaction, even if there seems to be a convergence towards the same outcome. It is notable in Olk's chapter that the acting subject or agent is not the child or children; it is clearly the political level versus the economic level – or to put it more antagonistically, voluntarism versus determinism.

We are in reality encountering the same problem in Vegard Johansen's chapter, even if it is not explicitly thematised. Johansen is studying distributive justice between generations at a societal level (not within families). This is a phenomenon that is found in all modern countries and one that varies between countries and between types of countries – in Johansen's chapter, it is demonstrated in an adapted version of Esping-Andersen's typology (Esping-Andersen, 1990). The results suggest that, once again, children are not given an agency role but rather they are fully dependent on the outcome of the interplay between market and welfare state, although clearly mediated by factors that help define the country types. In capitalist economies where the strongest guarantee for families' protection against poverty is to have a job – preferably two salaries – it is obvious that the market plays an important role; however, we also find that welfare state interventions are significant in warding off the most severe effects of a pure market economy. This is seen in Johansen's as well as in the chapter by Donald Hernandez, Nancy Denton, Suzanne Macartney, and Victoria Blanchard on poverty and human resources for children in the United States and a few European countries.

Again this chapter demonstrates the significance of both market and state but also that children are much more at risk under a pure market regime; the United States is not surprisingly an example of this fact because it is part of the country's ideology that state interference should be kept at a level that is lower than a European average and much lower than social democratic welfare states exemplified by the Nordic countries in Europe. The chapter by Hernandez et al. also makes it clear that many other factors play an important role such as education, employment, family composition, housing and command of language. All such factors find expression in the notion of class and to some extent race and ethnicity, whereas it is more difficult to perceive a systematic intergenerational cleavage that would cut through class and race factors. It seems clear though that the child poverty rate is much higher than the adult poverty rate in the United States and higher than in most European countries, mainly as a result of a different balance between market and state.

In the chapters mentioned so far, we find, in other words, outcomes that depend on market and state interventions, and this balance is in turn partly a result of political decisions about the role of the public. It is a choice between the primacy of economics and the primacy of politics – or rather some combination of letting the market decide and steering resources politically. This is a classical problematic and one which does not go away when the issue is children. A crucial question is then how we allow children to enter the stage as subjects or actors – not least for social studies of childhood that are quite committed to the idea of children as actors or agents. One might argue that some childhood researchers would find their identity as such exactly in an affirmation of children as actors. This is not necessarily true for macro-turned childhood scholars; nevertheless, several chapters are more or less explicitly dealing with this question.

As shown by Alison Watson, appalling reports and pictures of small children forced into armies in many places of the world no doubt tell us about a kind of participation, although often, one would surmise, without much consciousness about what they do. We know on the contrary about older children – from resistance movements during the Second World War for instance – who quite deliberately and often defiantly against will and wish of parents take part in dangerous actions. These are interesting cases that demonstrate that many children's capabilities are much stronger and more qualified than parents and other adults believe. They truly embody a children's agency that helps move society, for better or worse.

Whenever and wherever there are conflicts, there will be children who are sufficiently provoked so as to defend whichever values taught by adults. We have witnessed this in more contained conflicting areas such as on Cyprus, in Palestine and in Northern Ireland. Madeleine Leonard from Belfast writes about Northern Irish experiences from an area that has been in conflict for decades even if it these days seems to be abating. Leonard explicitly declares her 'orientation towards agency rather than structure' without diminishing the importance of structures; in fact, her chapter deals with 'how wider structural features of childhood impact on children's childhoods in contested spaces'. It is worthwhile noting that this preference for agency is not in conflict with a structure approach and also that it is not identical with an idealistic interpretation. Actually, children's resistance in these areas is a response to a highly concrete and for existence and survival threatening situation. At the same time, one cannot deny also that certain religious and/or ideological convictions are at stake. Structure and agency merge to a large extent, and by using Bourdieu's concept of *habitus*, Leonard succeeds in presenting children as both acting on their own initiative and as responsive to impacts from surrounding economic, political and cultural structures.

Most children are not involved in the kind of dramatic activities that comprise the backdrop, which Leonard and Watson (see below) write from – nevertheless, all children are engaged in everyday activities of some kind – be they organised or not. How are we to understand these daily activities within an agency-structure scheme? Maria Carmen Belloni's chapter reports about 11 to 13-year-old children's leisure activities, but already the title – Confiscated Time – leaves us with the assurance that they are not necessarily innocent or enclosed or set apart from adult society; it is at least suggested that children's leisure time may be something that can be taken away from them and controlled by adults and something that they are not allowed to keep for themselves, as the subtitle suggests. We find in other words that even at this mundane level children's activities take place under structured and structuring forms. However, we can hardly claim that what children do and the way they do it are massively influencing 'the way of the world', but it does suggest that children are an asset that is too costly to be left alone, and as contended by Belloni, there is no antithesis between structure and agency.

While leisure activities are in principle voluntary, school work is compulsory and universal. It encompasses all children within a certain age frame – typically 6–16 years of age, sometimes more, sometimes less depending on countries. If one only tries to imagine the current scope of children's school work, it constitutes one of the most massive, collective involvements of an age group ever seen in history, and one must wonder why it has not as such come to constitute a major focus for childhood scholars sharing an interest in agency. This is an activity that is *par excellence* determined by economic and political structures to an extent that it is found compulsory and universal in all modern countries – eventually, with more or less success, in all countries in the world. It is at the same time an activity that taken together represents an agency that is economically and politically significant and far-reaching. The question is what children's school work means – is it children's work, is it a manifestation of children's agency, does the result belong to children?

It can be argued, as Paul Close does in his chapter, that it represents both a highly overlooked activity and an activity that is imposed on children to a degree that from a strict definitional point of view might come to remind us of slave labour. As to its being overlooked, that is, as children's very own activities, it can interestingly be compared theoretically with the domestic labour debate about the character of housewives' work in private households. This debate effectively turned the attention to an overlooked 'occupation' that was massively performed by one population group – women – without being adequately recognised and rewarded. The allusion of it to slave labour may be rather a theoretically striking than a literally suitable construct in the sense that most children would probably continue to frequent the institution even if enrolment was made optional. At the same time, this could be seen as a choice that would only confirm their 'slave mentality', a notion that is not far away from Bourdieu's *habitus* (see Masculine domination by Bourdieu, 2001). With these discussions, we are coming close to discussions about children's role in production as also Qvortrup's chapter deals with, while claiming that children's compulsory work is changing its form and contents depending on mode of production but remains profoundly comparable because it is always system immanent or immanent to any prevailing mode of production (or *oikos*).

This hypothesis is one which touches on discussion about the value of children – which can be seen in terms of cultures, attitudes, politics and economics. As An-Magritt Jensen shows in her chapter, children's value is largely interpreted within frameworks of prevailing economies. Children may be valued and their worth assessed for what they give us emotionally or for what they contribute economically. At the bottom line, the production of children is clearly not a result of children's own negotiations, but nonetheless, a contested issue – personally and politically. It is a very concrete issue that to some extent divide women and men (mothers and fathers) but is also one which is highly pertinent at the level of economics and the polity – although sometimes in disguised form. It is an issue that is said to be private while at the end of the day it can hardly be circumvented that children are a public good, which many are eager to share but not so eager to contribute to. This imbalance is not necessarily one that has reached us as a common awareness – in particular not the growing number of free riders, as Qvortrup refers to in his chapter.

What are the chances and prospects for children to change this situation or to have it changed? Luigi Campiglio's chapter does not really bring children centre stage but rather leaves it to parents to act; nevertheless, it does bring children more in focus while taking up the issue of children as voters. This is an issue that has much to do with children's competence as political actors, and it has much to do also with questions of resource distribution raised in other chapters. Campiglio does not recommend that children become voters, but he does see a serious problem in the fact that the demographic development deprives children of ever larger shares of potential representatives among the electorate. It is difficult to prove a disinterest in children on the side of adults who do not have co-residing children, for instance the elderly. However, John Stuart Mill is quoted to that effect, and interestingly, his suspicion was confirmed by the German post-war chancellor Konrad Adenauer, who is known for the remark that politicians should forget about children, because they are not voters. Campiglio is significantly bringing children in play at the political stage, not directly as actors – voters – but as members of society who as such deserve a representation. By suggesting an extra vote for parents, one may argue that children's agency is 'vicariously' observed and the question of their subjectivity is brought into the debate at the interface of political and economic determination. However, perhaps, their subjectivity is not the most significant thing; others might argue that if they objectively speaking are getting their just part of resources, they are better helped.

A franchise reform that let parents vote on children's behalf may help bring childhood higher on the political agenda even though it does not necessarily give children themselves a feeling of co-determination. Could children's rights be an adequate answer to a desire for giving children a platform for influence? Can children's rights be understood as instruments to avert austere or other unwanted influences from the 'universalistic' world?

Alison Watson addresses the issue head on in her chapter on children and international law and clearly contends that structures are largely determining children's agency. Nevertheless, one must recognise that the consciousness about children's right to participate has increased throughout the 20th century, but it is still restricted to phenomena and occurrences of direct relevance to children or in which they are directly involved. The presence of wars and other conflict areas, of austerity measures, not to speak of economic recession reminds us that children can be and actually are situated in the midst of all too worldly calamities without having much hope for interference. They do though sometimes get involved nevertheless, as Watson points out, as child labourers and child soldiers, but these are examples of activities that politics and legislation do not allow, perhaps should not allow (see also the chapter by Leonard, this volume).

The question is in general terms when and under which conditions children have agency that is both allowed and recognised as crucial and with consequence for 'the way of the world'. In other words, activities that do not leave us in doubt that children by executing them are seen as included in society as participants in their own right; that childhood is indubitably perceived as an integrated category in the social fabric and that children, as far as the big society is concerned, are not merely seen to be in a waiting position until they become adults. The chapters therefore demonstrate that economy and politics are far from being alien concepts or phenomena to childhood. Indeed, childhood is for purposes deeply entrenched in the political economic fabric and the body social, exposed to a normalisation, as Giovanni Sgritta argues in another reprint that I am pleased to bring – published for the first time in English more than 20 years ago (Sgritta, 1987).

Even if Sgritta is perfectly aware of the diversification of childhood circumstances, he finds it appropriate to point to some general trends that seem to prevail in modern society. We live in a society the characterisation of which is powerfully said to be individualised, one in which the individual is claimed responsible for and setting the stage of his or her own life. Against this 'prime mover' is the dominant tendency towards institutionalisation of childhood or normalisation of childhood, which not only invokes the moment of the child's entry into a symbolic universe of rules and discipline, but also one that makes lifeworlds of children and adults more and more alike in terms of a 'liquidation of childhood' – a notion borrowed from the German sociologist Heinz Hengst (1981). Since Sgritta wrote the chapter, we have increasingly experienced children's institutionalisation (and normalisation) as exemplifying a mounting subsumption under a neo-liberal regime. The latter may currently be facing a deep crisis but is hardly likely to loosen its grip on the everyday life of children, while blurring and eventually abolishing the borderline between play and teaching, for instance. The difficulties for children (and their parents) to defending own interests are likely to be precarious because they do not constitute clear and well-defined interest groups, nor do they have a political constituency (see the chapter by Campiglio, this volume).

What is clear, however, is that childhood was and remains a contested terrain, which largely has been left to parents to preserve. This volume is meant as a reminder of the fact that childhood is a general interest and a public good, which should be studied and supported as such.

REFERENCES

Beck, U. (1986). *Risikogesellschaft: Auf dem Weg in eine andere Moderne.* Frankfurt am Main: Suhrkamp.

Bourdieu, P. (2001). *Masculine domination.* Cambridge: Polity.

de Lone, R. H. (1979). *Small futures: Children, inequality, and the limits of liberal reform. The carnegie council on children.* New York and London: Harcourt Brace Jovanovich.

Esping-Andersen, G. (1990). *The three worlds of welfare capitalism.* Cambridge: Polity.

Garbarino, J. (1986). Can American families afford the luxury of childhood? *Child Welfare, 65*(2), 119–140.

Hengst, H. (1981). Tendenzen der Liquidierung von Kindheit. In: H. Hengst, B. Riedmüller & M. M. Wambach (Eds), *Kindheit als Fiktion* (pp. 11–72). Frankfurt am Main: Suhrkamp (abridged version in The Sociology of Childhood, edited by J. Qvortrup, *International Journal of Sociology 17*(3), 1987, 58–80)..

Qvortrup, J., Corsaro, W. A., & Honig, M.-S. (Eds). (2009a). *The Palgrave handbook of childhood studies.* Basingstoke: Palgrave Macmillan.

Qvortrup, J., Corsaro, W. A., & Honig, M.-S. (2009b). Why social studies of childhood? An introduction to the handbook. In: J. Qvortrup, W. A. Corsaro & M.-S. Honig (Eds), *The Palgrave handbook of childhood studies* (pp. 1–18). Basingstoke: Palgrave Macmillan.

Sgritta, G. B. (1987). Childhood: Normalization and project. The Sociology of Childhood, edited by J. Qvortrup, *International Journal of Sociology, 17*(3), 38–57 (an extract from the author's 'Normalizzazione e progetto nella socializzazione dell'infanzia' in Sgritta, G. B. et al (Eds), Regale e socializzazione. Leoscher: Torino, 1984).

Zelizer, V. A. (2005a). *The purchase of intimacy.* Princeton and Oxford: Princeton University Press.

Zelizer, V. A. (2005b). The priceless child revisited. In: J. Qvortrup (Ed.), *Studies in modern childhood: Society, agency, culture* (pp. 184–200). Palgrave Macmillan: Basingstoke.

Jens Qvortrup
Editor

THE DEVELOPMENT OF *CHILDHOOD*: CHANGE AND CONTINUITY IN GENERATIONAL RELATIONS

Jens Qvortrup

INTRODUCTION

This chapter is not about the development of the child; I am making this clear from the outset because the title could easily be misinterpreted that way by the readers who are unacquainted with social studies of childhood. Although 'development' and 'child' are familiar concepts, which combined in notions of 'development of the child' or 'child development' are parts of a century long, successful and dominant discourse, the notion of 'development of childhood' is rather begging questions, such as if there at all is such a thing as a theory of childhood development and if we need it. To my mind the brief answer to the first question is 'no', but quite a few authors have made thoughtful formulations about it and about generational relations without necessarily having intended to be theory builders (cf. Alanen, 2009). The answer to the second question is 'yes', I believe we need such a theory to come to terms with how children's life worlds have changed and how they have related to contemporaries belonging to other generations – adulthood, youth and old age.

Structural, Historical, and Comparative Perspectives
Sociological Studies of Children and Youth, Volume 12, 1–26
Copyright © 2009 by Emerald Group Publishing Limited
All rights of reproduction in any form reserved
ISSN: 1537-4661/doi:10.1108/S1537-4661(2009)0000012006

Efforts to account for change and continuity of generational relations demand that we firmly distinguish between the family level and the societal level, which in turn requires a partly new terminology: 'development of childhood' (see Woodhead, 2009); 'minors, adults and old aged' as a sequel to 'children, parents and grandparents'; 'relationships' vs. 'relations' and others (see more below).

In theories of child development – as in everyday parlance – childhood is typically understood in terms of stage or *a period* in a person's life cycle. This chapter, written in a macro-sociological framework, assumes a much different understanding, namely that of childhood as a *permanent* structural *form* (see Qvortrup, 2009). Consequently, a macro-sociological under-standing does not look forward to adulthood (it is not anticipatory), nor does it follow the individual (it is not individualised). Childhood in this understanding is a social form or space which is imposed on or taken in possession by children – in principle from birth. At a certain age defined by a given culture, children leave this form or space and pass it on to new cohorts of children. They do not leave it exactly as they found it; childhood always changes – not, I would argue, as much as a result of children's plans and activities, but rather due to the societal changes that take place. Changes in the shape or form of childhood are primarily a result of changes in society at large. Such changes take place always but with varying rapidity and childhood changes accordingly. If this sounds deterministic, let me make it a bit clearer. The point is not the classical argument about striking a balance between socio-economic circumstances and human agency; it is rather that the human interventions that make observable *societal changes* are adults' rather than children's interventions. I do not by that say that children do not make a difference, but their activities do not count much among purposive changes at a societal level (see the chapter by Leonard, this volume). However, childhood as a structural form or children as a collectivity make much of a difference by their mere presence – whether they demographically are few or many. At a family level it is different; here children potentially have and eventually have got more and more of a say vis-à-vis their parents, but this is not at issue in this chapter.

Childhood as a structural form is a concept and a phenomenon that has not attracted much interest. One should not be surprised; in our individualistic world the concentration has been much more on *the child* and its growth and development and much less about the child's surroundings. That is in particular true, the larger the surroundings or contexts are – what we might call the *macro-parameters* of childhood. We seldom encounter questions about the development of childhood, whether we think back in history, anticipate our future – or simply place childhood in context here and now. In my view we should do exactly this – as a case in point, think, for instance, of the impact of the current financial crisis and recession on childhood compared with their impact on adulthood and old age.

When the notion of the *future* is invoked in connection with childhood – for instance, when talking about children as 'the generation of the future' – we are most likely having adulthood in mind: children as our future generation are the current generation of children who have become adults in the meantime! It is the anticipatory, although not necessarily the individualistic view. What we do not have in mind in the expression is childhood a generation ahead understood as the structural form or space of childhood as imagined decades in advance. Had this been the case, it would have been an example of contemplating the development of childhood from the shapes it assumes currently to what it may come to look like in, say, 2040. This would have been an interesting and productive idea, but it is not one that is entertained in phrases like 'childhood as our future' or 'childhood as our next generation'.

Our imagery is different when we look into our *past* and ask about childhood 100 years ago, for example. In this case our perspective is neither anticipatory nor individualistic, but in fact a structural one. We are not following individuals backwards and are not even interested in doing so – or rather: that may be a popular genealogical zeal for many people, and a specialism of psychoanalysis, which may find an interest in the history of historical personalities (see Erikson, 1962, on Luther; Miller, 1980, on Hitler). I would argue that contemplating the idea of childhood as a *past generation* (as opposed to discourses about childhood as our *future generation*) does not bring past adulthood to our minds, nor would we be thinking about adults in the past. Also, we would not come to think of childhood as a period of a particular individual's life cycle. In fact, most of us would rather have in mind a particular historical period's childhood as a structural form. We would be thinking of the general conditions of childhood at a particular historical juncture or during a certain period of the past, say the first decade of the twentieth century. There were without doubt at the time – as to day – a wide variety of childhoods and an historian studying the period might, of course, reveal this diversity. Yet, any discussion of 'childhood in the first decade of the twentieth century' will typically arouse an imagery of children's general life conditions at the time. Most of us would, I presume, come to think of a society characterised by low level of industrialisation, low level of technology, high birth rate and many children in a family, high mortality level, comparably short longevity, poor hygienic situation and rather modest health conditions, a lot of child labour, most people living in the country side, a short childhood in the sense of low level of education, etc. These characteristics, and many others could be mentioned, constituted the framework of childhood; they were the parameters that composed childhood as a structural form.

Interestingly, adults were influenced by the same parameters and so were young and old people at the time and thus we can talk also about structural forms or spaces of youth, adulthood and old age; similarly, we can talk about the development of youth, adulthood and old age. At any time generational units live side-by-side and are, in principle, impacted by the same parameters, although not necessarily in the same way or with the same intensity. It is this difference we must unravel – the difference in impact of the parameters, the difference in their reception and the response to their impact by different generations. In this respect, children are more defenceless and dependent than adults and even youth; in addition, an assessment of childhood must take into account also older and more powerful age groups' interests that are not necessarily compatible with those of childhood.

At any time in history there is and has been a connection between generations; in an effort to come to terms with the nature of the connections it is possible and fruitful to look for certain modal relations which are characteristic for certain eras – whatever they are called or however they are defined (e.g. mode of production or cultural hegemony). To the extent that we are able to locate certain modalities it should be possible to describe and understand the development of childhood in terms of both change and continuity. Childhood – understood as the outcome of prevailing parameters at any time – obviously changes because the values of the parameters change and because they interact with each other. Childhood nevertheless exhibits continuity to an extent that we are permitted to state that its forming parameters are in principle and qualitatively the same ones: in all societies we do have an economic parameter, even if it changes; in all societies we find an idea and a practice of the social; we always encounter a cultural climate even if it may be changing its impact on children. We can go on with political, technological and other parameters. Over and above these changes we must remember and take into account that, and how the parameters are embedded in intergenerational relations. Intergenerational relations are there at any historical and cultural juncture, but they are at the same time distinct by gradations determined by the dialectic of prevailing parameters.

PRIME MOVERS: LESSONS FROM ARIÈS
AND deMAUSE

A preoccupation with the development of childhood demands a historical perspective. Why, how and to which extent did childhood change – and to which extent are we permitted to claim a certain continuity? Social scientific scholarship about childhood obviously includes historians of childhood (who are different from historians of the child, cf. Berg, 1983; Wartofsky, 1981), and it has been blessed with a number of excellent ones (Cunningham, 2005; Gillis, 2009; Hendrick, 2009). Interestingly, though, none of the historians who have more or less devoted their life and career to the study of childhood has actually been builders of grand theories of childhood. To find such theories we have to go either to outsiders within history or to other disciplines like sociology (Zelizer, 1985) and anthropology (Mead, 1978).

Philippe Ariès and Lloyd deMause belong to the outsiders, even as historians. Surprisingly, for instance, Ariès did never pass the university examination as an historian and earned his living as a librarian in a tropical fruit company; he was, as he said in his memoirs, a 'Sunday historian' ('un historien du dimanche'): he used weekends and evenings to his creative history writing.

deMause was a self-established historian; he graduated in political science, trained later as a lay psychoanalyst, and called himself a 'psycho-historian' and his discipline for 'psychohistory' – an invention of his own and one that he has been pioneering.

While Ariès eventually got academic and collegial recognition, deMause is probably waiting for that to happen. His main work – actually a very long chapter in his edited book – was massively criticised and the reason was first of all his interpretation of history by means of what he called a psychogenic theory (deMause, 1974).

At first sight deMause is attractive; he used a great amount of empirical data – or data from many various sources – which enabled him to establish a 'periodisation of modes of parent–child relations', which runs as follows: (1) infanticidal mode (antiquity to fourth century AD); (2) abandonment mode (fourth to thirteenth century AD); (3) ambivalent mode (fourteenth to seventeenth centuries); (4) intrusive mode (eighteenth century); (5) socialization mode (nineteenth to mid-twentieth centuries); and (6) helping mode (begins mid-twentieth century) (see *ibid.*, pp. 51–54).

This evolutionary scheme is obviously crude but one which I, in principle, would be ready to accept provided more or less irrefutable evidence. In an answer to his many critics, he complains that 'not a single reviewer in any of the six languages in which the book was published wrote about any errors in my evidence, and none presented any evidence from primary sources which contradicted any of my conclusions' (deMause, 1988). However, the problem is not his evidence, even if it is correct. The problem is rather how he interprets his evidence in terms of his psychogenic theory. In that sense he is quite straightforward. Already in his original 'psychogentic theory of history' he posited that

> the central force for change in history is neither technology nor economics, but the "psychogenic" changes in personality occurring because of successive generations of parent-child interactions. (deMause, 1974, p. 3)

His theory was confirmed, if we are to believe his

> overall conclusion [...] that the history of childhood had showed slow and steady progress over time, and that it was an evolutionary process which was *determined mainly by psychodynamics within the parent-child relationship*, rather than primarily by economic factors (deMause, 1988, my italics)

and in his preface to a book published later he stated as one of his goals

> to show that childrearing evolution is an independent cause of historical change, with love as the central force in history, creating new kinds of personalities – new psychoclasses – that then change societies. (deMause, Emotional Life of Nations, 2002, p. 1 taken from download)

These quotes clearly suggest why deMause is not in many social scientists' good books. Even scholars who may be leaning to cultural interpretations – like for instance Ariès – would not accept that for instance economics and technology should not be playing a role in history.

deMause's substantive message is that children's life conditions have been steadily improved since antiquity – as one can, in fact, read it from his scheme earlier. The reason is not that society has changed but that parents have eventually acquired better human or caring qualities. From generation to generation parents seek to make it ever little better for their children than it was for themselves as children.

It is fully possible, in principle, to accept deMause's evolutionary scheme without endorsing his interpretation. The observation that children eventually, as history proceeds, experience more friendly and caring attitudes is one which many scholars have made for various periods of history (cf. Zelizer, 1985). Given his interpretation, deMause proves to be interested merely in parent–child relationships (and merely at the 'psycho-genetic' level!) and not in generational relations in a larger societal perspective.

Ariès was not alien to the idea that children came to be embraced with more and more commitment and love from parents; he used, for instance, the phrase 'the king-child' about a child in a small nuclear family running the risk of being spoiled, so even here his scepticism towards the modernity course reveals itself (Ariès, 1980; see the chapter by Jensen, this volume). He was not really interested in individual children or their *relationships* with their parents. He turned his attention, in stead, to how the *relations* between generations changed historically, and he did not like what he saw or what he chose to see. First of all he regretted that children, as he saw it, were more and more prevented from being participants in the large social fabric or not recognised for their participation, but actually I believe his concern was more about the former than the latter. An extreme example of this view was his story about children in Mediaeval Florence who were entrusted with the task of dragging stoned, bloody bodies away from the execution place; rather than being worried for the psychological impact on children, he chose to see the positive in the fact that children had a role and a function which no others could or would assume and he used this as a catalyst for a critique of modernity for failing to provide them with such a role (Ariès, 1994).

Ideologically Ariès was, as said in his memoir book (Ariès, 1990), 'a reactionary' and it is hard to avoid the suspicion that he took pleasure in cherishing the past nostalgically. He did not share deMause's rejection of material impacts on the development of childhood, but this did not make him a materialist; on the contrary, Ariès remained a classical mental historian, who attached much importance to cultural explanations (see the chapter by Olk, this volume), as when he interpreted what he saw as an increasing separation and isolation of children from adults (cf. below on severance of production and reproduction) as

> one of the aspects of the Reformation's great moral rearmament of mankind, whether the reformers were Protestants or Catholic, from the Church, the professional nobility, or the state. (Ariès, 1982, p. 7)

For Ariès, childhood was and is a cultural construction – or to be more correct: a mental construction or an idealistic construction. There is no mention by him of the economy or of modes of production as generic entities triggering changes; nevertheless, the gradual transformation of childhood did not happen by and of itself but as a result of external influences. That is already a more satisfying explanation, which of course is shared by many other scholars, for instance Zelizer (1985) in her classical book, in which she convincingly present her ideas about the new trend in late nineteenth and early twentieth century towards a sentimentalisation and a sacralisation of childhood – indeed very conspicuous features in the development of childhood.

There have been voices also to the effect that the change in childhood was a result of changes in economic demands (Caldwell, 1982; see also the chapter by Jensen, this volume). One could use the notion of the political economy of childhood to suggest – as I would do – that a number of factors were at play at the same time, of which the economy was not the least dominant.

THE TRANSITION OF CHILDHOOD TO INDUSTRIALISATION

Childhood changes incessantly, mostly step-by-step, sometimes by leaps and bounds. Childhood changes slowly or rapidly because *society* changes that way. In our imagery social change has over century-long stretches been long-winded, only to speed up with the onset of industrialisation and to accelerate by exponential rapidity during the recent decades. This pace of change makes profound impact on our way of life, on each and every category of people and their interconnections and indeed on childhood and the way in which generations relate to each other, as Mead (1978) has written insightful about (see also Davis, 1940).

Obviously, it is not time in itself which causes change; notions of *Zeitgeist* and the like are only begging the question. Changes come about as a result of interplay among human beings and their interaction with nature and means of production, that is, surroundings as found and shaped by adults, above all. The very presence of children – and thus childhood – influences our way of life; children's conscious being may turn the wheel of parental life, but hardly of societal life.

I do not intend to present a historical account of childhood in any detail; however, as a backdrop for discussing the transformation of childhood I shall have in mind the transition from pre-industrial to industrial society – that is, the last decades of the nineteenth through the first decades of the twentieth centuries.[1]

The transition to industrial society was not, of course, primarily a change in and of childhood but a massive shake-up of the economy with great impact on family and childhood. James Coleman speaks about it as transition from a *primordial social organisation* to a *purposively constructed social organisation*, that is more specifically a transformation of the economy from a 'set of weakly interdependent households, most of which produced most of what they consumed' to an economy 'in which most production took place in factories and most of what was consumed was purchased in the market', and as major indicators for this transformation are '[t]he movement of people off the land into cities and the movement of production from households to factories and other specialized workplaces' (Coleman, 1993).

Among other significant consequences of this societal upheaval were an increased 'proletarianisation' which can be interpreted as an accentuation of an already observable confrontation between two major social *classes* (in the Marxian understanding); it was a developing secularisation and individualisation which revealed itself among other things in an emergent educational regime and a democratic revolution, for instance, increased suffrage for both men and women.[2] These and other transformations constituted the framework for the further development of childhood: the demographic transformation reduced the numbers of children, who changed workplace from *manual work* in the country side and factories to *mental school* work, they were – like their parents – urbanised and moved into small apartments in the towns and were subjected to a strengthened family ideological regime, and as a result of all these changes they assumed a new position in the intergenerational structure.

The period we are talking about was in other words one, which fundamentally restructured and reshuffled various categories' position vis-à-vis each other – women and men, workers and capitalists, families with and without children – no wonder, therefore, that children's position also changed vis-à-vis other generational units. The main point – or the short version – is that the system immanent intergenerational connection *changed from children's relationship with parents to minors' relations to adults*. This is a crucial point to which I shall come back: it draws attention to the fact that beyond children's natural attachment to parents there is under a modern economy a significant connection between childhood and other generational units. It is a connection that has been almost overlooked under the strong regime of family ideology and trends towards familiarisation.

Severance of Production and Reproduction

From the point of view of changing generational relations, I shall, in particular, emphasise the severance of production and reproduction as quintessential. Most of the aforementioned consequences were subsumed this severance process which fundamentally altered the view and reality of who should carry responsibility for children. At first glance children were winners in an environment of increasing sentimentalisation (Zelizer, 1985; deMause, 1974) underlined by fewer children and smaller families; however, the severance also caused what Kaufmann (2005) calls a structural lack of consideration (Rücksichtslosigkeit) or a structural indifference (Gleichgültigkeit). Thus it seems that two worlds were established: a small one, the family, to which children 'naturally', as it were, belonged; and a 'big' world which was rather seen as hostile (Zelizer, 2005) or at least alien to children and childhood. This was a split that also furthered a view of children as a *private* rather than a *public good*. The question remains if this split at the end of the day was a blessing for children and for childhood? Perhaps even more pertinent is the question if the split in the long run was an advantage to society or, in particular, if the split might have aggravated the process towards an ageing society and our difficulties in meeting the requirements of an old population? At the bottom of this question lies, of course, the claim that generations at the end of the day are and remain interrelated and indispensable for each other.

The observation that production and reproduction drifted apart from each other during the process towards industrialisation is not new. It is contained in what Coleman wrote, but most candid was perhaps Kingsley Davis' portrayal of the split, when he in a famous article from 1937 wrote

> The thesis here maintained will be that the declining birth rate has resulted from a ripening incongruity between our reproductive system (the family) and the rest of modern social organization, ... The incongruity has been frequently recognized, but there are two contrasting views as to its nature. First, the view of the cultural lag theorists, who maintain ... that eventually it will adapt itself to the new situation. Second, my own view, that the kind of reproductive institution inherited from the past is fundamentally incompatible with present-day society and hence can never catch up'. (Davis, 1937, p. 290)

Davis is in this quotation asserting and authorising that in industrialisation there is a place for reproduction and another one for production; there is a place for emotions and one for rationality (cf. above Coleman on the change from primordial to purposeful organisation). By the same token he indirectly suggests that if there is now 'a ripening incongruity' then previously production must have been compatible with reproduction. What did the latter entail? Above all that producers and reproducers were basically the same persons in a locality; the fact that parents were typically producers as well left no doubt about a *shared responsibility* for children. Even persons who were producers without being parents were tacitly forced into an intergenerational responsibility which was in principle an endorsement of the system of intergenerational reciprocity over a life time: without sharing burdens and responsibilities for the common weal they could not count on provision and care in their old age. Hence one could not with impunity be a free rider in the system: a precondition for receiving assistance in old age was contributions made earlier. It is important to note that maintaining and sustaining any future production was dependent on reproduction of a renewed labour force, and the only persons available for doing the reproduction were male and female producers.

In modern society, as Davis indicates, the production sector takes no responsibility for reproduction. He is, in other words, suggesting that children are a private good and negating the idea of them as a public good. Does it mean that corporate society and children are irrelevant to each other? Does it mean that corporate society can be indifferent towards childhood? Does it mean, furthermore, that childhood and old age are without much mutual rapport? The problem is that since the onset of industrialisation we – adults in general and modern society as such – have acted as if business and childhood were at variance and have approached children as were they merely a part of the small world and not the large social fabric (see quote from Garbarino, 1986, on page xiv in my prologue this volume).

One consequence of the transition to industrialisation is that children in a sense have been excommunicated from the prevailing economy, as if they, in our imagery, were irrelevant for the economy as long as they were children (or as Ariès argued: they lost their right to be genuine participants). I wish to demonstrate that these are wrong answers. Intergenerational connections persist and children's role is as indispensable as before, as I shall argue later.

Discontinuity and Continuity: Changing Awareness of Economy, Family and Childhood

The development of childhood is activated by changes in the conditions for production and concomitant changes in our awareness about how various phenomena relate to each other. The changing connections between generations are particularly important to register in an account of children's changing position. Intergenerational connections in pre-industrial communities took above all the form of primary contacts because everybody lived close to each other in a small locality or community, even though they actually were included in both the reproductive and the productive spheres. The reason for this was obvious, because the economy was a household economy, or in another terminology, their *oikos* was of the household type.

I find this Greek term useful for comparative reasons.[3] *Oikos* can be used as a common, a generalised concept for any economic organisation – for households based on community or Gemeinschaft co-operation in a locality in pre-industrial society, as well as for what we might call a societal household (a national economy). In principle, all necessary economic processes take place in any *oikos*: production, reproduction, consumption, circulation and division of labour and everywhere one must 'economise' to maintain sustainability. Although, thus, in principle nothing has changed in terms of vital processes to accomplish – because all forms are indispensable forms for human survival – dramatic changes have taken place in *the way* the various *oikos* are organised.

In pre-industrial *oikos*, the household *oikos,* the connections among different functions were transparent, there was no separation between production and reproduction because those who produced were the same as those who reproduced, which meant that nobody was able, as mentioned, to be a free rider in the system or evade responsibility for common concerns. This implied a practical enforcement of a generational contract or covenant. In fact, children previously happened to be so deeply involved as both contributors and beneficiaries that Ariès found it appropriate to characterise it as a time and place where childhood had not yet been invented:

> In medieval society the idea of childhood did not exist' … the 'awareness of the particular nature of childhood, that particular nature which distinguishes the child from an adult … was lacking. (Ariès, 1962, p. 128)

Ariès not only mediates to us that insight about generational differentiation was hardly existing, because it barely existed in reality, but also that children and their activities were enmeshed and embedded in the community in which both parents and children lived and worked side-by-side. One is, therefore, justified in proposing that the work-divided differentiation was low – the nature of what children and adults did was in any case the same,[4] even if the activities were adapted to their bodily capacities.

When, to follow Ariès, childhood was 'invented' – and he points, in particular, to schooling as an important marker in this process – the way was paved for a growing attention to what children did. Historians' descriptions of child work in the nineteenth century is sufficient for us to realise at least two things: one, what children actually did – and they did, details aside, manual activities, as they had always done until this time and two, even if they largely shared kinds of activities with adults, it eventually came to clash with a new awareness about children. Some, but far from all, were alarmed of what was understood as an assault on children's bodies and minds. This reflected a new consciousness about children, as suggested by Ariès and many others (Zelizer, 1985; see earlier). Brunner is conveying the same message when he says that

> Only in the 18th century, the word family comes to penetrate the German everyday language and achieves this *particular emotionality* which we connect to it. (Brunner, 1980, p. 89; my italics; my translation from the German)

Not only childhood, but apparently also the family, according to Brunner, had to be invented as modernity progressed. With the changing economy – or *oikos* – also the division of labour and the rate of change increased. The traditional *oikos* was not at the time an issue but rather seen as a context for a 'natural' exchange of use values; it had not as such reached peoples' consciousness and therefore with industrialisation had to be addressed in a new way. As Levine says

> What to do with the economy has been a problem since we first became aware that we had one. *Our awareness of the economy is, however, a fairly recent development.* (Levine, 1995, p. 12; my italics)

The three quotations from Ariès, Brunner and Levine point in the same direction. They all speak of or allude to a lacking awareness – of, respectively, childhood, family and economy. I do not read this as if it merely took some social constructionism – or more precisely mental creativity – to establish childhood, family and economy. The fact was rather that incipient modernity – by means of a growing differentiating due to changing requirements of production – did away with the thus far dominant *oikos*, namely, what the Germans call 'das ganze Haus', that is, an extended household or an estate, as the case may be. This was a site for intimate family relationships resulting in reproduction as well as for production, but it was a productive activity that people did not realise as an economy, as an *oikos*.

To address Levine's point that it was not clear what to do with the economy when it rose to our awareness, it is tempting to say that severance of reproduction from production coincided with the demise of political economy to the advantage of what is now regarded as a classical liberal economy as pioneered by Alfred Marshall. Interestingly, further, this interpretation of the economy coincided with the ascendance of a number of child sciences such as paediatrics, developmental psychology and child psychiatry that all had their inaugurating assemblies during the last decades of the nineteenth century. It suited well also the portrayal of the period as one in which children were sentimentalised and subjected to an increased

protectionism – and therefore one which pleased deMause but displeased
Ariès while in a sense proved both of them right.

The problem was, to follow Kaufmann, that this was at the same time
accentuating an increased indifference towards childhood on the side of
corporate society. We observe in other words a paradox in the sense that
children are more and more embraced at the family level, whereas
simultaneously disregarded at the level of society – a paradox which accords
with Davis' 'increasing incongruity' thesis. To the extent that this thesis was
acceded by dominant economic and political forces it suggested a significant
change of childhood. However, one may ask if it was an interpretation which
served children well – or indeed, if it was a valid one? Was it true that
children, as it were, were thrown out of the serious social fabric – or did they
simply enter a changed version of the generational contract?

Relationships and Relations

Ariès and deMause disagree with each other on most accounts; perhaps
most significantly on perspective and level of analysis. Though deMause
insists to consider the family level and takes an interest merely in the
relationships between children and parents, Ariès informs us about the
larger context, including the relations between minors, adults and old aged.
The family is and always was the site for *relationships* between parents and
children and indeed beyond the psycho-genetic level; these are psychological
and sociological relationships which develop over time and differ from
culture to culture. Relationships at this level are unlikely to become
obsolete; however, as the *oikos* changes from a traditional household in
becoming a national economy, we come to observe that they are
accompanied by *relations* between generations – emerging with industrialisation and becoming more and more pronounced as we approach what
may be called a *global oikos*. Contrary to what Davis proposed childhood,
let alone the family, was not eclipsed from the 'modern social organisation',
but was adapted to it, as I shall say more about later.

Let me briefly explicate this terminology, which perhaps is more
unequivocal in the German language, which distinguishes between
Beziehungen and *Verhältnisse*. The former denotes close or primary
relationships between persons, be they relatives, peers or friends, whereas
the latter suggests *relations* between larger groups, collectives or categories;
the best example of the use of relations is in 'class relations' (in German
'Klassenverhältnisse'). There may well be a personal relationship between

a worker and a capitalist, but when we talk about class relations we have in mind the encounter between the working class and the capitalist class, in other words among categories that are seen as depersonalised entities, even when we talk about class consciousness (a class-for-itself relation vis-à-vis a class-in-itself relation).

The categories that we are talking about in this chapter are not class, gender or ethnic ones but *generational* categories, which are found at both the family and the societal level. At the family level we have as mentioned in mind primary relationships between children, parents and grandparents. As society develops into modernity and increasingly its divisions of labour, it does not suffice to use terms that merely pertain to the family level. To address the rather impersonal relations between younger and older, it is required to extend the discourse with notion of *relations between minors, adults and elderly* in addition to *relationships between children, parents and grandparents*. The new terms suggest that we are now dealing with larger generational categories, the members of which are not kinship-related. Far from all adults, for example, are parents or have home staying children.[5] The notion 'adults' thus include, besides parents, all adults who do not assume direct responsibility for children or share residence with them.

The problem is that even if the family level remains significant for generational contacts we have failed to come to terms with childhood as vital part at the level of society. Our lack of appreciation of the link between childhood, adulthood and old age – and between childhood, corporate society and the state – has caused a number of unintended consequences. Exactly as production and reproduction was severed, and childhood apparently separated from adulthood or the adult world, the family seems to have been disconnected from the larger economy because the latter relates to the individual employer and not the family, as Caldwell contended (see the chapter by Jensen, this volume). These understandings may be seen as a fatal misinterpretation: as a historical *faux pas* that has not been planned or 'directed' by anybody, but simply happened as a result of the development into a new *oikos*. It is true that childhood changed in the process, but not for that necessarily true that it was qualitatively different, as Davis indicated.

CHANGE AND CONTINUITY OF CHILDREN'S WORK

As discussed so far it has been emphasised that the world changes and the society alters as a result of forces on which children have little influence. *Childhood is developing* and *children's role is influenced* exactly because of worldly changes and societal alterations. As indicators of the transition to industrial society quite a few were aforementioned – from urbanisation over demographic transition to severance of production and reproduction, for instance. Most conspicuous among changes that directly involved children were the change in their main obligatory activities; in pre-industrial society children were typically performing manual work, whereas after the transition to industrial society they were all required to do mental work in schools. Seen in the light of the other major transformations this was not a trivial change, but how are we to understand it? What can we explain in terms of the development of childhood? What does it mean in terms of alterations of connections to other generations?

One of the distinguishing features of social studies of childhood is an eagerness to portray children as active persons and as agents in their own right (see the chapter by Belloni, this volume). Scholars in the field have produced an immense body of research that demonstrates children's activities in schools, in day care centres, on play grounds and many other arenas, and they have successfully corrected an ingrained impression of children's participation as chaotic to one that exhibit comprehensible patterns (see Corsaro, 2009; Thorne, 1993; Strandell, 1994; Gulløv & Højlund, 2003). This new understanding of children's play and interaction is and remains a major achievement.

It is on the background of this agency approach remarkable that scholars of social studies of childhood have been reluctant to accept *schooling as proper or real work*. It is interesting that the activities typically studied in schools have been observed in breaks or perhaps as clandestine interactions between pupils in the classes. Children studied in this way relate above all to each other, patterns of co-operation and conflict criss-cross small groups and cliques are revealed. The interchange between children is seen in terms of their contribution to constructing their own lives, as 'interpretive reproduction' with Corsaro's phrase. Children are significantly leaving an imprint on their own world, which would have been different without children's own activities and involvement. However, research has focussed on interactions between children at the cost of connections between pupils and staff, not to speak of efforts in understanding children's school work as a contribution to maintaining and sustaining society.

Schooling, thus, in the sense of the very activities performed by pupils as a part of the universal educational scheme is seldom studied or taken into account or thought of as a genuine children's activity. One wonders why? I have argued that schooling is worthwhile studying – not least in a macro-perspective; schooling does not exclude interactions with your school mates but is primarily pupils' exchange with institutions in an educational system of which teachers are merely one part; it is a necessary ingredient of the very socio-economic fabric in modern society. It becomes in other words a significant part of childhood's relation to adulthood as embodied in the prevailing socio-economic system.

My main thesis about schooling is that it represents a continuation of children's obligatory work in previous eras. Mental labour in current society corresponds to manual labour in pre-industrial society. In terms of indispensability there are hardly differences between the two forms, but while the *visibility* of manual work is obvious (and therefore also its being credited child workers), the usefulness of school work is opaque and abstract. In a sense one might argue that manual child work in pre-industrial society is producing use value within a scheme of simple production, whereas schooling is producing long-term exchange value within a system of extended production (in a Marxian sense; diachronic division of labour, see Qvortrup, 1995, 2000).

This difference as to visibility may help explain why apparently manual work is perceived as more useful than school work – despite the fact that schooling includes all children in an educational marathon stretching over many years, or to the extent that school work is generally contemplated as useful at all (see the chapter by Close, this volume).

Child Work and Connections between Generations

I have argued elsewhere for the thesis about schoolwork's usefulness (see Qvortrup, 1995, 2000) and shall not, therefore, detail this position. Important in this chapter's context is to emphasise change and continuity as to its placement in an intergenerational framework, and this is an argument which has much to do with my discussion above about production and reproduction.

Children were previously understood as an asset to families. In the traditional *oikos* there were two significant fertility motivations. (1) Children's potentials as a work force while they were still children, whereby they at least reduced the costs of their upbringing, perhaps even represented a surplus. (2) Children's indispensability as parents' best hope in due time for old age care and provision; this was a hope issued as a kind of intergenerational covenant and a very personal one between children, parents and grandparents. In the terminology introduced above we can speak about *relationships* between generations.

If we turn to industrial society – right until present time – schoolwork has replaced manual work. The two forms of child work are, of course, different as to their form and content and the instruments used for performing it; they also differ in terms of level of abstraction (present use value vs. future exchange value). More significant are the similarities; they are similar because both are obligatory; they are similar also because they both are *system immanent*, that is, they have the same meaning vis-à-vis the *oikos* in which they are deemed necessary and obligatory – in fact, that is the reason why they are *obligatory* forms of child work. The logic is clear: in an economy where manual functions dominate in the *oikos*, one will find that children are socialised to use their hands; similarly, in an *oikos* where mental and symbolic functions dominate, children must be trained to use their head. This necessary compatibility within prevailing *oikos* nevertheless produces a new kind of connection between generations in the move to a new *oikos* – it changes from *relationships* among persons to *relations* among categories (minor vs. adults or childhood vs. adulthood/old age). In other words, connections among generations remain, but the nature of them changes.

The reason for the changed nature of intergenerational connections is seen in the fact that school work does not – like classical child labour – favour parents specifically; it does not embody a rapport between children and parents. School work in stead enters an equation at the societal level; it is part of the modern *oikos*. It is to the benefit of each and every child/pupil/minor, of course, but above all it is of general worth and thus benefiting corporate society and society as a whole, that is, all adults and not merely parents. It is this general worth of school work that makes it depersonalised; it is not part of the intergenerational system of reciprocity at the family level but represents impersonal relations at a structural level. This change again implied that even if children's obligatory, *system immanent* work was not discontinued but merely transformed, parents were no longer able to perceive it as a motivation to give birth to children, because school work fundamentally pertains to the productive and not the reproductive sphere.

Furthermore, it is no longer biological offspring who provides and cares for old parents as a sign of a kinship *relationship*. Provision to and care of the elderly is now depersonalised and delivered by minors, who have become adults; provision in terms of pension is paid via the public purse or insurance companies. Care is typically delivered by salaried persons, above all women, who are not kin-related to the elderly, who receive care independent of their biological children. Hence, pretty much has changed, but nothing is new, however, in the sense that it now as before is the succeeding generations that provide and care for the preceding ones, but exactly the depersonalised nature forces us to think in terms of *relations* between generations rather than *relationships* within a family.

The Change in Children's Obligatory Activities and Its Prime Movers

It is not difficult to appreciate that the change in children's obligatory activities can be seen as a significant indicator of the development of childhood – in particular, as it is intertwined with a number of large scale indicators, as mentioned. There is no space here for addressing all questions about the background for the change but it is tempting at least briefly to return to questions about prime movers before continuing with assessing who were winners and losers.

As discussed earlier, the question of what causes historical changes is far from settled and will hardly be (see the chapter by Olk, this volume). Ariès is leaning towards idealistic explanations – culture, church and nobility. There is though historical evidence supportive of a more materialistic explanation (as favoured by the author of this chapter). It is striking, for instance, that – slightly dependant on the economic development of the country, of course – the time for the near completion of mass-scholarisation was by and large the same in all countries of Western Europe and North American, namely the period that this chapter has chosen as decisive – around the turn to the twentieth century. This remarkable coincidence or simultaneity happened despite a *politically* generated legislation that intended to and ideally should have made the completion of mass-scholarisation happen much earlier. Let us briefly compare experiences in Great Britain and Denmark, for instance, in this respect.

In Great Britain bills were issued against child labour as early as the beginning of the nineteenth century, accompanied by huge protests from owners of factories and coal mines. The most significant legislation to oblige children's schooling came in Britain only towards the very end of the nineteenth century. In Denmark, the order of the twin pieces of legislation was reverse. The bill obliging children to attend school until the age of confirmation was issued as early as 1814, whereas the bill against child labour was issued as late as 1872 – partly under the influence and fear of the 'social democrat Carl [*sic*] Marx' (Hornemann, 1872). It was remarkable that the initiative came from the employers' organization – a fact that, compared with Britain three quarters of a century before, can only be understood on the background of a maturation of the economy.

In both countries we saw child savers movements, which interestingly enough did not have much influence on enforcing legislation. British children continued to work despite legislation against it, whereas children in Denmark failed to attend school if more important work in the community was demanded. Even with legislation made to either effect, the significant fact was that only when necessary material conditions are available people are ready to follow suit and this is, of course, an answer to the question of prime movers. Another corollary is that, at the end of the day and when it favours them, people deliberately choose to adapt to the new dominant ways of production – in this case to the industrial economy.

Parents' acceptance of schooling was at the same time a favourable reception of the new *oikos*, which implied a new role for children. Parents had to recognise that children were no longer an economic asset – neither in the short nor in the long run; children had become an economic liability and the reaction was not long in coming – the birth rate adapted to parents' economic capability. Nevertheless, it is permitted to look at the transformations in a broader perspective, and that is what Kaufmann does when he suggests that scholarisation on a massive scale, as it happened at the time, was nothing less than the state's *colonisation* of a labour force that in Kaufmann's view belonged to parents (see also the chapter by Leonard, this volume). There was the truth in it that parents continued to be in charge of children's upkeep, even when they were scholarised – without being properly compensated for making this 'work force' available for the commonweal. The question is where the worth of children's school work is booked, because nobody will be so audacious as to suggest that it does not have a worth (see Qvortrup, 1995, 2000).

WINNERS AND LOSERS

I have been discussing childhood as it has developed in line with our societies' transformation from pre-industrial to industrial time. I have noted the large changes that both society and childhood have undergone. I have however, in particular, called attention to significant continuities in the transition, because they have typically, carelessly, but maybe unwittingly been obscured and hence remain difficult to observe. Above all I wanted to heighten the awareness of childhood as an integrated structural form – in terms of an intergenerational unit – even in our modern society.

Children (and childhood) have historically experienced a remarkable two-pronged fate. On the one hand, they have, as we have seen, been embraced with an increasing sentimentalisation to the point of sacralisation (Zelizer, 1985); on the other they have been subjected to a structural indifference (Kaufmann, 2005; see also the chapter by Sgritta, this volume). To the former corresponds their being a natural and indispensable part of a family with primary and warm *relationships* to parents and grandparents (in the 'haven in a heartless world', see Lasch, 1977). The latter matches up with exactly an indifferent corporate world, the interests of which are second to none and do not, as a matter of course, include children. This again was consistent with the claims that children were 'excommunicated' from the social fabric; their time and work was 'colonised' by the state in the service of not least corporate society with a merely half hearted recognition.

Ariès (1962, p. 412) interpreted schooling as 'a sort of quarantine', which 'removed the child from adult society' (p. 413) and he would agree with Benedict (1938) who talked about an increasing isolation of childhood from adulthood – one which historically coincided with and theoretically corresponded to the split between the reproductive and the productive spheres discussed earlier and alluded to by Davis (1937). Even if this observation is not necessarily consistent with the sentimentalisation thesis,[6] it contains the truth that not only is childhood (allegedly) beyond the interest spheres of corporate society and to some extent even that of the state, but it is also more and more distant to ever larger shares of adults. At the same time two opposing groups of adults have crystallised – those with and those without children (see the chapter by Jensen, this volume). The combination of lower birth rates and the extension of longevity has entailed a sharp increase in the proportion of all households without children. Coleman has for the USA shown an increase from 27 per cent in 1870 to 64 per cent in 1983.[7] During the same period the per capita income of minors relative to that of adults declined from 71 per cent to 51 per cent (Coleman, 1990, p. 590; Coleman, 1993, p. 6). The point is here that even if *children* do not in economic terms fall behind their *parents* (as long as they stay with them), *minors* lose ground to *adults* because more and more adults for ever longer periods live without children. This outcome demonstrates not only a lack of cohesiveness within the generational structure in society but is also a more and more irresistible invitation to a child-free life.

It is important to observe that in this intergenerational comparison, children and minors – although theoretically different – cover the same persons and same numbers within a given area, while 'adults' of course are a much larger group than 'parents', who currently share residence with their children; their 'excess' number expresses in a sense the growing distance between generations, that is, between minors and adults. Many would argue that relatively fewer children in an affluent society should give children a comparable advantage and lead to relatively more affluence among them. Exactly this is not happening because a decreasing share of households takes responsibility for children/childhood. Even if, despite this development, it cannot be claimed that minors' material conditions have worsened in absolute terms during the last century, or that children's welfare has deteriorated compared to that of their parents, Coleman's figures show that minors have done relatively worse than adults. This development does not contradict the sentimentalisation thesis, nor does it give empirical basis for predicting poverty among children. It nevertheless tells a story about supremacy of adulthood in that it represents a logical outcome to the advantage of increasing adult power and resources, given the demographic development and the displacement in distribution of responsibility among adults – from a situation where all adults, in principle, had to share this responsibility to one where it has become more or less optional. To this one can add a decreasing political influence (see the chapter by Campiglio, this volume).

This chapter has used the Greek term *oikos* as an overarching expression of economic householding under various circumstances; its forms differ, but its nature persists. It is not wrong to suggest that children also currently belong to a family household even if it is obvious that such a household has a different meaning than a family household had previously as it was the dominant *oikos* and combined productive and reproductive tasks. Therefore, it *is* wrong to say that they at present belong to the family *oikos*. The question is however in which way *minors* belong to the modern *oikos*, the modern national economy? We can phrase this question differently: are minors a private good or are they a public good?

There is no doubt that children in pre-industrial *oikos* were a *public good* in the sense that their involvement served the commonweal, however small that was; children were a clear response to classical fertility motivations and everybody profited from them – and the other way round: absence of children would clearly have jeopardised the maintenance and sustainability of the community. Currently, under a modern *oikos*, the answer is hardly different. The future of our society is unthinkable without *pupils' work* and without *succeeding generations' provision and care for the elderly* – in principle as ever. In this sense, they are a public good as they always were in line with its definition – as something that is common to and hence to be shared by the whole community; contrary to a *private good*, it is neither excludable nor rivalrous, which means that it is not consumed by merely one group of consumers. In this case, children are not 'consumed' merely by parents; whether it is seen as fair or not, they are available for the common good. The problem is that even if it is consumed by all it is not equally paid for by all.

Now, even if minors are a public good they are not a *free good* in the sense of being without budgetary implications. However, this seems to be the position of free riders, who appear to find it justified to enjoy a good without having contributed to its (re)production. We cannot be sure of what is an optimal number of children and it is probably impossible to arrive at such an imaginary number as long as there is a lack of coincidence between those who assume responsibility for their supply and those for whom they are in demand. We cannot, therefore, be sure that children *will* be reproduced in a number that corresponds to what is hypothetically required for societal sustainability. This proves our *oikos'* dependence on children and confirms their status as a public good. Children's school work is transformed into labour power demanded by corporate society and eventually into succeeding generations without which the old aged cannot survive. Everybody is ready to enjoy the gains thus made available through children, but not everybody is ready to share expenses for their upkeep. Employers may argue that they pay for the labour force when it is delivered; however, this is hardly an argument that motivates parents to have (more) children and therefore does not ensure that sufficient labour and tax payers will be reproduced. The trouble is in other words that the 'gains' in this sense is partly sent to the wrong address, namely to all individual adults and not merely to parents. It is a system in which rewards are disconnected from investments, and such a system is hardly viable.

In terms of winners and losers we may assert that – as long as it works – it is a system that in the short run favours those who do not contribute or do so comparably little. Also in the short run it is hardly harmful to individual children: as suggested their numbers have been reduced so as to match parents' material capabilities – a proof of parents' responsibility. However, since this is valued from the perspective of the family economy, nothing is said or considered about advantages or disadvantages to the modern *oikos* or from a structural point of view. As this analysis has indicated, it is wrong to suggest that the productive and the reproductive spheres are separable as were they independent of each other, exactly as the separation of childhood from adulthood (minors from adults) has been a doubtful development. The fact that spheres and generations have been allowed to co-exist in relative self-sufficiency has resulted in consequences that are both unintended and undesired. We can name a few of them: (a) a pension predicament; (b) a growing shortage of labour power befalling the modern *oikos* everywhere; (c) an ageing society, which the young members refuse to rejuvenate, because they don't have to and (d) within which increasing numbers of greying members leave their imprint on both the economic and political agenda – and therefore unwittingly jeopardise an already swaying architecture of childhood.

In its historical development and transformation childhood remains a segment in the equally transforming generational structure. It also keeps its significant place in the new *oikos*, even if this position has gone astray in our awareness. A sociology of childhood worth its name must come to terms with this structural position. Such a focus is not meant to overlook children's relationships with parents and grandparents, but it does entail an acceptance of childhood's continuous albeit changeable relation vis-à-vis other generational segments or forms; not least does it require an acknowledgement of the continuous worth of children's system immanent work. Our culture's sentimentalising and protective mood towards children is to be welcomed; an overprotected confinement to the small family may though have the price of overlooking childhood's indispensable relation to other generational segments.

NOTES

1. Another interesting transitory period to consider were the one observed by Ariès, but much less distinct and stretching over several centuries (fifteenth to seventeenth) in France. It has become famous due to Ariès, who saw the appearance of childhood in peoples' awareness – coming from nothingness.
2. The first decades of the twentieth century showed introduction of the right for women to vote in many countries.
3. I prefer it to Coleman's and Davis' terminology, which merely point to the differences between before and now.
4. These similarities were true for both girls and adult women and boys and adult men, whereas a gender difference was clear – and has remained until our days, but perhaps waning now.
5. It is though possible also to talk about *relations* between children and parents if our focus, for instance, is all children in society vis-à-vis all parents in society.
6. Because children and parents meet intensely in current small families; yet, they are typically separated in day time as both parents work and children frequent either day care centres or schools and leisure organisations.
7. In Scandinavia the proportion without children is as high as 3 in 4.

REFERENCES

Alanen, L. (2009). Generational order. In: J. Qvortrup, W. A. Corsaro & M.-S. Honig (Eds), *The Palgrave handbook of childhood studies* (pp. 159–174). Basingstoke: Palgrave Macmillan.

Ariès, P. (1962). *Centuries of childhood. A social history of family life.* New York: Vintage.

Ariès, P. (1980). Two successive motivations for declining birth rate in the West. *Population and Development Review, 6*(4), 645–650.

Ariès, P. (1982). *Barndommens historie.* (Abridged Danish translation of L'Enfant et la vie familiale sous l'ancien regime (1960) with preface to new French edition from Editions du Seuil: Paris, 1973). Copenhagen: Nyt Nordisk Forlag.

Ariès, P. (1990). *Ein Sonntagshistoriker.* Frankfurt Am Main: Hain.

Ariès, P. (1994). *Saint-Pierre oder die Süsse des Lebens. Versuche der Erinnerung.* Berlin: Verlag Klaus Wagenbach.

Benedict, R. (1938). Continuities and discontinuities in cultural conditioning. *Psychiatry, 1*(2), 161–167.

Berg, J. H. v. d. (1983). *The changing nature of man. Introduction to a historical psychology.* New York: W.W. Norton & Company.

Brunner, O. (1980). Vom 'ganzen Haus' zur 'Familie' im 17. Jahrhundert. In: H. Rosenbaum (Ed.), *Seminar: Familie und Gesellschaftsstruktur* (pp. 83–92). Frankfurt Am Main: Suhrkamp.

Caldwell, J. C. (1982). *Theory of fertility decline.* London: Academic Press.

Coleman, J. S. (1990). *Foundations of social theory.* Cambridge, MA: Belknap Press.

Coleman, J. S. (1993). The rational reconstruction of society. *American Sociological Review, 58*(February), 1–15.

Corsaro, W. A. (2009). Peer culture. In: J. Qvortrup, W. A. Corsaro & M.-S. Honig (Eds), *The Palgrave handbook of childhood studies* (pp. 301–315). Basingstoke: Palgrave Macmillan.

Cunningham, H. (2005). *Children and childhood in western society since 1500.* Pearson Longman: Harlow.

Davis, K. (1937). Reproductive institutions and the pressure for population. *The Sociological Review, 29*(3), 289–306.

Davis, K. (1940). The sociology of parent-youth conflict. *American Sociological Review, 5*(4), 523–535.

deMause, L. (1974). The evolution of childhood. In: L. de Mause (Ed.), *The history of childhood* (pp. 1–73). New York: The Psychohistory Press.

deMause, L. (1988). On Writing Childhood History. *The Journal of Psychohistory, 16*(2), Fall.

Erikson, E. H. (1962). *Young man luther: A study in psychoanalysis and history.* New York: Norton.

Garbarino, J. (1986). Can American families afford the luxury of childhood? *Child Welfare, 65*(2), 119–140.

Gillis, J. (2009). Transitions to modernity. In: J. Qvortrup, W. A. Corsaro & M.-S. Honig (Eds), *The Palgrave handbook of childhood studies* (pp. 114–126). Basingstoke: Palgrave Macmillan.

Gulløv, E., & Højlund, S. (2003). *Feltarbejde blandt børn – metodologi og etik i etnografisk børneforskning.* [Fieldwork among children – methodology and ethics in ethnographic child research]. København: Gyldendal.

26   JENS QVORTRUP

Hendrick, H. (2009). The evolution of childhood in Western Europe c.1400-c.1750. In: J. Qvortrup, W. A. Corsaro & M.-S. Honig (Eds), *The Palgrave handbook of childhood studies* (pp. 99–113). Basingstoke: Palgrave Macmillan.

Hornemann, E. (1872). 'Om Børns Anvendelse i Fabriker, særlig med Hensyn til vore Forhold' [On the use of children in factories, with particular respect to our circumstances]. *Hygieiniske Meddelelser og Betragtninger [Hygienic messages and considerations]*, 7(3), 151–194.

Kaufmann, F.-X. (2005). *Schrumpfende Gesellschaft. Vom Bevölkerungsrückgang und seinen Folgen.* Frankfurt Am Main: Suhrkamp.

Lasch, C. (1977). *Haven in a heartless world: The family besieged.* New York: Basic Books.

Levine, D. P. (1995). *Wealth and freedom. An introduction to political economy.* Cambridge: Cambridge University Press.

Mead, M. (1978). *Culture and commitment: The new relationships between generations in the 1970's* (Revised and updated edition). Garden City, NY: Anchor Press/Doubleday.

Miller, A. (1980). *Am Anfang war die Erziehung.* Frankfurt Am Main: Suhrkamp.

Qvortrup, J. (1995). From useful to useful: The historical continuity of children's constructive participation. In: Anne-Marie, A. (Ed.), *Sociological studies of children* (Vol. 7, pp. 49–76). Greenwich, CT: JAI.

Qvortrup, J. (2000). Kolonisiert und Verkannt: Schularbeit. In: Arbeit der Kinder, hrsg. von Heinz Hengst und Helga Zeiher. Weinheim: Juventa.

Qvortrup, J. (2009). Childhood as a structural form. In: J. Qvortrup, W. A. Corsaro & M.-S. Honig (Eds), *The Palgrave handbook of childhood studies* (pp. 21–33). Basingstoke: Palgrave Macmillan.

Strandell, H. (1994). *Sociala mötesplatser för barn: aktivitetsprofiler och förhandlingskulturer på daghem.* [Social meeting places for children: activity profiles and cultures of negotiation at day care centres]. Helsinki: Gaudeamus.

Thorne, B. (1993). *Gender play: Girls and boys in school.* New Brunswick, NJ: Rutgers University Press.

Wartofsky, M. (1981). The child's construction of the world and the world's construction of the child: From historical epistemology to historical psychology. In: F. S. Kessel & A. W. Siegel (Eds), *The child and other cultural inventions* (pp. 188–215). New York: Praeger.

Woodhead, M. (2009). Child development and the development of childhood. In: J. Qvortrup, W. A. Corsaro & M.-S. Honig (Eds), *The Palgrave handbook of childhood studies* (pp. 46–61). Basingstoke: Palgrave Macmillan.

Zelizer, V. A. (1985). *Pricing the priceless child. The changing social value of children.* New York: Basic Books.

Zelizer, V. A. (2005). The Priceless Child Revisited. In: J. Qvortrup (Ed.), *Studies in Modern Childhood. Society, Agency, Culture* (pp. 184–200). Basingstoke: Palgrave Macmillan.

DO IDEAS MATTER? CHANGES IN POLICIES CONCERNING CHILDREN AND FAMILIES IN GERMANY AND NORWAY

Thomas Olk

INTRODUCTION

Since the 1990s, the importance of childhood and children within the political agenda of advanced welfare states has grown rapidly. For example, in 1989 the Canadian House of Commons launched a resolution aimed at eliminating poverty among Canadian children by the year 2000. With the help of the National Children's Agenda and the National Child Benefit the situation of children should be improved. Nearly 10 years later in the UK, New Labour heralded the political goal to halve child poverty within 10 years and to eradicate it within 20 years. A wide variety of measures and programs like Sure Start and the National Childcare Strategy were started to improve the welfare and well-being of children. In 2002, a new paradigm was established in Germany concerning family policy. The aim was to improve the reconciliation of family and work, the material welfare of young families by a new parental leave scheme, as well as supporting the development of young children by increasing the number of places for children under the age of 3 in early childhood education and care.

Structural, Historical, and Comparative Perspectives
Sociological Studies of Children and Youth, Volume 12, 27–53
Copyright © 2009 by Emerald Group Publishing Limited
ISSN: 1537-4661/doi:10.1108/S1537-4661(2009)0000012007

Additionally, international organisations contributed to this trend. For example, the OECD (cf. 2001, 2006) propagated the development of early childhood education and care (ECEC) as an important contribution to a successful transition into the knowledge society. According to the Lisbon-Strategy, the EU announced new goals for policies concerning children and families as well as introduced benchmarks for evaluating the implementation of these goals in the member states. Finally, in an influential evaluation for the EU President, Esping-Andersen (cf. 2002) and his colleagues argued for a concept of a "child-centered social investment strategy."

This essay argues that the new political priorities, programs and measures just mentioned stand for the rise of a new political paradigm that will continue to gain influence in many countries in the near future. The new political paradigm is characterized by new political priorities and instruments as well as by a different interpretation of social risks and needs, not to mention a new social construction of the status of children and childhood in modern welfare states. Though under the old political paradigm children were rendered part of the private world of the family – and this means the responsibility of their parents – under the new political paradigm they are interpreted as the future human capital of societies and as an object of public investment. However, the relevance of the new political paradigm varies between countries. Although in some countries a rapid and far reaching change in political goals, instruments, and programs for children and families is taking place, in others it is not. In the latter the development is much more gradual and the protagonists of a competing political paradigm are neither successful in challenging existing values and orientations in policies for children and families nor in implementing a new normative reference system and new political strategy in this field.

Explaining Policy Change: The "Ideational Turn"

This raises the question as to how policy change takes place. In recent debates on policy change a plurality of explanations are under discussion. Whereas some approaches stress interest-based rationality and game-theoretic behaviour, others focus on institutional path-dependency and historically shaped patterns of development. From the perspective of historical institutionalism real policy change is rare. In the context of a given welfare architecture, existing national policy legacies, preferences, and a particular actor's problem-solving capacity, more often than not, social change takes place as a "within-regime" adjustment (cf. Pierson, 2001).

Historical institutionalism assumes that institutional constraints and the power of interests block radical policy change.

However, the examples aforementioned demonstrate that radical change in policies concerning children and families can happen in some countries under existing institutional constraints and policy legacies. Obviously, referring to external pressures and problems as well as to national policy legacies in institutional arrangements is not enough to explain policy change. This is the reason why in recent literature on policy change the importance of social-learning, ideas, and discourses for political analysis and explaining policy change is stressed (cf. Yee, 1996; Hall, 1993; Campbell, 1998; Schmidt, 2002; Schmidt & Radaelli, 2004, see Seeleib-Kaiser, 2002; Kuebler, 2007 for an analysis of family policies). This approach indicates that ideational processes are able to influence the way policy makers perceive problems as well as change their preferences. At the same time, the "ideational turn" does not neglect the relevance of institutional contexts or interests. Rather this approach is a specific variation of institutional analysis. This is the reason why it is labelled "discursive institutionalism" (cf. Schmidt, 2002). It is assumed that under specific conditions ideas and discourses are better able to explain political change than other approaches. This is the case when networks consisting of societal and state actors, confronted with new challenges, are successful in establishing a new definition of political problems and are able to link these new perceptions of problems to new political goals and innovative instruments. The ideational approach does not claim to explain every political change. Processes of social learning, ideas, and discourses are occasionally the decisive factors in explaining political change and some-times not. However, discourses can serve to bridge the gap between institutionalist and actor-centered analysis – and this means between structure and agency. Political change cannot simply be explained by referring to the reactions of policy makers on socioeconomic trends like the demographic challenge, the process of globalisation or the coming of the knowledge society. Depending on which discourses and political ideas are employed decision makers make sense of the given external pressures and problems which they need to identify as well as how they link these needs to political strategies and instruments.

In the following it is assumed that there is a certain correspondence between the predominant political paradigm, on the one hand, and the treatment of children and families as well as a specific discourse on the role of children in the society, on the other. Between both factors there is a close interaction: a certain kind of social and political practice of treating children and families is legitimized by specific social constructions of children and childhood. A new political paradigm in the field of policies concerning children and families can only be established by implementing new ideas and values concerning the role and status of childhood and children in the society. Of course, to explain the changes and continuities in childhood over time within a given society over time we need to include a wide variety of factors and processes. These include social, political, and economic processes that Allison James and Adrian James describe as "the cultural politics of childhood" (cf. 2004). "Taking place both through processes of continuity as well as change, the cultural politics of childhood comprises, therefore, both the many and different cultural determinants of childhood and children's behaviour, and the political mechanisms and processes by which these are put into practice at any given time" (James & James, 2004, p. 4). The analysis of the "cultural politics of childhood" must be engaged in the identification of processes "by which these cultural determinants and discourses are put into practice at any given time, in any given culture, to construct "childhood' in society" (James & James, 2004, p. 7). According to this, Adrian and Allison James identify law as a "key mechanism" of this process of construction and reconstruction of childhood within a given society. As far as the influence of political strategies in a narrower sense – that is, political programs, measures, and discourses – are focused on analysis, they speak of a "politics of childhood" (cf. James & James, 2004, 2005).

From the Family Responsibility Paradigm
to the Investing in Children Paradigm

As aforementioned this chapter assumes that in some advanced welfare states an existing "old" political paradigm in the field of policies concerning children and families was replaced by a "new" political paradigm. Each political paradigm is associated with a specific social construction of childhood and children (see Qvortrup, 2008; Olk & Wintersberger, 2007 for the position of children and childhood in the welfare state). In the following, both of the competing political paradigms will be presented.

The previously predominant paradigm is called the "family-responsibility paradigm" (cf. Jenson, 2004). According to this paradigm, parents are exclusively responsible for the well-being of their children. As dependent members of the family household, children have no direct relation to the welfare state. Their access to social security is guaranteed only indirectly via the entitlements of the male breadwinner. Under the rule of the male breadwinner family model it comes not only to a familiarization of the social rights of children but also to a familiarization of care. Whereas their material welfare has to be secured by the market capacity and income of the father, the provision of care is regarded as the obligation of the mother. The concrete form of the relationship between state and children is shaped by norms of family-solidarity and subsidiary (cf. Saraceno, 2004). To avoid weakening the primary responsibility of the parents for their children's welfare all state provisions for children and families are organized in a subsidiary manner. The state does not intervene except in extreme cases where families are not able to solve their problems on their own – for example, to protect children from neglect or violence by their parents or other adults as well as to guarantee the fulfilment of their basic needs and developmental opportunities. In so doing, the state does not focus on children's subjective rights and claims but rather on the duties of the parents to support their children. Income transfers and benefits respond to the needs of adults both in the context of their relationship to the labour force, and more specifically, in their capacity to earn enough income for themselves and their families.

This political paradigm is based on the norm of the "male-breadwinner-family-model," and means that the father's income alone must be sufficient to keep the family from falling into poverty. In accordance with this political paradigm the social construction of childhood defines childhood as a stage in life, which is situated in the private world of the family and the neighbourhood. Children are not rendered as full-fledged citizens but rather as "human becomings" who are destined to be engaged in activities which are appropriate for children (such as playing, etc.).

Given the rising participation of women in the labour market, the political claim of gender equality, the demographic challenge, and the coming of the knowledge-society, in the last few decades a competing political paradigm of increasing importance in many countries has emerged (cf. Jenson, 2004, 2006). According to this paradigm the well-being of the whole society depends on the welfare and well-being of children (cf. Esping-Andersen, 2005, 2008). It is assumed that future economic growth and prosperity require suitable investments in children in the here and now. For this reason, goals such as fighting child poverty and extending the number of places in facilities of early childhood education and care – especially for children under the age of three – have been gaining political relevance. Following this paradigm it is essential to support parents in investing in their children. To avoid child poverty protect against material insufficiency as well as to improve the conditions for investing in children, fathers *and* mothers need to participate in the labour market. Furthermore, it is not considered an acceptable option for single parents receiving social assistance to care for their children instead of participating in the labour market. The best possible way of supporting children policy under such conditions is to offer a suitable supply of places in childcare facilities and to improve the employability of fathers and mothers by securing access to income and work for both the parents.

The underlying social construction of childhood and children defines childhood as a stage in life, where children have the duty to prepare themselves for their future role as "citizen-workers of the future" (cf. Lister, 2004, 2006). Children are not rendered as dependent members of the family household, but rather as a human asset. The parents alone are not responsible for the welfare of their children; instead this responsibility is divided between the parents and the state. In this context the roles and responsibilities of mothers and fathers are becoming more and more equal, and there is a strong tendency toward "gender sameness." Though under this condition it is expected that mothers contribute to the family income by participating in the labour market, fathers are pushed to contribute to the development of their children by becoming more involved in their upbringing.

If and to what extend this new political paradigm of "investing in children" will be implemented in different countries depends on a plurality of factors (cf. Olk & Wintersberger, 2007). However, it is clear that factors like institutional arrangements and policy legacies or interests still play an important role. Nonetheless, the following analysis demonstrates that it is primarily the propagation of a new discourse about the role and status of children and parents in society which is responsible for the radical changes witnessed in several countries. Hence, it is above all the processes of social learning and discourse policies which can best explain a radical change in policies concerning children and families in some countries. To examine this approach I will analyse the children and family policies in both Germany and Norway with respect to the causes of political change.

The selection of these countries is legitimate for two reasons: First, the potential influence of the type of welfare regime on processes of political learning can be controlled. According to Esping-Andersen's (cf. 1990) typology. Germany can be assigned to the conservative welfare regime model and Norway to the social democratic model. Secondly, the dynamics of politics concerning children and families are different enough to demonstrate the importance of different factors causing policy change in these countries.

THE CASE OF GERMANY: "SUSTAINABLE FAMILY POLICY" – REFRAMING POLICIES CONCERNING CHILDREN AND FAMILIES

Until 2002 – the beginning of the second term of the red-green coalition under Chancellor Gerhard Schröder – no one would have guessed that a new paradigm regarding family policy and causing a radical change in political strategies and instruments would have been possible in Germany.

When the minister of family affairs, Renate Schmidt, took office a new concept under the title "sustainable family policy" was developed and implemented. This was the result of the huge discrepancy perceived between relatively high spending levels for programs and measures related to children and families, on the one hand, and their relatively small impact, on the other. Although Germany ranks relatively high in spending for families and children among European nations – with only Luxembourg providing a more generous child benefit package – the following deficits were found:

- The fertility rate in Germany was 1.35; a rate placing it in the lowest third in international rankings.
- German pupils ranked very low in international school achievement tests (PISA-test).
- Child poverty rates have been on the rise since the late 1980s.
- Last, but not least, compared to other nations, the rate of women's participation (especially mothers) in the labour market was relatively low.

To overcome the deficits of the old family policy a radical policy change was introduced. The new concept of "sustainable family policy" is oriented toward the following objectives:

- Fertility rate: to secure the demographic continuance an average fertility rate of 1.7 children per woman needs to be reached.
- Reconciliation of work and family: to increase the participation of women in the labour market as well as the implementation of measures aimed at increasing the fertility rate by means of a better reconciliation of work and family.
- Fighting child poverty: to eradicate children and family poverty the strategy of choice is not to increase social spending for families but rather to increase the labour market participation of both parents.
- Investing in education: to improve the conditions for future economic growth and to prevent children and family poverty, investments in education, especially by increasing the number of early childhood

education and care facilities and by expanding the number of all-day schools, needs to be realized.

To overcome the marginal status of family policy compared to other fields of policy as well as to make the new concept of family policy more convincing, the new paradigm of "sustainable family policy" was intentionally conceptualized as part of a strategy of economic modernization. For this reason it was interpreted as a strategy of "economization of the family policy discourse" (Leitner, 2008). The head of the department for family policy at the ministry of family affairs, Malte Ristau, argues in an article from June 2005 that the minister of family affairs, with the help of the new concept of "sustainable family policy," relies on "the economic charm of the family" (cf. Ristau, 2005, p. 19). Also the federal government's stance to the 7th Family Report in 2006 views this change of paradigms in the field of family policy as legitimated by economic arguments: "Families ensure the social growth as well as economic prosperity of our society. Germany cannot afford to waste important potentials for further growth and innovation." (BMFSFJ, 2006, p. XXIV).

Furthermore, the specific objectives of the concept of sustainable family policy must prove their economic viability. For example, increasing the birth rate addresses the labour shortage due to demographic change, an improvement of the system of early childcare and education contributes to the qualification of the future workforce, not to mention financially relieving the welfare state.

To increase the persuasiveness of the new concept and to gain allies within the civil society scientific experts were employed to communicate the new ideas. Two experts were particularly significant. First, the economist Bert Rürup, who advises the German government on economic issues, analyzed the demographic challenge. He concluded that a stabilization of the labour supply as a consequence of demographic trends could be reached by just increasing the birth rate and the labour market participation of women. From an economic perspective he argues for a reduction of opportunity costs, especially for educated women (cf. Rürup & Gruesco, 2003).

The sociologist Hans Bertram – simultaneously head of the independent expert commission of the 7th Family Report – stressed in his conclusion the existence of different family and work orientations of women. He argued for taking into account different biographical orientations of women by structuring policies concerning children and families to allow as many women as possible to have children regardless of their orientation toward work and career. In accordance with this line of thinking he advocates an intelligent mix of time politics, infrastructure, and financial transfers (cf. Bertram, Rösler, & Ehlert, 2005).

The strategic economization of the family policy discourse becomes quite evident when one considers that within the context of the new paradigm each family policy measure will be legitimized by verifying its economic efficiency. The central message is: sustainable family policy pays off![1]

The joint conclusion of all of these studies is that the new concept of sustainable family policy is in the genuine interest of enterprises, improves the conditions for economic growth, and thus, families represent a good investment!

To enforce a real policy change the minister of family affairs needed allies both at the state level and in civil society, because, traditionally speaking, family policy in Germany is a weak policy field. The ministry of family affairs is not fully responsible for all measures and programs related to children and families. For example, it is the ministry of financial affairs which is responsible for child benefits and family-oriented taxations. Complicating matters, the federal structure of the German state must also be factored into this equation. This means that the responsibility for family policy is dispersed between all three levels: federal, state, and local authorities. This fact alone makes it very difficult to develop a consistent family policy concept. Although the federal states (Bundesländer) are responsible for education, the local authorities are responsible for social services for families, children, and youths. Furthermore, as a consequence of a recent reform of the federalism the responsibilities of the state, especially in the field of education have been further weakened. As aforementioned, the federal ministry of family affairs, senior citizens, women and youth (BMFSFJ) is, traditionally speaking, a weak ministry with limited competencies and a small budget. Family affair ministers have no high priority in the Cabinet and their power depends on their relationship to the Chancellor and their public popularity. To improve its own power and its ability to persuade other powerful actors the federal ministry of family affairs constructed an alliance with societal actors who are both prominent in the public and influential; individuals from the economic sphere, unions, charities, churches, and sciences. The "Alliance for Families" served as a platform for joint activities (Mohn & von der Leyen, 2004).

These influential personalities have been used to help expand early childcare and education, introducing family-friendly work schedules in businesses as well as sustainable family policy. The "Local Alliances for Families" were initiated by the ministry of family affairs as a counterpart to the "National Alliance for Families" at the local level. The aim was to encourage local authorities, businesses, and nonprofit organizations to implement measures to improve the situation of families within a given community. At the present moment, there are 445 "Local Alliances for Families" in Germany. Allies in this movement are local businesses and the regional Chambers of Trade and Commerce.

All in all, with the help of the concept of sustainable family policy the ministry of family affairs managed to implement a new paradigm of policy concerning children and families, to identify new target groups with new social needs and to involve new political actors. For example, by highlighting the reconciliation of family and work, the needs of working mothers and caring fathers, and the needs of young children (especially those under the age of three) these issues have been made the focus of attention. Furthermore, additional resources for a sustainable family policy were mobilized by activating new social actors like businesses, business associations, unions, churches, charity organizations and chambers of trade and commerce.

Such measures are most important in the context of the new social policy for children and families: increasing the number of places in early childcare and education for children under the age of three and the new parental leave scheme.[2]

First, the legislation concerning the expansion of early childcare for children under the age of three (Tagesbetreuungsausbaugesetz) was launched in January 2005. With the help of this law roughly 230,000 additional places for children under the age of three are to be created by 2010 – and thus closing in on the international standard. These provision rates in Germany fell far behind the other European nations – especially compared to the Nordic countries. In 1998, the provision rate in Western Germany was 2.8% and approximztely 36.3% in Eastern Germany; total 7% (cf. Jurczyk, Olk, & Zeiher, 2004; Rauschenbach, 2006; Spieß, Berger, & Groh-Samberg, 2008). In accordance with this law local authorities who are responsible for financing early childcare and education are requested to identify the need for childcare at the local level and to offer no fewer than the number of places for children of this age whose parents are either both gainfully employed, single parent, are participating in vocational courses or in integration measures organized by the new social assistance for long-term unemployed (Hartz IV[3]). To implement this law 1.5 billion Euro p.a. have been calculated till 2010 (cf. Meysen & Schindler, 2004).

In addition to the reform of the system of early childcare and education for children under the age of three Minister Schmidt aimed at reforming the parental leave scheme during her term. The previous parental leave scheme offered only a very small flatrate compared to wages and incomes (300 €)

with the consequence that the opportunity costs for the parent who interrupts his/her gainful employment to care for the child were very high. In practice, it was primarily the mothers (more than 90%) who made use of the old parental leave scheme. Thus the central aim of the new parental leave scheme is to reduce the opportunity costs associated with raising a child – especially for highly educated women. As such mothers or fathers who interrupt their employment to care for their child should receive 67% of their former wages for up to 12 months. To motivate fathers to take more responsibility in caring for their child(ren) initially three months of paid parental leave were reserved for them.

Owing to the early federal elections (which took place in 2005 instead of 2006) it was not possible to launch the new parental leave scheme during the red-green coalition's second term. However, the newly formed CDU/CSU and SPD coalition took up the former coalition's initiative and the new minister of family affairs Ursula von der Leyen (CDU) has continued with the family policy of her predecessor Renate Schmidt (SPD). Thus, the German Bundestag adopted the law concerning the new parental leave in September 2006, and which went into effect in January 2007. The amount of the new parental leave is 67% of the average net income of the person who cares for the child – with a maximum of 1,800 Euro per month. Parents who did not work in the months before giving birth are eligible to receive a monthly payment of 300 Euros. The parental leave can even be divided between the two parents. However, two months are reserved for the parent who continued working, which is usually the father (the so-called "daddy quota"). Lone parents are eligible for a parental leave of up to 14 months. The new parental leave scheme persues several different aims: The primary aim is to reduce opportunity costs for the caring parent. Second, by reducing the duration of the new parental leave to a maximum of 12 months per person mothers shall be better integrated into the labour market. Thirdly, incentives for giving birth to more children should be induced. By this it was accepted that above all families with higher incomes profit more from this law than poor people who have even fewer benefits than under the previous system (they receive 300 Euro per month, but only for 14 months instead of 24 months).

Concerning the "daddy quota," conflict between different interest groups has emerged and there was an intensive public debate on this issue. Some members of the CDU/CSU protested against the introduction of the daddy months arguing that the state is not allowed to intervene into the private sphere of the family. However, contrary to the previous conflicts there was no party cleavage, instead only a conflict within the CDU/CSU. As the

CSU – a Bavarian regional party – holds a veto in the German Bundesrat (the Chamber of the Federal States) a political compromise was negotiated. Given the strong political consensus across all political parties and given the wide acceptance of the new parental leave scheme in the public, the opponents were not able to prevent the passing of the new law.

After having implemented the new parental leave, the minister of family affairs started a new initiative to expand early childcare, especially for children under the age of three. The new legislation aimed at supporting children (Kinderförderungsgesetz), which took effect in January 2009, will increase the provision rate for children under the age of three from the present 14% to 35% by 2013. Thus around 500,000 new places in crèches and child minders need to be created. The federal government is contributing a share of four billion Euros to the total costs of 12 billion Euros (cf. BMFSFJ, 2008).

All in all with the help of the new concept of "sustainable family policy" the ministry was able to enforce a new social construction of childhood and to establish a new type of parental responsibility. The new policy for children and families is oriented toward the adult-worker-family-model. Fathers *and* mothers shall be engaged in gainful employment to prevent families from falling into poverty, to stabilize the supply of labour in a situation of demographic aging, and finally, to strengthen the economic security of women. Children are no longer rendered as dependent members of their family, but as a "public good"and as an object of investment in their human capital. At the same time, we are witnessing a far-reaching reconstruction of childhood. As a consequence of the expansion of early childcare for children under the age of three the construction of a "learning childhood," even in the very early stages of life, is being implemented. However, so far there is a strong discrepancy between ambitious political goals, on the one hand, and the real situation, on the other. Nearly no effects of the sustainable family policy can be measured. For example, despite the new parental leave the expected increase in births did not take place. According to preliminary estimations, in 2008 approximately 675,000 children were born – ca. 8,000 or 1.1% fewer than 2007. Solely in Eastern Germany there was a slight increase in the fertility rate. According to experts this trend is caused by the new parental leave (cf. Amann, 2009). Furthermore, at the time being the increase in the number of places in publicly subsidized daycare is nothing but a political aim. Given the monetary restrictions at the local level and the dispersed responsibilities at different federal levels it is not guaranteed that it will be able to create 500,000 new places within four years.

THE CASE OF NORWAY: A DUALISTIC MODEL OF POLICIES CONCERNING CHILDREN AND FAMILIES

Policies concerning children and families in Norway are shaped by the specific "cultural construction of Norden" (cf. Sørensen & Stråth, 1997) as well as by the ideas and values concerning the status and role of children and families in Norwegian society. It is a central part of the Norwegian social model and a specific version of the social democratic welfare regime (cf. Esping-Andersen, 1990). Furthermore, the "Nordic protestant ethic," the specific geography of the country, and the dominance of the traditional industries like fishing, agriculture, forestry, and shipping continue to exert a strong influence. Thus, it is no surprise that such principles as independence, autonomy, individuality, and personal freedom still play an important role within the society and culture. Traditionally speaking, children were and are considered citizens with their own needs, interests, and rights, and childhood was accepted as a stage of life with its own inherent value (cf. Satka & Eydal, 2004; Nilsen, 2008).

Thus, from the very beginning in Norway the interests and needs of the children played an important role in the process of conceptualizing policies concerning children and families. The characteristic of the Norwegian welfare state as a proponent of the social democratic welfare regime, above all its universalism, makes it relatively easy to include children into the policy agenda (cf. Greve, 2000; Hemmerling, 2007; Risa, 1999; Wagner, 2006). During the period of welfare state expansion after World War II generous financial transfers for children and families as well as the expansion of the public school system took center stage. The Norwegian welfare state has aimed at guaranteeing social security, equality, and an adjustment of life chances for all members of the society – including children

When it comes to the material provision of children and families instruments such as taxes and child benefits certainly have to be mentioned. Like in many other countries, the Norwegian welfare state uses the tax system to redistribute resources between families with and without children. Different child-related tax deductions were established. However, tax deductions tend to produce unintended effects in the sense that privileged population groups profit more from it than poorer groups. This is the reason why in 1970 Norway replaced child-related tax deductions with child benefits (cf. Skevik & Hatland, 2008, p. 102).

Consequently, today child benefits are the most important financial provision for families and children. In 2005, the amount of the child benefit was 970 NOK (approximately 120 €) per month and those living in the arctic regions were eligible for an additional 320 NOK (approximately 40 €) for every child. The additional benefit for lone parents of children aged 1–3 was 660 NOK (approximately 83 €) per month (cf. Skevik & Hatland, 2008, 102 f.). There has been effectively no increase in the child benefit since the early 1990s. This is at the very least a result of the increasing of the age limit from 16 to 18 in 2000, the financial burdens that emerged from the expansion of public childcare and the introduction of the cash-for-care benefit. In other words, there is a form of redistribution between different social benefits for children and families that enjoy a high level of public acceptance.

Public Daycare for Children in Norway

Given the Norwegian welfare state's longstanding stance toward the needs of children it is all the more surprising to find out that the expansion of public daycare in Norway was implemented much more slowly than in many other European countries – especially compared to the other Scandinavian nations Denmark and Sweden. Until the 1970s, public daycare was mainly a phenomenon of the big cities; 80% of children in public daycare lived in cities. Reasons for this include the specific geographic and climatic conditions in Norway, the dispersed settlements in the country, the late urbanization and industrialization as well as the traditional dominance of industries like fishing, agriculture, forestry, and shipping (cf. Korsvold, 1991, p. 230 ff.). Under these conditions until the late 1960s married women mostly stayed at home, the farm, or went into family businesses. Furthermore, the climatic living conditions outside of the cities were for a majority of the population quite difficult. Even pre-school age children contributed to the family economy by doing domestic work. There was a strong belief that parents were exclusively responsible for their children, thus the family and the home were considered to be the most appropriate place for children.

As such, the first law regarding kindergartens in 1975 viewed them as institutions that need to provide an appropriate environment for children and should operate very closely with the parents (cf. Nicolaysen, 2000). The task and aim of the kindergartens were oriented toward the needs of children and pedagogical concepts; other rationales like gender equality or a better reconciliation of family and work were at best seen as secondary.

Under pressure from the increased participation of females in the labour market as well as the processes of industrialization and urbanization, politicians negotiated the "Norwegian compromise" (cf. Korsvold, 1991) regarding the rationale of the kindergartens. Given the fact that there was a sceptical orientation toward nonfamilial childcare, on the one hand, and an increasing proportion of working mothers dependent on a sufficient supply of public childcare, on the other, kindergartens were conceived as institutions that were directly oriented toward the needs of the children. Given the specific Norwegian construction of childhood and children this means that kindergartens have to support the development of the child by enabling free play and social learning as well as by considering the individual needs of each child (cf. Strand, 2006). Everyday life in public kindergartens should approximate as closely as possible the family life and the traditional lifestyle of Norwegian children at home as well as offer opportunities to spend time and play in nature.

The Ambivalence of the Norwegian Policy Concerning Children and Families

Generally speaking, all of the Scandinavian countries were considered proponents of the social democratic welfare regime type in that they combined the principle of universalism with a strong emphasis on social services. However, when it comes to social services Norway is an exceptional case. Although Norway offers a generous social services package for the elderly, those services targeting children, especially under the age of three, were at that time underdeveloped (cf. Anttonen & Sipilä, 1996). The main reason for this lies in the fact that the rationale for childcare services in Norway is – as aforementioned not conceptualized with respect to goals like gender equality or female labour market participation, but rather with respect to pedagogical aims. Nevertheless, in the late 1980s full coverage was proclaimed as a common goal of Norwegian family policy. However, the right to childcare was not introduced for two reasons: First, the political autonomy of the local governments should be secured. Second, the freedom of choice between the dual-earner family model and a traditional breadwinner model should be obtainable. This can be seen as another manifestation of the fact that the Norwegian policy does not privilege a specific model of family life, but instead pursues a "dualistic family policy" model under which both models of family life are to be encouraged (Ellingsæter, 2003; also Ellingsæter & Gulbrandsen, 2007).

The result of this was that the proportion of children in public daycare in Norway increased more slowly than in Denmark or Sweden. Although Denmark and Sweden managed to close the "care gap" by expanding public daycare, until only recently a substantial care gap existed in Norway (Ellingsæter & Gulbrandsen, 2007, p. 654; see also Leira, 2006). Although since the late 1980s, there has been a marked expansion of public daycare, the supply did not meet the increased demand. Ellingsæter and Gulbrandsen (cf. 2007) argue that this slow expansion cannot be explained by political strategy. Instead, they consider this the result of interactive processes between supply and demand on the childcare market. Following their line of argumentation, the decisive factor does not involve the policies, but rather "mothers' agency." This means that the driving factor was not so much a political strategy but the urgent demand for public daycare especially by well-educated mothers. Adding to the considerable increase in female employment since the middle 1980s, there was a sharp rise in the number of full-time working mothers. In contrast to this, the provision rate increased from a mere 2% in the 1960s to 20% in the 1980s. When faced with the insufficient supply of public childcare in the 1980s many parents' initiatives were implemented to compensate for this shortage (cf. Leira, Tobio, & Trifiletti, 2005). As a consequence, the hesitant policy toward public childcare gave rise to private facilities that were supported by the state. Since the middle 1970s, there are approximately as many private facilities as there are public. Furthermore, only since the 1980s has the percentage of full-time places regularly increased (78% in 2005).

In the 1990s there was a strong increase in the provision rate for public childcare. Though in the early 1990s merely 36% of children under the age of 6 were in public childcare, by 2000 the number had climbed to 52%. However, this impressive increase does not have as much to do with the expansion of the number of places in public childcare, but rather is primarily attributable to the expansion of the parental leave scheme in 1993 and the lowering of the school age from 7 to 6 in 1997.

Before 1993 the duration of the parental leave was 24 weeks (30 weeks at 80% of the normal wage). The parental leave reform in 1993 extended compensation to 42 weeks at full wage or 52 weeks at 80% wage (cf. Skevik & Hatland, 2008, p. 98f.). Additionally, with the lowering of the school age to six meant that an entire age cohort was taken from the market. This means that since 1997 the political aim is to guarantee a place to all children between 1 and 5 years of age if the parents request one. When it comes to trends in the childcare market the increase in the number of places during the 1990s for children over three years of age was significant, whereas the number of places for children under the age of three hardly increased at all.

The Cash-for-Care Reform

The goals and rationale of the policies concerning children and families remained contested between the left- and right-wing political parties in the years that followed. Whereas the left-wing parties preferred the dual-worker family model and emphasized the goal of gender equality, the right-wing parties were oriented toward the traditional breadwinner family model and the goal of optimizing choice for parents (cf. Ellingsæter, 2006). The social democratic government supported the dual-breadwinner model with the parental leave reform and the expansion of early childcare and education. Afterwards, the center minority Government, with the help of two other right-wing parties attempted to support choice for parents by introducing the cash-for-care reform to restore balance in the dualistic family policy in Norway.

This reform pursued three goals: First, parents should be allowed to spend more time caring for their children. Second, families should be offered a real choice between different care arrangements. Third, the realization of a just distribution of financial transfers between families with different care arrangements (cf. Ellingsæter, 2003; Skevik & Hatland, 2008, p. 103f; Ellingsæter, 2006). The cash-for-care benefit was launched in August 1998 for one-year-olds and in January 1999 for two-year-olds. All families are eligible whose children do not have an all-day place in public daycare. The amount of the cash-for-care benefit is 3,000 NOK (approximately 400 €); that corresponds to the cost of an all-day place at a public daycare facility. This hotly contested reform was preceded both by controversies in the public and between the political parties. Although the left-wing parties feared a roll back of the progress in gender equality, the more central- and right-wing parties criticized the lack of alternatives and the lack of choice in a policy which exclusively supports the dual-earner family model.

Interestingly enough, the effects of the reform were limited. Though most of the parents made use of the new cash-for-care benefit, there were only very small changes in the patterns of labour market participation by mothers. A study that was conducted shortly after the introduction of the reform showed that one year later just as many mothers with children between the ages of 1 and 2 were unemployment as before the reform – namely 25% or 26% – and the average weekly working hours of mothers decreased only slightly from 23.9 to 22.4 h (cf. Ellingsæter, 2003, p. 426). Furthermore, there were no discernable effects of the reform regarding fathers. Ellingsæter found that there are no simple causal effects in the complex field of social practises within families and that financial incentives sometimes have unintended consequences. Furthermore, family policy measures like the cash-for-care reform promote a wide variety of aims, some of which conflict to varying degrees with one another. For example, with the cash-for-care reform the choice with respect to different family models should be secured as well as make it possible for parents (most often mothers) to spend more time with their children. Furthermore, a clear separation between working- and nonworking mothers was assumed. Contrarily, the orientations of mothers are much more complex, and this means that many mothers combine full- and part-time work over the course of their lives.

Since the labour market situation in Norway for mothers at the time of the reform was very good and mothers' interest in gainful employment and nonfamilial daycare was on the rise, mothers did not use the cash-for-care benefit to stay at home, but to pay for childcare facilities in a tense private market. Nearly one decade after the introduction of the cash-for-care benefit there is a sharp decline in the percentage of parents who make use of the benefit. The percentage went down from 74.8% of parents with children between the ages of 1 and 2 in 1999 to 47.8% by the end of 2006 – a decrease of 27% (cf. Ellingsæter & Gulbrandsen, 2007, p. 661). To a certain extent this decline was caused by the expansion of places in public daycare for these age groups. Even the reform caused a contrary effect with respect to the demand for public daycare: whereas directly after the introduction of the reform the percentage of one- and two-year-olds in public daycare briefly went down, today the percentage of users is higher than before the reform took effect and the demand is still rising. Estimates show that the percentage of children in these age groups in public daycare increased from 37% in 1999 to 62% in 2006 (cf. Ellingsæter & Gulbrandsen, 2007, p. 662).

With respect to the supply and demand in the field of public daycare, it can be said that in the meantime the traditional scepticism of the Norwegian population toward public daycare has diminished. It should be noted that the high quality of the public daycare has also played a role in its increasing acceptance in Norway. Public daycare institutions are strictly controlled, there are clear norms for pedagogical quality, good staff/child ratios, and suitable surroundings. The parents also have a great deal of trust in the public daycare system, and prefer public daycare centers to all other forms of supply (like family centers, child minders, nannies, etc.). For this reason Ellingsæter and Gulbrandsen (cf. 2007) argue that the dynamic development in the field of public daycare in recent times is caused by the "mothers' agency" factor – this means by the extremely close interrelationship between demand and supply.

In 2003, a new political initiative changed the situation. The government and the opposition made an agreement both on reducing the price of places in daycare centers and at the same time offer a place to anyone who wanted to make use of daycare centers. As a consequence there was an expansion as never before in small children's enrolment at childcare centers and a subsequent reduction in use of the cash-for-care benefit. In the following years the close connection between female work participation and use of childcare centers was weakened. According to Gulbrandsen (cf. 2009), this agreement turned the relation between the supply of public subsidized daycare and mother's agency around. So far the pressures had come from well-educated mothers in the work force. After the reform all political parties including the parties of the center and the right wing supported the aim of guaranteeing a place in public daycare for everyone who asks for it. In some sense this can be interpreted as a radical political change. However, this radical political change is not a result of a coherent political concept or strategy but is more an unintended consequence of negotiations between political parties under conditions of party competition.

However, it remains to be explained why the development in the field of child and family policies in Norway was – at least till the recent past – much more continuous than in Germany with its long period of political blockade and its recent "political revolution?" The answer seems to be that the strong party cleavages in Norway prevented an overcoming of the traditional political discourses and ideas, and thus the establishment of a new cognitive and normative reference system and interpretation of external challenges and problems. Accordingly, Ellingsæter (cf. 2007) demonstrates that state interventions, as a reaction to increase female employment and the development of new needs, are becoming increasingly complex, more diverse, and produce new policy mixes. These complex policy packages rest on different normative rationales and ideologies. For example, measures like parental leave schemes, Daddy quota, and the expansion of public daycare are legitimized by the principle of gender equality. The Daddy quota intends to help redistribute the care-giving time between mothers and fathers so that it is possible for both of them to participate in gainful employment as well as to raise the child(ren). The aim is – in the same sense as public daycare – to support the dual-earner/dual-carer family model. Contrary to this, the aim of the cash-for-care benefit is to promote the principle of choice. The goal of these measures is to give the parents the opportunity to implement "good childcare" and elevate the perceived value of parental care in the society. This will be fostered by providing a choice as well as by obtaining a just distribution of financial transfers between those parents who make use of public childcare and those who do not. Although measures like this are introduced in a gender neutral manner, the implicit rationale is to support the traditional breadwinner model. In the Norwegian party system these different policy paradigms are heavily debated and are most likely irreconcilable. Coalitions led by the social democrats tend to support the adult-worker-family model, whereas the politically right-wing and enter parties adhere to measures and programs promoting choice which means that they continue to believe that the best place for children is at home.

Furthermore, in Norway there are significant obstacles impeding the introduction of a "radical social investment revolution." In this particular context there are two relevant reasons: First, the rationale of investing in human capital – especially that of children – influenced policies both in Norway and other Scandinavian countries much earlier than in countries with a liberal or conservative welfare regime. However, these investment-oriented policies were balanced by the equally strong orientation toward the principles of security and equality. Second, the specific Norwegian interpretation of the aim of public kindergartens made sure that the principle of social investment was balanced by the strong commitment to children's needs and rights. Though in many countries, including Germany, efficiency-oriented learning, cognitive stimulation, and school readiness are increasingly gaining support and influence in pedagogical concepts of early childcare and education, the influence of these or similar concepts in Norwegian kindergartens is thus far rather weak. As aforementioned, kindergartens in Norway are designed to be safe and stimulating environments for children. Although free play and social learning take center stage, education and school preparation play a relatively minor role. Nilsen (cf. 2008) and Kjørholt (cf. 2005) have extensively analyzed the dominating social construction of a "good childhood" and its intimate relationship to the pedagogical concepts and the daily life in Norwegian kindergartens.

CONCLUSION

This essay argues that we are currently witnessing a profound paradigm change in the field of policies concerning children and families in many welfare states. The "family-responsibility paradigm" is being replaced by the "investing-in-children paradigm." This paradigm change corresponds with a change in political ideas and images concerning the status of children and families in society. Although in the family-responsibility paradigm children are rendered incomplete and insufficient "human becomings," who are engaged in activities appropriate for children in the private world of the family, in the investing-in-children paradigm they are interpreted as a public good, as human assets which represent a good investment. However, it should be noted that this radical policy change is not taking place in all countries. Nevertheless, as this comparative analysis of children and family policies has shown, under specific conditions things like ideas, values, and discourses can play an important role in policy change. Furthermore, as we have seen in the case of Germany it is possible to establish a new political discourse concerning the status and role of children and families in society as well as change the interpretations of needs and preferences of influential political actors. Until recently, the family policy in Germany was oriented toward the traditional breadwinner family model and a social construction of childhood, which interprets children as dependent parts of the private world of the family. Under these conditions, family policy in Germany adhered to a policy package characterized both by a dominance of financial transfers and a deficit of social services. Consequently, Germany was, at the beginning of the 21st century, confronted with a backlogged demand regarding the reconciliation of family and work for working mothers and public daycare (especially for children under the age of three). It was under these conditions that the political actors in the ministry of family affairs identified the need for a radical change. They established the new concept of a "sustainable family policy." However, in the multiple-actor system of the federal republic of Germany – with its distribution of power between the federal state, "Bundesländern," and local governments, not to mention the relevance of nonprofit organizations – to achieve actual political change it is decisive to find political partners and built advocacy coalitions. It is precisely for this reason that the ministry of family affairs attached such great importance to attracting influential scientific experts as supporters for both formulating and implementing the new concept of sustainable family policy as well as to build alliances with different actors from all sectors of society. The rationale underlying this concept of family policy is that investing in children is advantageous not only for children, but for the whole of society as well. The new policy model was presented as a comprehensive strategy of economic modernisation to convince both other political actors and the public. However, up till now the new political concept could not cause strong effects. As demonstrated, no increase in birth rate took place and the expansion of public financed daycare takes time. Hence, it remains unclear whether there will be long-term improvements in the living conditions of children and families.

In opposition to this, in Norway – as a proponent of the Scandinavian welfare regime – a strong expansion of the public daycare system took place without any radical changes in the ideas and discourses concerning children and family policies. Several reasons can be given for this: First, although Norway was a relative latecomer in the field of expanding public childcare facilities compared to countries like Sweden and Denmark, it was nonetheless much further along than Germany. Norway, in contrast to Germany, has reached the Barcelona benchmark (provision rate for children under the age of 3: 33%). Since the middle of 1980s, there has been a steady increase in the number of public daycare places in Norway. This trend was driven by a high demand for female employment and a strong preference for public daycare among Norwegian mothers. Second, there was no need for a radical change in the ideas and values concerning children and families because of the strong traditional commitment of the Norwegian society to children's needs and rights. Given the relevance of children in Norwegian society as well as for the further development of Norwegian identity the investment in children was still a traditional aim of Norwegian policies for children. As a consequence, it was not necessary to "discover" children – as it was in Germany – as important citizens. Furthermore, the social construction of childhood in Norway works as an effective barrier against the influence of the new social investment ideology and the exclusive definition of children as "citizen-workers of the future."

However, policies concerning children and families underwent a profound change over the past few decades. Instead of a radical change there was a step-by-step modernization which began at the end of the 1970s. As demonstrated in this essay, this change cannot be explained by the introduction of a new political paradigm and a new social construction of children and childhood, but by the reaction of the Norwegian state to the preferences of mothers and the increasing demand for nonfamilial childcare – even for very young children (mothers' agency). Not until 2003, all political parties negotiated a broad political agreement concerning the expansion of the public daycare system. Since then not only well-educated mothers but also low-income families made use of public daycare. Instead of introducing a new political model of a "good childhood" and a "good family life" – like in many other countries – the normative foundation of the Norwegian policy concerning children and families remains the same. The political package for children and families in Norway is characterized by a combination of public daycare and a cash-for-care benefit. This is both a result of a political compromise between the parties of the left, on the one hand, and the parties of the center and the right wing, on the other, and seems to be in perfect harmony with the preferences of Norwegian parents. The positive attitudes toward the cash-for-care reform – which have not changed since 1999 – seem to measure attitudes toward the principle of freedom of choice (cf. Gulbrandsen, 2009). As a consequence, it can be summarized that the principle of freedom of choice is strongly rooted in the Norwegian population whereas paternalism – from the left as well as the right wing of the political spectrum – is not appreciated. In so far in Norway we are witnessing a change in behaviour but no radical change in political ideas and discourses.

NOTES

1. In the meantime a number of studies calculating the economic benefit of family policy measures have been commissioned by the ministry of family affairs (BMFSFJ). For example, different analyses by the German Institute for Economic Research (DIW) calculate the positive economic effects of the expansion of facilities for early childcare and education at all levels of the federal state (central government, federal states, and local authorities). Furthermore, in different studies Prognos-AG calculated the economic effects of family friendly measures for small- and mid-range businesses. All these studies are available on the ministry for family affairs homepage (www.bmfsfj.de).

2. Complementary to these new measures in the field of family policy in Spring 2002 the initiative "Future, Education and Care" – 2003–2007 (IZBB) – was launched by the federal state. As a reaction to the results of the PISA study and the deficits in the supply of after school care the federal government developed the goal of increasing the number of all-day schools. Four billion Euro were spent by the federal government to enable the Länder to make a quarter of approximately 40,000 schools in Germany an all-day school by 2007.

3. The so-called Hartz IV law came into effect in January 2005. In this law, the insurance for the long-term unemployed and the system of social assistance were unified. The law was part of the shift to the concept of activating social policies in the field of unemployment and social assistance and was characterized by the new principle of "no rights without responsibilities."

REFERENCES

Amann, S. (2009). Wie das Elterngeld wirklich wirkt, *Spiegel Online* 2009, Spiegelnet GmbH. Available at http://www.spiegel.de/wirtschaft/0,1518,623066,00.html. Retrieved on 13.05.2009.

Anttonen, A., & Sipilä, J. (1996). European social care services: Is it possible to identity models? *Journal of European Social Policy*, *6*(1), 87–100.

Bertram, H., Rösler., W., & Ehlert, N. (2005). *Nachhaltige Familienpolitik. Zukunftssicherung durch einen Dreiklang von Zeitpolitik, finanzieller Transferpolitik und Infrastrukturpolitik.* Gutachten im Auftrag des Bundesministeriums für Familie, Senioren. Berlin: Frauen und Jugend.

BMFSFJ. (2006). *Familie zwischen Flexibilität und Verlässlichkeit. Perspektiven für eine lebenslaufbezogene Familienpolitik.* Berlin: Siebter Familienbericht.

BMFSFJ (2008) *Pressemitteilung* des Bundesministeriums für Familie, Senioren, Frauen und Jugend zum Kinderförderungsgesetz (KiföG), Berlin, 28.09.2008.

Campbell, J. L. (1998). Institutional analysis and the role of ideas in political economy. *Theory and Society*, *27*(3), 377–409.

Ellingsæter, A. L. (2003). The complexity of family policy reform. The case of Norway. *European Societies*, *5*(4), 419–443.

Ellingsæter, A. L. (2006). The Norwegian childcare regime and its paradoxes. In: A. L. Ellingsæter (Ed.), *Politicising parenthood in Scandinavia. Gender relations in welfare states* (pp. 121–144). Bristol: The Policy Press.

Ellingsæter, A. L. (2007). 'Old' and 'new' politics of time to care: Three Norwegian reforms. *Journal of European Social Policy*, *17*(1), 49–60.

Ellingsæter, A. L., & Gulbrandsen, L. (2007). Closing the childcare gap: The interaction of childcare provision and mothers'agency in Norway. *Journal of Social Policy*, *36*(4), 649–669.

Esping-Andersen, G. (1990). *The three worlds of welfare capitalism.* Cambridge, NY: The Polity Press.

Esping-Andersen, G. (2002). A child-centred social investment strategy. In: G. Esping-Andersen, D. Gallie, A. Hemerijck & J. Myles (Eds), *Why we need a new welfare state* (pp. 26–67). Oxford: University Press.

Esping-Anderson, G. (2005). *Children in the welfare state. A social investment approach.* DemoSoc Working Paper no. 2005–10. Barcelona. Available at http://www.recercat.cat/bitstream/2072/2045/1/DEMOSOC10.pdf, 7th July 2009.

Esping-Andersen, G. (2008). Childhood investments and skill formation. *International Tax and Public Finance*, *15*(1), 19–44.

Greve, B. (2000). Family policy in the Nordic countries. In: A. Pfenning & T. Bahle (Eds), *Families and family policy in Europe. Comparative perspectives* (pp. 90–103). Frankfurt Am Main: Peter Lang.

Gulbrandsen, L. (2009). The Norwegian cash-for-care reform. Changing behaviour and stable attitudes. *Nordisk Barnehageforskning*, *2*(1), 17–25.

Hall, P. A. (1993). Policy paradigms, social learning, and the State. The case of economic policymaking in Britain. *Comparative Politics*, *25*(3), 275–296.

Hemmerling, A. (2007). *Der kindergarten als Bildungsinstitution. Hintergründe und Perspektiven.* Wiesbaden: VS Verlag für Sozialwissenschaften.

James, A., & James, A. L. (2004). *Constructing childhood. Theory, policy and social practice.* Basingstoke, Houndmills: Palgrave Macmillan.

James, A., & James, A. L. (2005). Introduction: The politics of childhood – an overview. In: J. Goddard, S. McNamee, A. James & A. L. James (Eds), *The politics of childhood. International perspectives, contemporary developments* (pp. 3–12). Basingstoke, Houndmills: Palgrave Macmillan.

Jenson, J. (2004). Changing the paradigm: Family responsibility or investing in children. *Canadian Journal of Sociology, 29*(2), 169–192.

Jenson, J. (2006). The LEGO™ paradigm and new social risks: Consequences for children. In: J. Lewis (Ed.), *Children, changing families and welfare states* (pp. 27–50). Cheltenham, UK: Edward Elgar.

Jurczyk, K., Olk, T., & Zeiher, H. (2004). German children's welfare between economy and ideology. In: A.-M. Jensen, A. Ben-Arieh, C. Conti, D. Kutsar, M. Ghiolla Phádraig & H. W. Nielsen (Eds), *Children's welfare in ageing Europe* (Vol. 2, pp. 703–770). Trondheim: Norwegian Centre for Child Research.

Kjørholt, A. T. (2005). The competent child and the "right to be oneself": reflections on children as fellow citizens in an early childhood centre. In: A. Clark, A. T. Kjørholt & P. Moss (Eds), *Beyond listening: Children's perspectives on early children's services* (pp. 151–175). Bristol: Policy Press.

Korsvold, T. (1991). Kindergarten und Kulturvermittlung. Entwicklung und Eigenarten des norwegischen Kindergarten-Modells. *Pädagogische Rundschau, 45*(2), 227–237.

Kuebler, D. (2007). Understanding the recent expansion of Swiss family policy: An idea-centred approach. *Journal of Social Policy, 36*(2), 217–237.

Leira, A. (2006). Parenthood change and policy reform in Scandinavia, 1970s–2000s. In: A. L. Ellingsæter (Ed.), *Politicising parenthood in Scandinavia. Gender relations in welfare states* (pp. 27–52). Bristol: The Policy Press.

Leira, A., Tobio, C., & Trifiletti, R. (2005). Kinship and informal support: Care resources for the first generation of working mothers in Norway, Italy and Spain. In: U. Gerhard, T. Knijn & A. Weckwert (Eds), *Working mothers in Europe. A comparison of policies and practices* (pp. 74–96). Cheltenham, UK: Edward Elgar.

Leitner, S. (2008). Ökonomische Funktionalität der Familienpolitik oder familienpolitische Funktionalisierung der Ökonomie. In: A. Evers & R. G. Heinze (Eds), *Sozialpolitik. Ökonomisierung und Entgrenzung* (pp. 67–82). Wiesbaden: VS Verlag für Sozialwissenschaften.

Lister, R. (2004). The third way's social investment state. In: H. Lewis & R. Surender (Eds), *Welfare state change. Toward a third way?* (pp. 157–181). New York: Oxford University Press.

Lister, R. (2006). An agenda for children: Investing in the future or promoting well-being in the present? In: J. Lewis (Ed.), *Children, changing families and welfare states* (pp. 51–66). Cheltenham, UK: Edward Elgar.

Meysen, T. & Schindler, G. (2004) *Ausbau der Kindertagesbetreuung – Ein Gesetzentwurf zwischen Einigkeit und Reizthema.* Deutsches Institut für Jugendhilfe und Familienrecht e.V., Juni-Juli, pp. 277–344.

Mohn, L. & Leyen, U. von der (eds.), (2007). *Familie gewinnt: Die Allianz und ihre Wirkungen für Unternehmen und Gesellschaft.* Bundesministerium für Familie, Senioren, Frauen und Jugend. Bertelsmann Stiftung: Gütersloh.

Nicolaysen, B. (2000). The kindergarten movement in Norway in historical-comparative perspective. In: A. Pfenning & T. Bahle (Eds), *Families and family policy in Europe. Comparative perspectives* (pp. 289–304). Frankfurt Am Main: Peter Lang.

Nilsen, R. D. (2008). Children in nature: Cultural ideas and social practices in Norway. In: A. James & A. L. James (Eds), *European childhoods. Cultures, politics and childhoods in Europe* (pp. 38–60). London: Palgrave.

Olk, T., & Wintersberger, H. (2007). Welfare states and generational order. In: H. Wintersberger, L. Alanen, T. Olk & J. Qvortrup (Eds), *Childhood, generational order and the welfare state: Exploring children's social and economic welfare* (Vol. 1, pp. 59–90). Odense: University Press of Southern Denmark.

Organisation for Economic Cooperation and Development (OECD). (2001). *Starting strong: Early childhood and care.* Paris: OECD.

Organisation for Economic Cooperation and Development (OECD). (2006). *Starting strong II: Early childhood education and care.* Paris: OECD.

Pierson, P. (Ed.) (2001). *The new politics of the welfare state.* Oxford: Oxford University Press.

Qvortrup, J. (2008). Childhood in the welfare state. In: A. James & A. L. James (Eds), *European childhoods. Cultures, politics and childhoods in Europe* (pp. 216–233). Basingstoke, Houndmills: Palgrave Macmillan.

Rauschenbach, T. (2006). Wer betreut Deutschlands Kinder? Eine einleitende Skizze. In: W. Bien, T. Rauschenbach & B. Riedel (Eds), *Wer betreut Deutschlands Kinder? DJI-Kinderbetreuungsstudie* (pp. 10–24). Beltz: Weinheim/Basel.

Risa, A. E. (1999). Familienpolitik in Norwegen. In: C. Leipert (Ed.), *Aufwertung der Erziehungsarbeit. Europäische Perspektiven einer Strukturreform der Familien- und Gesellschaftspolitik* (pp. 245–258). Frankfurt/Main: Opladen, Leske und Budrich.

Ristau, M. (2005). Der ökonomische Charme der Familie. *Aus Politik und Zeitgeschichte.* Beilage zur Zeitschrift, Das Parlament' 23–24 (6 June), pp. 16–23.

Rürup, B., & Gruesco, S. (2003). *Nachhaltige Familienpolitik im Interesse einer aktiven Bevölkerungsentwicklung.* Gutachten im Auftrag des Bundesministeriums für Familie, Senioren. Berlin: Frauen und Jugend.

Saraceno, J. (2004). De-familialization or re-familialization? Trends in income-tested family benefits. In: T. Knijn & A. Komter (Eds), *Solidarity between the sexes and the generations transformations in Europe* (pp. 68–86). Cheltenham, UK: Edward Elgar.

Satka, M., & Eydal, G. B. (2004). The history of Nordic policies for children. In: H. Brembeck, B. Johansson & J. Kampmann (Eds), *Beyond the competent child. Exploring contemporary childhood in the Nordic welfare societies* (pp. 33–61). Roskilde: Roskilde University Press.

Schmidt, V. A. (2002). Does discourse matter in the politics of welfare state adjustment? *Comparative Political Studies, 35*(2), 168–193.

Schmidt, V. A., & Radaelli, C. M. (2004). Policy change and discourse in Europe: Conceptual and methodological issues. *West European Politics, 27*(2), 183–210.

Seeleib-Kaiser, M. (2002). A dual transformation of the German welfare state? *West European Politics, 25*(4), 25–48.

Skevik, A., & Hatland, A. (2008). Family policies in Norway. In: I. Ostner & C. Schmitt (Eds), *Family policies in the context of family change. The Nordic countries in comparative perspective* (pp. 89–107). Wiesbaden: VS Verlag für Sozialwissenschaften.

Sørensen, Ø., & Stråth, B. (Eds). (1997). *The cultural construction of Norden.* Oslo: Scandinavian University Press.

Spieß, K. C., Berger, E.M., & Groh-Samberg, O. (2008). *Die öffentlich geförderte Bildungs- und Betreuungsinfrastruktur in Deutschland: Eine ökonomische Analyse regionaler und nutzergruppenspezifischer Unterschiede.* Innocenti Working Paper 2008-03, UNICEF Innocenti Research Centre, Florence.

Strand, T. (2006). The social game of early childhood education. The case of Norway. In: J. Einarsdottir & J. T. Wagner (Eds), *Nordic childhoods and early education. Philosophy, research, policy, and practice in Denmark, Finland, Iceland, Norway and Sweden* (pp. 71–99). Greenwich, CT: Information Age Publishing.

Wagner, J. T. (2006). An outsider's perspectives. Childhoods and early education in the Nordic countries. In: J. Einarsdottir & J. T. Wagner (Eds), *Nordic childhoods and early education. Philosophy, research, policy, and practice in Denmark, Finland, Iceland, Norway and Sweden* (pp. 289–306). Greenwich, CT: Information Age Publishing.

Yee, A. S. (1996). The causal effects of ideas on policies. *International Organization, 50*(1), 69–108.

CHILDREN AND DISTRIBUTIVE JUSTICE BETWEEN GENERATIONS ☆

Vegard Johansen

INTRODUCTION

The causes and variations of social and material welfare form a widespread theme. Classical sociology attended primarily to social class, whereas modern sociology looks at variables such as gender, ethnicity, sexuality and physical and mental ability. Generation or age is proposed as an additional variable to social and material inequalities. Statistical offices have divided income by age brackets and accounted for 'age-related' public spending for decades, but it is only relatively recently that generational variations have been theorized. Structure-oriented scholars within social studies of child-hood have suggested comparing and confronting the condition of children vis-à-vis the condition of adults and the elderly.

This chapter considers the question of distributive justice between age groups or generations in terms of material welfare. The first section is

☆This chapter presents a long summary of my doctoral thesis: *Children and distributive justice between generation: A comparison of 16 European countries*. My work on the thesis was made possible through the project *Children's welfare: money, time and space*, funded by the Research Council of Norway and initiated by Professor Jens Qvortrup and Professor An-Magritt Jensen. The thesis was defended in January 2009 at the Norwegian University of Science and Technology in Trondheim, Norway. The full text is available for free at the following address: http://ntnu.diva-portal.org/smash/record.jsf?pid = diva2:132665

Structural, Historical, and Comparative Perspectives
Sociological Studies of Children and Youth, Volume 12, 55–79
Copyright © 2009 by Emerald Group Publishing Limited
All rights of reproduction in any form reserved
ISSN: 1537-4661/doi:10.1108/S1537-4661(2009)0000012008

theoretical and presents the synchronic generation perspective. It discusses the relevance of analysing social and material inequalities between contemporaries such as children, adults and the elderly (Qvortrup, 1987, 1999, 2003; Wintersberger, 2005; Olk & Wintersberger, 2007).

The second section is also theoretical. It examines allocation principles relevant to welfare studies of generations and children. John Rawls' theory of justice-as-fairness is particularly useful. Rawls (1999) points to patterned principles of justice such as the difference principle, equal outcome and equal opportunity.

The third section explores material welfare in 16 European countries. The chosen indicators of material welfare are disposable income and social benefits. Several studies over the past decades have revealed child poverty, old age poverty and increased public spending on the old compared to younger age groups (Preston, 1984; Sgritta, 1996; Thomson, 1996; Esping-Andersen & Sarasa, 2002; Lynch, 2004). This empirical-oriented section is based on masses of data collected from a wide variety of sources, including Eurostat, OECD, Statistics Norway and an array of statistical and academic reports.

A SYNCHRONIC GENERATION APPROACH

This section presents the synchronic generation approach. The structure-oriented approach contends that childhood is an element in the social structure, not just a period in an individual's life-cycle. Generational analysis, in the sense of comparing the condition of children at large with the conditions of adults and the elderly, is a quite recent development.

The first part distinguishes between the main innovations in social studies of childhood: agency and structure. Next, I use ideas taken from structure-oriented child scholars to define the generation groups: childhood, adulthood and old age. Finally, I make a clear distinction between diachronic and synchronic approaches to studies of generational relations.

Social Studies of Childhood

Childhood has been analysed from a variety of different perspectives. Developmental psychology understands the ageing process through stages, where one stage follows another with regard to mental and social development. Sociology is more focused on the social and cultural context and how children adapt to society. Though Piaget's stage theory assumes that the child has a certain universal nature which predisposes it to develop in identifiable stages (Woolfolk, 2004), Parsons' socialization theory explores how institutions shape the growing child who comes to internalize the values and rules of adult society (Corsaro, 1997).

Social studies of childhood in the 1980s represent a break from both socialization theories and stage theories. They criticize these traditional studies for underestimating children's capacities and activities, for over-concentration on (adult) outcomes, and for not considering the importance of children and childhood to society. The social studies define childhood as a cultural, economic and social construction, and children are recognized and studied as particular persons or agents, as well as being used as unit of analysis in statistics (Qvortrup, 1987; Corsaro, 1997; James, Jenks, & Prout, 1998).

Over the past decades, a variety of theories and methods have been applied to social studies of children and childhood. I will briefly point out the division between agency- and structure-oriented research. Agency-oriented child research focuses on children's subjectivity and agency. Qualitative research methods are preferred in such studies on children's competences, contributions and creativity. In contrast, the structure-oriented approach includes quantative methods at a societal level of analysis (macro-analysis) (Corsaro, 1997; James et al., 1998; Olk & Wintersberger, 2007).

This chapter perceives childhood in structural terms, that is, as a permanent and dynamic structure of society. First, the permanence of childhood is recognized by the simple fact that its members are continually being replaced. Even though children become adults individually, they are still a feature of all social worlds. Next, the structural childhood is defined by economic, political, social, cultural and ideological parameters. These external parameters change over time and thus recreate childhood. In principle, children, adults and old people are exposed to the same external parameters, but their impact might differ between the three groups (Qvortrup, 1999, 2003).

The structural approach argues that it is relevant to think of children as a category (Qvortrup, 2003; Olk & Wintersberger, 2007). This involves downsizing within-group differences and emphasizing common features distinctive for children, for example, compared to adults. Of greatest importance is the fact that children form the last large and compact population group to be excluded from full citizenship: children have civil rights, but their citizenship does not cover vital areas such as politics, civil and criminal law, economics, and social responsibilities.[1]

Childhood, Adulthood and Old Age as Generation Groups

Generation is a valuable concept to the social sciences, but it is difficult to work with. The term 'generation' has many loose meanings, and intergenerational issues are discussed broadly. One important distinction is between diachronic and synchronic generation approaches (see next section). Other distinctions include family and society, and longitudinal and structural approaches.

Generation analysis at the family level refers to kin ties between children, parents, grandparents and great-grandparents, and it is quite easy to separate generations. It is more difficult to tell when one generation begins and another ends when the societal level is used. Generation analysis at the societal level refers to a range of rather different phenomena such as contemporaries (all people alive at the same time), broad groups of coevals (young and old), birth cohorts (all people born at about the same time), or coevals sharing a social position (Ryder, 1965; Abrams, 1970; Thomson, 1996).

At the societal level, a distinction has been suggested between longitudinal definitions and structural definitions of generations (Wintersberger, 2000; Taskinen, 2004). Those concerned with the large-scale processes which impact on children's daily lives and welfare prefer a structural understanding of generation. This definition assumes that childhood, adulthood and old age 'relate and interact with each other in particular ways under various historical and societal circumstances' (Wintersberger, Alanen, Olk, & Qvortrup, 2007, p. 15).

The economic formation is a key factor in composing society. A central element in the economic formation is the mode of production and its respective division of labour. When positioning childhood vis-à-vis adulthood and old age in the course of history, theorists have been particularly concerned with the division of labour (Qvortrup, 1999; Wintersberger, 2005). They argue that children take part in the kinds of activities that are dominant in the respective mode of production. In pre-modern society, children's integration and valuable role are demonstrated by historical documentation of their involvement in manual labour (Qvortrup, 1987). By contrast, even though many teenagers combine part-time work and schooling (Jensen et al.,

2004; Phádraig, 2007), the main activity of children in modern and developed societies is attending school.

One might categorize children's changing roles in the economy as a shift from inclusion to exclusion. However, it is also feasible to interpret the shift from classic child labour (manual activities) to school work (mental activities) in a different manner: given an understanding of labour as something more than work for wages, scholarization and human capital formation might be perceived as 'child labour adapted to the conditions of an advanced capitalist society' (Olk & Wintersberger, 2007, p. 63). This latter understanding recognizes that children's manual labour was useful and that children's mental activities are useful. One difference, however, is that in pre-modern society the economic payoffs of children's manual efforts took place when children were still children. The economic returns of children's mental efforts take place after they have completed their education, when they have become adults and can engage in income-earning activities.

In modern society, the phrase 'the generational division of labour' refers to the sequence of education, paid work and pension (Wintersberger, 2005; Phádraig, 2007). This points to different main activities; childhood is characterized as the time of education, adulthood as the time of paid work, and old age as the time of retirement. This suggests the following substantive definitions of the three structural groups: an understanding of *childhood as a generation group* is to define 'children' as those who are in the obligatory educational regime; *adulthood as a generation group* is to define 'adults' as those constituting the workforce (working or non-working, for example, students, the unemployed, the disabled, etc.) and *old age as a generation group* is to define 'the elderly' as those who are retired.

Rather than 'generation', some scholars prefer terms related to 'age' (age brackets, relative age status and age groups). I favour 'generation' for two reasons. First, generation suggests a shared position in society at large: for example, to talk about an age group above 65 years old is something different from talking about the elderly as those who have retired. Secondly, the term 'generation' is more robust when referring to changing societal circumstances compared to age: for example, to talk about childhood in terms of school-leaving age would make childhood longer than it was 100 years ago (e.g. 14 years compared with 18 years), whereas to talk about it in terms of voting age, childhood would have become shorter (e.g. 20 years compared with 17 years). Thus, in theoretical and historical discussions of children and childhood, age brackets become artificial.

Diachronic and Synchronic Approaches

There are different approaches to the study of generational relations, and a central distinction is between diachronic and synchronic approaches. In general, a diachronic approach is used in the study of a phenomenon or event as it changes through time, whereas a synchronic approach is used in the study of a phenomenon or event at a particular time. Different generational relations are illustrated in Fig. 1, which divides 'historical time' up into 30-year intervals, thus showing relations between the categories childhood, adulthood and old age.

Fig. 1 shows that childhood, adulthood and old age are not only periods for individual persons (the children of the 1980s become adults in 2010), but also that these categories have permanence (childhood, adulthood and old age may be observed empirically at different historical times). The arrows (A–E) track different types of studies of generational relations.

Arrows A and B illustrate the passing of an individual or a group of people from one category to another. One might also compare A and B, that is, compare groups of people born at different periods. Life stage theories (Piaget, in Woolfolk, 2004), life course theories (Elder, 1999) and cohort theories (Ryder, 1965; Thomson, 1996) are important in this respect. Such approaches are future-oriented, suggesting that childhood experiences are of primary interest when they are used to understand adult outcomes.

Arrow C illustrates the ability to compare the position of different categories by historical time, for example, to compare childhood in the 1920s, 1950s and 1980s. The lifespan account is concerned with inequalities over life times, and this model rejects comparisons of co-existing age groups (Daniels, 1988).

Arrows D and E illustrate the synchronic generation approach. They show the ability to make cross-sectional comparisons of generational relations, as well as historical comparisons. The synchronic approach is a

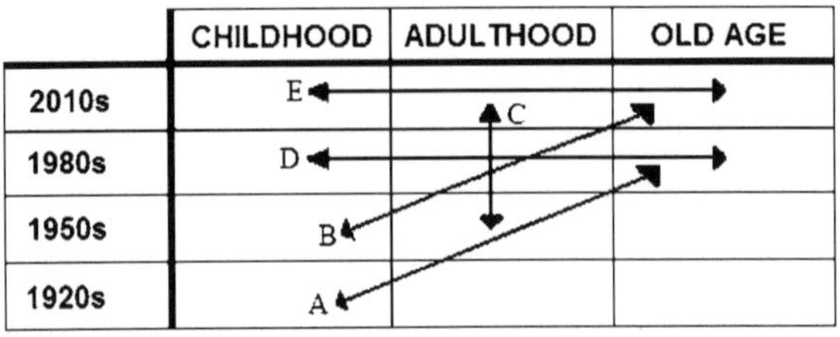

Fig. 1. Model of Generational Relations. *Source:* Developed from Qvortrup (2003).

legitimate and widely applied perspective. Luxembourg Income Studies (LIS), Eurostat and OECD use a synchronic approach in their masses of income data, and this approach is also central to *social studies of childhood* and their aim of comparing children's life conditions with other groups such as adults and the elderly.

DISTRIBUTIVE JUSTICE

Distributive justice has been a favoured theme of research and philosophy for more than 2,000 years. It is associated with problems concerning the appropriate distribution of goods, such as money, education, civil and political rights and opportunities (Barry, 2000). The first part differentiates between procedural and social justice. The next presents John Rawls and his theory of justice. The third part discusses four arguments regarding children and distributive justice. The final part points out allocation principles of relevance to cross-sectional comparisons of the material welfare of children, adults and the elderly.

Social Justice

It is common to distinguish between procedural justice and social justice. Procedural theorists find that the requirement of justice is satisfied if certain rules are adhered to. An example is Nozick (2000) and his entitlement theory. To Nozick, any pattern of the distribution is just provided it has the appropriate history: the justice of a distribution is determined by rules of just acquisition and transfer.

Scholars working within the tradition of social justice are interested in outcomes more than procedures. Social justice involves the use of patterned allocation principles in comparison with actual distributions of resources in a society, for example, quality of life, income and wealth and public transfers. Various allocation principles are proposed to guide how resources should be shared among the members of a given society.

Social justice theories dominate the discourse and will also be the focus in this chapter. The concept most often used in the context of justice is *equality*. Egalitarian theorists find equal opportunity and low levels of inequalities in outcome desirable (Lamont, 2003). *Need* is another central criterion. Needs are basic necessities or requirements in respect of a minimum level of money for food and clothing, as well as adequate housing, education, health care and opportunities for employment (Marshall, 1997). The principle of *merit* refers to demonstrated ability or achievement and is advocated by the Greek philosophers Plato (1996) and Aristotle (1985). The primary principle of utilitarianism is 'the greatest happiness of the greatest number'. Its leading thinkers, Bentham and Mill, find that the just distribution is the one that *maximizes societal utility* (Barry, 2000). Those working within the tradition of *desert-based* principles emphasize the responsibilities of people, and consider distributive systems just in so far as they reward people according to their productive efforts or contributions (Lamont, 2003).

Entitlement, merit, desert, utility, need and equality are all relevant for a discussion of distributive justice. Many of these principles are considered by John Rawls and his theory of justice-as-fairness, presented in a range of texts from the 1950s to the revised edition of his famous book, *A Theory of Justice*, published in 1999.

John Rawls and Justice-as-Fairness

John Rawls' (1999) theory is a mixture of both procedural and social elements. He wishes to show that justice is about the rules which should run social practices, but he also discusses the outcomes produced by these rules. His theory emphasizes the role of societal institutions since they are decisive in respect of the revision of laws and the allocation of duties and rights, as well as influencing the production of goods and services, and the distribution of welfare.

Rawls seeks to identify universal guidelines or principles on justice that are accepted by all citizens. He uses the contractarian method: making the principles of justice an object of the original agreement. The construction of a hypothetical original position involves accounts of the parties' rationality, knowledge and psychology, as well as the conditions under which these persons meet.

Rawls' ensures that the parties meet on equal terms by placing them behind the 'veil of ignorance', where they are unaware of their place in society (e.g. class, fortune, abilities, intelligence, psychology, age, colour and gender) and their 'conception of the good' (e.g. beliefs about ethics, religion, politics and the good life). But Rawls wants them to be rational actors who promote self-interest. To do this, he gives the parties a 'thin conception of the good', which allows them to assume that they normally prefer more than less primary goods (health, physical strength, material resources and influence), and that they should protect their liberties, widen their opportunities and enlarge their means to promote their purposes in life. Furthermore, they have some knowledge about human society, laws, political affairs and economics. A final point is their psychology: the parties are free from envy, they accept incentives and inequalities and they are risk-averse.

These are the essential features that describe the original position and the parties. The other issue is the presentation and discussion of the principles that the parties would choose to govern their future relationships. Rawls derives two principles:

(1) Each person is to have an equal right to the most extensive total system of equal basic liberties compatible with a similar system of liberty for all.
(2) Social and economic inequalities are to be arranged so that they are both
    (a) to the greatest benefit of the least advantaged, consistent with the just savings principle and
    (b) attached to offices and positions open to all under conditions of fair equality of opportunity (Rawls, 1999, pp. 266–67).

The first principle is about liberty and the second is about wealth and income. This text is about material welfare, thus the second principle is of most relevance. Principle 2b specifies *equal opportunity* and is before 2a, *the difference principle*. According to Rawls, an inequality is unjust except in so far as it is a necessary means to improve the position of the worst off.

Rawls concludes that equality and need are central criteria of distributive justice. His theory has been acclaimed, but also criticized. For one thing, it is argued that the design of the original position ensures the principles Rawls favours. For another thing, the chosen principles are judged and measured with competing principles. Nozick (2000) presents a libertarian answer to Rawls' theory, Wolff (1977) criticizes Rawls for constructing justice from existing practices and thus protecting the status quo, and Dworkin (1981) tries to amend some of the shortcomings in justice-as-fairness regarding envy, efforts and compensation.

Over the years, Rawls has replied to various 'attacks'. Following the former presentation of allocation principles, I focus on utilitarianism, desert-based theories and egalitarianism. The principle of maximizing societal utility is a significant contribution. In his response to utilitarian thinkers, Rawls stresses that it is ethically troublesome to use individuals as means to utility and to justify disadvantages to some by pointing to the advantages for others. Desert theorists find efforts to be enough, and they disagree with Rawls' claim that unequal rewards are justified only if this improves the position of the least advantaged. In his response, Rawls focuses on the fact that social life is a joint activity in which talents can only be realized in cooperation with the less talented. Egalitarians, however, criticize the difference principle for tolerating vast inequalities between rich and poor. Rawls responds that, if inequalities benefit the least advantaged, this will bring about a natural tendency towards equality and also provide incentives for hard work.

In addition to criticism regarding the design of the original position and the choices of principles, the theory of justice-as-fairness has been criticized for 'lacks' of perspectives. Some feminist scholars pass the judgement that Rawls fails to account for the injustices found in patriarchal social relations (Okin, 1989), some scholars interested in international relations criticize Rawls for considering nation states and not the global redistribution of resources (Singer, 2002), and researchers working on the rights and duties of children claim that Rawls ignores this population group. The challenge of producing good reasons for including children in discussions of distributive justice is my next focus.

Four Arguments on Children and Distributive Justice

I have investigated several acknowledged theories of distributive justice, and they are all adult-centred. Plato (1996) argued that children had not developed sufficiently to be just people. Children, like women, foreigners and slaves, were a private matter to Aristotle (1985). The utilitarian Mill saw children as pre-moral beings, liable to follow bad ideas or custom blindly. Desert-based principles direct attention to qualities in an individual's past actions and are irrelevant to questions of children and distributive justice. In Nozick's entitlement theory it seems to be self-evident that children should be excluded, as he writes about animal rights but nothing about children's rights (Bojer, 2000). Finally, John Rawls states that his theory of justice is limited to 'the rights and duties of normal adults as free citizens' (*ibid.*).

Despite this exclusion of children from theories of distributive justice, a diversity of allocation principles are used in empirical analyses of child welfare. A theory or model might be applied more broadly than its producer intended, and some researchers are considering children's inclusion in theories of distributive justice. Without being exhaustive, I will present four arguments on children's rights to and needs for distributive justice.

The first argument is that although Rawls (1999) might state that his theory of justice concerns adults only, in his text children are guaranteed justice too. The minimal requirements defining a moral person refer to 'a capacity', and children are capable of realizing a moral personality in time. Thus, as Rawls says that moral people have the right to justice, he argues that children are to receive the full protection of the principles of justice. Also, Rawls comments that the parties to the social contract would want to insure themselves against situations in which their powers are less developed (childhood). If parents and guardians are capable, they are to exercise the rights of children. In situations in which parents are unable or unwilling to serve their children's best interests, public authorities have a right and duty to intervene.

A second group of arguments regarding children and distributive justice is about children's needs. Hilde Bojer (1993, 2000) has written extensively on the issue, and she has three suggestions for a balance of the economic responsibility of children between parents and the state. First, since children, parents (and society) might have contradictory preferences in terms of how care for children should be organized, it is important to account for children's interests when formulating public policy. Secondly, since children represent budget constraints in time and financial costs (Folbre, 1994; Bojer, 2000; Jensen, 2003), parents should be compensated by public policies for some of their costs of having children: with the arrival of a child, parents must spend less time on paid work and pay for childcare and reduce the time spent in leisure. The final suggestion is a policy geared towards ensuring every child the necessary resources to develop his or her capabilities. It is particularly important that public authorities intervene in those instances when parents themselves are unable to secure their child's resources.

The third approach to children and distributive justice involves a discussion about citizenship and the Convention on the Rights of the Child (CRC) (United Nations, 1989). There are three positions on children and citizenship: (a) to ignore children because they lack political and civil rights, (b) to argue that all people (men, women and children) are citizens and (c) to present arguments on children's 'co-citizenship'. According to the latter, adults enjoy all civil, political and social rights and responsibilities essential to citizenship, and children have the benefit of some of these rights and responsibilities. The rights of children are expressed in the CRC (*ibid.*), which has been ratified by all countries except for the USA and Somalia. As such, the paragraphs of the CRC might be said to express the 'universal' rights of children, the rights and responsibilities of parents, and the responsibilities of the state vis-à-vis parents and children. The CRC finds that the best interests of the child should be the primary consideration, and that securing children's upbringing, education and social and material welfare is both a state and parental responsibility. Thus, according to the CRC, children should be dealt with seriously in matters of the public allocation of resources.

A fourth and final argument on distributive justice is to consider children's contributions. With regard to future prospects, it is argued that children represent a public good (Folbre, 1994): the children of today are the workers of the future, and the payoffs from children's future work will be transferred to the national economy (and all those living in it). Since future prosperity depends on the number and quality of workers, many scholars argue for social investments in families and children (Preston, 1984; Hinrichs, 2002; Esping-Andersen & Sarasa, 2002). For one thing, parents carry the costs of children disproportionately, and public policies might eliminate the constraints on having children (e.g. by reducing the time and financial costs of children). For another thing, children are recognized to be collective assets, and public policies might help to ensure that every child is born with optimal opportunities to be productive workers in the future (e.g. by reducing child poverty).

One could also ask if children contribute in the here and now. There are many teenagers who combine income-generating part-time work and schooling, and many children contribute in the form of housework. In Norway around 2000, approximately 60 per cent of 16-year-olds had paid work, and more than 70 per cent of children from 9 to 15 years of age participated in household chores on a daily basis (Jensen et al., 2004). Paid work and household tasks are still minimal activities compared to children's main activity, which is school. In Norway, it is calculated that children spend 3.8 h daily (any day including holidays and Sundays) on school and paid work, and this amount of time is somewhat less compared to adults' use of time in employment (4.4 h on daily average) (*ibid.*). Few would deny that children perform an important task with their schoolwork, as our society would soon cease to function if children did not do it (Qvortrup, 1995; Olk & Wintersberger, 2007).

Relevant Allocation Principles

The earlier section presented some arguments for considering children when decisions about distributive justice are made. This section points out allocation principles of relevance to cross-sectional comparisons of the material welfare of children, adults and the elderly in rich countries. The resource or good being focused on here is disposable income and how it is spread among different age groups.

Merit and desert are irrelevant to a study of children. If we were to reward financially children for their contributions and performance, should we differentiate according to grades, time spent on schoolwork, or some other criterion like future prospects? It might also be argued that utilitarianism and entitlement theories are irrelevant to the study of children and distributive justice (Bojer, 1993). Thus, I am left with the patterned notions of need, equality and equal opportunity, allocation principles related to Rawls' (1999) theory of justice.

Needs are to some extent relative. One example is that adequate housing, education and level of money depends on the society one lives in. Another example is that children, adults and the old differ in their needs because of variations in activities and social roles. This calls for unequal welfare policies. Even so, those advocating the principle of need claim that there is some objectivity of needs (as compared to the subjectivity of wants). Rawls (1999) agrees with this. His search for a principle ensuring everyone's basic and essential needs is answered by *the difference principle*, which states that inequalities are justified if they improve the position of the least well off. This is well suited for empirical investigations of the magnitude of low income and wealth among children, adults and old people.

The next allocation principle is *equality*. The connection between justice and equality is complex; justice often implies equality, but some theorists wish to justify inequalities (e.g. the difference principle). In its strictest form, the principle of equality says that all people should have the same level of resources, be it in the form of material goods, happiness or power. This is seldom demanded. But many scholars find that the removal of gross social and economic inequalities represents an improvement, and the ideal of low levels of inequality is central to many modern welfare states. I decide to use the criterion *low level of inequality* when discussing the material welfare of children, adults and the elderly.

The final allocation principle is *equal opportunity*. This refers to the removal of impediments or obstacles that stands in the way of an individual realizing her potential. Rawls (1999) proposes that one's place of birth, social status and family influences are matters of luck that might unduly influence the amount of benefits received in life. Other theorists asserting an opportunity-based egalitarianism are Arneson (equal opportunity for welfare), van Parijs (equalizing opportunities) and Sen (capabilities) (Barry, 2000).

EMPIRICAL STUDIES OF BENEFITS AND INCOME

The synchronic generation approach and allocation principles derived from Rawls' theory of justice can be used as a platform for empirical comparisons of material welfare between children, adults and the elderly. In this final section I ask about inequalities between the chosen groups in terms of disposable income and social benefits, using statistics from Norway and EU-15. EU-15 refers to the member countries in the European Union before the accession of 10 candidate countries in 2004, that is, Austria, Belgium, Denmark, Finland, France, Germany, Greece, Ireland, Italy, Luxembourg, Netherlands, Portugal, Spain, Sweden and the United Kingdom.

Before I turn to the statistics, I would like to mention five issues of relevance to my empirical analyses. First, even if 'generation' is preferred theoretically, I shift to the term 'age group' in empirical examinations of income divided by age brackets. Second, the empirical analyses do not correspond accurately to the theoretical aims of the synchronic generation approach: whereas income can be divided according to age brackets, comparative data on social benefits do not isolate children as a group. Thus, the aim of placing children in the larger generational structure is unattainable in international comparisons of social policy. Third, it is important to be aware that comparative international data are 'out of date', and less relevant when drawing lessons of current performances. Fourth, quantitative nation comparisons imply inevitable trade-offs, and much of the contextual reality of individual nations is sacrificed for the sake of broader generalization. Fifth, the limited number of observations (16 cases) makes it difficult to maintain the theoretical assumptions of OLS regression, for example, non-normal residual distributions pose a threat, a single case might have substantial impact on the parameters, and it is likely that relevant variables are omitted, as using only 16 cases places tough restrictions on the number of explanatory variables that can be included in the analysis.[2]

In the following pages, I have discussed various topics using indicators of disposable income and public transfers. To understand the differences between the countries being considered, I examined dimensions such as economic performance (GDP per capita), age structure (share of children and the elderly) and a modified version of Esping-Andersen's (1990) famous classification of welfare states (Social Democratic regimes, Conservative, Liberal and Southern European regimes). The first part is about disposable income divided by age brackets, and the second about public transfers to the old and families with children.

Disposable Income Divided by Age

Theorists of justice refer to various distributions of goods. The term material welfare points to a state or condition of doing or being well with reference to resources or possessions, and income is by far the most frequently applied indicator of material welfare (Canberra Group, 2001). Based on current practices, the validity of results and the availability of data, I choose disposable income (net income after direct taxes and transfers) as my main pointer of material welfare.[3]

By using equivalence scales and selecting age brackets, I am able to compare the position of children, adults and those in old age in the income distribution. Empirical studies necessarily involve some randomness when splitting the three groups. Children are theoretically defined as those who are in obligatory education, and 18 or 19 years of age marks the end of obligatory education in most Western countries. At the time of writing this section, the closest age group in the Eurostat database was 0–15 years of age. The category of old people is theoretically defined as those who have retired. Empirically this corresponds to effective retirement ages, but they vary in the countries examined here (OECD, 2005). The most common official age of retirement in this group of countries is 65 years of age, and 65 years or older is also an available statistical category in the Eurostat database. The category of adults is defined as those of employable age. Based on the available statistics, the onset of adulthood is 16 and the end point is 64.

There are two concerns, in particular, when dealing with income data divided by age brackets. First, equivalence scales are widely used, but the choice of scale has vital consequences when comparing the positions of the various age groups. The data used are weighed according to the EU scale. Compared to another pragmatic scale, the OECD scale, the EU scale decreases the likelihood that families with children are classified as poor and increases the chances of elderly people being classified as poor.

Secondly, choices regarding key components of the income concept also have impacts when comparing the positions of different age groups. Excluded areas such as the informal economy, benefits in kind and unpaid work taking place in the home might matter, and the exclusion of wealth (savings and assets) is of particular interest. The actual consumption of a household may be smaller or larger than its disposable income because of variations in wealth. Old people often have positive wealth, whereas families with children usually have debts to pay off (loans on apartments and student loans). The consequence of leaving out wealth is that the 'old' are doing less well in the distribution of income, whereas the 'young' are statistically doing better. Eurostat (1998) has calculated that the simple inclusion of the value or cost of owning an apartment to the definition of disposable income reduces the percentage of old age poverty.

Table 1 presents three indicators of inequality and poverty in 16 European countries. The Gini coefficient gives inequality across countries,

Table 1. The Gini Coefficient for the Entire Population (2004), Relative Median Position by Selected Age Groups (2000–2001)[a] and Relative Poverty by Selected Age Groups (60% of the Median Income in One Year) (2004).

	Gini	Median Position			Relative Poverty			
	All	0–15	16–64	65+	All	0–15	16–64	65+
Mean	29	93	107	84	15	17	14	20
Social democratic								
Denmark	24	99	105	76	11	9	10	17
Finland	25	98	106	78	11	10	10	17
The Netherlands	27	89	106	97	12	18	11	7
Norway	25	99	108	73	11	8	10	19
Sweden	23	98	109	79	11	11	10	14
Liberal								
Ireland	32	91	109	66	21	22	17	40
UK	35	87	113	80	18	22	15	24
Conservative								
Austria	26	87	107	85	13	15	11	17
Belgium	26	100	106	79	15	17	13	21
France	28	95	104	89	14	14	13	16
Germany	28	93	104	95	16	20	14	15
Luxembourg	26	89	104	97	11	18	11	6
Southern European								
Greece	33	100	106	78	20	20	18	28
Italy	33	90	104	95	19	26	18	16
Portugal	38	86	109	82	21	23	18	29
Spain	31	85	107	88	20	24	17	30

Sources: Förster and d'Ercole (2005) and Eurostat (2007).
[a]It should be noted that I use various sources on median position. Norwegian, Danish and Swedish figures on median positions are calculated by Förster and d'Ercole (2005, pp. 68–71). The statistics cover the year 2000, and the age groups are 0–17, 18–65 and 66+. Statistics for other countries are derived from Eurostat.

the median position gives inequalities between age groups ((Disposable median income of the age group/National median disposable income)*100), and relative poverty gives the shares of different age groups with a disposable income less than 60 per cent of the median disposable income.

I start my comments with cross-country variations in inequality and poverty rates for the population as a whole. Descriptive analyses of the Gini coefficient and poverty rate show that the Social Democratic and the Conservative regimes have substantially less inequality and poverty compared to the Liberal and Southern European regimes.

- The average level is 29 per cent on the Gini coefficient. Denmark, Norway, Finland and Sweden have the lowest levels of inequality (Gini = 23–25), whereas the Southern European and Liberal countries have high levels of inequality (Gini = 31–38). Most of the countries being examined have experienced an increase in inequality since the late 1980s (Eurostat, 2007).
- The mean poverty rate for all countries is 15 per cent and the median is 14. There are obvious cross-country differences. For the whole population, poverty rates are lowest in the Social Democratic countries and Luxembourg (11–12 per cent), whereas the Southern European and Liberal countries have high poverty rates (18–21 per cent).

The table also distinguishes between age groups. Descriptive analyses of median positions and poverty rates indicate that adults are better off than children, and children are better off than the elderly. This conclusion might be questioned. The use of the EU scale and neglect of wealth affects the 'statistical positions' of the elderly negatively (high poverty rates and low median position) and children positively (low poverty rates and high median position)

- A division by age shows that the risk of poverty is highest for the elderly (20 per cent) followed by children (17 per cent) and lowest for adults (14 per cent). Child poverty varies from 8 (Norway) to 26 per cent (Italy), adult poverty rates vary from 10 (Nordics) to 18 per cent (Southern Europe), and old age poverty rates vary from 6 (Luxembourg) to 40 per cent (Ireland).
- The median is a measure of central tendency. The adult percentage of disposable income is highest in the United Kingdom at 113 per cent and the lowest figures are 104 per cent. Children's median position varies from 100 per cent in Belgium and Greece to 85 per cent in Spain. The median

position of the elderly varies from 66 per cent in Ireland to 97 per cent in the Netherlands and Luxembourg.

One might also perform cross-country comparisons. Based on Rawls' (1999) theory, I suggest that the just society is characterized by low levels of inequality in the total population and between age groups (equality), as well as low poverty rates for all age groups (the difference principle). This criterion gives the following result: Finland, France, Sweden and the Netherlands score very well; the remaining Social Democratic and Conservative countries are close to the top group; Ireland and Portugal come out particularly low and the remaining Liberal and Southern European countries are close to the bottom group.

Thus far, it looks like the proposed welfare regime typology might help to explain cross-country variations in poverty and inequality. Multivariate analyses are used to control for effects of other relevant variables on cross-country differences in child poverty and old age poverty.[4] On child poverty, I find that the proposed regime typology, family and child benefits and GDP per capita show significant effects. On old age poverty, the effects of old age benefits and the regime typology are important.

First, GDP per capita shows GDP on a purchasing power parity (PPP) basis divided by population.[5] My result indicates that wealthy countries have lower child poverty rates than less wealthy countries. This agrees with analyses showing that economic performance is crucial to the size of social benefits for both families and children. The missing statistical correlations between GDP per capita and old age poverty also correspond to variations in spending on old age benefits: less wealthy countries prioritize the elderly, thus reducing cross-country differences regarding the size of old age benefits.

Secondly, an increase in the size of family and child benefits in PPP per capita produces a decrease in child poverty rates, and an increase in old age benefits in PPP per capita produces a decrease in old age poverty rates. This is in accordance with former studies showing the important role of public transfers in reducing poverty rates (Sgritta, 1996; UNICEF, 2005).

Finally, the regime typology is based on the premise of cross-country differences on the dimensions of the state, the market and the family. Differences were expected since the regimes are based on unlike 'traditions of welfare' and pursue different goals in their social policy (Esping-Andersen, 1990; Castles & Ferrera, 1996). The lowest child and old age poverty rates were found in the Social Democratic and Conservative countries. The Social Democratic countries pursue equality and de-familiarize welfare responsibilities, whereas the Conservative countries have high social spending, and family benefits encourage motherhood. The position of the Southern European regime, with its high child poverty and average old age poverty, is explained by a system of public allocation strongly favouring the elderly and their interests. The Southern European countries spend comparatively little on social benefits and maintain a sustained adherence to traditional familial welfare responsibilities. The Liberal countries have the highest child and old age poverty rates. This is explained by their strong market-orientation and a social policy based on means-testing and modest universal transfers.

The final topic concerning disposable income is children and equal opportunity. My discussion concentrates on what characterises children living at the risk of poverty. This is a topic that goes beyond the synchronic generation perspective since it explores within-group differences, but it is central when exploring child welfare. Protecting children from income poverty is important, since a wide range of evidence demonstrates that poverty affects children negatively not only while they are children, but also in their subsequent adult lives (Hinrichs, 2002; Esping-Andersen & Sarasa, 2002). My investigation of poverty rates for different types of households shows that the chief peril to child poverty is parental unemployment. In addition, the main risk groups for child poverty are children living with single parents, young parents, ethnic parents and parents of low levels of education.

Public Transfers

Having discussed income, I turn to public transfers. Theorists of justice diverge on the role of the state with regard to its impact on reducing economic inequalities. Bentham, Mill, Nozick and desert theorists are minimal state adherents. Rawls and egalitarian thinkers are proponents of the welfare state. Most empirical studies show broad public acceptance of the majority of existing welfare programmes (Johansen, 2009).

Over the past decades, statistical offices have accounted for public spending to those in old age, and such data have been used in many empirical studies. In addition to data on old age benefits, there are other indicators used in discussions of 'age-related' spending. I will give three examples based on national statistics for Norway. The first indicator is *public spending by age groups*. This indicator divides public spending in Norway according to which age groups the expenses were meant for and the

actual consumption of the different services (Toresen, 2006). A second
indicator separates the population by age and calculates *net transfers from
taxes and expenditures* (total transfers minus taxes and duties). Since adults
(19–63) work, they are net taxpayers, whereas children (0–18) and the old
(64+) receive more in transfers than they pay in taxes (Pension Commission
Norway, 2004). A third indicator separates the population by age and
presents calculations of *net transfers by income*, that is, the difference
between 'gross income' and 'disposable income' (Canberra Group, 2001).
This indicator tells us that old people (67+) are net receivers and younger
age groups (0–15 and 16–66) are net taxpayers (Statistics Norway, 2003).

These indicators are available for Norway, but not for other countries.
My approach is to investigate the system of *social benefits* in 16 European
countries. This is a common and acknowledged practice in studies of public
transfers and their effects: data are available on-line at OECD and Eurostat,
they are regarded as providing concise overviews of social expenditure at the
programme level, and they are published in a wide range of relative and
absolute standards. This permits sensitivity analyses.

The decision to focus on social benefits also has its weaknesses. One
concern is that I do not account for how or by whom public expenses are
financed. Another, more important concern is that the available data do not
allow me to separate out children as a distinct group. This breaks with the
synchronic generation approach. Still, I find that the discussion of *family
and child benefits* and *old age benefits* serves a purpose. The study of social
benefits informs us about the position and importance of families with
children vis-à-vis the elderly in social transfer systems, and it informs about
changes in past decades, and it suggests reasons for the differences between
welfare states.

I begin with descriptive analyses of the sizes of 'old age benefits' and
'benefits for families and children' over the past decades. From the 1960s till
the mid-1980s, there seems to have been a trade-off between more spending
on the elderly and less spending on families with children (Preston, 1984;
Sgritta, 1996; Thomson, 1996). From the 1980s to 2003, old age benefits as a
share of total social benefits grew extensively whereas the level of family and
child benefits remained stable. This general finding conceals cross-country
variations: in nine countries, the gap between old age benefits and family
and child benefits increased; in three countries the gap decreased and four
countries showed no particular development.

Complementing the descriptive analysis, I use multivariate regression to
understand cross-country differences in the size of 'benefits for families and
children' and 'old age benefits'.

The analyses show that the Social Democratic and Conservative regimes spent significantly more on both old age benefits and family and child benefits compared to the Southern European regime. These findings imply that some of the observed cross-country differences in the size of social benefits should be sought in the state's role in the management and organization of the economy.

The chief explanatory variable of variances in family and child benefits was GDP per capita, whereas this variable matters less to old age benefits. Thus, less wealthy countries give priority to the elderly. The importance of wealth in spending on family and child benefits is important, especially if one takes into account the current financial crisis.[6]

The most vital predictor of old age benefits was the share of old people in the population. The share of children does not matter to variations in family and child benefits. It seems that large elderly populations create both a need for more welfare spending and a political constituency to 'fight' for their share of resources (Preston, 1984; Thomson, 1996). Since the 1950s, studies have demonstrated political passivity among the young and political activity and knowledge among the elderly, as well as widespread and consistent differences in the attitudes and loyalties of people in different age groups (Abrams, 1970; Eurobarometer, 2005). Few rational politicians would ignore the huge political potential residing among old people. This is important as the proportion of old people continues to increase in all the countries examined here, in particular in Southern Europe.

A final theme investigated is population ageing. Ageing is agreed to be one of the crucial tests of European welfare states in the 21st century. It is caused by decreased fertility rates, longer life expectancy and migration. Looking at total fertility rates, a multivariate analysis indicates interesting correlations between fertility rates and ideal fertility, female employment and family and child benefits. First, empirical studies show that women would prefer to have more children than they actually end up having (Fahey & Spéder, 2004). My analysis shows a positive statistical relationship between cross-country differences in desired and actual fertility rates. Second, the analysis shows a positive relationship between the shares of women aged 25–54 participating in the workforce and total fertility rates. This result is in accordance with other studies (Castles, 2001; Jensen, 2003). Thirdly, the analysis reveals a positive link between the size of family and child benefits and fertility rates. This finding is supported by a number of studies (Esping-Andersen & Sarasa, 2002; Jensen, 2003; d'Addio & d'Ercole, 2005), whereas other studies indicate that public policies have little impact on fertility rates (Gauthier, 2000; Bagavos & Martin, 2001). As such, it would be an overstatement to propose that my test has provided clear-cut evidence of a link between public spending and fertility rates. But it gives an indication of a correlation.

NOTES

1. Some scholars insist that it is "always' necessary to speak of 'childhoods' (and not childhood). They emphasize the diversity of childhood experiences according to class, gender, ethnicity, health, place of residence or disability. Accordingly, they argue that it is more accurate to talk of many childhoods across cultures and within these cultures (James et al., 1998).

2. In my doctoral thesis, I have compared results from OLS regression with Robust regression and results from models without influential cases (Johansen, 2009). This solves some of the problems with non-robust results from OLS estimates. For broader discussions on regression analysis with Small N, see Hamilton (1992). See also Esping-Andersen and Przeworski (2001) and their discussion of quantitative cross-national research methods. The latter chapter also includes sections on the advantages and negative sides of multivariate regression.

3. According to the Canberra Group (2001), income distribution influences 'well-being and people's ability to acquire the goods and services they need to satisfy their needs'. This group of experts argues that the concept of disposable income is the best indicator for describing the opportunities of households and individuals (*ibid.*). It is also common to use subjective measures of the quality of life and satisfaction of needs.

4. In my thesis I also investigate cross-country variations in median positions (median incomes as a percentage of the national median income) through multivariate regression analyses. The model on children and the model on elderly people's median positions were poorly specified, showed little explanatory powers, and there were obvious problems with the assumptions of OLS analysis. Thus I was unable to provide any explanation of cross-country variations in the median positions of children and the elderly (Johansen, 2009).

5. PPP is an artificial currency which reflects differences in national price levels that are not taken into account by exchange rates, and allows meaningful volume comparisons of economic indicators across countries (Magnien, 2002). GDP per capita is a cornerstone indicator of the economic performance of countries, and an acknowledged indicator in comparison with welfare states and countries (Lynch, 2004).

6. Developments in Sweden and Finland in the 1990s might illustrate this point. As a response to economic difficulties, both countries cut social protection expenditures from 1992 till 2001 (from 34 per cent of GDP to 25 in Finland and from 35 to 29 per cent in Sweden). Although the share of family and child benefits was reduced over the period, the elderly were protected from cuts. In fact, expenditures earmarked for the elderly rose from 29 to 33 per cent of total social benefits in Finland and from 34 to 38 per cent in Sweden (Eurostat, 2007).

REFERENCES

Abrams, P. (1970). Rites de passage: The conflict of generations in industrial society. *Journal of Contemporary History*, *5*(1), 175–190.

Aristotle (1985). *Nicomachean ethics*. Indianapolis, IN: Hackett Publishing Company.

Bagavos, C., & Martin, C. (2001). *Low fertility, families and public policies*. Vienna: European Observatory of family matters and Austrian Institute for Family Studies.

Barry, N. (2000). *Modern political theory*. New York: Palgrave Macmillan.

Bojer, H. (1993). Barn og rettferdig fordeling. *Tidsskrift for Samfunnsforskning*, *36*(1), 93–104.

Bojer, H. (2000). Children and theories of social justice. *Feminist Economics*, *6*(2), 23–39.

Canberra Group. (2001). *Final report and recommendations* (Available at ⟨http://www.lisproject.org/links/canberra/finalreport.pdf⟩). Ottawa: The Canberra Group.

Castles, F. (2001). *The future of the welfare state: Crisis myths and crisis realities, re-inventing society in a changing global economy* (Available at ⟨http://www.utoronto.ca/ethnicstudies/Castles_paper.pdf⟩). Toronto: University of Toronto.

Castles, F., & Ferrera, M. (1996). Home ownership and the welfare state: Is southern Europe different? *South European Society and Politics*, *1*(2), 163–185.

Corsaro, W. (1997). *The sociology of childhood*. London: Sage.

d'Addio, A., & d'Ercole, M. (2005). *Trends and determinants of fertility rates: The role of policies. Social employment and migration*. Working Papers, 27, OECD Publishing, Paris.

Daniels, N. (1988). *Am I my parents' keeper? An essay on justice between the young and old*. Oxford University Press: New York.

Dworkin, R. (1981). What is equality? Part 2: Equality of resources. *Philosophy and Public Affairs*, *10*(4), 283–345.

Elder, G., Jr. (1999). *Children of the great depression: Social change in life experience* (25th Anniversary edition). Colorado: Westview Press.

Esping-Andersen, G. (1990). *The three worlds of welfare capitalism*. Cambridge: Polity Press.

Esping-Andersen, G., & Przeworski, A. (2001). Quantitative cross-national research methods. In: N. J. Smelser & P. B. Bates (Eds), *International encyclopedia of social & behavioral sciences* (pp. 12649–12655). New York: Elsevier Science.

Esping-Andersen, G., & Sarasa, S. (2002). The generational conflict reconsidered. *Journal of European Social Policy*, *12*(1), 5–21.

Eurobarometer. (2005). *The Lisbon Agenda. Eurobarometer* 62.1. Available at ⟨http://ec.europa.eu/public_opinion/archives/ebs/ebs_215_en.pdf⟩.

Eurostat. (1998). *Statistics programming committee recommendations on social exclusion and poverty statistics*. Luxembourg: Eurostat.

Eurostat. (2007). *Living conditions and welfare* (Available at ⟨http://epp.eurostat.ec.europa.eu/portal/page?_pageid = 3134,70318806,3134_70394008and_dad = portaland_schema = PORTAL⟩).

Fahey, T., & Spéder, Z. (2004). *Fertility and family issues in an enlarged Europe*. Luxembourg: Office for Official Publications of the European Communities.

Folbre, N. (1994). Children as public goods. *American Economic Review*, *84*(2), 86–90.

Förster, M., & d'Ercole, M. (2005). *Income distribution and poverty in OECD countries in the second half of the 1990s. OECDs social employment and migration*. Working Papers, 22, OECD Publishing, Paris.

Gauthier, A. (2000). *Public policies affecting fertility and families in Europe: A survey of the 15 member states* (Available at ⟨http://ec.europa.eu/employment_social/eoss/sevilla_en.html⟩). Sevilla: Low Fertility, Families and Public Policies.

Hamilton, L. (1992). *Regression with graphics: A second course in applied statistics.* Belmont, CA: Wadsworth Inc.

Hinrichs, K. (2002). Do the old exploit the young? If so is enfranchising children a good idea? *Archives européennes de sociologie, 43*(1), 35–58.

James, A., Jenks, C., & Prout, A. (1998). *Theorizing childhood.* Cambridge: Polity Press.

Jensen, A.-M. (2003). *Fra nyttebarn til byttebarn: Barns verdi og demografi.* Oslo: Gyldendal.

Jensen, A.-M., Kjørholt, A. T., Qvortrup, J., Sandbæk, M., Johansen, V., & Lauritzen, T. (2004). Childhood and generation in Norway: Money, time and space. In: A.-M. Jensen, A. Ben-Arieh, C. Conti, D. Kutsar, M. Phádraig & H. Nielsen (Eds), *Children's welfare in ageing Europe* (Vol. 1, pp. 335–402). Trondheim: Norwegian Centre for Child Research.

Johansen, V. (2009). *Children and distributive justice between generations: A comparison of 16 European countries.* Doctoral theses at Norwegian University of Science and Technology (NTNU) 2009, 10. Trondheim: NTNU.

Lamont, J. (2003). Distributive justice. *The Stanford Encyclopedia of Philosophy.* Available at ⟨http://plato.stanford.edu/archives/fall2003/entries/justice-distributive/⟩

Lynch, J. (2004). *The age of welfare: Patronage, citizenship, and generational justice in social policy. Center for European studies.* Working Paper, No. 111. Harvard University, Cambridge.

Magnien, F. (2002). *The measure of GDP per capita in purchasing power standards (PPS): A statistical indicator tricky to interpret* (Available at ⟨http://www.oecd.org/dataoecd/48/44/1960906.doc⟩). Paris: Meeting of National Accounts Experts.

Marshall, G. (1997). *Oxford dictionary of sociology.* New York: Oxford University Press.

Nozick, R. (2000). The entitlement theory. In: R. Solomon & M. Murphy (Eds), *What is justice? Classic and contemporary readings* (pp. 301–309). New York: Oxford University Press.

OECD. (2005). *Key statistics: How active social policy can benefit us all* (Available at ⟨http://www.oecd.org/dataoecd/31/16/34530748.pdf⟩). Paris: Meeting of Social Affairs Ministers.

Okin, S. M. (1989). *Justice, gender, and the family.* New York: Basic Books.

Olk, T., & Wintersberger, H. (2007). Welfare states and generational order. In: H. Wintersberger, L. Alanen, T. Olk & J. Qvortrup (Eds), *Childhood, generational order and the welfare state: Exploring children's social and economic welfare* (pp. 59–83). Odense: University Press of Southern Denmark.

Pension Commission, Norway. (2004). *Modernisert folketrygd: Bærekraftig pensjon for framtida.* NOU, No. 1. Oslo: Finansdepartementet.

Phádraig, M. N. G. (2007). Working children and the 'Descholarization' of childhood. In: H. Wintersberger, L. Alanen, T. Olk & J. Qvortrup (Eds), *Childhood, generational order and the welfare state: Exploring children's social and economic welfare* (pp. 201–225). Odense: University Press of Southern Denmark.

Plato (1996). *The republic.* Copenhagen: Copenhagen University.

Preston, S. (1984). Children and the elderly: Divergent paths for America's dependents. *Demography, 21*(4), 435–457.

Qvortrup, J. (1987). Introduction. *International Journal of Sociology, 17*(3), 3–37.

Qvortrup, J. (1995). From useful to useful: The historical continuity of children's constructive participation. *Sociological Studies of Children, 7*(1), 49–76.

Qvortrup, J. (1999). *Childhood and societal macrostructures: Childhood exclusion by default. Child and youth culture.* Working Paper, No. 9, Odense University, Odense.

Qvortrup, J. (2003). *Barndom i et sociologisk generationsperspektiv.* Working Paper, No. 123-03, University of Aarhus, Aarhus.

Rawls, J. (1999). *A theory of justice.* Oxford: Oxford University Press.

Ryder, N. (1965). The cohort as a concept in the study of social change. *American Sociological Review, 30*(6), 843–861.

Sgritta, G. (1996). The golden age of child poverty: Facts and reason. In: Wintersberger, H. (Ed.), *Children on the way from marginality towards citizenship. Childhood policies: Conceptual and practical issues* (pp. 67–99, Eurosocial Report, No. 61) Vienna: European Centre for Social Welfare Policy and Research.

Singer, P. (2002). *One world: The ethics of globalization.* New Haven: Yale University Press.

Statistics Norway. (2003). *Required statistics to COST A19: Children's welfare. Oslo: Division for Income and Wage Statistics, Statistics Norway.*

Taskinen, S. (2004). *Generations* (Available at ⟨http://www.oif.ac.at/sdf/generations_taskinen. pdf⟩). Wien: Austrian Institute for Family Studies.

Thomson, D. (1996). Justice between generations and the plight of children. In: Wintersberger, H. (Ed.), *Children on the way from marginality towards citizenship. Childhood policies: Conceptual and practical issues* (pp. 43–66, Eurosocial Report, No. 61) Vienna: European Centre for Social Welfare Policy and Research.

Toresen, J. (2006). *Offentlige velferdsutgifter: Nivå og aldersfordeling 1981–2002.* Oslo: Norsk institutt for by- og regionforskning.

UNICEF. (2005). *Child poverty in rich countries.* Innocenti Report Card, No. 6. Florence: Innocenti Research Centre.

United Nations. (1989). *The convention on the rights of the child,* adopted by the General Assembly of the United Nations on 20th November. Available at ⟨http://www.unicef. org/crc/⟩.

Wintersberger, H. (2000). Family issues between gender and generations. In: S. Trnka (Ed.), *Family issues between gender and generations.* Seminar Report, Official Publications of the European Communities, Luxembourg.

Wintersberger, H. (2005). Work, welfare and generational order: Towards a political economy of childhood. In: J. Qvortrup (Ed.), *Studies in modern childhood: Society, agency, culture* (pp. 201–220). Basingstoke: Palgrave Macmillan.

Wintersberger, H., Alanen, L., Olk, T., & Qvortrup, J. (2007). Introduction. In: H. Wintersberger, L. Alanen, T. Olk & J. Qvortrup (Eds), *Childhood, generational order and the welfare state: Exploring children's social and economic welfare* (pp. 9–27). Odense: University Press of Southern Denmark.

Wolff, R. (1977). *Understanding Rawls: A critique and reconstruction of a theory of justice.* Princeton: Princeton University Press.

Woolfolk, A. (2004). *Pedagogisk psykologi.* Trondheim: Tapir Akademisk Forlag.

POVERTY AND HUMAN RESOURCES FOR CHILDREN IN THE UNITED STATES AND SELECTED RICH COUNTRIES

Donald J. Hernandez, Nancy A. Denton, Suzanne Macartney and Victoria L. Blanchard

INTRODUCTION

Children must rely on adults to provide the economic and human resources essential to assure their well-being and development, because it is the adults in their families, communities, and the halls of government who determine the nature and magnitude of resources that reach children (e.g., Bronfenbrenner, 1979; Haveman & Wolfe, 1994). In view of this dependence of children on adults, this chapter has three main goals. The first is to portray the extent to which children in the United States and other selected rich countries experience limited access to economic resources, compared to the adults in each country. The second is to focus on key family circumstances of children which reflect human resources available in the home and which influence the level of economic resources that parents have available to provide for their children. The third is to draw attention to

Structural, Historical, and Comparative Perspectives
Sociological Studies of Children and Youth, Volume 12, 81–113
Copyright © 2009 by Emerald Group Publishing Limited
ISSN: 1537-4661/doi:10.1108/S1537-4661(2009)0000012009

differences among the race, ethnic, and immigrant groups that are leading the demographic transformation of rich countries around the world.

CHILD POVERTY: LIMITED ACCESS TO ECONOMIC RESOURCES

The survival, comfort, and self-respect of both children and adults depend on their having access to adequate levels of nutrition, clothing, housing, education, health care, and other amenities of modern life. Two society-wide, institutional spheres provide the means to access these essential goods and services: the market economy and government. From the market economy, individuals can obtain income to pay for these material goods and services mainly in return for work they perform in the labor market. From government, individuals can obtain income through social transfers of public resources in the form of cash to pay for essential goods and services, or in the form of near-cash benefits, such as food stamps in the United States, or in-kind benefits such as health care.

Because children are legally barred from most labor market activities, and because children as a social category often are not eligible to receive public income transfers, it is children who constitute the majority of persons who depend completely on others to assure their economic well-being. Although children directly obtain resources mainly from family members, these resources are originally obtained by parents from either the economy or government. It is useful, therefore, to assess the extent to which economic resources available in children's families originate from market or from public sources. This is particularly the case for children in low-income families who live in poverty, because the current well-being and future prospects of these children are of interest and concern not only to the children themselves and to their parents, but also to the broader society as well.

Children in low-income families may experience serious deprivation in such basic areas as nutrition, clothing, housing, early education, and health care. Thus, results concerning child poverty have important implications, because children who grow up in poverty, and who may lack access to high quality early education and health care, experience negative consequences during childhood in the areas of socioemotional and cognitive development, and during later years as they complete fewer years of school and earn lower incomes during adulthood (Duncan & Brooks-Gunn, 1997; Edmunds & Coye, 1998; McLoyd, 1998; Sewell & Hauser, 1975; Shonkoff & Phillips, 2000; Takanishi, 2004).

MEASURING POVERTY IN THE UNITED STATES

More than a decade ago, in response to increasing public controversy, the U.S. Congress asked the National Research Council of the National Academy of Sciences to convene a Panel on Poverty and Family Assistance to address rising concerns about the official poverty measure.[1] The panel's " ... major conclusion is that the current measure needs to be revised: it no longer provides an accurate picture of the differences in the extent of economic poverty among population groups or geographic areas of the country, nor an accurate picture of trends over time" (Citro & Michael, 1995, p. 1).

The panel recommends that new poverty thresholds " ... represent a budget for food, clothing, shelter (including utilities), and a small additional amount to allow for other needs (e.g., household supplies personal care, non-work-related transportation)" (Citro & Michael, 1995, p. 4). The Panel also recommends a revised family income measure defined " ... as the sum of money income from all sources together with the value of near-money benefits (e.g., food stamps) that are available to buy goods and services in the budget, minus expenses that cannot be used to buy these goods and services. Such expenses include income and payroll taxes, child care and other work-related expenses, child support payments to another household, and out-of-pocket medical care costs, including health insurance premiums" (Citro & Michael, 1995, p. 5).

Two additional panel recommendations are that the poverty threshold " ... should be adjusted to reflect the needs of different family types and to reflect geographic differences in housing costs" (Citro & Michael, 1995, p. 5). Pursuing in the late 1990s an alternative to the official approach in measuring poverty, the Economic Policy Institute (EPI) in Washington, DC developed "basic family budgets" for more than 400 U.S. communities including most components recommended by the NAS Panel, but using a somewhat different and generally more generous set of procedures (Bernstein, Brocht, & Spade-Aguilar, 2000; Boushey, Brocht, Gundersen, & Bernstein, 2001).

Recently, Hernandez, Denton, and Macartney (2007a) use the broad framework recommended by the NAS Panel, setting thresholds based on the cost of food, housing, and other necessities as they vary across geographic localities and by family size, and calculating family resources based on a measure of family income that has been decreased by an amount equal to nondiscretionary expenses for work, health care, and federal taxes. It does so taking account of income of all family members in the home, where cohabiting parents both are counted as family members. These estimates use or adapt the EPI procedures using Census 2000 data (IPUMs 5% microdata file prepared by Ruggles, et al., 2008) and provide the basis for the results reported here.

BASIC BUDGET POVERTY AND OTHER POVERTY MEASURES

To assess child poverty in the United States, this chapter presents results for the "Baseline Basic Budget Poverty Rate," which takes account of the costs of food, housing, other necessities, and transportation for work. The Baseline Basic Budget Poverty Rate based on Census 2000 data for the income year of 1999 indicates that 21.3% of children ages 0–17 lived in poverty. Since the Official Poverty measure suggests that 14.8% were poor, the number of children living in poverty according to the Baseline Basic Budget Poverty measure is 44% greater than indicated by the Official measure, that is, 14.6 million, instead of 10.1 million.

To compare poverty levels across rich countries, researchers from the Organization for Economic Cooperation and Development (OECD), the United Nation's Children's Fund (UNICEF), and others have for nearly two decades relied on a measure based on 50% of national median post-tax and transfer income using data from the Luxembourg Income Study (LIS) and other sources (Oxley, Dang, & Antolin, 2000; Bradbury & Jantti, 2001; Smeeding & Torrey, 1988; UNICEF, 2005). The LIS-based measure most comparable to the Baseline Basic Budget approach indicates a child poverty rate of 23.5% in 2000 (UNICEF, 2005; Hernandez et al., 2007a). Thus, the Baseline Basic Budget Poverty measure yields a result slightly lower than the LIS-based approach that is widely used for international comparisons (21.3% vs. 23.5%).

However, neither the Baseline Basic Budget Poverty measure nor the LIS approach in measuring poverty takes into account the costs of Early Childhood Education and Care (ECEC). In rich European countries, children generally have access to and participate in formal early child education and care arrangements funded by the national government. Further, in these countries, parents of infants and toddlers can care for these very young children at home because of government-guaranteed, job-protected, paid maternal or paternal leave arrangements (Neuman & Bennett, 2001). Thus, for comparisons involving rich countries other than the United States, it is not necessary to take into account the costs to families of Early Childhood Education and Care, but for the United States the NRC Panel recommended that these child care costs be included in calculating the poverty rate.

However, the NRC Panel recommended that child care costs be taken into account only for families in which there is no stay-at-home parent to care for the children and at a level that provides only for the minimum care necessary for the parent to hold down a job, not for care involving educational enrichment (Citro & Michael, 1995). Yet research indicates clearly that early childhood education programs promote school readiness and educational success (Haskins & Rouse, 2005). Past research also has found that many mothers who are not in the workforce would seek employment, and many employed mothers would work more hours, if child care were available at reasonable cost. This seems to be especially true for mothers who are young, single, and with low educational levels or little income (Presser & Baldwin, 1980).

For these reasons, we calculate a second Basic Budget Poverty Rate that includes costs related to Early Childhood Education and Care for all children regardless of parental work, based largely on the state-level estimates made by the Children's Defense Fund (CDF) of center-based child care costs to families.[2] This expanded Basic Budget Poverty measure reflects European standards for universal parental leave and early education, although our cost estimates do not address the cost implications of differences between typical center-based care and *high-quality* center-based programs, an important distinction in light of recent research showing that the quality of many early education programs leaves considerable room for improvement (Clifford et al., 2005b; Pianta et al., 2005; Clifford, Bryant, & Early, 2005a; Early et al., 2005).

Given a recent estimate that a high-quality preschool program may cost $8,000 per child a year (Haskins & Rouse, 2005), whereas the CDF locality-based estimates indicate that the costs of actual programs range from $3,540 to $7,848 a year, our approach using CDF data tends to substantially underestimate the costs of a high-quality preschool program in most localities across the nation as of Census 2000. Our estimate also allocates the cost of center-based care for very young children, whereas in European countries the cost of paid maternal/paternal leave for many new parents assured by national governments is likely much higher. Thus, our approach tends to underestimate costs for very young children compared to comparable benefits provided in European countries.

At the same time, there is a trend in the United States among individual states to enact voluntary universal prekindergarten (pre-K) programs.

Currently, three states (Florida, Georgia, and Oklahoma) offer voluntary universal pre-K programs in which parents can enroll their four-year-old children, and four states (Illinois, Iowa, New York, West Virginia) are phasing in such programs (Pre-K Now, 2007). In addition, some parents receive subsidies from government programs targeted to enroll children in low-income families in child care or early education programs, and some parents may prefer to remain at home to care for their own children.

For these reasons, and particularly for these states, the Basic Budget Poverty Rate that includes early education costs tends to somewhat overestimate current poverty compared to our estimates from Census 2000. Insofar as the precise magnitude of these countervailing tendencies to underestimate and to overestimate the costs of child care and early education cannot be measured, the results presented here should be viewed as approximate. Child poverty calculated from Census 2000 rises from 21.3% for the Baseline Basic Budget Poverty Rate to 32.4% when the costs of Early Childhood Care and Education (ECEC) also are taken into account, which is more than twice the level of 14.8% indicated by the official poverty measure.

It is instructive to compare results for the "Baseline Basic Budget Plus ECEC Poverty Rate" to a "200% Poverty Rate" that is calculated as the percent of children who fall below twice (below 200%) of the Official Poverty threshold. Recognizing limitations of the Official approach in measuring economic deprivation, major government programs for children increasingly are setting eligibility criteria at levels higher that the Official Poverty threshold.

For example, households that are eligible for food stamps can have a gross monthly income up to 130% of the federal poverty threshold (USDA, 2007). The eligibility thresholds for the State Children's Health Insurance Program (SCHIP) in 2006 also were set substantially above the Official Poverty threshold in every state. In particular, 26 states use 200% of the Official Poverty threshold as the upper income eligibility standard; 9 states set the standard in the lower range 140–185%; however, 6 states set the standard in the higher range 235–280%, and 9 states set the standard in the much higher range 300–350% (Herz & Peterson, 2007). Moreover, the proportion of children and families below 200% poverty also is often used in policy discussions (Annie E. Casey Foundation, 2006).

The value of 32.4% for the "Baseline Basic Budget Plus ECEC Poverty Rate" is close to the 35.7% value for the "200% Poverty Rate". Taken together, the comparisons to the LIS-based approach and the "200%

Poverty" approach suggest that the "Baseline Basic Budget Plus ECEC Poverty Rate" is an appropriate benchmark both for international comparisons and for policy discussions in the United States.

INTERNATIONAL COMPARISONS
OF OVERALL CHILD POVERTY

The UNICEF Innocenti Research Centre recently used the LIS data to develop comparative child poverty rates for 25 rich countries between 1999 and 2001 (UNICEF, 2007; see the chapter by Johansen, this volume). The poverty rates were in the low range 2–9% for 9 of these countries in Northern Europe (Denmark, Finland, Norway, and Sweden), in Western Europe (Belgium, France, Netherlands, and Switzerland), and in the Czech Republic. The rates were somewhat higher at 11–12% in Australia and Greece, and higher still at 13–16% in other countries of Northern and Western Europe (Austria, Iceland, Ireland, and United Kingdom), Southern Europe (Italy, Portugal, and Spain), Eastern Europe (Hungary and Poland), and in Canada, well as the Pacific nations of Japan and New Zealand.

The LIS-based measure for the United States in the UNICEF study registers a poverty rate of 21.7%, which is one-third higher than the next highest rate of 16.2% for the United Kingdom. But taking into account early childhood education and care, the Baseline Basic Budget Plus ECEC Poverty Rate of 32.4% is double the rate experienced by children in the United Kingdom, and approaches 1 of every 3 children in the United States.

It is important to note that the NAS Panel also recommended that the cost of out-of-pocket medical care expenses, including health insurance premiums, should be taken into account in measuring poverty (Citro & Michael, 1995, p. 11). In the European context, such information is unnecessary because all rich countries other than the United States provide universal access to government-funded national health care systems (in the United States such a program exists currently only for persons age 65 and older). Thus a more complete poverty measure for the United States including costs for health care would yield a child poverty rate greater than the Baseline Basic Budget Plus ECEC Poverty Rate of 32.4%, and the gap separating child poverty in the United States from other rich countries would be even larger. Additional international comparisons are discussed later in the context of more specific topics.

HOW SOCIAL TRANSFERS AFFECT
CHILD POVERTY

To what extent are child poverty rates reduced in the United States and other rich countries by social transfers of public resources to families with children? An analysis for the United States assessing the effect of Food Stamps, Housing Assistance, Energy Assistance, and School Meals indicates that taking into account these programs would act to lift no more than 2% of children out of Baseline Basic Budget Poverty (Hernandez et al., 2007a). In other words, these social transfers might reduce the Baseline Basic Budget Plus ECEC Poverty Rate from 32% to 30%.

Similar results are reported in a recent LIS study. According to this research, social transfers act to reduce child poverty in the United States by only 3%, that is, the LIS estimates the recent child poverty rate in the United States to be 22.2%, and without social transfers the rate would have been 25.2% (Gornick & Jantti, 2009). Only two of the 12 other countries in this study experienced reductions in child poverty rates due to social transfers as small as 2–4%, the Netherlands and Switzerland, but in these 2 countries the child poverty rates (taking account of social transfers) are only, 7–9%, that is, only one-third to one-half the level of the United States. Social transfers act to reduce child poverty in Canada and Germany by 7%, in Australia, Denmark and Norway by 10–12%, in Finland, Poland, Sweden, Israel, and the United Kingdom by 14–17%.

Thus, social transfer programs in the United States are less effective in reducing child poverty than are the corresponding programs in 10 of the 12 other countries in the recent LIS study, and in the 2 countries where the effect of social transfers is similar in size to the United States, the child poverty rates are much lower than in the United States.

POVERTY FOR CHILDREN COMPARED TO ADULTS

The child poverty rate exceeds the adult poverty rate by a substantial margin in the United States, and in many other but not all countries (Gornick & Jantti, 2009; and additional unpublished results provided by Jantti; see also the chapters by Jensen and Qvortrup, this volume). The Baseline Basic Budget Poverty Rate and recent LIS-study results indicate that the poverty rates for children are, respectively, two-fifths greater than for the adults in the United States (21.3% vs. 14.9% in present study, and 22.2% vs. 15.6%

in the LIS study). Not surprisingly, compared to the Baseline Basic Budget Poverty Rate, because children are more likely than the general population to live in families with young children (see the chapter by Qvortrup, this volume), the gap in the United States between children and adults in their Baseline Basic Budget Plus ECEC Poverty Rates is larger; children are three-fifths more likely than adults to live in poverty according to the Baseline Basic Budget Plus ECEC Poverty Rate (32.4% vs. 20.1%). Among the other 12 countries included in the recent LIS study, only for children in the United Kingdom is the ratio of child to adult poverty higher than in the United States (1.7 vs. 1.6) (Gornick & Jantti, 2009; and unpublished results provided by Jantti).

More importantly, the poverty gap including the costs of ECEC that separates children and adults in the United States is 12% (32.4% vs. 20.1%), nearly twice the size of the next largest gap of 7% in the United Kingdom (19.1% vs. 12.1%) and 7.6% in Poland (19.6% vs. 12%), and approximately 3–4 times the size the 4.2% gap in Canada (15.6% vs. 11.4%) and the 3.7% gap in Israel (18% vs. 3.7%). Excess poverty among children compared to adults is in the much lower range 1–2% in Germany (9% vs. 8.3%), the Netherlands (6.5% vs. 4.5%) and Switzerland (8.9% vs. 7.3%), whereas child poverty rates are lower than adult rates in Australia (11.9% vs 12.4%), Denmark (2.7% vs. 6.1%), Finland (3.1% vs. 6.1%), Norway (3.7% vs. 7.3%), and Sweden (4.3% vs. 7.3%).

Across countries, then, the child poverty rate of 32% in the United States is approximately half again greater than in Poland (20%) and the United Kingdom (19%), twice as high as child poverty in Canada (16%), and approximately 3–12 times greater than in the other countries in the LIS study.

It is important to note that these results take into account social transfers (except for the United States, although social transfers have a small effect of no more than 3% in this country) (Hernandez et al., 2007a; Gornick & Jantti, 2009). The child poverty rate in the United States (including costs of ECEC but ignoring social transfers) of approximately 30% is, compared to LIS-based market-based measures for other countries, notably higher in the United Kingdom (34.2%), Israel (34.2%), and Poland (36.2%). But these three countries also are the three in the recent study for which the effects of social transfers are largest. As a consequence the actual child poverty rates in these countries are only approximately two-thirds to one-half as large as the Baseline Basic Budget Plus ECEC Poverty Rate in the United States (18–20% vs. 32%).

RACE-ETHNICITY AND IMMIGRANT ORIGINS: POVERTY IN THE UNITED STATES

Children in various race-ethnic and immigrant origin groups can differ greatly in their poverty rates, both in the United States and in other rich countries. For example, in the United States, children in immigrant families (children who are foreign born or have at least one foreign-born parent) are substantially more likely than children in native-born families (children and parents born in United States) to be poor, at 47.9% vs. 28.7%, respectively, using the Baseline Basic Budget Plus ECEC Poverty Rate. Large differences also are found within these broad groups.

Among children in native-born families in the United States, for example, the Baseline Basic Budget Plus ECEC Poverty Rate ranges from a low of 21–23% for Whites and Asians, to 42–45% for Mexican-origin Hispanics, Native Americans, and Native Hawaiian and other Pacific Islanders, to 53–60% for Blacks, and Puerto Rican Hispanics.

Among immigrant origin groups, the range is still wider. More than 50% of children in immigrant families are poor according to the Baseline Basic Budget Plus ECEC Poverty Rate among children with origins in Cape Verde, Central America (El Salvador, Guatemala, Honduras), Haiti, Albania, Indochina (Cambodia, Thailand), West Asia (Afghanistan, Bangladesh, Saudi Arabia), and Africa (Senegal, Eritrea), and this rises still higher for children with origins in Mexico (62%), Dominican Republic (64%), Laos (61%), Yemen (67%), Sudan (68%), and Somalia (85%).

At the opposite extreme, this poverty rate is in the low range 16–19% for children in immigrant families with origins in the Australia and Canada, and some countries in Europe (United Kingdom, Ireland), Asia (Taiwan, Philippines, India, Sri Lanka), and Africa (Tanzania, Zimbabwe, Union of South Africa). But even among immigrant groups in the United States with the lowest poverty rates, the rate is higher than among children living in other rich countries reporting LIS poverty rates (UNICEF, 2007; Gornick & Jantti, 2009).

INTERNATIONAL COMPARISONS OF POVERTY BY IMMIGRANT STATUS

Recent research using the LIS and other sources estimate child poverty for children in immigrant and native-born families in selected rich countries, although results must be treated with caution, because available data allow for only somewhat crude measurement of immigrant status, and the quality of the immigrant data varies across rich countries (Smeeding, Wing, & Robson, 2009). Results indicate that children in immigrant families experience higher poverty rates than children in native-born families. The differences are 12–13% in England (28.8% vs. 15.6%) and in France (18.5% vs. 6.1%) and a smaller 6–7% in Australia (19.7% vs. 13.5%) and Germany (14.5% vs. 8%).

Thus, children in both native-born and immigrant families in Australia, France, and Germany, and in native-born families in England and Wales, are equally or less likely than children in the United States to live in poverty, even compared to children in the United States who are Whites or Asians in native-born families, and compared to children in the United States in immigrant families with origins in most immigrant sending countries (exceptions are children with origins in the fewer than a dozen countries noted earlier).

The effects of social transfers on child poverty vary greatly across these four countries and the United States. For children in both immigrant and native-born families in the United States, social transfers reduce child poverty by no more than 2% in this study. In Germany, social transfers reduce market-based poverty by 7% for children in both immigrant and native-born families, and the effect rises to 12% in Australia. But in France and in England social transfers are most effective in reducing market-based poverty, and they are especially effective for children in immigrant families, at 30% for the England, and 38% for France. As a result, the poverty gaps (after taking account of social transfers) that separate children in immigrant and native-born children in France and in England, while substantial, are only 12–13%, compared to 19% in the United States.

OVERCROWDED HOUSING

Housing costs represent the largest single expenditure category for families month after month, year after year (Boushey et al., 2001). Families with low wages and below-poverty incomes may double-up with other family members or nonrelatives to share housing costs and make scarce resources go further, leading to overcrowded housing conditions. Overcrowded housing can make it difficult for a child to find a quiet place to do homework, and it can have negative consequences for behavioral adjustment and psychological health (Evans, Saegert, & Harris, 2001; Saegert, 1982). Children are characterized here a living in overcrowded housing if they live in a home with more than one person per room (U.S. Census Bureau, 1994). The proportion living in overcrowded housing can be viewed as one measure of the extent to which children's families have access to decent housing.

Nearly 1-in-5 children in the United States (18%) live in overcrowded housing, but there are enormous differences across groups. Among children in native-born families, only 7% of Whites live in overcrowded conditions, but the proportions are twice as large for Asians (16%), three times greater for Blacks and mainland-origin Puerto Ricans (22–23%), approximately 4 times greater for most other native-born race-ethnic groups (26–32%), and more than 5 times greater for Native Hawaiian and other Pacific Islanders (40%). At least one-fourth of children in most immigrant groups live in overcrowded housing, but this rises to more than one-half for children with origins in Pakistan/Bangladesh (51%), Central America, Cambodia, and Laos (59–61%), Mexico (67%), and the Hmong (82%).

Among rich countries with comparable data, in Australia and the United Kingdom children are less likely than in the United States to live in over-crowded housing (10–13% vs. 18%), whereas the proportion is somewhat higher in France (23%), and much higher in Italy (45%) (results here and later comparing the circumstances in 7 other rich countries to the United States are drawn from Hernandez, Macartney, & Blanchard, 2009). In most of these countries there are large differences in rates of overcrowding between children in native-born and immigrant families, particularly families with origins in low- and middle-income countries (LMICs), that is, families from comparatively poor countries in Africa, Asia, and Latin America. Among children in native-born and immigrant families in Australia, including those with LMIC origins, only 9–12% live in overcrowded housing, essentially the same rates as in the United Kingdom and the United States among children in native-born families (10–11%).

The rate of overcrowding is approximately twice as high among children in native-born families in France (19%) and in immigrant families generally in the United Kingdom, although this rises to one-third (33%) for immigrant families with LMIC origins. Much higher are the rates of overcrowding for children in native-born families in Italy (43%) and in immigrant families, especially those with LMIC origins, in the United States (44% and 53%), France (49% and 60%), and Italy (57% and 64%).

FAMILY HOMEOWNERSHIP

Homeownership is another measure that reflects access to housing, and although it does not necessarily reflect the quality of housing, it does represent for a family an investment in and commitment to the neighborhood and community in which the family lives. Two-thirds (67%) of children in the United States live in family-owned homes. Although the rate of homeowner-ship is 16–19% greater for children native-born than in immigrant families, more than half of the children in immigrant families (55%), including those with LMIC origins, live in family-owned homes (52%).

In fact, only for 8 immigrant origins does the proportion fall below 50%. The proportion is as low as 25% only for children with origins in the Dominican Republic, a group highly concentrated in the very expensive New York metropolitan housing market. Four-fifths or more (42–48%) live in family-owned homes among children in immigrant families with origins in Mexico, Central America, Cambodia, Pakistan/Bangladesh, Afghanistan, and the Hmong, and Blacks from Africa.

Across five rich countries, Australia, France, Italy, the United Kingdom, and the United States, the proportion of children in native-born families living in family-owned homes is uniformly high, in the range 58–71% (Hernandez et al., 2009). More than one-half of children in immi-grant families, including those with LMIC origins, also live in family-owned homes in four of these countries. The proportions fall in Italy to 49% for children of immigrants, and to 37% for those with LMIC origins, and the corresponding proportions in France are approximately 10% less at 36% and 25%, respectively.

FAMILY COMPOSITION

Children depend most immediately and directly on the parents and other family members in their homes for the nurturance and economic resources they require. Most children live with two parents, most have other dependent siblings in the home, and some also have grandparents, other relatives, or nonrelatives in the home who can either augment or draw on the resources of the child's nuclear families. Children in various rich countries and in race-ethnic and immigrant origin groups sometimes differ substantially in their family composition, with consequences for their well-being.

Two-Parent and One-Parent Families

Children living with two parents tend, on average, to be somewhat advantaged in their educational success, compared to children in one-parent families (Cherlin, 1999; McLanahan & Sandefur, 1994). Nearly three-fourths (74%) of children in the United States have two parents in the home. Children in immigrant families are substantially more likely than children in native-born to live with two parents (82% vs. 71%), although there are large differences within each group, particularly the native-born group.

Most likely to live with two parents among children in native-born families are Whites (80%), Asians (74%), and Native Hawaiian and other Pacific Islanders (72%). The proportion falls to two-thirds (65%) for Native American children, three-fifths (59%) for most Hispanic groups, one-half (48%) for mainland origin Puerto Ricans, and two-fifths (39%) for Black children. The range is much narrower among children in immigrant families. For most immigrant origins, between 75% and 95% live with two parents. The proportion is as low as 63–70% only for children in immigrant families with origins in the Dominican Republic, Haiti, Jamaica, and other English-speaking Caribbean nations which have a long tradition of one-parent families in the context of cohabiting partnerships.

The vast majority of children in other rich countries with comparable data also live with two parents, regardless of immigrant status (Hernandez et al., 2009). Focusing on children in native-born families, the proportions living with two parents are in the range 74–78% in Australia, Germany, and the United Kingdom (similar to the United States at 74%), and this rises to 88–92% in France, Italy, and the Netherlands. In France and Italy, the proportions living with two parents are identical for children in native-born families and in immigrant families with LMIC origins, whereas children in immigrant families with LMIC origins are more likely than those native-born families to live with two parents, by 3–5% in Switzerland and Germany, and by 7–9% in the Australia, the United Kingdom, and the United States.

Only in the Netherlands are children in immigrant families with LMIC origins less likely than those in native-born families to live with two parents (75% vs. 89%). This difference is accounted for mainly by children with origins in the Dominican Republic, Suriname, Congo, Ethiopia, Ghana, Somalia, Angola, and the Netherlands Antilles. Most of these countries are either Caribbean nations with long traditions of one-parent families, or they are African countries where single parents, often the mothers, are fleeing with their children as refugees to escape severe economic disturbances or civil wars.

Overall, then, children in immigrant families in these eight rich countries are generally more likely than children in native-born families to live in strong two-parent families, and the exceptions tend to prove the rule, because they often involve single mothers who have with enormous difficulty and in the face of great hardships left their country of birth to escape with their children to the Netherlands.

Siblings in the Home

Brothers and sisters in the homes of children can not only be beneficial but also a liability. Siblings provide companionship that may last a lifetime, but they also must share available family resources. Insofar as parental time and finances are limited, these resources must be spread more thinly in families with larger numbers of siblings than in families with fewer siblings (Blake, 1985, 1989; Hernandez, 1986; Poston & Falbo, 1990).

Children in immigrant families are slightly more likely than children in native-born families to live in homes with 4 or more dependent siblings aged 0–17 (18% vs. 13%). Among children in native-born families the range is from 10–11% for children in White and Asian families to 14–19% for most other groups, and 22% for Native Hawaiian and other Pacific Islanders. For children in immigrant families, the proportion is in the range 5–16% for many origins, but this rises to 20–28% for Mexico, Haiti, Thailand, Pakistan/Bangladesh, Afghanistan, Iraq, Irael/Palestine, other West Asia, and for Blacks from Africa, and it rises to 32% for Cambodia, 38% Laos, and 75% the Hmong. Children with these origins are especially likely to experience both the benefits and the disadvantages of living in families with larger numbers of siblings.

There is also a great variation in various rich countries in the number of siblings in the home. For example, the proportion living in families with three or more dependent siblings among children in native-born families ranges across 7 countries from only 7% in the Netherlands, to 16% Italy, 20% Germany, 26% Switzerland, 32% France, and 36–38% the United States and Australia. Except in Australia, children in immigrant families with LMIC origins in these settlement countries are more likely to live in large families (by 6–9% in most countries) but especially in Germany and France, where the difference is 27% (Hernandez et al., 2009).

PARENTAL EDUCATIONAL ATTAINMENTS

It has long been known that children whose parents have completed fewer years of schooling tend, on average, to themselves complete fewer years to school and to obtain lower paying jobs when they reach adulthood (Blau & Duncan, 1967; Featherman & Hauser, 1978; Sewell & Hauser, 1975; Sewell, Hauser, & Wolf, 1980).

Parents Graduating from College

Children in native-born families are only 4% more likely than children in immigrant families to have fathers who have graduated from college (32% vs. 27%).[3] But there is a large 28% difference in the proportion with fathers not graduating from high school, at 12% for children in native-born families, and 40% for children in immigrant families. As is true for other statistical indicators reported here, there are large differences within each group.

One-third of White children in native-born families have a college graduate father (32%), but the proportions are even higher among Asians in native-born families (44%). Many immigrant groups are as likely as Whites in native-born families to have a college graduate father, and the proportions are much higher for children with many origins in Europe, Asia, and Africa, most notably for children with origins in Japan (60%), Taiwan (79%), India (73%), Iran (67%), and Whites from Africa (62%).

Parents Not Graduating from High School

At the lower end of the educational distribution, in the United States only 6–10% of White and Asian children in native-born families have fathers who have not graduated from high school, but this rises to 13–24% for most Hispanic groups in native-born families and Native Americans. Among most immigrant groups, the proportion with fathers not graduating from high school is in the low range 1–10%, but the range is much higher for island-origin Puerto Rican children (37%) and for children in immigrant families with origins in Dominican Republic, Haiti, Cambodia, Laos, Thailand, Vietnam, and Iraq (33–45%), and higher still for Central America, Cambodia, and the Hmong (48–53%), and especially Mexico (69%).

Parents with Less Than Nine Years of School

Many immigrant origins most likely to have fathers not graduating from high school also have high proportions who have not entered let along completed high school. The proportion with fathers completing only 0–8 years of school is 5% or less for most groups, but it is 2–4 times greater for children with origins in Dominican Republic, China, Vietnam (13–19%), and 5–9 times great for children with origins in Central America, Cambodia, Laos, Thailand (24–30%), and Mexico (45%) and for the Hmong (41%).

Parents whose education does not extend beyond the elementary level may be especially limited in the knowledge needed to help their children succeed in school. Immigrant parents often have high educational aspirations for their children (Hernandez & Charney, 1998; Kao, 1999; Rumbaut, 1999), but they may have little knowledge about the U.S. educational system, particularly if they have themselves completed only a few years of school. Parents who have completed few years of schooling may, therefore, be less comfortable with the education system, less able to help their children with school work, and less able to effectively negotiate with teachers and the educational system.

International Comparisons of Parental Education

Children in immigrant families with LMIC origins across six other rich countries (France, Switzerland, Germany, Australia, United Kingdom, and Australia), as in the United States, tend to have parents with lower educational attainments than children in native-born families, but also as in the United States, there is enormous variability across immigrant origins. The pattern of education differences for specific origin countries varies, however, depending on the settlement country, suggesting that labor migration by persons with limited education from LMICs is likely to occur from nearby continental regions both for the United States and for affluent European countries. In contrast, immigrants with LMIC origins who have the highest levels of education are more likely to have the resources needed to immigrant over longer distance to improve their economic circumstances (Hernandez et al., 2009).

Thus, for example, children in immigrant families with origins in Mexico are more likely to have parents with higher educational attainments if they live in Europe than in the United States, whereas children with origins in Africa are more likely to have parents with higher educational attainments if they live in the United States than in Europe. In each of these settlement countries, then, it is important that government devote special attention to immigrant groups with low parental education, but the specific groups will vary from one settlement country to the next.

PARENTAL EMPLOYMENT

Parent's paid work is the primary source of income for most children
(Hernandez, 1993), and most children live in families with strong work
ethics.

Father's Employment

The vast majority of children in the United States with fathers in the home
have fathers who work for pay. The proportion is at least 87% for nearly all
native-born and immigrant groups. The proportion is slightly lower at 83%
for island-origin Puerto Ricans. Even among children in immigrant families,
the proportion falls below 87% only for children with origins in Cambodia
(76%), Laos (83%), Thailand (80%), Iraq (85%), and the Hmong (75%).
Many of the immigrants from these countries are refugees who left their
country to escape the Vietnam War or other conflicts, and some of these
parents no doubt have experienced severe traumas that limit their capacity
to work.

The vast majority of children in native-born and immigrant families with
LMIC origins who live in the United States and seven other rich countries
with available data have fathers who are employed (Hernandez et al., 2009).
Among children in native-born families, the proportions with employed
fathers ranges from 83–86% in Australia, France, and Italy to 89–98% in
Germany, the Netherlands, Switzerland, the United Kingdom, and the United
States. The proportions with employed fathers among children with LMIC
origins are within 1–8% of the corresponding rates for children in native-born
families in Australia, Italy, Switzerland, the United Kingdom, and the United
States, whereas this expands to 12–14% in France and Germany and 21% the
Netherlands. But even in these latter 3 countries, the vast majority (72–80%)
of children with LMIC have employed fathers.

Mother's Employment

Children are less likely to have employed mothers than employed fathers
across eight rich countries with comparable data (Hernandez et al., 2009).
Among children in native-born families the smallest difference of 14% is
found in France (86% vs. 72%), whereas the largest differences of 37–38%
occur in Italy (85% vs. 47%) and Switzerland (98% vs. 61%). Differences in

the remaining five countries are in the range 22–27%. Still, between approximately one-half and three-fourths of children in native-born families live with working mothers in these eight rich countries.

Among children with LMIC origins, the proportions with working mothers are somewhat lower (8–15%) in four countries, but this rises to 23% in the United Kingdom, and 33–37% in France, Germany, and the Netherlands. Nevertheless, the proportion of children with LMIC origins who have working mothers is no less than approximately one-third in France and Germany (31–35%), approximately 40% in several other countries, and higher still at 48–52% in Australia and Switzerland, and 61% the United States.

More detailed results for the United States indicate that Black children in native-born families (79%) and children in immigrant families with origins in Haiti (77%), Jamaica (83%), and the Philippines (82%) are most likely to have employed mothers. Among most native-born groups in the United States, 72–74% have working mothers, and among most immigrant groups the proportion is in the range 60–75%. Fewer than one-half (44–47%) have an employed mother only among children in immigrant families with origins in Japan, Afghanistan, Iraq, and other West Asia, and the proportion is substantially lower only for children with origins in Pakistan/Bangladesh (38%).

Strong Family Commitment to Work
Children in both native and immigrant families live with fathers and mothers who are strongly committed to work for pay to support their families. The vast majority has employed fathers and large majorities have fathers working full-time year round. A majority also has employed mothers, and many have mothers who work full time. Clearly, children in native-born and immigrant families live in families with a strong work ethic, regardless of race-ethnicity and immigrant origins. Results not presented here do indicate, however, that substantial proportions in various groups have fathers who are not able to find full-time year-round employment (Hernandez, Denton, & Macartney, 2007b; Hernandez et al., 2009).

LANGUAGE ENVIRONMENTS
AND SKILLS OF CHILDREN

In most countries a single language, or at most two or three official languages, provide the basis for communicating in families, schools, neighborhoods, work sites, and other settings, and children in native-born families with parents who speak the national language(s) learn this vital communication skill as a matter of course. But insofar as immigrants may arrive with limited skill in the native language of their adopted homeland, language use and language skills merit special attention here.

Most children in the United States who live in immigrant families, that is, families with at least one foreign-born parent, grow up in complex language environments that can help promote the development of English language skills, whereas a smaller proportion lives in linguistically isolated households in which parents and other family members speak little or no English. Children in native-born families, that is, families with parents born only in the United States, typically learn English from the earliest ages, but with rising immigration they also are increasingly in contact with children who may speak another language occasionally or frequently.

Studies of immigrant acculturation have long used English language fluency as a key indicator of cultural integration into American society. The role of language is critical for at least two reasons (Alba & Nee, 2003). First, because important aspects of the heritage culture are embedded in the native language of parents, the reduced use or loss of fluency in their native language can lead to a loss of the heritage culture. Second, parental use of their native language typically involves interaction with peers from their origin culture, whereas use of English often engages parents with English speakers embedded in American culture.

Insofar as nearly 1 in 4 children (24%) in the United States lives in an immigrant family (calculated by the authors with Current Population Survey data), similarities and differences in language (and culture) among children are essential in understanding the opportunities and constraints experienced by diverse social groups. This section presents basic information regarding language use and fluency for children and their parents.

Family Language Environment

The language skills of parents have important implications for language acquisition by their children. Because children are exposed to language first by their parents, children living with parents who are English fluent are most likely to themselves become fluent English speakers at an early age, whereas children living with parents who are English language learners are most likely to be limited in their English skills and to be classified by schools as English language learners. Intermediate in their chances of being classified by schools as English language learners are children with one English fluent parent and one English language learner parent.

The English language skills of parents may have additional important implications because parents who are English language learners are less likely than fluent English speakers to find well-paid full-time jobs. They also are less able to help their children study for subjects taught in English. Moreover, to the extent that education, health, and social institutions do not reach out to parents and children in the heritage language of the parents, both parents and children may be cut off from access to important public and private services and benefits.

In view of the importance of language use and fluency, and in light of data available from the American Community Survey (Ruggles et al., 2008), results presented here for the United States classify English language skills as follows. Parents or children are classified as English fluent if they speak "only English" or if they speak English "very well," whereas parents or children are classified as English language learners if they speak English "well," "not well," or "not at all." This corresponds to the approach used by the Census Bureau to classify persons for the purpose of distinguishing households that are "linguistically isolated" from other households.

In addition, for the purpose of portraying the social and economic circumstances of children in immigrant families according to English language skills of parents in the home, three groups of children are distinguished. First are children living with English fluent parents only. Second are children living with one English fluent parent and one English language learner parent. Third are children with English language learner parents only.

Parental Language Use and Fluency

Not surprisingly, essentially all children in native-born families have parents who speak English. However, 1-in-10 lives with parents who also speak another language at home. The proportion with parents speaking both English and another language at home is only 3–4% among children in native-born families who are White or Black. But this rises to 19–21% for Asians and Native Americans, 34% for Native Hawaiians and other Pacific Islanders, 50–57% for most Hispanic groups, and 91% for children in island-origin Puerto Rican families, that is, children with least one parent born on the island of Puerto Rico.

The vast majority (95%) of children in immigrant families also live with parents who speak English at home, with 14% speaking only English, and the

remaining 81% speaking both English and another language. Thus, only a
small minority (5%) of children in immigrant families have parents who speak
no English at home. Even among children with immigrant origins who are
most likely to have parents who speak no English at home, the proportions are
small at 11% for Mexico and Somalia and 6–8% for Guatemala, Honduras,
El Salvador, Cuba, and Dominican Republic. Thus, parents in every immigrant group are learning and using English, the language of their adopted
homeland.

Among children in native-born families, at least 99% have a parent who
speaks English fluently, and at least 98% live with English fluent parents
only, with the lone exception of island-origin Puerto Ricans, among whom
15% live with mixed-fluency parents, and 26% live with English language
learner parents only. Many parents in immigrant families who speak English
are, however, English language learners who do not speak English fluently.
Overall, two-fifths (41%) of children in immigrant families live with English
fluent parents only, about the same as the proportion (43%) living with
English language learner parents, whereas the remaining children (16%) live
with both an English fluent parent and an English language learner parent.
Thus, more than one-half (59%) of children in immigrant families have a
parent who is an English language learner, and nearly as many (56%) have
a parent who is a fluent English speaker.

Both the challenges and the opportunities experienced by children in
immigrant families with parents who are English language learners are widespread, insofar as children with English language learner parents only
account for 25% or more among children with most specific immigrant
origins. Despite differences in English language fluency, it is clear that
children in immigrant families live with parents who are committed to
language integration in America, as reflected in the near universal use of
English and the substantial levels (at least 36%) who speak English fluently
in most specific immigrant groups.

Children's Language Use and Fluency

Like their parents, most children (98–100%) of children in various native-
born and immigrant groups speak English. Also like their parents, many
children speak an additional language at home. Among children in native-
born families, the proportion speaking both English and another language is
only 2–3% for Whites and Blacks, but this rises to 9–16% for Asians, Native
Americans, and Native Hawaiian and other Pacific Islanders, to 25–31% for

most specific Hispanic groups, and to 70% for children in island-origin Puerto Rican families.

Among children in immigrant families, the proportion speaking English and another language at home is less than 30% only for those with origins in countries where English is widely spoken (with the exception of Italy), and it reaches as high as 80% or more for those with origins in Mexico (90%), Dominican Republic (88%), Hmong ancestry (90%), Yemen Arab Republic (88%), and Central America, Colombia, Ecuador, Uruguay, Nepal, Somalia, Albania, Bosnia, Commonwealth of Independent States other than the Russian Federation, and Ukraine (80–86%).

Overall, the vast majority of children in native-born families (99%) and in immigrant families (81%) speak English fluently. Even among the group least likely to speak English fluently, children in immigrant families with origins in Mexico are two and one-half times more likely to be fluent English speakers than to be English language learners (72% vs. 28%). In fact, more than one-half (52%) of children in immigrant families both speak another language at home and speak English fluently, including the 63% of children with origins in Mexico who speak English very well and also speak Spanish at home.

These high levels of English language use and fluency among children in all immigrant groups indicate that these children are becoming linguistically integrated into English-speaking society.

Household Linguistic Isolation

Although most children in various immigrant groups speak English fluently, and many also live with English fluent parents, approximately one-fourth (27%) of children in immigrant families live in linguistically isolated households, where no over the age of 13 speaks English fluently. The proportion is highest among children in immigrant families with origins in Mexico (40%) and Somalia (42%), and in Central America, Dominican Republic, Ecuador, Uruguay, China, Indochina, Sudan, Albania, Bosnia, and the Commonwealth of Independent States other than the Russian Federation (27–32%).

Children in these families may experience a high degree of isolation from English-speaking society because not even adolescent children in these households speak English proficiently. These children and families present both special challenges and opportunities for schools. The challenges are reflected in the need to design policies and programs that will most effectively educate these children in immigrant families and that will engage their parents through outreach in the languages of the families.

International Comparisons for Language Spoken at Home

In the recent study of eight rich countries focusing on children in immigrant families with LMIC origins, three had data available regarding children in immigrant families who speak a language at home other than the settlement country language (Hernandez et al., 2009). The proportion is 56% in Australia and 73–77% France and the United States. The proportions are especially high for children in Australia with origins in Vietnam and China (92–95%), in France for children with origins in Cambodia, Laos, and Turkey (82–90%), and in the United States for children with origins in several countries emerging from the former Soviet Union, as well as Mexico, Colombia, and various countries in Central America (82–93%).

Although many children in immigrant families speak the heritage language of their parents at home, most also speak the settlement country language with their parents. In France, for example, only 20% of immigrant parents use the heritage language exclusively in speaking with their children, although this is slightly higher at 26% for immigrant parents from Morocco, and a slight majority at 56% for Turkish parents. The corresponding proportions in the Netherlands are 20% for Turkish immigrants and 29% for Moroccan immigrants. In the United States, insofar as only a tiny proportion of children in immigrant families (2% or less for most origins) have parents who speak only a language other than English, it is reasonable to conclude that the vast majority speak both the heritage language and English with their children. These results suggest that not only in the United States, but also in France and the Netherlands, and perhaps in other rich countries as well, most immigrant groups are becoming linguistically integrated into the settlement society, and parents are learning the language of the settlement society along with their children.

IMMIGRANT FAMILIES PUTTING DOWN DEEP ROOTS

The deep roots of many children in immigrant families in their adopted homeland are reflected not only in their own and in their parents' English fluency, but also in their levels of citizenship in the settlement country.

Parental Citizenship

Nearly three-fifths (59%) of children in immigrant families in the United States live with at least one parent who is an American citizen. The proportion rises from 34% for children with English language learner parents only, to 73% for children with mixed-fluency parents, to 80% for those with English fluent parents only. Children in immigrant families with English language learner parents only who are least likely to live with American citizen parents include those with origins in Mexico, Central America, Argentina, Brazil, Venezuela, and Japan (11–29%). Among children with English fluent parents only, and with mixed-fluency parents, at least 60% have an American citizen parent, with the lone exceptions of children if they live with mixed-fluency parents with origins in Guatemala (59%) and India (55%).

Many of these parents are naturalized citizens, and the greater the English fluency among parents, the more likely they are to be naturalized. Overall, nearly one-half (45%) of children in immigrant families have a parent who is a naturalized citizen, at 31% for those with only English language learner parents, 49% for mixed-fluency parents, and 58% for only English fluent parents. The corresponding proportions for children in immigrant families with origins in Mexico, the largest immigrant group, are 21%, 38%, and 49%, respectively. Insofar as the requirements to become a naturalized United States citizen include the ability to read, write, and speak ordinary English, it is not surprising that the proportion with naturalized parents is higher among children with parents with higher levels of English fluency.

The high proportions with naturalized parents among children with at least one English fluent parent, and the substantial proportions with naturalized parents even among children with English language learner parents only suggest that parents in immigrant families have a strong commitment in becoming naturalized American citizens. Recent research indicates, in fact, that naturalizations are increasing. Between 1990 and 2005, among all legal permanent foreign-born residents, the percent naturalized climbed from 38% to 52% (Passel, 2007).

The overall proportions of children in immigrant families with specific origins who have at least one American citizen parent (including the substantial proportions with parents who are American citizens because they were born in the United States) are at least 40% and as high as 90%, indicating a strong and permanent commitment to the United States by these parents.

Results for four other affluent countries with available data also indicate that many children in immigrant families have at least one citizen parent

(Hernandez et al., 2009). For children in immigrant living in Australia, Italy, the Netherlands, and Switzerland, and who have origins in low- and middle-income countries, at least 1-in-10 and often at least one-fourth of children with specific national origins have at least on citizen parent. Thus, available data indicates that immigrants in diverse rich countries have a permanent commitment to their adopted homeland.

Children's Citizenship

Children in immigrant families are even more likely than their parents to be American citizens. The vast majority (82%) of children in immigrant families are American citizens because they were born in the United States. Taking account of naturalizations, the proportion is still higher (86%). The proportion of children in immigrant families who are American citizens is very high, regardless of parental English fluency, at 79% for those with English language learner parents only, and 90–93% for those with at least one English fluent parent.

At least two-thirds of children in immigrant families are American citizens for each specific origin that can be estimated in the American Community Survey. Even among children in immigrant families with English language learner parents only, the proportion who are American citizens falls below 50% only for those with origins in Canada, Argentina, Uruguay, Venezuela, Japan, Kenya, Germany, Belarus, Moldova, and France (16–47%). Insofar as children with these origins are among the groups most likely to have parents who have resided in the United States less than 10 years, as these parents continue to have additional children, the proportion of children with these origins who are American citizens born in the United States will rise substantially above 50%.

Thus most children in immigrant families, and most children with most specific origins, share precisely the same rights and privileges as do citizen children in native-born families. Still, one or both parents of children in immigrant families may be excluded from eligibility for important government benefits and services because of the parent or parents' foreign birth.

The proportion of children in immigrant families with LMIC origins who are citizens of the settlement society is about the same in Australia as in the United Sates (80–85%), and approximately one-half (49%) in Italy, whereas in Switzerland which does not have birthright citizenship the proportion falls to one-third (34%) (Hernandez et al., 2009). However, the vast majority of children in immigrant families with LMIC origins are second generation children born in the settlement country, not in their parents' country of birth. The proportion second generation is only 27% in Australia, but this rises to 63–68% Italy and Switzerland, 74% the United States, and 87–88% France and the Netherlands.

Thus, as second generation children, most children in immigrant families in these countries are likely to have a strong commitment to the country in which their parents have settled, not only because these children were born in the settlement country, but also because they will likely spend most or all of their life in this country, attending the schools, learning the language, and customs as their own native-born experience (Hernandez et al., 2009).

LOOKING TO THE FUTURE

High levels of immigration, particularly from low- and middle-income countries, are bringing large changes in the race-ethnic composition of the population of the United States and other rich countries. In the United States, race-ethnic minorities are projected by the U.S. Census Bureau to become the majority population, and this transformation will occur first among children. In 2030, the baby-boom generation born between 1946 and 1964 will be in the retirement ages of 66–84 years old. The Census Bureau's projections indicate that by 2030, 72% of the elderly will be white non-Hispanic, compared to only 56% for working-age adults, and 49% for young children (U.S. Census Bureau, 2004). As a result, as the growing elderly population of the predominantly white baby-boom generation reaches the retirement ages, it will increasingly depend for its economic support during retirement on the productive activities and civic participation (i.e., voting) of working-age adults who are members of racial and ethnic minorities. Many of these workers will, as children, have grown up in immigrant families.

The same general trends are found for other rich countries with recent population projections. For example, the total proportion of the population that is "non-Western" is projected to roughly double between 2000/2001 and 2050/2051 from 9% to 25% in England and Wales, from 7% to 18% Germany, and from 9% to 17% the Netherlands (Coleman, 2006). Similarly, the proportion of the total population of the United States, that is race-ethnic minorities, is projected to grow between 2000 and 2050 from 31% to 50% (U.S. Census Bureau, 2004).

Across the same period, the populations of rich nations will be aging, because of low rates of natural increase, particularly among the non-immigrant population. The "elderly dependency ratio", that is, persons ages 65 and over calculated as a percent of persons in the working ages 15–64, will roughly double for Germany, France, Italy, Netherlands, and the United Kingdom from 21–29% for various countries in 2005 to 39–66% in 2050 (Eurostat, 2006), and for the United States from 24% in 2000 to 47% in 2050 (U.S. Census Bureau, 2004).

In short, the well-being and development of children whose parents are immigrants, especially those from non-Western developing countries who may differ from nonimmigrants in their appearance, language, religion, and culture, will have important consequences during the next several decades for rich countries with large immigrant populations. As these children become adults, they will represent an increasing share of the labor force, the political community (see the chapter by Campiglio, this volume), and the next generation of parents.

Consequently, aging nonimmigrant populations will depend increasingly during their retirement on the economic productivity of workers who often were reared by immigrants from low- and middle-income counties, and which often are non-Western in their cultural heritage. Thus, the success of immigrants and their children in their adopted homeland is important not only to immigrant families but to all residents in the immigrant destination countries, and the success of children and parents in immigrant families will depend on the extent to which they are welcomed and integrated into the culture, the schools, and the other institutions of the towns, cities, and countries where they live.

CONCLUSION

Children rely on their parents, other adults, and governments to provide for their economic and social needs. Poverty rates for children in many rich countries are comparatively low, often less than 5% in Nordic countries, and less than 10% in other European countries, but this rises to 16–20% in countries such as Canada, the United Kingdom, and Poland, and still further in the United States when the cost of early education and child care are taken into account to approximately one-third (32%). Although social transfers from governments to families substantially reduce market-based poverty in many high-poverty countries, these public policies and programs act to reduce poverty in the United States by no more than 3%.

Poverty rates among children and adults in many rich countries are quite similar, within 3% of each other. But in rich countries with high poverty rates, children often are substantially more likely than adults to live in poverty, with differences of 7% in Canada, the United Kingdom, and Poland that rise to an excess of 12% in child poverty in the United States (32% vs. 20%). High poverty rates can lead to overcrowded housing conditions as families double-up to make scarce economic resources go further.

Child poverty within different countries also often varies across race-ethnic and immigrant origin groups. Limited parental education in some groups, as well as limited native language skills among parents, can lead to low-paid work and poverty levels incomes. Despite these difficulties for some race-ethnic and immigrant origin groups, the vast majority of children in diverse groups in the United States and the other rich countries studied here live in strong two-parent families with fathers, and often mothers, working for pay to support themselves and their children.

Available evidence also suggests that immigrant groups are putting down deep roots in their adopted homelands. Rates of homeownership and citizenship often are high, and children of immigrants often are born in and citizens of the settlement country. The well-being and success of these children in adapting to their parents' new homeland is critical, not only for the children and their parents, but also for the broader society, because as time passes these children will form a rapidly increasing share of the next generation of adults, that is, the adults who be called on to support the rapidly aging native-born populations of these countries.

Rich countries differ greatly in the extent to which they provide for children and adults on an equal footing, and they differ greatly in the extent to which they assure economic resources are available to children in various race-ethnic and immigrant groups. Insofar as the current well-being and future success of children depend on the extent to which they receive necessary economic resources, those countries which invest not only in their older population but also in their children – all of their children – will reap the important benefits associated with living in a society where all children may lead happy lives and, as the decades go by, become productive adults.

NOTES

1. Discussion of poverty in this chapter draws substantially on research reported in Hernandez et al. (2007a), which also summarizes the evolution of poverty measurement in the United States and Europe.

2. For results using two alternative approaches that are more restrictive (see Hernandez et al., 2007a).

3. Results for mothers are broadly similar to fathers and are not discussed separately here.

ACKNOWLEDGMENTS

The results presented here are from Census 2000 and from the American Community Survey for 2005–2007 (Ruggles et al., 2008) unless otherwise indicated. Additional indicators for children can be retrieved at www. albany.edu/csda/children, by clicking on "data" and then the title of this chapter. This website also presents extensive information for additional age groups, and for specific states and metropolitan areas. The authors wish to acknowledge and appreciate support from the William and Flora Hewlett Foundation, the Foundation for Child Development, the Annie E. Casey Foundation, the National Institute of Child Health & Human Development (5 R03 HD 043827-02), and the Center for Social and Demographic Analysis at the University at Albany (5 R24-HD 04494301A1). The authors alone are responsible for the content and any errors of fact or interpretation.

REFERENCES

Alba, R., & Nee, V. (2003). *Remaking the American mainstream: Assimilation and contemporary immigration*. Cambridge, MA: Harvard University Press.

Annie E. Casey Foundation. (2006). *The Annie E. Casey Foundation 2006 KIDS COUNT DATA BOOK*. Baltimore, MD: Annie E. Casey Foundation.

Bernstein, J., Brocht, C., & Spade-Aguilar, M. (2000). *How much is enough? Basic family budgets for working families*. Washington, DC: Economic Policy Institute.

Blake, J. (1985). Number of siblings and educational mobility. *American Sociological Review*, *50*(1), 84–94.

Blake, J. (1989). *Family size and achievement*. Berkeley, CA: University of California Press.

Blau, P. M., & Duncan, O. D. (1967). *The American occupational structure*. New York: Wiley.

Boushey, H., Brocht, C., Gundersen, B., & Bernstein, J. (2001). *Hardships in America: The real story of working families*. Washington, DC: Economic Policy Institute.

Bradbury, B., & Jantti, M. (2001). Child poverty across twenty-five countries. In: B. Bradbury, S. P. Jenkins & J. Micklewright (Eds), *The dynamics of child poverty in industrialized countries* (pp. 62–91). Cambridge: Cambridge University Press.

Bronfenbrenner, U. (1979). *The ecology of human development: Experiments by nature and design*. Cambridge, MA: Harvard University Press.

Cherlin, A. J. (1999). Going to extremes: Family structure, children's well-being, and social sciences. *Demography*, *36*(4), 421–428.

Citro, C. F., & Michael, R. T. (Eds). (1995). *Measuring poverty: A new approach*. Washington, DC: National Academy Press.

Clifford, R. M., Barabarin, O., Chang, F., Early, D., Bryant, D., Howes, C., Burchinal., M., & Pianta, R. (2005b). What is pre-kindergarten? Characteristics of public pre-kindergarten programs. *Applied Development Science, 9*(3), 126–143.

Clifford, R. M., Bryant, D., & Early, D. (2005a). What we know about pre-kindergarten programs, Principal. Vol. September/October, 21–24.

Coleman, D. (2006). Immigration and ethnic change in low-fertility countries: A third demographic transition. *Population and Development Review, 32*(3), 401–446.

Duncan, G. J., & Brooks-Gunn, J. (Eds). (1997). *Consequences of growing up poor*. New York: Russell Sage Foundation.

Early, D., Barbarin, O., Bryant, O., Bryant, D., Burchinal, M., Chang, F., Clifford, R., Crawford, G., Weaver, W., Howes, C., Ritchie, S., Kraft-Sayre, M., Pianta, R., & Barnett, W.S. (2005). *Pre-kindergarten in eleven states: NCEDL's multi-state study of pre-kindergarten and study of state-wide early education programs (SWEEP)*. NCEDL Working Paper, Chapel Hill, NC.

Edmunds, M., & Coye, M. J. (1998). *America's children: Health insurance and access to care*. Washington, DC: National Academy Press.

Eurostat (2006). EU25 population aged 65 and over expected to double between 1995 and 2050. Eurostat News Release, Vol. 129, Eurostat, Luxembourg.

Evans, W. G., Saegert, S., & Harris, R. (2001). Residential density and psychological health among children in low-income families. *Environment and Behavior, 33*(2), 165–180.

Featherman, D. L., & Hauser, R. M. (1978). *Opportunity and change*. New York: Academic Press.

Gornick, J. C., & Jantti, M. (2009). Child poverty in upper-income countries: Lessons from the Luxembourg Income Study. In: S. B. Kamerman, S. Phipps & A. Ben-Arieh (Eds), *From child welfare to child wellbeing: An international perspective on knowledge in the service of making policy*. New York: Springer Publishing Company.

Haskins, R., & Rouse, C. (2005). Closing achievement gaps. *The Future of Children, Policy Brief*, Spring, Princeton-Brookings, Princeton, NJ.

Haveman, R., & Wolfe, B. (1994). *Succeeding generations: On the effects of investments in children*. New York: Russell Sage Foundation.

Hernandez, D. J. (1986). Childhood in sociodemographic perspective. In: R. H. Turner & J. F. Short, Jr. (Eds), *Annual review of sociology* (Vol. 12, pp. 159–180). Palo Alto, CA: Annual Reviews.

Hernandez, D. J. (1993). *America's children: Resources from family, government, and the economy*. New York: Russell Sage Foundation.

Hernandez, D. J., & Charney, E. (Eds). (1998). *From generation to generation: The health and well-being of children in immigrant families*. Washington, DC: National Academy Press.

Hernandez, D. J., Denton, N. A., & Macartney, S. E. (2007a). Child poverty in the U.S.: A new family budget approach with comparison to European countries. In: H. Wintersberger, L. Alanen, T. Olk & J. Qvortrup (Eds), *Childhood, generational order and the welfare state: Exploring children's social and economic welfare, volume 1 of COST A19: Children's welfare* (pp. 109–140). Odense: University Press of Southern Denmark.

Hernandez, D. J., Denton, N. A., & Macartney, S. E. (2007b). *Children of immigrants – The U.S. and 50 States: National origins, language, and early education"*. In: *Child Trends & Center for Social and Demographic Analysis, University at Albany, SUNY: 20047 Research*

Brief Series, March. Publication #2007-11, 1–9. Available at http://mumford.albany.edu/children/researchbriefs_new_1.htm

Hernandez, D. J., Macartney, S., & Blanchard, V. L. (2009). *Children in immigrant families in eight affluent countries: Their family, national, and international context.* Florence, Italy: UNICEF Innocenti Research Centre.

Herz, P., & Peterson, C. L. (2007). *State Children's Health Insurance Program (SCHIP): A brief overview CRS Report for Congress.* CRS Report for Congress, Order Code RL30473, Congressional Research Service, Washington, DC.

Kao, G. (1999). Psychological well-being and educational achievement among immigrant youth. In: D. J. Hernandez (Ed.), *Children of immigrants: Health, adjustment, and public assistance* (pp. 410–477). Washington, DC: National Academy Press.

McLanahan, S., & Sandefur, G. (1994). *Growing up with a single parent: What hurts, what helps.* Cambridge, MA: Harvard University Press.

McLoyd, V. (1998). Socioeconomic disadvantage and child development. *American Psychologist, 53*(2), 185–204.

Neuman, M., & Bennett, J. (2001). *Starting strong: Early childhood education and care.* Paris: Organization for Economic Co-operation and Development.

Oxley, H., Dang, T. T., & Antolin, P. (2000). Poverty dynamics in six OECD countries. *Economic Studies* (30), 2000/I.

Passel, J. S. (2007). Growing share of immigrants choosing naturalization. *Pew Hispanic Center Report*, Pew Hispanic Center, Washington, DC. Available at http://pewhispanic.org/files/reports/74.pdf. Retrieved on 24 May 2008.

Pianta, R., Howes, C., Burchina, M., Bryant, D., Clifford, R., Early, D., & Barbarin, O. (2005). Features of pre-kindergarten programs, classrooms, and teachers: Do they predict observed classroom quality and child-teacher interactions? *Applied Developmental Science, 9*(3), 144–159.

Poston, D. L., Jr., & Falbo, T. (1990). Scholastic and personality characteristics of only children and children with siblings in China. *International Family Planning Perspectives, 16*(2), 45–54.

Pre-K Now (2007). Votes Count: Legislative Action on Pre-K Fiscal Year 2008. Available at http://www.preknow.com//documents/LegislativeReport_Sept2007.pdf. Retrieved on 19 May 2008.

Presser, H. B., & Baldwin, W. (1980). Child care as a constraint on employment: Prevalence, correlates, and bearing on the work fertility nexus. *American Journal of Sociology, 18*(5), 1202–1213.

Ruggles, S., Sobek, M., Alexander, T., Fitch, C. A., Goeken, R., Hall, P. K., King, M. & Ronnander, C. (2008). Integrated Public Use Microdata Series: Version 4.0 [Machine-readable database]. Minnesota Population Center [producer and distributor], Minneapolis, MN. Available at http://www.ipums.org

Rumbaut, R. G. (1999). Passages to adulthood: The adaptation of children of immigrants in Southern California. In: D. J. Hernandez (Ed.), *Children of immigrants: Health, adjustment, and public assistance* (pp. 478–545). Washington, DC: National Academy Press.

Saegert, S. (1982). Environment and children's mental health: Residential density and low income children. In: A. Baum & J. E. Singer (Eds), *Handbook of psychology and health, Vol II. Issues in child health and adolescent health* (pp. 247–271). Hillsdale, NJ: Lawrence Erlbaum Associates.

Sewell, W. H., & Hauser, R. M. (1975). *Education, occupation and earnings.* New York: Academic Press.

Sewell, W. H., Hauser, R. M., & Wolf, W. C. (1980). Sex, schooling, and occupational status. *American Journal of Sociology, 83*(3), 551–583.

Shonkoff, J. P., & Phillips, D. A. (2000). *From neurons to neighborhoods: The science of early child development.* Washington, DC: National Academies Press.

Smeeding, T. M., & Torrey, B. B. (1988). Poor children in rich countries. *Science, 42,* 873–877.

Smeeding, T., Wing, C., & Robson, K. (2009). Differences in social transfer support and poverty for immigrant families with children: Lessons from the LIS. In: E. L. Grigorenko & R. Takanishi (Eds), *Immigration, diversity, and education.* London: Routledge/Taylor and Francis Group.

Takanishi, R. (2004). Leveling the playing field: Supporting immigrant children from birth to eight. *Future of Children, Special Issue on Children of Immigrants, 14*(2), 61–79.

U.S. Census Bureau. (1994). Housing of lower-income households. *Statistical brief,* SB/94/18. Available at http://www.census.gov/aspd/www/statbrief/sb94_18.pdf. Retrieved on 9 January 2006.

U.S. Census Bureau. (2004). *U.S. interim projections by age, sex, race, and hispanic origin.* Available at http://www.census.gov/ipc/www/usinterimproj/. Retrieved on 16 March 2005.

UNICEF. (2005). Child poverty in rich countries, 2005. Innocenti Report Card No. 6, UNICEF Innocenti Research Centre, Florence, Italy.

UNICEF. (2007). An overview of child well-being in rich countries. Innocenti Report Card No. 7, Innocenti Research Centre, Florence, Italy.

USDA. (2007). *USDA food stamp program: Food stamps make America stronger.* Available at http://www.fns.usda.gov/cga/FactSheets/food_stamps.htm. Retrieved on 13 July.

CHILDREN'S AGENCY IN POLITICALLY DIVIDED SOCIETIES: THE CASE OF NORTHERN IRELAND

Madeleine Leonard

Fuelled by the theoretical underpinnings of the 'new sociology of childhood', a plethora of studies have emerged emphasising and demonstrating the active agency of children in the varied contexts of their everyday lives. This collective approach with its increasingly multidisciplinary converts provides a welcome redress to studies that position children as objects rather than subjects in the research process. Rather than taking for granted the adult viewpoint, this relatively new perspective highlights the myriad of ways in which children practice agency and produce unintended or negotiated outcomes. By granting children conceptual autonomy (Thorne, 1987), children are constituted as 'persons in their own right'. Yet at the same time, childhood itself is a structural phenomenon. In other words, it is both structured and structuring (Qvortrup, 1987). While children have agency, they are also influenced by social structures over which they have limited control. Their everyday actions impact on these structures, but these structures also impact on their everyday actions, so that neither structure nor action exist independently, rather both are interrelated (Giddens, 1977). The purpose of this chapter is to explore this interrelationship by critically examining the macro framework in which children's agency in politically divided societies is expressed using Northern Ireland as a case study. The chapter looks at four core macro-level contexts – politics,

Structural, Historical, and Comparative Perspectives
Sociological Studies of Children and Youth, Volume 12, 115–138
Copyright © 2009 by Emerald Group Publishing Limited
ISSN: 1537-4661/doi:10.1108/S1537-4661(2009)0000012010

economics, education and culture – and examines how children are constrained by the power relationships within these realms. However, while
structures are constraining, they are also enabling (Giddens, 1984), and
the final section of the chapter examines the ways in which children have the
ability to impact on the world around them through their actions as well as
being prone to reproduce that world.

STRUCTURE AND AGENCY: TWO SIDES
OF THE SAME COIN?

Childhood is often defined in contrast to adulthood. Each becomes
meaningfully linked so that it is difficult to understand what childhood is
without looking at adulthood or vice versa. Each becomes what the other is
not. In a similar vein, structure and agency are often characterised in
contrast to each other. The meaning of each becomes dependent on the
meaning of the concept which it is set against. Hence, structure becomes
defined as 'constraint while agency becomes defined as freedom, structure is
regarded as static while agency is regarded as active; structure becomes
defined as collective while agency becomes defined as individual' (Hays,
1994, p. 57). This way of conceptualising structure and agency often
underplays the interconnections between the two. Up until the 1980s,
children were primarily considered within developmental psychology and
functionalist socialisation frameworks. The former presented childhood as a
natural and universal phase of human life with adulthood being seen as the
logical endpoint of childhood. The latter adopting teleological frameworks
viewed childhood as a preparation for adulthood and focused in particular
on the importance of socialisation in reproducing stable adult personalities.
In both approaches, children were considered mainly in terms of presumed
future outcomes. In breaking with these approaches, the 'new sociology of
childhood' sought to emphasise children's agency and to consider children's
lives in the here and now rather than as future projects. This has resulted in
a plethora of qualitative studies that highlight children's position as active
agents. Indeed, in developing a new paradigm for the sociology of
childhood, Prout and James (1997) specifically recommend ethnography
as a preferred method for uncovering and understanding children's daily
lives. This has led Qvortrup (1999, p. 3) to express concern that the
'adherents of the agency approach are gaining the upper hand'. Qvortrup
warns that researchers also need to employ structural approaches to fully

understand and illuminate the broader landscape of childhood. He reminds us that childhood is a particular and distinctive form of every society's social structure. Rather than a transient phase, it is a permanent social category shaped by macro forces. While of course children practice agency throughout their childhood and ethnographic studies have been crucial in challenging adults' conceptions of children as irrational, immature and so on, nonetheless, Qvortrup argues that these studies have been less useful in illuminating the position of childhood in macro societal structures. These wider societal forces position children as a minority group conditioned by resilient power relations based on generation, and they have been relatively immune from children's individual or collective agency. In other words, children act as agents under specific structural conditions. Of course, this does not render children's agency as meaningless. Like adults, children actively produce certain forms of social structure, while simultaneously, social structures produce certain types of childhood (see the chapter by Qvortrup, this volume). Hence, structures are enabling as well as constraining (Giddens, 1984). Indeed over the past two decades, adults are becoming increasingly aware of childhood as a structural form and of the durability of power differentials between adults and children and are increasingly working with children to develop a rights-based agenda to further their collective interests. This could be seen as an example of the collective agency of children although it also illustrates how this agency takes place against a backdrop where existing hierarchies between adults and children structure the conditions under which children practice their agency. One could question whether participating in these recurring forms of social interaction make children agents (Hays, 1994, p. 63).

Recognising the constraints under which agency is practiced does not necessitate dismissing the potential impact of agency on social structures. Agency implies that alternative choices are always possible, and while choices may create and recreate structures, they have the capacity under certain conditions to transform structures. In the remainder of this chapter, I will consider how the dual processes of structure and agency impact on children growing up in politically divided societies. I will draw on fieldwork carried out in Northern Ireland, which illustrates my orientation towards agency rather than structure (Leonard, 2006a, 2006b, 2006c). While these accounts situated Northern Ireland's children within wider political and economic frameworks, the impact that these wider frameworks had on their everyday lives was not my primary concern. Yet, these accounts demonstrated how children 'habitually' reproduce prevailing patterns of social life (Bourdieu, 1990). This chapter will elaborate in more detail how wider structural features of childhood impact on children's childhoods in contested spaces. While the primary focus will be on Northern Ireland, other societies experiencing protracted political conflict will be referred to in order to demonstrate the commonality of the condition of childhood for children living in disputed territories and the strategies they employ to engage with wider structures.

CHILDREN AND THE POLITICAL SYSTEM

It seems obvious to state that children in divided societies are born in places already rife with adult conflicts. Often the origins of conflict can go back to hundreds of years, and therefore, these societies may be characterised by recurring generations of children subjected to the impact of intense divisions not of their own making. English invasions in Ireland began in the 12th century and sparked off more than seven centuries of Anglo-Irish struggle marked by fierce rebellions and harsh repressions culminating in the 1916 Easter Rebellion that led to independence in 1921 for the 26 Southern countries (including three located geographically in the north but acceded to the south to ensure a Protestant majority in the north) and six northern countries that continue to remain part of the United Kingdom. Hence, adults may also be affected by political disputes that occur beyond their control. However, since the implementation of universal suffrage that formally legalised their adult positioning, they can impact directly on political systems through their ability to vote for political representatives committed to prolonging or ending political conflict. Northern Ireland has been characterised by extremist politics for many decades although extremist politicians from both sides now form the majority representatives committed to finding a peaceful solution to the Northern Ireland conflict by their change of strategy involving the establishment of shared government.

Children by contrast have little scope for influencing the political systems under which they grow up because of the ongoing failure of electoral systems to extend the vote to children. Indeed, a review of the history of suffrage reveals the ongoing positioning of children as the 'other'. Before 1918, the right to vote was generally applicable to males over 25 years of age. However, after First World War, the majority of European States extended suffrage to women and gradually lowered the voting age to 18 years of age, hence positioning children under the age of 18 as the only group with no voting rights other than immigrants without full citizenship (Hinrichs, 2002; see also the chapter by Campiglio, this volume).

As Semashko (2004, p. 5) points out, 'becoming a nation's citizen from birth, a child becomes a voter only after 18 years, as if in the intervening years the child lives outside society, is not its member, does not have problems or needs, and does not do anything of social importance'.

Of course, there were exceptions to this general trend. In Northern Ireland, for example, up until the civil rights marches of 1968, only property owners had the vote and they had one vote for each property they owned. Since the majority of property owners were Protestant, this voting system ensured that Protestants maintained their power base within Northern Ireland. This had particularly skewed effects in places like Derry where despite a majority of non-property holding Catholics living in the city, the political representatives came predominately from Protestant property holding backgrounds. The civil rights marches that took place in 1968 were premised on the belief that voting is an essential component of a group's ability to self-protect, but as with the case in the majority of the world's countries, there was an inability to extend this reasoning to the realm of childhood.

The failure to extend the vote to children under 18 years of age is often premised on the view that they would cast their vote frivolously or that they would be unduly influenced by their parents or other adults responsible for their care. This illuminates dominant macro discourses around childhood, which define children as sites of absence. It brings to the fore, the relational position of adults to children, where the former are considered as active, rational, mature and competent and the latter as passive, irrational, immature and incompetent. These discourses render the macro institutions that shape children's lives such as the educational system and the economy as undemocratic. The ongoing absence of children within electoral systems encourages politicians to pay little more than lip service to children's issues. This structural positioning of children as non-electors often means that children become a low priority issue for many governments.

Yet, politicians from parties influenced by competing ideologies often converge around dominant discourses around childhood, which position children as innocent and in need of protection. Politics in contested spaces are often fought around specific images of childhood. In the United Kingdom, these images came to the fore during the Boer War and First World War where soldiers' vulnerability was traced to inadequate care and nutrition in early life (Fildes, Marks, & Marland, 1992). Hence, Brocklehurst (2006) argues that the institutionalisation of childhood especially around care and health originated from links made between a population's health and the national interest in times of crisis particularly during war situations. This led to a popularisation on the home front of an ideal, healthy childhood and gradually evolved into a range of welfare structures premised on the separation of children from adults, with children being identified as having specific childlike needs. These changes built on other macro changes wrought by the industrial revolution. A combination of pressure from male workers and philanthropists restricted and banned female and child employment and ushered in new discourses around gender and childhood depicting both with essentialist characteristics. A range of institutions emerged to protect and exclude the child from the adult world. The purity, vulnerability and innocence of children became major icons in Second World War propaganda especially in Nazi and Soviet accounts, which produced images of children imploring adult protection (Clarke, 1997). Stephens (1997) develops a similar approach in her analysis of American children during the Cold War. Macro discourses invoking images of children as innocent beings provided the rationale for the development of a powerful nuclear defence system justified on the basis of the need to protect vulnerable American children from foreign enemies. By positioning children as 'icons of emergencies', ongoing wars and conflicts in faraway places become humanised through projecting images of vulnerable children caught up in situations that are not of their making (Burman, 1994).

Most of these accounts draw on macro discourses that position children as future citizens. Hence, both war and peace become necessary for the 'sake of the children'. Wars are fought in the name of children and peace is sought for the protection of children. In the process, essentialist identities are constructed rendering men as warlike, women as peacemakers and children as unwitting pawns used by adults to support war or seek peace. Children's 'natural' non-political characteristics permeate concepts of war and peace. Dominant representations of child soldiers render them as being duped by adult political activists, having no choice with their reluctant participation resulting in them attaining premature adulthood (Boyden, 2003; Hamilton, 1995). Throughout the 'troubles', street rioting has been a dominant form of political protest. However, when children riot, the political significance of the activity is often devalued or unacknowledged. Carter (2003, p. 276), for example, argues that street rioting involving young people in Belfast is little more than 'localised entertainment, rather than the promotion of a specific political agenda or resistance against oppression'. In a similar vein, Jarman and O'Halloran (2001) coined the phrase 'recreational rioting' to describe the participation of children rioting in Belfast. As they put it (2001, p. 17), 'it has no obvious political aspiration, requires no spark (besides boredom) and is seen as exciting and enjoyable for the young people involved'. While these motivations explain some children's participation, focus group discussions with teenagers who engage in this practice suggest that for some young people, rioting is a way of establishing and reproducing sectarian-ethnic identities based on maintaining territorial claims over competing space (Leonard, 2009a). Moreover, the term is rarely extended to cover incidents where adults are involved in street rioting. Hence, the term is a label rather than a description of an activity, and the label itself reduces children to non-political beings. Indeed, children's understandings of and involvements in long-term political conflicts remain under-theorised and under-researched (Stephens, 1997).

Instead, children are located as 'zones of peace' (Bellamy, 1999). The embodiment of children as innocent and in need of protection provides the impetus for movements for peace, movements that are often led by adults in the name of children. In Northern Ireland, the deaths of three children including a baby of four weeks of age led to the creation of the 'Peace People' in 1976. The movement was led by two women, the mother and aunt of the deceased children who went on to receive the Nobel Prize for peace in 1996. Brocklehurst (2006, p. 108) argues that 'mothers and children together created a powerful yet infantilized and feminine construct'. She documents how Mo Mowland, the former Secretary of State for Northern Ireland, justified her perseverance through the long drawn-out process that led to the Good Friday Agreement on the basis that she was doing it for the children who had known nothing else. The document outlining the conditions of the Good Friday Agreement that was delivered to every home in Northern Ireland as a prelude to a referendum on its adoption utilised an imagery of an idealised family on its cover. The husband, wife, male and female child are seen as a close, supportive and happy unit looking out at the sun rising signifying a new dawning for Northern Ireland. Of course, children themselves were excluded from voting for or against the referendum. This leads to a somewhat paradoxical situation whereby the location of children as non-political provides the rationale for political acts. Children's 'child-like' qualities are manipulated for political purposes. They become a valuable asset to attaining political objectives. Discourses around 'children are our future' bring children into politics in ways that continue to ignore the underlying power relationships between adults and children, which is in itself deeply political, and as Swartz and Levett (quoted in Cairns, 1996, p. 154) point out, 'too many adults appear to fool themselves into thinking that peace will be achieved by targeting children in an attempt to nurture the flowering of a desocialized and reified innocent essence'. This subsequently structures the conditions under which children practice their agency. How the power of adults is subsequently used in the aftermath of long-term political conflicts often reveals the politicization of childhood through ongoing practices that render children as a non-political group. Hence, peace reconstruction makes passive use of children as future projects and continues to marginalise or exclude their active agency in terms of influencing agenda setting. The impact that this positioning has on the subsequent agency of children in one politically divided locality in Belfast will be discussed in the section 'The interface between structure and agency in Belfast'.

CHILDREN AND THE ECONOMIC SYSTEM

Along with the realm of politics, the world of economics is considered as part of the public sphere making it difficult for children to practice agency given their location within the private sphere of the family (see the chapter by Jensen, this volume). Within most economies, children are not considered as economic agents (Levison, 2000). Rather their economic activity is often constrained by the location of childhood within appropriate spaces such as family units. The majority of modern welfare states are dependent on the reproduction of children as dependent beings. This journey towards dependency can be traced back to the middle of the 19th century in England where children were progressively removed from the world of work outside the household resulting in the exclusion of children and childhood from the adult world of politics and economics (Hendrick, 1997; see also the chapter by Qvortrup, this volume). Childhood became redefined as a universal essentialist category based on notions of children as innocent beings in need of protection. Idealist constructions of the family emerged facilitating policies that increasingly situated children as dependents within 'loving' family units in the process ignoring the diversity of such units and the underlying power relationships on which they were based. Parents were positioned as caretakers 'rightly' making decisions on behalf of children since they were considered as having their best interests at heart (Archard, 1993). In the process, children's entitlements to provision and protection outweighed their right to participation (Wyness, Harrsion, & Buchanan, 2004).

The privatisation of childhood is fundamental to understanding how children in Northern Ireland (and indeed elsewhere) structurally and spatially relate to the economic sphere. Migration and displacement often accompany political conflicts. In Northern Ireland, during the period 1969–1972, an estimated 60,000 people were forced out of their homes resulting in the increasing segregation of space into localities dominated by one or other of the two main communities (Darby & Morris, 1974). A

Northern Ireland Housing Executive (1999) Report revealed that 98% of their local housing estates in Belfast are dominated by residents who are over 90% Catholic or Protestant. These segregated working class spaces have been disproportionately affected by the conflict (Fay, Morrisey, & Smyth, 1999; Murtagh, 2001). While adults are often constrained within these spaces, their structural position as adults gives them scope for greater mobility compared to children whose structural position within the confines of childhood enhances their immobility. Hence, children often become trapped in sectarian spaces. Within these spaces, Catholic nationalists and Protestant unionists live by and large separate lives. However, adults have the opportunity to transcend these spaces through their involvement in paid employment. The latter brings Catholic and Protestant adults together in mixed employment environments. By contrast, children's location as recipients of adult care precludes their participation in paid employment. Northern Ireland, as is the case in the majority of developed societies, has in place a legislative framework that curtails and excludes the involvement of children in paid work based on the premise of sheltering them from the harsh realities of the adult world and prioritising their work as school pupils. This deepens their economic dependency on poor adults. It also impacts negatively on their opportunities to engage in shared leisure pursuits located outside their immediate localities. Many children cannot afford to travel to mixed leisure spaces located in less segregated parts of the city. They have little recourse but to roam the streets with nothing to do. This in turn incurs disapproval from a range of adults in their respective communities including parents, neighbours, paramilitaries and the police (Leonard, 2006c). It also enhances the reproduction, maintenance and strengthening of negative stereotypes between communities. Many children have limited opportunities to meet or positively engage with members of the other community. Their location in residentially segregated areas, economic dependency on adults and exclusion from the labour market, premised on local and global conceptions of childhood, preclude their ability to transcend sectarian boundaries. Hence, the pauperisation of childhood (Jensen, 1994), which characterises childhood as a structural form across the world (Vleminckx & Smeeding, 2001), has specific local effects in Northern Ireland. I am not simplistically suggesting that children's involvement in paid employment would by itself challenge their economic dependency within the family or lead to the erosion of the complex web of factors, which separate the two main adult communities in Northern Ireland. What I am suggesting is that dominant conceptions of children and their childhoods in relation to their economic positioning add an additional layer to the structural constraints under which they practice their agency in this particular contested society.

CHILDREN AND THE EDUCATION SYSTEM

The educational system is a further crucial component for reproducing childhood as a structural form. The withdrawal of children from the labour market led to their increasing location within schools. Childhood became progressively regulated through the establishment of children's universal duty to attend schools for the most part of their childhoods. While national legislation differs from country to country, the majority of the world's children particularly in developed societies are obligated to spend significant amounts of their time within school environments (Qvortrup, 2000). Schools are a primary site for the reproduction of discourses on children, which emphasise supposedly natural characteristics such as incompetence and immaturity, hence needing tuition from adults about the dispositions necessary for entry to adulthood. While these processes are global, education also needs to be set within its local social and political context (Popkewitz, 2000). Education historically has played a key role in state formation and nation building (Gellner, 1983). State efforts to monopolise education become one of the battlegrounds for a nation's secession and one of the first areas to be reformed (Brocklehurst, 2006). The creation of the separate entity of Northern Ireland in 1921 turned the educational system into an arena of contestation between the state and the churches leading to the provision of separate schools for Protestant and Catholic children. This legacy remains in place today with around 95% of children in Northern Ireland attending schools that are segregated on the basis of religion. In a review of education in areas of ethnic conflict, Bush and Salterelli (2000) outline some of the functions of education in contested states. They argue that education emerges as an arena for creating and preserving positions of economic, social and political privilege. In Northern Ireland, debates around the 11-plus, which is an examination taken by children in the final year of primary school to determine whether they should transfer to a grammar or secondary school, are fought along traditional party lines, with unionist/loyalist parties supporting the retention of selection and nationalist/republican parties opposing this. The system was abolished by republican Sinn Fein's education minister in 2009 amidst a great deal of controversy with some grammar schools indicating that they will retain some form of academic selection. The ongoing politicization of education in Northern

Ireland does little to challenge the ongoing segregation of children along class as well as religious lines and looks set to remain a divisive challenge for the newly devolved power-sharing government.

Another important function of education is how it can be used as a means of manipulating history for political purposes (Bush & Salterelli, 2000). In Northern Ireland, this led to the privileging of British as opposed to Irish history (Murray, 1985). Indeed, Murray (1985) discusses the alternative 'three R's' that permeated the school system, religion, ritual and rivalry. As transmitters of nationalist discourses, teachers' own ideologies may feed into the teaching of history so that children may be encouraged to align themselves with strongly held views propagated by teachers. For example, Spyrou (2001) outlines how teachers in southern Cyprus emphasised Greek over Cypriot identity particularly in the aftermath of the Turkish invasion in 1974. Encouraging children to construct a strong sense of 'Greekness' allowed teachers to draw on discourses relating to 'others', particularly the Turks as core enemies. Cairns (1996) outlines how prominent 'terrorists' in Northern Ireland outlined the nationalistic tones of the teaching of history they received in schools as one of the motivating factors for subsequently joining a paramilitary organisation. Hence, schools may play a key role in identity formation. In exploring educational policy in Israel from the 1948 transition to statehood and the educational reforms in the late 1960s, Levy (2005) outlines how the schools contributed to the marking out of ethnic boundaries between Arabs and Jews. She concludes that educational policy often 'reveals the interplay between nationalism, ethnicity and citizenship in multiethnic societies, which underlies the making of modern states and ethnicized societies' (2005, p. 272).

Schools are also sites for peacebuilding initiatives suggesting that states acknowledge their key role in the politicisation of their inhabitants. Through its educational policies, particularly through citizenship programmes, states may universalise the particularistic core social relationships within their boundaries. Many states experiencing conflict transmit notions of universal citizenship through schools as a way of emphasising national belonging over ethnic identity. In Northern Ireland, one of the core aims of citizenship education is to encourage children to reflect on the competing rights of different groups and how such rights may be if not resolved then managed through notions of universal rights and responsibilities (Weinstein, Freedman, & Hughson, 2007; McEvoy, McEvoy, & McConnachie, 2006). Local and Global Citizenship became a statutory curriculum requirement for all secondary level schools in Northern Ireland in September 2007. The programme draws on wider European and human rights discourses on citizenship and aims to increase cultural awareness, reduce prejudice and challenge stereotypes held by each respective ethnic group. Hence, schools may play a pivotal role in the transmission of universal values to consciously manipulate and transform political identities (Spyrou, 2000).

Utilising schools as a location for conflict resolution tells us a number of things about states' conceptions of childhood. Firstly, it indicates that children are already considered as political beings in that they have already been subjected to the particularistic views of their own families and communities. It also suggests a rather passive model of childhood whereby children are considered as empty vessels likely to mimic the views of adults in their households and localities. The malleability of children is extended to the school sphere whereby the educational system supported by the state is considered as an effective mechanism for encouraging or coercing children to 'unlearn' particularistic values and 'relearn' universalistic values through teachers as holders of state-endorsed knowledge. Of course, teachers may not necessarily transmit the universal overarching ideologies that underpin citizenship programmes. Preliminary evaluation of the piloting of Local and Global Citizenship in Northern Ireland (CCEA, 2006) reveals the unease some teachers feel about bringing politics overtly into the classroom. Many teachers choose to implement a 'culture of silence' whereby core divisions within Northern Ireland are not discussed, and in practice, citizenship education was found to focus on less contentious issues such as environmental or 'third world' issues.

However, it is teachers not pupils who have the power to implement silence in relation to topics discussed. It is teachers who are agenda setters within school systems. It is teachers who can confront or avoid sensitive issues. In the process, the reification of national identity may lie in what is not said rather than what is discussed. Of course, children are not mere puppets within educational systems. They do not passively respond to views transmitted by teachers but actively negotiate and co-construct the messages they receive (Spyrou, 2000). However, they do so within a framework that endorses the power relationships between adults and teachers in the wider society. This accords teachers, by virtue of their adult status, holders of more appropriate knowledge than the children in their charge. Hence, classroom debates often result in a process whereby 'good' pupils come to gradually accept what the teacher already knows (Edwards, 1990). As a result, children's experiences and views on ethnic conflict and its resolution may be dismissed as naïve and unsophisticated (Leonard, 2007). One of the core recommendations of teenagers in a study of how politics could be made more meaningful to their everyday lives was their call for independent political education in schools as a way forward (Finlay & Irwin, 2004). Other research into young people's views on their contribution to the peace process revealed that they considered themselves as onlookers rather than valued participants in conflict resolution (McCabe & Bourke, 2002). Similarly, citizenship programmes in Northern Ireland remain adult centred and children are rendered invisible at the decision-making stages of these initiatives (CCEA, 2006). Hence, the positioning of children within power structures in schools influences the enabling and constraining opportunities they have to accept, question or contest the messages they receive.

CHILDREN AND CULTURE

The structural location of children in the overlapping political, economic and educational spheres in Northern Ireland also impacts on their scope for agency in relation to culture. In exploring 'the sticky problem of culture', Hays (1994, p. 58) questions the tendency to dichotomise culture as hidden, internal and requiring interpretation with structure defined as external, publicly assessable and open to scientific operation. Her analysis locates culture as part of social structure. Culture is often narrowly reduced to the beliefs and values of social groups. However, culture also has a material presence. It is embodied in people's everyday practices and relationships. It structures gestures, actions, interactions, speech and rituals and feeds into artefacts and institutions. It is a producer and product of all these forms of being. It has a historical basis. Culture does not emerge from nowhere. New cultural trends do not appear at random. Rather culture is profoundly resilient. As Hall (1990, p. 225) puts it, 'cultural identities come from somewhere, they have histories. But like everything else which is historical, they undergo constant transformation. Far from being eternally fixed in some essentialised past, they are subject to the continuous "play" of history, culture and power'. Hence, culture is socially constructed by history, by past and present relations between groups, and as Hays (1994, p. 68) succinctly puts it, 'culture influences not only what we think about but how we think about it'.

One way of illuminating the specificity and heterogeneity of culture is to draw on Bourdieu's (1990) notion of 'habitus'. The 'habitus' refers to taken-for-granted ways of thinking about and acting upon the social world. According to Bourdieu, people habitually reproduce the structures of everyday life. In other words, their past history, their culture and their past experiences impact on their current state of mind and behaviour (Bourdieu & Wacquant, 1992). This does not mean that their behaviour is therefore rendered as predictable. Since people are agents, alternative choices are always possible. However, this agency is practiced within the field of structurally provided possibilities, and therefore to some extent, subsequent choices are likely to reproduce existing structures. But this complementary relationship may at times be an antagonistic one in that the reproduction process 'is never fully stable or absolute and, under particular circumstances, the structured choices that agents make can have a more or less transformative impact on the nature of structures themselves' (Hays, 1994, p. 65).

While power relations are at the heart of Bourdieu's notion of the habitus, he pays more attention to class than other forms of domination. Hence, he pays little attention to generational power processes. However, because habitus is regarded as linked to individual history, then Bourdieu indirectly locates generational relationships at the centre of his analysis. For example, he outlines the impact of socialisation both within the family and in educational systems on the internalisation of the dispositions that underline the reproduction of the habitus. As he puts it, 'The habitus acquired in the family is at the basis of the structuring of school experiences ... , the habitus transformed by the action of the school, itself diversified, is in turn at the basis of all subsequent experiences'. The family, the school and their location in specific places produce a 'cultured habitus' (Bourdieu, 1967, p. 344) and a form of cultural capital which under certain conditions can be transformed into human and economic capital. Elsewhere, I have criticised Bourdieu's dismissal of sub-cultural capital and its relevance to teenage culture (Leonard, 2008). None-theless, his recognition of the importance of upbringing and social environment is a useful way of conceptualising how the habitus creates dispositions to act, interpret experiences and think in a certain way. He argues (Bourdieu & Wacquant, 1992, p. 133) 'experiences will confirm habitus because most people are statistically bound to encounter circumstances that tend to agree with those that originally fashioned their habitus'. At the same time, the insights he provides into the dynamic but recurring workings of the habitus enable us to view children's involvement in cultural reproduction as one not reduced to mere mimicry but one where children are capable of simultaneously producing, reproducing and transforming their everyday worlds.

THE INTERFACE BETWEEN STRUCTURE
AND AGENCY IN BELFAST

I now want to bring together the macro and micro worlds of children's everyday lives in North Belfast to illustrate the importance of structure as well as agency in influencing the framework in which they make sense of the choices they make. I have outlined thus far how children are marginalised from the formal sphere of politics by their total exclusion from suffrage and their ongoing marginalisation in setting political agendas (see the chapter by Campiglio, this volume). They have been utilised in the past to justify conflict and peacebuilding but in a passive rather than active capacity. Yet, children have to live with the decisions made by adult political actors in the states they reside. The conflict in Northern Ireland has resulted in wide-spread residential segregation particularly in working class areas. This separation is enhanced by the educational system that continues to divide the majority of children along religious and class lines. Their generational positioning as children vis-à-vis adults lends another layer of structure to the intertwined realms of their everyday lives. Their economic dependence on adult family members and restricted ability to engage in paid employment curtails their spatial mobility both within and outside their local communities. I now want to turn to how this combination of structural factors impacts on the agency of children drawn from two interface areas located in Belfast. Elsewhere, I have focused on the active strategies pursued by these children in negotiating and renegotiating their ethnic-sectarian identities (Leonard, 2006a, 2006b, 2006c). While I located children's accounts within the specificities of the wider society of Northern Ireland, my core intention was to demonstrate their active agency. Eighty children from the two main communities took part in the research, which used a combination of qualitative methods including writing essays, producing maps of typical movements and focus group discussions. Hence, the research was firmly located within the paradigm outlined by Prout and James (1997) describing children's daily lives in a specific sociocultural context using ethnographic methods that facilitated an agency-orientated perspective. The children did not constitute a representative sample of children in Northern Ireland but were specifically drawn from areas that have and continue to experience disproportionate levels of sectarian conflict. It might seem surprising then that I am choosing to focus on an atypical group of children to demonstrate the relationship between structure and agency. However, 'the point is that no child can evade the impact of economic or spatial forces, nor ideologies about children and the family – let alone political and economic ideologies and realities' (Qvortrup, 2000, p. 79).

In the first phase of the research, children wrote an essay describing the nice and not so nice aspects of growing up in North Belfast. The exercise was deliberately general and aimed to capture children's broad attitudes to growing up in their locality rather than being steered in advance towards particular topics. Despite not being mentioned, the conflict in Northern Ireland formed a core aspect of their essays on the not so nice aspects of growing up in North Belfast. The second phase of the research involved asking children to draw maps on their typical movements over a typical week. On their maps, children were asked to situate where their house was located, where their school was positioned, where they worked (no child had a part-time job), where they shopped and where they spent their leisure time. Once the maps were completed, children were asked using blue and red stickers to indicate where they felt safe and where they felt less safe. This aspect was not introduced in advance as the intention was to gain an insight into typical movements rather than guiding young people towards thinking of movements in terms of safety and risk. Moreover, safety and risk were not defined and it was left to the young people to determine their own meanings of safe and less safe places. However, as with the first exercise, the conflict in Northern Ireland dominated accounts of safety and risk. In the final phase of the research, children were divided into groups of four to six and took part in focus group discussions on two separate occasions. The focus group discussions centred on the themes outlined by the young people in their essays and maps and their identification of the positive and negative aspects of growing up in North Belfast. To explore the interplay between structural factors and children's agency, the remainder of the chapter will attempt to apply Bourdieu's concept of the 'habitus' to illustrate the impact of macro processes on children's lifeworlds within this specific context.

I want to explore children's location in three overlapping spheres – the family, school and the locality. According to Bourdieu (1990), the habitus is not an essentialist mode of thinking but a generic one. This suggests that children's dispositions are likely to be partly shaped by the influential adults in their lives and by dominant discourses around the positioning of childhood in modern society. Families, for example, remain prime sites for the socialisation of children. Within families, children are predisposed towards certain ways of behaving. While families differ in composition, they generally are structured around power relationships between adults and children endorsed by the wider society and supported by a range of practices and institutions that uphold these generational power relationships. While I do not intend to locate children as mere dupes within families, passively reproducing parental attitudes and values, nonetheless, it seems likely that children will be influenced to varying degrees, by parental taken-for-granted assumptions about the everyday world. Within North Belfast, families play a role in developing, maintaining, reproducing and challenging attitudes and behaviours premised on sectarian differences. The majority of the parents of the teenagers who took part in the research were born in North Belfast. They have experienced their own childhoods against a backdrop of sectarian violence. During focus group discussions, some children discussed their perception of parents holding strong political views based on nationalism/ republicanism or unionism/loyalist ideologies. Some parents had been imprisoned for political beliefs and some children had family members who had been killed or wounded due to the political conflict. While some children discussed parents' friendship patterns made at work as transcending sectarian boundaries, for the majority, the main collective experience produced a range of overlapping fields based on defining differences between 'us' and 'them'.

By viewing the habitus as a 'complex system of distributed cognitions', Connolly (2006, p. 146) is able to demonstrate how ways of thinking and behaving are also mediated by relationships, objects and events within schools, and it is to this location that I now turn. In relation to Northern Ireland, the separation of schooling along sectarian lines reinforces notions of difference. Schools reflect dispositions based on religious identity. Different sports are prioritised within schools. Emblems based on religious differences permeate school corridors and classrooms. While each school had developed some cross-community initiatives, children often had no control or say over who participated in such schemes. Hence, in practice, participation was often linked to good behaviour with 'well-behaved' classes qualifying for cross-community programmes as a reward for good behaviour. Hence, some children who took part in the research had never been selected for participation in these projects. Schools played a role in promoting a culture of tolerance, but teachers controlled the environment under which sectarianism and tolerance were discussed and at times engaged in a 'culture of silence', which enabled the ways of thinking and acting upon the social world emanating from children's everyday lived experienced in their family and surrounding locality to flourish. The locality itself further mediates the ways in which teenagers think and behave. Flags, wall murals and graffiti based on competing territorial claims adorn each neighbourhood. Hence, sectarian culture based on difference becomes embodied in the physical landscape. Throughout the focus group discussions, teenagers tended to position themselves in terms of in-groups and out-groups based on perceived political differences. They curtailed their movements on this basis, with many implementing self-imposed restrictions on their everyday mobility. These ways of thinking and behaving have been accumulated over time and come to represent instinctive taken-for-granted ways of engaging in everyday life. Given this context then, it is unsurprising that some of the teenagers who took part in the research internalise and reproduce recurring forms of sectarianism as part and parcel of their everyday lives.

Bourdieu's notion of the habitus has been criticised for its seemingly latent determinism (Jenkins, 1992), and the account outlined above may be accused of reflecting structure without agency. However, Bourdieu sees habitus as 'potentially generating a wide repertoire of possible actions, simultaneously enabling the individual to draw on transformative and constraining courses of action' (Reay, 2004). Hence, while the habitus predisposes individuals towards certain ways of behaving, it simultaneously allows for individual agency. If we turn to the family dispositions outlined above, it seems that children often have little autonomy to oppose traditional sectarian mindsets. Studies of adults' daily movements in this particular interface suggest fear and avoidance of the ethnic other were commonplace daily occurrences. Over three-quarters of the adults surveyed indicated that they would not out of choice enter an area dominated by the other sectarian groups (Shirlow, 2003). This geographical immobility was reflected in adults' usage of the two leisure centres servicing the overall area where both are located in Protestant areas. Eighty four percent of adults stated that they would not use these leisure centres for fear of being attacked or harassed by the other community (Bairner & Shirlow, 2003). During focus group discussions, children spoke of how their parents transferred these apprehensions to their spatial mobility opportunities curtailing their children's usage of these spaces. However, children did not always accept adults' definitions of daily risks and often transcended the boundaries set by adults; therefore, for example, at times, they inhabited spaces defined as no-go areas without adults' knowledge. They developed rules and practices that demonstrated their competency in defining and negotiating their own safety in public spaces. For example, in using leisure centres, children adopted a range of strategies, such as concealing their Catholic identity from perceived Protestant peers, utilising the leisure centre in groups rather than as individuals and utilising local street knowledge to acquire information about how to handle risky situations. At times, teenagers reported how 'carrying on' such as throwing other teenage users into the pool without knowledge of ethno/sectarian background enabled the short-term suspension of traditional sectarian identities.

In other ways, children did not passively follow the sectarian outlook of their families but played a central and active role in either maintaining sectarian identities, appropriating sectarian practices in new ways or challenging taken-for-granted sectarian assumptions. Children utilised the streets to gain autonomy from adults and utilised the streets as places where they could interact with peers. At times, children established their own networks and developed their own rules of engagement. Hence, children's relationship to the locality was much more nuanced than one linked simply to the wider political framework. For example, in their stories on 'what's nice about growing up in North Belfast', some children exhibited a strong affinity with nature in their geographical descriptions of the local area and saw nature in a much broader context than one reduced to the segregated nature of each respective interface locality. Hence, while street corners, shops and local leisure spaces were depicted as belonging to one side or the other, the mountains surrounding the area were presented as belonging to no one group, and in this way, children produced messier constructions of space than one reduced to sectarian identity.

Many children felt that they held more tolerant attitudes towards the other community compared to their parents. Some children questioned parental attitudes towards the 'troubles' as old-fashioned and outdated. Children discussed their more diluted forms of sectarian identity by indicating that they would consider marrying someone from the other community despite their perceptions that parents would disapprove of such unions (Leonard, 2009b). Within schools, children confronted their positioning as innocent and incompetent by developing a range of strategies for dealing with attending school in a risky location. In some cases, they confronted and challenged teachers' attempts to protect them by not giving them full information about dangerous political situations that were developing outside in the immediate locality while they were within the confines of school space (Leonard, 2006b).

Children reworked the embodiment of sectarian culture in new ways through their consumption of hairstyles, jewellery and designer clothes, all of which were utilised to emphasise a sectarian identity separate from the traditional markers utilised by adults in the locality. But they also utilised consumption to define and create other identities not based on sectarian difference. Some children used clothes to break with tradition and habit and forge an element of individuality (Featherstone, 1991). Other children used clothes to form new relationships with peers that seemed immune from sectarian labelling. Children moved within and between the fields of the family, school and locality working out the game to be played in each setting and at times modifying their behaviour accordingly. At the same time, they reproduced, at least to some degree, the structural framework in which they are already located. Hence, the wider structural features of growing up in North Belfast placed limits on young people's capacity to fully transcend sectarian divisions. Since young people continue to grow up in territorial enclaves segregated by religion and class and since they continue to be educated in schools segregated by religion and class, identities based on in-group and out-group affiliations remain resilient. However, this is not to reduce the habitus to a deterministic position. As Harker (1984, p. 126) reminds us 'the habitus ... is no more fixed than the practices which it helps to structure'. Hence while children embodied the rules and expectations of their local culture, they retained a sense of agency, which at times produced messier and more contradictory forms of sectarian identities.

CONCLUSION

States create children and children create states. The construct of the ideal child or the ideal childhood infiltrates the heart of 'western' political systems. Much of the state's business involves maintaining the separation of adults from children and the location of children in spheres deemed necessary to protect their innocence and monitor their journey towards adult citizenship (see the chapter by Qvortrup, in this volume). Theoretical assumptions about what constitutes the political often results in the categorisation of children as non-political subjects. Yet, the location of children as non-political beings is in itself a political act. Children's location as innocent and in need of protection has valuable political currency. It has provided a rationale for war and peace processes. In demonstrating how these themes are played out in the context of Northern Ireland, I utilised Bourdieu's concept of the habitus as a fruitful approach for linking the macro to the micro. Children's lives in Northern Ireland are partly the product of wider historical, political, economic, educational and cultural factors, which links together childhood as a structural form encouraging a set of attitudes and practices around the positioning of children as immature, incompetent and non-political. Hence, the habitus of the global field informs local attitudes, practices and institutions, which in turn inform understandings of the global. Dispositions, attitudes, behaviours and practices are also partly determined by the specificity of growing up in a particular locality in Northern Ireland. Here, I have focused on the production, reproduction and reformation of ethnic sectarian identity. The habitus produces individual and collective practices. Individually and collectively, teenagers in North Belfast are partly influenced by the normative expectations surrounding definitions of the 'other' resulting in a range of culturally inherited dispositions that come to be seen as second nature. Teenagers carry around a storehouse of cultural and subcultural knowledge in their heads, which in turn informs their everyday practices. These dispositions are durable and transportable (Bourdieu, 1977). Yet, within every habitus lie the seeds of or potential for social change (Fuchs, 2003). Hence, the habitus should not be viewed as overdetermining agency (Morrison, 2005). Alternative choices are always possible. In an attempt to move beyond the conceptual quagmire whereby structure impacts on agency and vice versa, Hays (1994) develops the notion of 'structurally reproductive agency'. In her view, structurally reproductive agency 'is made possible under particular historical circumstances – when portions of what were once deeper social structures become particularly malleable and provide occasion for significant collective refashioning' (Hays, 1994, p. 64). Understanding children's agency as 'structurally reproductive agency' necessitates engaging with the array of macro structures that construct and reconstruct childhood within and across different societies. The habitus like childhood is in a constant process of becoming. Northern Ireland has embarked on a peace process that is transforming the political structures of the wider society and its institutions, and this should impact on the habitus described here and change the rules under which existing games are played. Moreover, children's agency is given more weight with the ongoing emergence of rights-based discourses that are feeding in to some of the major institutions that structure children's everyday lives. At a local level, this could further enhance a break with history and encourage the emergence of more tolerant attitudes and practices and lead to a set of different taken-for-granted dispositions that reflect wider structural changes. At the same time, the messy relationship between structure and agency is likely to continue to provoke heated debate. In relation to childhood in general, a central dilemma remains in that children continue to be anchored in historically durable generational relationships based on power, and it is within this framework that their agency is practised.

REFERENCES

Archard, D. (1993). *Children: Rights and childhood*. London: Routledge.
Bairner, A., & Shirlow, P. (2003). When leisure turns to fear: Mobility and ethno-sectarianism in Belfast. *Leisure Studies, 22*(2), 203–221.
Bellamy, C. (1999). *The state of the world's children 1996*. Oxford: Oxford University Press.
Bourdieu, P. (1967). Systems of education and systems of thought. *Social Science Information, 19*(3), 338–358.
Bourdieu, P. (1977). *Outline of a theory of practice*. Cambridge: Cambridge University Press.
Bourdieu, P. (1990). *The logic of practice*. Cambridge: Polity Press.

Bourdieu, P., & Wacquant, L. (1992). *An invitation to reflexive sociology*. Chicago: University of Chicago Press.

Boyden, J. (2003). The moral development of child soldiers: What do adults have to fear. *Journal of Peace Psychology, 9*(4), 343–362.

Brocklehurst, H. (2006). *Who's afraid of children? Children, conflict and ethnic relations.* Aldershot: Ashgate.

Burman, E. (1994). Innocents abroad: Projecting Western fantasies of childhood onto the iconography of emergencies. *Disasters: Journal of Disaster Studies and Management, 18*(3), 238–253.

Bush, K., & Salterelli, D. (2000). *Two faces of education in ethnic conflict*. Italy: United Nations Children's Fund, Innocenti Research Centre.

Cairns, E. (1996). *Children and political violence*. London: Blackwell.

Carter, T. F. (2003). Violent pastime(s): On the commendation and condemnation of violence in Belfast. *City and Society, 15*(2), 255–281.

Clarke, T. (1997). *Art and propaganda in the twentieth century: The political image in the age of mass culture*. London: Weidenfeld and Nicolson.

Connolly, P. (2006). The masculine habitus as 'Distributed Congition': A case study of 5- to 6- year-old boys in an English inner-city, multi-ethnic primary school. *Children and Society, 20*(2), 140–152.

CCEA – Council for the Curriculum Examinations and Assessment. (2006). *Local and global citizenship at key stage 3, preliminary evaluation findings*. Northern Ireland: University of Ulster.

Darby, J., & Morris, G. (1974). *Intimidation in housing*. Belfast, Northern Ireland: Community Relations Council.

Edwards, D. (1990). Classroom discourse and classroom knowledge. In: C. Rogers & P. Kutnick (Eds), *The social psychology of the primary school* (pp. 49–69). London: Routledge.

Fay, M., Morrisey, M., & Smyth, M. (1999). *Northern Ireland's troubles: The human cost*. London: Pluto Press.

Featherstone, M. (1991). *Consumer culture and postmodernism*. London: Sage.

Fildes, V., Marks, L., & Marland, H. (1992). *Women and children first: International and infant welfare 1870–1945*. London: Routledge.

Finlay, E., & Irwin, G. (2004). *We have a voice: Young people and political engagement*. Belfast: Democratic Dialogue.

Fuchs, C. (2003). Some implications of Pierre Bourdieu's works for a theory of social self-organisation. *European Journal of Social Theory, 6*(4), 387–408.

Gellner, E. (1983). *Nations and nationalism*. Oxford: Blackwell.

Giddens, A. (1977). *Studies in social and political theory*. New York: Basic Books.

Giddens, A. (1984). *The constitution of society*. Cambridge: Polity Press.

Hall, S. (1990). Cultural identity and diaspora. In: J. Rutherford (Ed.), *Identity, community, culture, difference* (pp. 222–237). London: Lawrence and Wishart.

Hamilton, C. (1995). Children in armed conflict – New moves for an old problem. *The Journal of Child Law, 7*(1), 5–19.

Harker, R. (1984). On reproduction, habitus and education. *British Journal of the Sociology of Education, 5*(2), 117–127.

Hays, S. (1994). Structure and agency and the sticky problem of culture. *Sociological Theory, 12*(1), 57–72.

Hendrick, H. (1997). Constructions and reconstructions of British childhood: An interpretive survey, 1800 to the present. In: A. James & A. Prout (Eds), *Constructing and reconstructing childhood* (pp. 34–62). London: Falmer.

Hinrichs, K. (2002). Do the old exploit the young? Is enfranchising children a good idea? *Archives of European Sociology, XLIII*(1), 35–58.

Jarman, N., & O'Halloran, C. (2001). Recreational rioting: Young people, interface areas and violence. *Child Care in Practice, 7*(1), 2–16.

Jenkins, R. (1992). *Pierre Bourdieu*. London: Routledge.

Jensen, A.-M. (1994). The feminisation of childhood. In: J. Qvortrup, M. Bardy, G. Sgritta & H. Wintersberger (Eds), *Childhood matters: Social theory, practice and politics* (pp. 59–75). Aldershot: Avebury.

Leonard, M. (2006a). Teenagers telling sectarian stories. *Sociology, 40*(6), 1117–1133.

Leonard, M. (2006b). Segregated schools in segregated societies: Issues of safety and risk. *Childhood, 13*(4), 145–164.

Leonard, M. (2006c). Teens and territory in contested spaces: Negotiating sectarian interfaces in Northern Ireland. *Children's Geographies, 4*(2), 225–238.

Leonard, M. (2007). Children's citizenship education in politically sensitive societies. *Childhood, 14*(4), 487–504.

Leonard, M. (2008). Social and cultural capital among teenagers in Northern Ireland. *Youth and Society, 40*(2), 224–244.

Leonard, M. (2009a). What's recreational about 'recreational rioting'? Children on the streets in Belfast. *Children and Society, 35*(1), 97–114.

Leonard, M. (2009b). It's better to stick to your own kind: Children's views on cross community marriages. *Journal of Ethnic and Migration Studies, 35*(1), 97–114.

Levison, D. (2000). Children as economic agents. *Feminist Economics, 6*(1), 125–134.

Levy, G. (2005). From subjects to citizens: On educational reforms and the demarcation of the "Israeli-Arabs". *Citizenship Studies, 9*(3), 271–291.

McCabe, D., & Bourke, T. (2002). *Interim report for the Northern Ireland fund for reconciliation*. Dublin: The Training Trust.

McEvoy, L., McEvoy, K., & McConnachie, K. (2006). Reconciliation as a dirty word: Conflict, community relations and education in Northern Ireland. *Journal of International Affairs, 60*(1), 81–106.

Morrison, K. (2005). Structuration theory, habitus and complexity theory: Elective affinities or old wine in new bottles? *British Journal of Sociology of Education, 26*(3), 311–326.

Murray, D. (1985). Identity: A covert pedagogy in Northern Irish schools. *Irish Educational Studies, 5*(2), 18–27.

Murtagh, B. (2001). *The politics of territory*. London: Palgrave.

Northern Ireland Housing Executive. (1999). *Community relations and community safety*. Belfast: Northern Ireland Housing Executive.

Popkewitz, T. (2000). *Educational knowledge: Changing relationships between state, civil society and the educational community*. New York: Albany Press.

Prout, J., & James, A. (1997). A new paradigm for the sociology of childhood? Provenance, promise and problems. In: A. James & A. Prout (Eds), *Constructing and reconstructing childhood, contemporary issues in the sociological study of childhood* (pp. 7–33). London: Falmer Press.

Qvortrup, J. (1987). Introduction to the sociology of childhood. *International Journal of Sociology, 17*(2), 3–37.

Qvortrup, J. (1999). *Childhood and societal macrostructures: Childhood exclusion by default.* Working Paper no 9. Child and Youth Studies. Odense University, The Department of Contemporary Cultural Studies.

Qvortrup, J. (2000). Macroanalysis of childhood. In: P. Christensen & A. James (Eds), *Research with children: Perspectives and practices* (pp. 77–97). London: Falmer Press.

Reay, D. (2004). It's all becoming a habitus: Beyond the habitual use of habitus in educational research. *British Journal of Sociology of Education, 25*(4), 431–444.

Semashko, L. (2004). Children's suffrage as a key way of improvement of children's well-being in an age of globalization. *Electronic Journal of Sociology.* Available at http://www.sociology.org. Accessed online on 2 July 2009.

Shirlow, P. (2003). Ethno-sectarianism and the reproduction of fear in Belfast. *Capital and Class, 80*(3), 77–95.

Spyrou, S. (2000). Education, ideology and the national self: The social practice of identity construction in the classroom. *The Cyprus Review, 12*(1), 61–81.

Spyrou, S. (2001). Being one and more than one: Greek cypriot children and ethnic identity in the flow of everyday life. *disClosure, 10*(1), 73–94.

Stephens, S. (1997). Nationalism, nuclear policy and children in cold war America. *Childhood, 4*(1), 103–123.

Thorne, B. (1987). Revisioning women and social change: Where are the children? *Gender and Society, 1*(1), 85–109.

Vleminckx, K., & Smeeding, T. (2001). *Child well-being, child poverty and child policy is modern nations.* Bristol: The Policy Press.

Weinstein, J., Freedman, S. W., & Hughson, H. (2007). School voices: Challenges facing education systems after identity based conflicts. *Education, Citizenship and Social Justice, 2*(1), 41–71.

Wyness, M., Harrsion, L., & Buchanan, I. (2004). Childhood, politics and ambiguity: Towards an agenda for children's political inclusion. *Sociology, 38*(1), 81–99.

CONFISCATED TIME: ARE CHILDREN ALLOWED TO MANAGE THEIR OWN TIME?

Maria Carmen Belloni

A NECESSARY SPECIFICATION

Major merits of New Childhood Sociology are that it has introduced into sociology three fundamental points: (a) studying children as social actors, contrary to the view customarily held of them; (b) defining childhood not as a transitional phase, a state that people leave behind, but as a permanent structure of society – wherein, however, constant turnover occurs, so that childhood changes over time and in different types of society (James, Jenks, & Prout, 1998; Qvortrup, 1991, 2004); (c) considering children as essential part of a historically and socially constructed relationship with adults (Alanen, 2001), following the generational perspective already indicated by Mannheim (Mannheim, 1952).

This specification is important because it enables us to differentiate the characteristics of childhood with respect to not only different historical periods (Ariès, 1960) but also the local contexts in which children are embedded, thereby deterring excessively generalized, or conversely indivi-dualized, considerations on their characteristics. The anchoring of analysis to structural elements of the local context also makes it possible to reduce the antithesis (in my opinion artificial) between approaches that treat the

Structural, Historical, and Comparative Perspectives
Sociological Studies of Children and Youth, Volume 12, 139–165
ISSN: 1537-4661/doi:10.1108/S1537-4661(2009)0000012011

child principally in terms of agency and others that would have him/her disappear into the social structure. Even should we wish to consider children as subjects producing a culture – transmitted and reproduced essentially among themselves though connected with that of society as a whole (Corsaro, 1997) – the fact remains that their culture assumes different features and is subject to different influences according to the structure and the organization of the local setting that children live: the material resources available to them, the way in which households organize their everyday routines, the structures and agencies with which children enter relations, demographic composition, public discourses on childhood and so on. For these reasons, it is always advisable when analyzing childhood to also consider the characteristics of the adult society in which children live, as well as the ways in which it is organized, because childhood inevitably establishes dependency relations with the world of adults.

In regard to specific research on children, I believe it is important to reconstruct their effective spaces of action. Reconstructions of this type are rare and are perhaps taken too much for granted. I contend instead that the organization of children's everyday lives is an important indicator of the structural context in which they act. For the organization of childhood routine – as we shall see – is closely connected with that of adults. It reflects the constraints and the opportunities conditioning how children arrange their activities and the contexts in which these develop, the normative systems that regulate them and the accessible physical spaces that importantly condition their performance. It is within this scenario that children act and can use the various degrees of autonomy granted to them, developing their relationships with both their peer group and other generations.

I shall clarify this assertion by citing two studies – among the many in the ample literature on the subject – on the use of spaces by children. Attention to practised spaces is very important for my analysis here, because these spaces, as the dimensions in which everyday life takes material form, are structures that summarize the complex system – of relations, rules and spheres action – within which childhood is embedded.

The first example is an essay by Helga Zeiher (2004), where she, analyzing the play activities of two groups of children, illustrates the relationship of planning adopted by adults in creating spaces for childhood and some derived important consequences for children. Differently planned places and spaces could in fact prompt children both to adopt different models of temporality and different ways to conduct relations among peers and therefore also different models to devise their courses of action. Also important is the fact that the different urban locations of play spaces reinforce distinctive components of class cultures such as orientation to the future, skills and capabilities.

The second study that I cite (Rasmussen, 2004) likewise shows how analysis of spaces of children/for children yields understanding of how the sense of belonging, responses to institutionalization, appropriation of spaces and autonomy come about within a specific configuration of the spaces, public structures, time schedules and social representations within which children act.

These examples highlight how empirical analysis of specific cases enables us to grasp how childhood is always socially constructed in different ways in different social and cultural settings. If one considers the situation of a large Italian city, for instance, it is difficult to find conditions similar to those described in the above-mentioned studies. The contexts in which the children described in those studies act have features very different from Italian ones and likewise very different are the everyday lifestyles of the children – their spaces of agency, autonomy and their relationships with adults.

Against this background, I shall describe the everyday life of children in a specific Italian city (Turin)[1] of metropolitan size situated in one of the most developed and industrialized geographical areas of the country, the destination of various migratory waves (first from the poorer regions of Italy, today from European and extra-European areas of underdevelopment). My aim is a modest one in light of the more detailed analyses conducted on childhood. Or better, this study is preliminary to addressing the question of whether and how children can be considered real social actors, as competent subjects able to pursue courses of action. Yet, reconstructing action scenarios is nevertheless useful. The research described here produced nothing more than a description of the behaviours of children aged between 7 and 10 (elementary school) outside school hours, obtained by examining the time-use diaries compiled by the children themselves.[2] As is obvious from the characteristics of the survey instrument, it can be used to reconstruct how children's everyday lives are organized in a specific context and to a certain extent also the 'structural' mechanisms that give rise to specific behaviours, individual and above all collective, but it cannot be used to identify the evaluations, the reasonings or negotiations that, within a given range of possible choices, lead to outcomes revealing the actual mechanisms with which agency is exercised.[3] It is undoubtedly true, however, that a survey of this kind can contribute to knowledge of the conditions and local contexts in which children act and therefore make their actions fully intelligible. Moreover, as I shall describe in more detail below, the 'objective' recon-struction of time organization can furnish a summary indicator of the social space within which children's autonomy is realized, since it is through the possibility of arranging time autonomously that non-dependence from external agents is asserted.

THE TEMPORAL STRUCTURE OF SOCIETY AND THE TIMES OF CHILDREN

In the research referred to here, time was used to measure childhood's activities or, in other words, as an instrument with which to quantify the duration of the various activities of children and their organization across the day, the places in which they are performed and the relationships between people in doing them. But quantification of everyday time also makes it possible to determine the type of temporal structuring in which children are embedded. The temporal organization in which, since early age, children participate constitutes, in fact, the principal dictate of their socialization and in parallel the normative framework within which their courses of action take place. This is very evident in the cases studied by Zeiher in Berlin. The randomness of encounters in the play space, or the need to organize them on the basis of the precise management of appointments, defines diverse strategies of action.

The analysis of the time of children, even in its more descriptive form with the scant motivational content that necessarily derives from time-use diaries, in any case aids understanding of the ways in which children act through definition of the main structural contexts in which they do so. Comparison between the time structuring of adults and that of children reveals, in fact, a powerful mechanism used by adult society to exercise control over childhood and thereby profoundly influence the features that it assumes. If we consider the structuring of everyday time in contemporary society, for children, it is perhaps the conditioning factor that they are least able to change. It will therefore be useful to consider briefly some characteristics and dimensions of the structuring of time in contemporary societies, seeking to show how it conditions the time of children.

The main factor structuring adult life is the *schedule*. This has important consequences for the relationship of individuals with the time/space system, because the schedule is able to define the entire organization of everyday life (Giddens, 1984; Zerubavel, 1981). The time structure that has arisen in Western societies since the industrial age comprises three main dimensions that most directly affect the ways in which childhood and relationships between children and adults are structured.

Firstly, the schedule is a *complex normative system* comprising different types of temporal regulation (the schedules of organizations and institutions), each with its own logic and predominant among which are those to do with the world of work. The regulation that derives from scheduling therefore introduces a rigidity and a compulsoriness, which lie at a level above spontaneous behaviour and which are thought to respond better to children's biological needs. Children must respect the schedules of the institutions (school or after-school activities) in which they spend large part of their everyday time. They are also subject to the constraints imposed by the schedules of the adults with whom they come into contact and on whom they depend to perform the majority of their activities. The post-Fordist organization of work, however, has introduced margins of flexibility to render labour more adaptable to just-in-time production systems in industry, to adjust workers to an increasingly globalized market, to respond to the demands of the now predominant tertiary sector and, in the best of cases, to enable reconciliation among the numerous, often conflicting, schedules that are present in a specific area. However, flexibility is not contrary to scheduling; rather, it is an adjustment device and consequently gives collective time a density and a continuity deriving from the accumulation and over-lapping of the segments of regulation (individual schedules).

For children, immersion in a system dominated by the schedule (in function of the adult organization) subjects them to a structure of constraints that often reinforce one another and greatly restrict the possibilities of choice. Schools have opening hours that are still more inflexible than those of many organizations. Teaching timetables impose precise times when lessons must begin and end. The low margins of flexibility in the entry and exit times of many schools respond more to the work/life reconciliation needs (among different schedules) of families than[4] to those of the children. And they mean that children must spend periods of supervised waiting, which consist in suspended temporality rather than fully lived time. Added to school opening hours are other time systems: the work schedules of parents (of the mother and the father), which may entail an extension of school time for their children (a prolongation of normal school opening hours), and those of other training agencies (extra-school cultural courses, sports training courses and similar, leisure activities for children, religious instruction and the like). These are chosen mainly by the parents to balance their work schedules or to supplement/anticipate training or for personal or health care (medical facilities).

Secondly, other consequences for the lives of children derive from the structuring of time systems/schedules into a plurality of *social times*. These constitute temporal spaces with their own characteristics and rules and with specific meanings for those who experience them and specific connotations in collective social representations. In industrial societies, the main axes along which social times have been traditionally arranged are those between leisure time and work time and between public time and private time. As a rule, also for children, quotidian time oscillates between these two axes of sense and issuing norms and regulations. But the status of leisure (i.e. time unconstrained by external controls) is improperly attributed to time free from schooling.[5] For children, real leisure can only be accomplished outside institutionalized settings, these being generally recreational or educational structures subject to the control/management of specialized adult practitioners. It is only outside an institutional context, in fact, that children cannot only play but also find a private dimension not subject to constant control of their selves and possessions by institutions.[6] In the above-cited study by Rasmussen, the children felt truly 'free' only when they returned home.[7] In the Turin survey, the children stated[8] that they preferred to organize themselves in their play, rather than being led by an adult (Belloni, 2005). Nevertheless, the full capacity of children to arrange their own time (the necessary condition for their achievement of leisure) is further conditioned by the fact that they are not regarded as subjects with genuine decision-making abilities/possibilities. Often, in fact, also the use of their time outside school by children is decided by their parents in consideration of other factors (their own constraints, concerns about education or training).

The mitigation of the hours system, through flexibilization of work schedules, the increasing density of time and the overlapping of social activities and times through multi-tasking characteristic post-Fordist society often impose even more binding rules on children. Childish leisure (in the proper sense) may, for instance, not find sufficient space for realization, because it is often transformed – especially among the middle and middle-upper classes – into merely free time filled with other institutionalized and controlled activities guided by experts, often intended to impart skills deemed (by adults) necessary for success in adult life.

Thirdly, social times and schedules, moreover, turn into socially constructed *collective rhythms*, which in themselves are social principles of regulation and organization. Social rhythms determine the scheduling of activities (particularly cardinal ones), the sequencing of breaks and intervals, the length of social times, their fragmentation and therefore the pace of societies as a whole. On the contrary, they constitute benchmarks and anchoring points in the everyday organization of individuals and groups. It is these rhythms that differentiate among economic cultural domains. Also, children are subject to these regulatory systems. They adapt to the temporal cadence of society in general, which often forces their biorhythms, although these are likely to require less fragmentation, less speed and less rigidity. The obligation to participate in a particular configuration of social rhythms inevitably produces a particular mode of living in time, oriented towards some activities rather than others and situated in particular contexts of action. This, too, means that childhood differs according to the local reality in which it is embedded.

In post-industrial societies also, social rhythms have undergone change of status in recent years. The reduction of the boundaries of social times, their overlapping and the proliferation of schedules all have contributed to destabilizing local tempos, although distinctive cadences still persist (for instance, the socially constructed schedules for mealtimes, returning home, the duration of the day, attending events, exchanging visits and going to sleep, which differ among countries and often also within them). For children, this means that external temporal regulations diminish, whilst domestic ones increase, or those of the immediate reference group. The elements of collectively recognized stability are reduced, and dependence on the family's rhythms increases. It may therefore happen that children depend more closely on their own households, strengthening the presence of familial or peer group micro-organizations that are difficult to synchronize with those of other households.

THE NATIONAL AND LOCAL ITALIAN CONTEXT

I believe that childhood can only be thoroughly understood if it is considered within its specific context. Consequently, the following description of an Italian case requires a brief summary of its structural setting. Although Italy belongs among advanced Western countries and shares many features with those of Europe, it differs from the latter, and particularly those of North Europe, in many respects that may affect the lives of children.

Schematically, the most salient features of what one may call Italy's 'exceptionality' concern its welfare system, situation of women, demographic structure and certain cultural aspects closely intertwined with them. However, these features vary according to the local situation, particularly so in the situation to which the following description of children's everyday lives refers.

According to Esping-Andersen's (1990) well-known classification, Italy belongs among the countries with conservative-corporative welfare regimes.

This means that it does not pursue real policies in support of families (although the family is assumed to be the fundamental unit of the society) and that family and childcare services are often not only inadequate but also 'traditional', in that they place heavy responsibility on parents, especially on women/mothers. Moreover, Italy has notable differences within its interior. Its various geographical areas, above all along the north/south axis, exhibit marked .imbalances of development, to which correspond equally marked imbalances in the delivery of services, especially those to the person and children. An important difference concerns the supply of school services, which are particularly scant in the South of Italy, where nurseries and full-time (elementary) school are quite absent. In the North, and in the city of Turin in particular, although the supply of public early childhood services is inadequate (though above the average for Italy), elementary school is the main service catering to children aged between 6 and 10, from the morning until the mid-afternoon. Moreover, the Turin municipal administration has a long tradition of investments in children's services, ranging from places for playing, organized structures for reading and playing ('ludoteche'), child training centres to services co-managed or available on request like crèches, babysitters on call and similar. Alongside the public supply – both because of the above-mentioned inadequacy of early childhood services and because of the widespread prolongation of working hours into the evening (and therefore after school closing times) – there is a flourishing supply of private childminding services that cover the entire day from before 8:00 (a.m.) until after 7:00 (p.m.).

The situation of Italian women is indubitably connected with the country's welfare system. Although female labour market participation in Italy is still below the level of other European countries,[9] recent years have seen the massive entry of women into employment, although with considerable and persisting disparities between the North and South. Unlike in other countries, part-time work in Italy is infrequent among women,[10] who face problems of work/family reconciliation, which often induce them to seek jobs with shorter and more compact working hours, such as teaching and public sector employment. In the city considered here, a large part (73%) of women between 25 and 44 years old with children are in employment, and they generally have rather long work schedules, although a bit shorter than those of men.[11]

Another feature of the Italian family system is the strong persistence of imbalanced gender roles that strongly penalize women. Even in dual-earner families, the predominant model of the domestic division of labour imposes a workload on women heavier than the average in Europe (Istat, 2008) – with limited contributions by fathers above all to core housework but also, albeit to a slightly lesser extent, to childcare. In this case, too, the differences among economic geographical areas are substantial, and they are largely due to the greater labour market exclusion of women in the South and partly due to the persistence of more traditional family models. Nevertheless, even in a context more favourable to egalitarian family models like Turin, the gender gap is still wide: for example, the domestic workload of women living with a partner is here two hours more than that assumed by the partner, whilst women devote forty minutes more to childcare (Del Boca & Saraceno, 2007).[12]

Another characteristic crucial for the following analysis is the structure of the family. In Italy, this has altered profoundly in recent years because of a fall in the birth rate,[13] which has produced marked demographic change. Couples now habitually have one or two children and at an increasingly advanced age.[14] Small families – many with only one child – are therefore very common. The proportions have consequently changed among the generations, to the detriment of the younger ones, so that the Italian population is currently one of the most elderly in the world.

The structural features just briefly described are not disconnected with a particular system of values, beliefs and attitudes that can be considered on the one hand the cultural matrix and on the other the basis for the stability of the general structure. Certain relations between structural and cultural aspects contribute to creating what we can call the 'exceptionality' of the Italian case, in which the family and its workings are placed at the centre of a system of constraints and unwritten rules characterized by the strong rigidity of roles, gender imbalances and ambiguity in relationships among generations (above all towards the younger one).

The welfare model currently in Italy, which gives families little support, together with the persistence of a division of family labour not inspired by gender equality, can be linked with the scant propensity/possibility of career for women in the labour market[15] and correspondingly with the large investment of time made by women in domestic work, as well as with the adoption of strategies to curb human and material costs (mainly in terms of time and management), among which a reduction in the number of offspring.

What are the implications of the above-described situation for childhood? The burden carried by families (and women in particular) in everyday housework and caring causes lack of time, or rather, a severe shortage of capital consisting in free time. Although kinship networks (especially grandparents) are still important sources of help for families, above all at the beginning of the family life cycle (in the presence of young children), they are not enough to make up the time deficit. Two consequences ensue: children are increasingly expelled from non-institutionalized spaces and exchanges between children and parents are confined to marginal times or subject to 'colonization' of the night,[16] with the consequent impact on child biorhythms.

Of particular importance for definition of the characteristics of childhoods is analysis of demographic changes. The advent of a new population age structure, a phenomenon especially marked in Italy, has significant consequences for the everyday lives of children. The increasing frequency of couples with only one child, or at most two,[17] is changing the relationships between generations and the parent/children relation. Moreover, children have fewer opportunities to relate with their peers in the private sphere, and not in institutionalized settings, under the supervision of adults with specific competences.

Furthermore, a child is today a rare commodity.[18] The current public discourse on childhood in Italy well testifies to this: children, in fact, are subject to not only large economic investments (the child is one of the main targets of advertising) but also strong emotional pressures, assumptions of responsibility, anxieties, fears concerning dangers external to the family and projections into the future. Indicators of these phenomena are the widespread recourse to early training, surveillance and assistance protracted until adolescence and beyond and fears of physical and relational risks.

Finally, in addition to sociodemographic aspects, brief consideration is required of spatial ones. Also in this regard, Italy is an interesting case, because it takes tendencies apparent in other European regions to the extreme. In Italy, high residential density and car ownership make the large cities, and also those of smaller size, unsuited for the unsupervised use of spaces by children. Public spaces fraught with danger, often of difficult access to the weakest segment of the population, and the limited extent of parks or playgrounds therefore provoke the increasing exclusion of children from urban spaces. Although many cities – among them Turin – have launched projects to restore the urban environment to children,[19] the use of external space as an autonomous daily experience, without the supervision and protection of adults, is still greatly limited. This, too, is indubitably an indicator of the close dependence of children on adults.

THE EVERYDAY ORGANIZATIONS
OF CHILDREN AND FAMILIES

Many of the above considerations apply to the everyday behaviour of adults and children when examination is made of how they employ their time.[20]

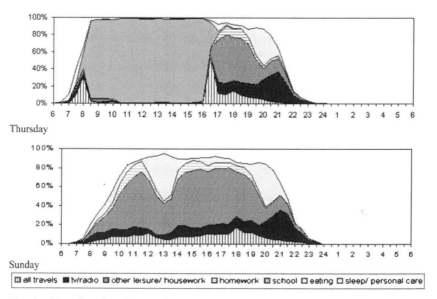

Thursday

Sunday

| □ all travels ■ tv/radio ▨ other leisure/ housework □ homework ▨ school □ eating □ sleep/ personal care |

Fig. 1.   Day Graphs of Everyday Time. Elementary School Children. *Source:* The
use of time of children in Turin, 2003 (Belloni, 2005).

First considered is the organization of the day in relation to scheduling
(Fig. 1). If we compare its set of characteristic dimensions (consistency,
arrangement, relations among social times), we note similarities between
children and adults. It may be said that the day rotates around a central
time – compact, long, non-negotiable and generalized – which for children is
represented by the school and reproduces the structure of adult working
time. It also reproduces the duration of the latter: 8 hours exactly, and even
more, if homework and after-school courses are added (8 hours 21 minutes).
We may therefore state that the preponderant part of children's everyday
time (at least on weekdays) is constricted time, as it is for adults.[21] Its
constricted nature (or, in other words, its strong regulation by rules external
to the child) emerges not only from the preponderance of this time over the
others but also from the stability of its arrangement: the schedule is repeated
every day of the week and also regulates biorhythms across the various days
of the week. Indicative of this is the sleep/wakefulness pattern, whose
changes over the week are very similar to those of adults (especially if male
adults are considered). Children seem to participate in some sort of
collective regulation on school days: they all get up early at around 7.30
a.m., and they all go to bed at between 9.00 and 9.30 p.m.. But on Saturdays

and Sundays, each of them follows his/her own rhythms: they get up at different times, some even sleep until 10 or 11 a.m., and they prolong the day until 10 p.m. in the evening or even later. We may say that on Saturdays and Sundays, children mostly follow 'their own times', as can also be deduced from their more relaxed relationship with their bodies and their biological functions and from the greater amount of time (2 hours altogether) devoted to sleeping, eating and washing.[22]

Overall, therefore, at least during the week, children precociously adhere to a time schedule similar to that of adults and characterized, as we have seen, by long duration and the preponderance of regulated activities (school-like work), density of time with scant possibility for interruption (centrality of the regulated schedule) and repetitiveness of unvarying rhythms (routine). Nevertheless, the sharing of the same temporal rules does not always ensure satisfactory integration between the time organizations of children and those of their families. Indeed, incompatibilities often arise and cause two main problems: one of organizational type and the other related to inter-generational relationships within the family. The parents must adopt strategies of organization and conciliation so that they can furnish the care and surveillance required (and socially defined) by the young age of their children and fulfil the relationship with their children in correspondence to the relational models adopted by the family. The children must adapt to the schedules defined by the adults and to the relationships made possible with both adults and the peer group, within a system of constraints and opportunities mainly manifest in the regulation (structuring) of everyday time.

One constraint is undoubtedly the difficulty of children in moving freely around city space because the urban environment is (or is believed to be) dangerous and therefore out of bounds to children. The coincidence of the beginning of the school day (8 a.m.) and the start of the working day for the majority of parents obliges families to solve the problem of accompanying children to school (and of collecting them in the afternoon, Table 1) by manoeuvring within the margins of flexibility provided by their schedules,

Table 1.   People Who Accompany and Collect Children to and from
School (in Percentage) – Elementary School.

	Father	Mother	Relatives	Childminder	Neigbours	Siblings	Alone	Friends	Others	Total
Accompanying	3.7	52.5	7.1	0.9	1.6	1.8	1.8		0.6	100
Collecting	19.8	51.2	16.4	3.4	5.2	3.3	1.6		0.8	100

Source: The use of time of children in Turin, 2003 (Belloni, 2005).

often by dividing the task between the father and mother – the latter, however, being the parent who most frequently assumes this task. But when the clash of schedules cannot be resolved, it is the children who must adjust their rhythms to the external constraints. It thus happens that many of them (between 15% and 20%) enter school early (even from 7 a.m. onwards), where they are supervised until lessons begin.[23]

The opposite problem, which arises because of the mismatch between the end of the school day (4 p.m.)[24] and the end of the majority of working days (which may be much later, even at 7 or 8 p.m.),[25] requires the adoption of even more complex strategies and organizational choices that once again obviously impact on children. The most widespread solution is that of steering children towards activities such as sports training or arts and crafts, which enable prolongation of children's schedules beyond school hours (and which may even last until 7.30 p.m.), at either their schools or other equipped facilities. This solution is in many cases obligatory for parents, being dictated by the rigidity of schedules or by the unavailability of family members or friends. In other cases, it instead serves the projections of adults on their children by adhering to a model of anticipatory training based on the precocious acquisition of skills considered useful, if not essential, for future success. In this way, the days of children become extremely dense with activities, and their times grow even more structured. The more this structuring increases, the more it reduces the chances of children being able to manage their own time.

The mass media often depict the children of contemporary societies as small victims of a dense organization of time, which obliges them to be very – excessively – busy. Our data largely confirm this image of mass media. Children are on average very busy; in fact, they engage in numerous structured activities and for a large amount of time, and this obliges them to spend long periods away from home, in situations of constant exposure of the self in public. Not surprisingly, therefore, at times, above all, on their return home, they take 'hinge-time' or 'transition time', which is denoted with largely uninformative phrases like 'I'm resting'.[26] Because of this dense organization of time, everyday leisure time is reduced to two and a half hours.

The average figure, obviously, conceals diverse situations that confirm the existence of a plurality of childhoods, of different ways of being a child, even in the same city setting (Table 2). As said, only a small minority of children (12%) are 'idle', so to speak, in that they do not engage in extra-school courses during the week, either on or off school premises.[27] And it is the children of the most deprived neighbourhoods who do not engage in any courses at all. The majority of children are instead rather busy after school in that they engage in one (24%) or two courses (30%). But the 'super-busy'

Table 2.   How Much Time Children Would Want to Spend in Activities
(in percentage) – Elementary School.

No. of Activities	Playing at Home			Playing Outdoors		
	More time	Less time	It's ok	More time	Less time	It's ok
0	38	16	46	50	23	27
1 o 2	49	7	45	59	7	33
3 or more	49	4	48	62	4	34
	Sports			Foreign language courses		
	More time	Less time	It's ok	More time	Less time	It's ok
0	53	20	27	36	21	43
1 o 2	59	9	31	23	22	55
3 or more	57	6	37	20	33	47
	Computer			Music, theater, painting courses		
	More time	Less time	It's ok	More time	Less time	It's ok
0	50	12	38	54	22	24
1 o 2	43	10	46	45	16	39
3 or more	49	11	40	42	17	41

Source: The use of time of children in Turin, 2003 (Belloni, 2005).

children, those involved in three or more courses, make up more than one-third of the sample (34%), and they live in elite neighbourhoods.[28] Comparison between children who engage in structured after-school activities and those who do not shows that such activities take time away from play – which is what we can regard as the freest and most 'natural' activity of children. And in fact, it is the children who are busy after school who declare they would like to have more time to play at home, especially out of doors.[29] But it would be incorrect to draw unequivocal conclusions from these data, which are ambiguous in several respects. Whilst it is true that participating in numerous extra-school courses increases the degree of everyday constriction and subtracts time from play, it nevertheless furnishes intellectual stimulation, and it enables children to make friends, to engage in not rigorously educational activity with other children and to share non-scholastic time with peers, for which opportunities are otherwise rather rare. This is somehow perceived by children themselves, because those who do not participate in structured after-school activities, unlike the others – perhaps out of curiosity or by imitation or desire for assimilation[30] – would like to have more out-of-school commitments. These children want to participate in activities that might seem not particularly attractive, such as language courses (perhaps because the majority of them are foreigners), and they are the only ones who would prefer to play less.

We now briefly consider other consequences of the saturation of everyday time. The direct consequence of the long hours of children's school and out-of-school activities, and of their parents' jobs, is a reduction of relational time among family members. Also, the time which children spend with their mothers, although longer than that spent with their fathers, is rather limited. This is partly due, as said, to the fact that mothers rarely have part-time jobs and that their working hours are often as long as those of the fathers. It thus happens that the composition of adult schedules, in the presence of opportunities offered by specific local contexts, and probably mediated by particular models of family relationality, gives rise to a pattern of daily organization by Italian families with small children, which differs markedly from those in other European countries. Whereas, in fact, parents in other countries tend to stagger their working hours, opting for their rationaliza-tion and organization, in Italy, they tend to have them overlap and instead seek to maximize the relational time spent together by all the members of the family (Carriero, Ghysels, & van Klaveren, 2009), exploiting the opportu-nities available locally (as we have seen, public or private services for childhood or relatives, above all, grandparents).

What impacts do these family strategies have on the time of children? It is evident that the time during which children are in 'custody' is prolonged both by resorting to institutionalized structures and by relying on relatives (and much more rarely friends). Nevertheless, this allows the creation of a stretch of time shared by all the family members – although concentrated in the late afternoon and evening – when the entire household is once again assembled. This, in fact, is the only occasion when the entire family is together during the day, because there are no other opportunities. The children eat the lunch at school, and when lessons finish, it is their mothers who usually pick them up and take them to their various after-school activities and supervise them at home until the return of their fathers, who generally have longer working hours.

An often overlooked consequence of the fact that the family unites only in the evening is that this type of organization conditions the activities reali-zable by children and restricts their possibility to self-determine their time. In sharing the stretches of time made free on conclusion of the complex interweaving of daily schedules, children find themselves in situations that they are unable to choose and control. It is likely that by imitation or because of the desire for co-participation – which translate into practices of sharing family spaces and activities – that children often spend the evening in front of the television. In fact, the peak viewing time for children on weekdays is between 8.00–8.30 and 9.30 p.m. (and on Saturdays and Sundays between 9.00 and past 10.00), whilst afternoon (after school) television programmes, which are mainly devoted to children, are much more infrequently watched.

TIME CHOICES AND CONTROL

The research data just outlined therefore confirm that children and adults generally adhere to the standard time structure. The data also highlight that the everyday organizations of children and adults must reach a conciliation among different needs within a complex system of constraints. However, the endeavour to reconcile the demands of the two populations does not take place on an equal footing, given the evident imbalance of power when the rules are fixed (even if adults are in their turn constrained and must resolve the not minor conflicts among their different schedules). Hence, as we have seen, children must often select from a range of options restricted by the situation in which they happen to be. Their above-described television watching habits are indicative in this regard. If children wanted to play with friends at that time, how could they do so if there were no adult to accompany them? At what other time of the day could they be with their mothers and fathers? And what relationship could they have with them, in the evening, after a long day of work and commitments, if they did not adjust to the adult time allocated to evening television watching?

The hypothesis developed of children's dependence on the time system of adults has two main corollaries: one concerns the relationships of children with other people (adults and children) (Table 3) and the other their relationship with external spaces. We have seen that the constraints imposed

Table 3.   People with Whom Children Spend Time (Generic Mean, in Hours and Minutes) – Elementary School.

	Alone	Only Children	Children and Adult	Only Adults
Thursday	1:03	1:08	9:48	2:04
Saturday	2:08	2:42	4:12	4:12
Sunday	2:02	2:20	4:24	3:42

Source: The use of time of children in Turin, 2003 (Belloni, 2005).

by the schedules of children and adults combine to reduce the physiological and leisure time of children, influencing free-time activities and their arrangement across the day. We also know that the dependence of children on adults is also manifest in the need for them to be accompanied in their movements. This is a very powerful constraint, and it conditions children's opportunities to meet their peers outside institutionalized contexts. In fact, on a normal weekday, less than half of children (45%) are able to meet friends outside these contexts. In unstructured or 'freer' contexts, therefore, only children with brothers and sisters can spend at least some of their daily time with other children.

In this case too, however, to be noted is the ambiguity inherent in the situations in which children habitually find themselves. In general, children pursue relationships with their peers in institutionalized contexts, and therefore, in situations of restricted freedom and autonomy. But one should not underestimate the fact that these contexts offer the main – often the only – opportunity for children to have such relationships. Institutional contexts therefore represent not only the principal frames within which relationships are conducted but also quite the only situations in which those among peers can be developed in continuous, not fragmented, times, and in which the rules of being together and of relationality can be learned. This also concerns relations with adults and which consist primarily in relations with institutional figures, given the brief time spent by children with their parents or relatives. From this derives another indubitable limitation on autonomy due to the fact that children have few opportunities to be alone with their peers. Instead, they spend almost all of their everyday time (around 12 hours, excluding the circa 10 hours of sleep) subject to the 'control' of adults, although this is sometimes accompanied by the presence of other children.[31]

This lack of autonomy is evident in the scant opportunities for children to appropriate the external spaces and places of the city; opportunities that are conditioned, as said, in the first instance by the availability of adults to accompany them (Table 4). And it is undoubtedly influenced by the constraints (perhaps at times excessively internalized) imposed by the structure of cities and the way in which urban spaces are organized, functional above all to rapid traffic flows and devoid of places directly accessible to children.[32] In fact, children are excluded from use of the city. Their time during the day is mainly spent in closed environments and in a few well-known places: more than eight hours (8 hours 18 minutes) between the school and the premises of after-school courses and only three-quarters of an hour in the open (including journeys).

Table 4.   Places Where Children Spend Time (Generic Mean, in Hours
             and Minutes) – Elementary School.

	Indoor, Domestic	Commercial, Entertainment	Study, Sports, Religious	Outdoor Places	Car	Other Means of Transport
Thursday	4:24	0:06	8:18	0:47	0:20	0:03
Saturday	9:26	0:50	0:23	1:35	0:41	0:02
Sunday	8:30	0:19	0:39	2:10	0:50	0:06

Source: The use of time of children in Turin, 2003 (Belloni, 2005).

Comparison among the days of the week adds further information with
which to understand the extent to which children adapt to adults' time
organization. Like adults, children participate in three types of daily
organization: that of weekdays, that of Saturday and that of Sundays and
holidays. A powerful time-giver for the first type of day is the school, with its
opening hours, and it is substantially constrained by time to which all the
members of the family are subject. The second type and the third type of day
are instead less structured and therefore grant children greater self-
determination. Nevertheless, although these types of days are less conditioned
by the temporal rigidities dictated by institutions, they are not entirely exempt
from the constraints deriving from childhood, in which dependence on adults
and the family is manifest mainly in the other-directedness of time.[33]

Time rules are relaxed on Saturday and Sunday. The pressure of (school,
work) schedules diminishes, and children reappropriate their time, at least to
some extent, and they radically modify the organization of their days. They
re-appropriate the rhythms of their bodies, devoting more time to elementary
physiological activities such as eating and sleeping, and they devote
themselves to activities chosen autonomously (albeit within the constraints
due to their non-dominance of space) and expand their time devoted to
leisure. Their main activities become play and watching television.

Focusing mainly on time organization – and trying to deduce the meaning
attributed to time by children – we may say that the expansion of leisure
time (which increases by around four hours), which takes place in these two
days, evidences its substantial destructuring (Table 5). And we can fully
grasp the importance of this change of register if we consider the different
symbolic status of what is here called 'leisure'. Leisure activities, in fact,
have three main features: they have a recreational content, they are not
undertaken in institutionalized contexts and they are not developed in an
other-directed way. This also explains why, on school days, we find so little

Table 5.   The Children's Everyday Time (Generic Mean, in Hours and
Minutes) – Elementary School.

	Thursday	Saturday	Sunday
Sleeping, eating	11:23	13:15	14:03
School	7:58	0:10	0:00
Homework	0:21	1:03	0:50
Shopping	0:04	0:34	0:04
Domestic aid, pets	0:05	0:20	0:16
Social participation, religion	0:11	0:07	0:25
Sociality	0:07	0:31	0:42
Sports	0:24	0:59	1:10
Play	0:53	2:31	2:20
PC, videogame	0:07	0:17	0:14
Reading	0:10	0:21	0:18
TV, music	1:02	2:02	1:48
Journeys	0:49	1:01	1:07
Other	0:19	0:40	0:34

Source: The use of time of children in Turin, 2003 (Belloni, 2005).

leisure in the everyday time of children, so little play and so few relational
activities or ones involving exercise. It is indubitable, in fact, that not only
does school time comprise periods expressly devoted to play but also that all
activities, including scholastic ones, can be experienced by children in terms
of play. Children, moreover, engage in exercise and sport at schools and at
after-school facilities, where they also pursue relations and social interactions.[34] But the substantial difference in this case is that these activities
develop in institutionalized contexts, under the direct supervision and
direction of adults: that is, entirely outside the domain of leisure as defined
here. On non-school days, these activities instead mainly respond (again
within a set of constraints) to a logic characterized by choice, so that we can
expect them to change their meaning by children.

It is play that expands to the greatest extent during leisure time (it increases
by about two hours). Notwithstanding the limitations of our data (which
concern behaviour, not perception evaluation), the predominance of play not
only in leisure time (around half of it) but also in the entire daily time of
wakefulness (around one-third) enables us to state that it significantly
conditions Saturdays and Sundays, it gives them general meaningfulness,
although the ways in which choices are made are, as we shall see again,
subject to constraints. Although the constraints imposed school hours
diminish, there are nevertheless those other constraints – less coercive

regarding the general daily time but perhaps subtler because of their lower visibility and irksome to children[35] – due to dependence on family organizations. An example is the long time (almost one hour) spent by children on Saturdays in commercial premises while their parents do the weekly shopping. These constraints become particularly evident if we consider the places in which leisure activities are undertaken. It is mainly on Sunday, when parents are free from work and domestic commitments, that children can be accompanied to external spaces, which thus become accessible and can be frequented for a longer time (just lesser than two and a half hours). By contrast, on Saturday – a semi-work day for adults – children fall back on leisure activities undertaken mainly indoors (above all, television).

Separate discussion of television viewing is required, given the importance of the issue in public discussion and in the specialist literature. It would be beyond the scope of this article, which is essentially centred on analysis of time structures, to examine the symbolic and valorial aspects inherent to exposure to television. Moreover, on the basis of our data, we can say nothing about the programmes watched or about their popularity. The only considerations possible concern patterns of television viewing. Generally, for adults, watching television is classified as a leisure activity, given its predominantly recreational content and its position in time when adults are free of other commitments. It is more difficult to interpret this activity in regard to the problem of children's self-determination of their daily time. Children make use of television in different ways and they prove able to distinguish them. In more than half (53%) of cases, television watching is a choice dictated by interest in the programme, but in more than one-third (35%), it is a 'forced choice' ('When I don't know what to do'), dictated mainly by the impossibility of accessing other forms of leisure. Watching television is apparently a free activity, in that it is independent of the availability of adults: the television is close at hand, in the home, often even in the child's bedroom. The only possible constraint is denial of permission to watch by parents, if it does. In reality, however, also this leisure choice is not disjoint from the degree of structuring of everyday time and from the margins of autonomy that make the consequent choice of activities possible. Television watching is relatively limited on weekdays, and because daily time is a zero-sum game, this is explained by the scant time available after school. It increases, as to be expected, with the expansion of free time (i.e. on Saturday and Sunday), but it is not easy to determine to what extent this depends on the contingent situation or on effective freedom of choice. The fact that television watching increases particularly on Saturday – a day, as we have seen, not entirely free for adults (and in many cases neither for their children) and during which children spend much less time outdoors than on Sunday (children are often obliged to remain indoors under the supervision of their mothers as they 'catch up' with the housework not done during the week) – suggests that watching television is probably a 'fall-back' solution, however pleasant, in the absence of other alternatives. Moreover, the fact that peak television viewing is always in the evening, both during the week and at weekends, suggests that it is often either the simplest and most practicable way to spend time with the other members of the family or a way to 'kill time' because there is nothing else to do.

The variations of other leisure activities do not allow particularly significant findings to be added to those already discussed. Some caveats are in order regarding the interpretation of sport, which, although it is included in the same survey category, has important semantic variations. It assumes different meanings on the different types of day, oscillating between characterizations in terms of leisure and others in terms of coerced time. During the week, in fact, the term 'sport' refers mainly to structured activities (the after-school courses frequently mentioned), while on Saturdays, it may cover both structured courses (mainly football courses for males, or in winter, skiing lessons for children spending the weekend out of town) and non-structured exercise. On Sunday, we can suppose that sports activities are largely free, but the time recorded as being devoted to them is not always entirely reliable (especially in cases when the weekend is spent out of town). Nor, however, do these activities – which should more closely match children's needs for movement and expressiveness – represent genuinely selected time or real leisure, above all, when they take the form of training courses. The entirely reliable description now quoted – taken from a recent best-selling novel in Italy – should prompt reflection: "Alice Della Rocca hated the ski school. She also hated the alarm clock at half past seven in the morning during the Christmas holidays, and her father staring at her over breakfast and nervously jiggling his leg, as if to say, get on with it ... The appointment was at the ski lift ... Alice's classmates were already there, like identical toy soldiers muffled up in their uniforms and numbed by sleep and the cold ... Nobody felt like talking, and Alice least of all" (Giordano, 2008, p. 11–12).

CONCLUSIONS

An important finding from the foregoing analysis is that when children and their ways of life are studied using a sociological approach, account of the characteristics of adult society must be taken. Childhood is closely dependent on the previous generations (above all, parents, as well as grandparents, albeit to a lesser extent), and its features can only be understood in terms of inter-generational relationships. The space for freedom, autonomy and consequently responsibility available to children is defined in relation to the set of constraints and opportunities defined by the adult generations. These constraints and opportunities, in their turn, have a complex configuration that derives from both the structural and the symbolic dimensions. The former dimension is tied to the organizational situation of households and, more generally, to the social organization in which they are embedded (the local system of services, the national welfare system). Everyday organizations, as we have seen, perhaps inevitably push towards forms of constriction imposed on children owing to the frequent lack of other practicable solutions. The mechanism that operates in this case is quite evident and brings to light the material constraints, more or less quantitatively important, of contemporary societies. This study has illustrated some results of this approach.

The second dimension is intangible, and it is connected with the set of collective social representations and public discourses concerning childhood and society as a whole and the public image of childhood obtaining in a particular context. Negative collective representations (sense of insecurity, fear of risk, mistrust and similar) may influence the relationship between the generations and the characteristics assumed by childhood. The particular sense of responsibility created in parents induces a protectiveness that often turns into possessiveness. This article has not analyzed these mechanisms, but indicators can be considered the surveyed behaviours of the children, which also mirror parental attitudes of closure towards the outside and retreat into the private sphere (their children's scant relationships with the peer group, rare use of urban spaces).

A further consideration is that the extent to which childhood depends on the previous generation is not uniform even among societies with similar characteristics (Alanen, 2001). Not even in Western societies, characterized by the same production systems and by similar levels of development, do the relationships between generations – especially when they concern the initial phases of the life course – assume the same forms and expressions. It has been emphasized that a different organization of the welfare system or of working time may give rise to particular structures of relationality and dependence. Some patterns of behaviour in Italy – or, better, in a specific area of it – described here, such as the tendency of families to use few neighbourhood or friendship networks for the care and supervision of their children, or the tendency of children to comply with the evening routines of adults, are probably not referable to other countries of Europe. The contexts in which children live are therefore essential for the definition of different types of childhood. Moreover, the different patterns of protection and control developed by parents influence inter-generational relationships and the different degrees of autonomy and responsibility granted to children.

A final consideration concerns the high level of institutionalization to which childhood is subject in our societies. We have seen that the control exercised on children exposed to highly structured contexts is a constant and widespread feature and that it restricts the autonomy of children. However, some research results also signal the ambiguity of this relationship. The daily organization of children highlights, on the one hand, how strong structuring makes days repetitive, predictable, pre-defined and not directly governable by the subjects. On the other hand, however, where real conditions are not created to allow autonomous management of time and spaces by children (especially in urban settings), the lack of structured activities outside school hours does not seem to increase children's control over their own time. Comparison – not reported in this article – with other areas of Italy, where schools are only open in the morning, does not find that days are characterized by the greater self-determination of children or by broader relations among peers. Rather, it shows an increase in the time devoted to watching television, often alone. Moreover, as we have seen, non-participation in spaces of structured time, such as after-school courses, often produces feelings of exclusion and in effect reduces opportunities for children already in disadvantaged circumstances. Different kinds of institutionalization probably alter the sense attributed by children to this type of experience. In this case, too, the diversity of situations must be set in relation to differences among ways of belonging to childhood.

NOTES

1. The research (March 2003) analyzed 721 children from the second to fifth year of elementary school and 708 from the first to third year of middle school. In addition, 280 children (aged 5–6) from six infant schools were also interviewed. The methodologies adopted were time-use diaries, questionnaires and drawings (only for infant school children). Here, I only analyze the elementary school children. The research on children was conducted simultaneously, and using the same research design, with another survey on the entire city population (in its turn parallel with a nationwide study on the use of time conducted by ISTAT). This has enabled cross-referencing to be made with the national situation and also comparison of the children's diaries with those of the adult population of the same city.

2. The research adopted the standard time-budget methodology. In the time-use diaries, children noted, in their own words and for 24 hours a day and in succession, the duration of the activities performed (principal activities) and activities performed simultaneously if present (secondary activities), the locations where the activities took place and the people present or interacting. Post-codification of the short narratives allowed statistical elaboration.

3. The research referred to here was followed by another survey, which is now in progress. On the basis of the findings of the previous inquiry, this second one seeks to identify the ways in which children construct their spaces of autonomy and how the constraints to which they are subject are interiorized and justified as established norms.

4. The long duration of school opening hours, however, does not exclude conflict with the work schedules of parents (the school closes at a time in the afternoon when most parents are still at work). This conflict between two schedules is one of the problems most difficult for families to manage, as we will illustrate later. The most frequent solutions are a reduction of working hours by the mother or prolongation of the children's schedule through the use of private schools or facilities that look after children for the time necessary.

5. As I have written elsewhere (Belloni & Carriero, 2008), I use the term 'leisure', although is conceptually incorrect with reference to children (it defines in fact, with the birth of industrial work, unpaid and unconstrained time), by analogy with the concept as defined by sociology for adults.

6. Although situations of everyday 'normality' are very different from the total institutions described by Goffman, they are nevertheless able to attribute similar control functions to institutional spaces (locker inspections, checks on personal possessions, discipline in the use of the spaces, surveillance on gestures and language, etc.) that make the self always 'in public'. Obviously, the degree of control in these cases is less than in total institutions (for instance, a boarding school), because it is exercised only for the limited period when they are frequented. Nevertheless, true leisure is driven ever further away.

7. 'When "free time" is spent in an institutional context, it is not experienced as quite free' (Rasmussen, 2004, p. 169).

8. These statements were collected by the questionnaires that accompanied the time-use diaries.

9. The employment rate of female between 15 and 64 years old in Italy is 45%, with marked disparities between economically developed and less developed areas (in South Italy is 30%) (Istat, 2006).

10. In Italy, part-time working hours indicate shorter hours than national labour contracts. They can be vertical (shorter working time in the day) or horizontal (generally fewer days in the week). In the labour contracts of Public Administration, there are generally shorter times (six hours for six days), so that workers usually stop at 2 p.m. In the school, the working hours are mostly in the morning (but there are some differences between primary and other levels of school). Short hours are the main cause of feminization in the Public Administration.

11. The daily duration of working time for women in couples with children is, on average, 6 hours 37 minutes (that of men is 8 hours 4 minutes). The percentage of women engaged is 65.6% against 72.6% among men (Del Boca & Saraceno, 2007)

12. Domestic work time is divided within couples resident in Turin as follows: for men 1 hour 6 minutes (specific mean, participation 69%), for women 3 hours 40 minutes (specific mean, participation 96.8%); time spent on care for children aged under 13: for men 1 hour 12 minutes (specific mean, participation 67%), for women 1 hour 42 minutes (specific mean, participation 83%) (Del Boca & Saraceno, 2007).

13. Italy is the country with the lowest birth rate in Europe (1.3%). A hypothesis is that the unbalanced housework influences the fertility of Italian women (Boeri, Del Boca, & Pissarides, 2005). The recent slight increase has been due to the change of the structure of immigration from low development areas. This has recently consisted of family immigration, giving rise only in most recent years to the presence of a second generation of immigrants.

14. The average age of the first child is 31. The current precariousness of employment among young people can be considered one of the main causes of the postponement of procreation age.

15. This contrasts sharply with the constant rise in female education levels (which are now higher than male ones) and with the better academic performance by females at school.

16. As Melbin said years ago (Melbin, 1987), 'in our societies, a new time organization generated a kind of "colonization" of the night (a day extension into the night) that produced relevant consequences on the everyday life. It seems to me that the same is now happening for children'.

17. Notwithstanding the different relationship that it establishes, the presence of two children is often not enough to increase interaction time between siblings, especially if they attend different schools (with different opening hours, locations, etc.).

18. About the discourse on childhood, see mainly James et al. (1998) and Jenks (1996).

19. A broad network of Italian cities is involved in the 'Sustainable Cities for Children' project that carries forward the European strategy to promote a child-friendly environment (set out in various documents following the 1989 Convention on the Rights of the Child). Moreover, there are numerous local schemes, also Agenda 21, aimed at making cities more children-friendly. Among the most important of these, though they are still relatively rare, are schemes to create protected routes for children to go to school unaccompanied (Tonucci, 1996; Baraldi & Maggioni, 2000).

20. In the following description of the data, the reference is mainly to the research conducted in Turin on time use by children (see note 1). Only considered here are children aged between 7 and 10 (elementary school), so as to restrict the treatment to a population homogeneous on the autonomy/dependence dimension, while the 11–13 age band (lower secondary school) is more subject to the variability of family rules (Belloni, 2005).

21. For short, the adult's data are not reported here.

22. In fact, from the two extra hours devoted to physiological activities, which appear in the time budgets of children for Saturday and Sunday, one must deduct around three-quarters of an hour for lunch, which is included in school time during the week.

23. It is significant that the children in our sample usually denoted this time in their diaries with the expression 'I'm waiting'. I have elsewhere called this time 'suspended' (Belloni, 2005).

24. Note that reference here is to a city where all-day school predominates. Matters are different in other geographical areas of Italy, where school hours are generally only in the morning.

25. As said before, the female part-time work is rare. Women can conciliate hours because of their a bit shorter working time.

26. Expressions written in time-use diaries and collected from focus groups in our ongoing research.

27. Every school studied had a programme of courses (at least one), which they either directly organized or hosted on their premises.

28. Data collected by the questionnaire accompanying the time-use diaries.

29. Data collected by the questionnaire accompanying the time-use diaries.

30. Many of the children who did not engage in out-of-school activities were immigrants.

31. For a more detailed description of these aspects, see Belloni and Carriero (2008).

32. About children and public spaces, see Valentine (2004).

33. Control over time seems to be one of the areas in which parents continue to exercise most power (at least for these age bands). Bargaining on rules instead appears to be much more favourable to children (see, e.g., negotiation on permission to watch television) or it may not even be necessary. Also, access to consumption to goods is an area in which the desires of children and those of their parents often coincide.

34. 'Sociality', as an activity in itself, is a weakness of surveys on the use of time and is in fact the category least usable. This is regardless of the specific problems posed by the study of childhood. For these reasons, it is not examined here.

35. An ongoing research project I quoted in note 3 reports that children find it irksome to accompany adults when they do the shopping. Above all, they are distressed by the noise, confusion and crowds of markets.

REFERENCES

Alanen, L. (2001). Childhood as a generational condition: Children's daily lives in a central Finland town. In: L. Alanen & B. Mayall (Eds), *Conceptualizing child adult relations.* London: Routledge/Falmer.

Ariès, P. (1960). *L'enfant et la vie familiale sous l'ancien régime.* Paris: Plon.

Baraldi, C., & Maggioni, G. (Eds). (2000). *Una città con i bambini.* Roma: Donzelli.

Belloni, M. C. (Ed.) (2005). *Vite da bambini. La quotidianità dai 5 ai 13 anni.* Torino: Ed. Archivio storico della città di Torino.

Belloni, M. C., & Carriero, R. (2008). Childhood: A homogeneous generational group? In: A. Leira & C. Saraceno (Eds), *Childhood: Changing contexts.* Comparative Social Research (Vol. 25, pp. 293–324). Bingley: Emerald Group Publ.

Boeri, T., Del Boca, D., & Pissarides, C. (2005). *Women at work: An economic perspective.* Oxford: Oxford University Press.

Carriero, R., Ghysels, J., & van Klaveren, C. (2009). Do parents coordinate their work schedules? A comparison of Dutch, Flemish, and Italian dual-earner households. *European Sociological Review, 1*(13), 69–85.

Corsaro, W. A. (1997). *The sociology of childhood.* Thousand Oaks, CA: Pine Press.

Del Boca, D., & Saraceno, C. (2007). Lavorare e fare famiglia a Torino. In: M. C. Belloni (Ed.), *Andare a tempo. Il caso Torino: una ricerca sui tempi della città* (pp. 151–170). Milano: Angeli.

Esping-Andersen, G. (1990). *The three worlds of welfare capitalism.* Princeton: Princeton University Press.

Giddens, A. (1984). *The constitution of society.* Cambridge: Polity Press.

Giordano, P. (2008). *La solitudine dei numeri primi.* Milano: Mondadori.

ISTAT. (2006). *Rilevazione sulle forze di lavoro.* Roma: ISTAT.

ISTAT. (2008). *Time use in daily life. A multidisciplinary approach to the time use's analysis* (online version). Roma: ISTAT.

James, A., Jenks, C., & Prout, A. (1998). *Theorizing childhood.* Cambridge: Polity Press.

Jenks, C. (1996). *Childhood.* London, New York: Routledge.

Mannheim, K. (1952). The problem of generations. In: *Essays on the sociology of knowledge.* London: Routledge & Kegan(original German, 1928).

Melbin, M. (1987). *Night as frontier.* New York: The Free Press, McMillan Inc.

Qvortrup, J. (1991). *Childhood as a Social Phenomenon – an Introduction to a Series of National Reports. Eurosocial report,* Vol. 36. Vienna.

Qvortrup, J. (2004). I bambini e l'infanzia nella struttura sociale. In: H. Hengst & H. Zeiher (Eds), *Per una sociologia dell'infanzia* (pp. 25–44). Milano: Franco Angeli.

Rasmussen, K. (2004). Places for Children–Children's Places. *Childhood, 11*(2), 155–173.

Tonucci, F. (1996). *La città dei bambini.* Roma: Laterza.

Valentine, G. (2004). *Public space and the culture of childhood.* Hants, UK and Burlington, USA: Ashgate Publ.

Zeiher, H. (2004). Regimi sociali del tempo e organizzazione individuale dell'esistenza. In: H. Hengst & H. Zeiher (Eds), *Per una sociologia dell'infanzia.* Milano: Franco Angeli.

Zerubavel, E. (1981) *Hidden rhythms.* Chicago and London: University of Chicago Press.

MAKING SENSE OF CHILD LABOUR IN MODERN SOCIETY

Paul Close

INTRODUCTION

The sociology of childhood is fraught with problems, not least those centred on the idea, notion or concept of 'childhood', and in particular, the issue of how to define, distinguish and identify 'childhood' for sociological purposes. The study, analysis and understanding of childhood hinge upon how 'childhood' is defined, either explicitly or implicitly, one problem being the plethora of quite diverse approaches in both popular and sociological discourses. While there cannot be a correct definition of 'childhood', there can be a best definition, such as for sociological purposes, those of making sense of 'childhood' in particular and of social life, relationships and experience in general.

For me, the best approach to defining 'childhood' means taking into account popular, everyday notions, while not being slavishly bound by these; recognising how children's social activities and contribution seem to be widely misrepresented in both popular and sociological accounts, doing so in a way which compounds children's relatively marginal structural position in modern societies; and acknowledging the sociological benefits of counting some, if not all, of children's everyday activities as *productive labour*.[1]

My approach to defining 'childhood' is at odds with that of Chris Jenks in his *Childhood* study[2], even though Jenks argues 'that play is [...] an

Structural, Historical, and Comparative Perspectives
Sociological Studies of Children and Youth, Volume 12, 167–194
Copyright © 2009 by Emerald Group Publishing Limited
ISSN: 1537-4661/doi:10.1108/S1537-4661(2009)0000012012

important component of the child's work as a social member', and 'that a sociology of childhood should arise from the constitutive practices that provide for the child and the child-adult relationship' (Jenks, 1996, pp. 27–29). While Jenks's study makes a major contribution to the sociology of childhood, in particular to the 'social constructionist' perspective, it is striking how he devotes a considerable amount of space to the issue of conceptualising childhood without, however, making it unambiguously clear what he means by 'childhood'.

Jenks does not explicitly define 'childhood' and only implies a definition through a scattering of clues, from which it is possible to ascertain that his approach is remarkably conventional. For Jenks, 'childhood' is above all distinct from 'adulthood':

> Childhood [...] refers to a life phase as well as to the age group defined as children, but is also a cultural construction, part of the social and economic structure of communities. (Jenks, 2005b)

Childhood is a socially, culturally and economically constructed separate phase in the life cycle. It is the phase that precedes, and prepares children for, adulthood.

For Jenks, the separation of childhood, or of *childhoods*, and adulthood within the life cycle is the key to the sociological task of making sense of both phases and of the relationship between them:

> to abandon a shared category of the child is to confront a daunting paradox. If as adults we do just that, what happens to the concept of 'childhood' through which we, as adults, see ourselves and our society's past and future. If, as we have argued here, the concept of 'childhood' serves to articulate not just the experience and status of the young within modern society but also the projections, aspirations, longings and altruism contained within the adult experience then to abandon such a conception is to erase our final point of stability and attachment to the social bond. (Jenks, 1996, p. 136)

Jenks argues for abandoning the view of childhood as a shared, or common, category for all adults, and instead for the view that there is a diversity of childhoods on the way to adulthood. But, the danger here is of distracting attention from how children tend to share certain socially important, even fundamental, and so sociologically significant aspects of their lives, relationships and experiences and, moreover, how they do so not only with one another but also with adults.

Jenks's approach to 'childhood' is representative of a view that is far more widely held both within sociology and elsewhere, as reflected in Ivar Frønes' contribution to Jenks's relatively recent *critical concepts* book

(Jenks, 2005a):

> The members of an age group, unlike social classes and generations, do not have stable interests, since for the individual an age group is a life phase he or she must pass through […]. In an agrarian society, and in early industrial society, children had a direct significance for production […]. The trajectory from the working child to the educated child is part of an all-embracing [historical] process […]. Although educational institutions [in modern society] serve other purposes than the education of children, we will define modern childhood and youth as a phase for the acquisition of competences or qualifications. It follows that during this time, children are of no direct economic benefit to parents (or to others), and indeed are for them even a burden economically. Any future benefit from this education will accrue to the society at large. (Frønes, 2005, p. 236)

For me, however, there is another approach to defining 'childhood', one with sociological advantages. This approach means shifting away from an emphasis on the (not inconsiderable) life cycle and other differences between childhood and adulthood to an emphasis on the similarities, especially those similarities that are nevertheless differentially represented, assessed and rewarded by adults with significant personal, experiential and social consequences. This alternative approach means shifting to an emphasis on, in particular, *the child's work* – of which, for Jenks, a component is *play* (Jenks, 1996, p. 27) and through which, for me, children's social lives, relationships and experiences are crucially shared with not only one another but also adults.

It means, more precisely, shifting to an emphasis on how *the child's work* in not only agrarian society and early industrial society but also modern society is largely productive. It means re-viewing *the child's work* as directly productive, even in modern society. It means regarding the dichotomy, contrast and separation implied by the 'trajectory from the working child to the educated child' view of childhood as misleading, including for sociological purposes. It means recognising how within, for instance, *educational institutions in modern society* and through *the acquisition of competences or qualifications*, children are directly engaged in productive work - in, that is, (productive) *labour*.

Just as adults perform 'work', participate in productive activities and so engage in (productive) labour, children do the same, albeit with a range of differences (from adults) and a great deal of variety vis-à-vis the content entailed. Some of children's play will be a component of their labour, as will some of their family, or domestic activities[3] and, perhaps primarily, some of their (formal) educational activities, or schoolwork.

Nonetheless, what is then pivotal in shaping children's social lives, relationships and experiences is how their labour is represented, assessed and rewarded by adults, in particular relative to adults' own labour. The way in which children's labour, contrary to its basic similarities with adults' labour, is differentially represented, assessed and rewarded will be crucial in determining children's shared experience and development during the process through which they are transformed into fully social, socialised adults.

CHILD LABOUR

In everyday life itself and in accounts of everyday life, such as by sociologists, children's labour tends to be masked, ignored or sidestepped, as reflected in how it is labelled and is *not labelled*. In popular discourses and representations, children's commonplace (productive) labour tends not to be labelled and categorised as such. This is exemplified by the approach of, for instance, the International Labour Organization (ILO), according to which – for the purpose of the *Convention Concerning the Prohibition and Immediate Action for the Elimination of the Worst Forms of Child Labour* (ILO, 2009a) – a child is anyone 'under the age of 18' (Article 2) and:

> 'Economic activity' [...] encompasses most productive activities undertaken by children, whether for the market or not, paid or unpaid [...]; it excludes chores undertaken in the child's own household and schooling [...]. 'Child labour' is a narrower concept than 'economically active children' [sic] [...]. The concept of 'child labour' is based on the ILO Minimum Age Convention, 1973 [...], which represents the most comprehensive and authoritative international definition of minimum age for admission to employment or work, implying 'economic activity'. (ILO, 2006, p. 6)

The ILO use the terms 'child labour' and 'child employment' interchange-ably – as synonyms – where child labour is 'children's work which is of such a nature or intensity that it is detrimental to their schooling or harmful to their health and development' (ILO, 2006). Similarly, the *New World Encyclopedia* defines child labour as:

> the employment of children under an age determined by law or custom [...]. Child labor, the employment of children under a specified age [...] can include factory work, mining, quarrying, agriculture, helping in the parents' business, having one's own small business (for example selling food), or doing odd jobs [...]. The most controversial forms of work include the military use of children and child prostitution. Less controversial, and often legal with some restrictions, [is] agricultural work outside of the school year (seasonal work). (New World Encyclopedia, 2009)

Essentially, Carolyn Tuttle, an economist specialising in the study of women's and children' labour, tells us:

> The term 'child labor' generally refers to children who work to produce a good or a service which can be sold for money in the marketplace regardless of whether or not they

are paid for their work. A 'child' is usually defined as a person who is dependent upon other individuals (parents, relatives, or government officials) for his or her livelihood. (Tuttle, 2001)

And the *libertarian* economist Thomas DeGregori declares, 'I am against child labor' and so for 'getting children out of the workplace and into schools', where 'they can grow to become productive adults' (DeGregori, 2002).

According to these views, a child is a dependent person who may or may not perform 'child labour', the latter being identified as those activities that are performed in the production of goods and (provision of) services for exchange, sale and purchase on the market. Child labour is employed labour, or paid labour, or at least is conducted under the conditions of employed (paid) labour, even though the children involved may be actually paid very little or nothing at all. Child labour is carried out in the same locations as adult (paid) labour: in factories, mines, quarries and family businesses such as shops. It does not include children's activities in the 'household and schooling' (ILO, 2006, p. 6). Those who are against child labour are in favour of 'getting children out of the workplace and into schools', where children 'can grow to become productive adults' (DeGregori, 2002).

This popular approach to 'child labour' can be otherwise readily gleaned from newspaper reports such as Michael Simmons' *Guardian* account of a *global march against child labour* with the aim of presenting 'a petition comprising 30,000 British and Irish schoolchildren's footprints' to Britain's Prime Minister, Tony Blair. The march set off from Manila, the Philippines, in January 1998 and headed for Geneva where the ILO was preparing a 'new convention against child labour' in response to the way in which many 'school-aged children [...] are forced', whether 'through wretched family circumstances or unscrupulous employers, to work' (Simmons, 1998). Simmons reports,

> At least 250 million school-aged children are [...] trapped in hard labour and servitude [...]. The Prime Minister will be told that the marchers want governments to act immediately to end child labour and to insist that no child under 14 should be forced to work full-time. They want it recognised that forcing children of primary-school age to work is a violation of their human rights [...]. The exploitation of children is at its most stark in poorer countries, but also has an impact on richer countries [through imported] items produced by child labour [... Many] children are forced into the drugs trade, while others become bonded labour, slaves for life. (*ibid.*)

The labour that Simmons and the *global march against child labour* has in mind is that performed by children in the production of goods and (the provision of) services through either paid employment (no matter how

---

meagre the pay) or slavery – goods and services that are variously owned, controlled, consumed and exchanged on the market not by the children themselves but instead by others such as employers. This labour is either employed (paid) labour or slave labour, in contrast to, for instance, (unpaid) *primary school* activities.

While the child labour to which Simmons refers may be most evident in poorer countries, it would seem to be far from unknown in richer ones. In the same year as the *global march*, Anne Caborn writing in *The Observer* drew attention to how a '15-year-old undertaking heart monitoring duties in a Scottish hospital [...] highlighted the issue of child labour' throughout the United Kingdom (Caborn, 1998). Caborn explains,

> The law prohibits under-13s from working. The only exceptions may be where councils allow a younger child to do light farm work for a parent. A child of 13 is allowed to do a job, but not hazardous or heavy work [...]. The law also lays down when a child can work: not before 7 am and after 7 pm, and for a maximum of two hours on a schoolday or a Sunday [... But, research] by the Low Pay Unit into child employment [...] suggests that [...] the national figure [for employed schoolchildren is] 2 million [and that] many are as young as 10 [...]. The idea of schoolchildren working to supplement the family income is [a major] issue nationally. (*ibid.*)

The 'work' that children under the age of 13 are not allowed to do under the law is that associated with employment. It is employed (paid) work, or paid labour, and in the United Kingdom, with exceptions, children do not have the right to engage in this kind of activity. Children are denied the right, which is enjoyed by the over-13s and so by all adults, to *freely* engage in employment, in employed (paid) labour, in paid labour, in 'labour'.

CITIZENSHIP AND EXCLUSION

This means, however, that the under-13s are denied a right – the so-called *right to work* – which is enshrined as a human right in the 1948 *Universal Declaration of Human Rights* (UDHR) and the *International Covenant on Economic, Social and Cultural Rights* (ICESCR), adopted by the UN General Assembly on 16 December 1966 and in force from 3 January 1976 (UN, 1948; UN, 1976a). Article 23 of the UDHR states, 'Everyone has the right to work, to free choice of employment, to just and favourable conditions of work and to protection against unemployment', and Article 6 of the ICESCR informs us that the States Parties 'recognize the right to work, which includes the right of everyone to the opportunity to gain his living by work which he freely chooses or accepts, and will take appropriate steps to safeguard this right' (UN, 1976a, Article 6).

As of February 2009, the ICESCR had 160 States Parties and a further seven signatories. The United Kingdom, ratified this Covenant in 1976, and was a State Party along with all the other 26 Member States of the European Union (EU) and the other 46 Member States of the Council of Europe (CoE), obliged as all the governments of these countries are to ratify the CoE's *Convention for the Protection of Human Rights and Fundamental Freedoms* (or the *European Convention on Human Rights*, ECHR). Thirty-two UN Member States were not States Parties to the ICESCR. These included the United States, the government of which had signed in 1977 without having subsequently ratified (UN, 2009a).

In the United Kingdom, as in all other modern societies, children's exclusion from the right to do paid labour, with exceptions, equally with adults is accompanied by a raft of other, similar exclusions. For instance, although Article 12 of the UN's *International Covenant on Civil and Political Rights* (ICCPR), which came into force on 23 March 1976 (UN, 1976b), and as of February 2009 had 164 States Parties, including all Member States of the EU and the CoE, 'gives people the rights of liberty of movement and freedom to choose their residence, both of which are incompatible with slavery' (BBC, 2007b), these rights are denied to children, or more precisely to people under the *age of majority*, the chronological point at which in law people cease to be minors, or children, and become adults.

The age of majority is the point at which, in law, people assume control over themselves and their actions and decisions, resting these things from their parents or guardians. At this point, parents (or guardians, in lieu of parents) lose control over and responsibility for their children, their children's activities and their children's affairs in general. In England, Wales and Northern Ireland, the age of majority is 18; in Scotland, it is 16; in Mississippi, New York and the District of Columbia in the United States, it is 21; in Japan, it is 20; in American Samoa, it is 14; in Chile, it is 18 for males and 15 for females; while in El Salvador, it is 25 for males and 17 for females.

While the relationship between the age of majority and what people are allowed in law to do for the first time is far from simple, the age of majority tends to be a *major* turning point in the process by which people acquire the full range of statutory rights in modern societies. In general, people acquire a set of socially important rights for the first time, rights associated specifically and distinctively with adulthood, such as those that allow them to get married, enter into binding contracts, vote, drive motor vehicles and consume alcoholic drinks. That is, on reaching the age of majority, people acquire a list of legal, citizenship, civil, political, economic and social rights from which children are categorically excluded. Accordingly, one way of viewing childhood is that children are relatively, but significantly, statutorily excluded and as a result socially marginalised in modern societies, in particular, with regard to citizenship rights.

This form of exclusion poignantly reflects and greatly reinforces children's social marginalisation overall. Along with a few other categories of people in modern societies, most notably non-nationals, or aliens, children are not (full) citizens, do not enjoy (full) *citizenship*. While children, like aliens, may have some citizenship rights, they are statutorily denied 'the right' to enjoy the full range of these rights, and consequently are not, in this socially important and sociological significant sense, 'citizens'. Only adults are or can be citizens; children are not and cannot be. All children may be 'nationals' (of at least one nation-state), but no children – at least in modern societies – are 'citizens':

> there is a sociologically useful distinction to be drawn between the mere possession of (some) citizenship rights and the acquisition of the full range of citizenship rights, and [therefore] it is [...] apposite to employ the label 'citizen' in a way which pinpoints and highlights this distinction. Citizens are those who, having attained the full range of citizenship rights, are (in the legal of formal sense) full members of a 'national community'. Those who have not gained full [...] citizenship rights within a *national community* [Barbalet, 1988, p. 18] are not 'citizens' – they are instead 'non-citizens'. (Close, 1995, p. 69)

Citizenship 'is an *internally oriented* relationship which people as individuals have with the nation-state of which they have full formal membership' by virtue of their nationality (as recognised by that nation-state) followed by 'their enjoyment of the full range of citizenship rights granted, guaranteed or enforced by the state' (*ibid.*, p. 2). In that children do not enjoy the full range of citizenship rights, they will be non-citizens, will not be full members of the *national community* and will be in a socially important, and sociologically significant, way marginalised relative and in relation to adults.

This approach to 'citizenship' is alluded to by T. H. Marshall, for whom citizenship is

> a status bestowed on all those who are full members of a community. All who possess the status are equal with respect to the rights and duties with which that status is endowed [...]. Citizenship [accompanies] a [...] community [...] of free men endowed with rights and protected by common law. (Marshall, 1950, pp. 28–29, 40–41)

Similarly, for Rainer Baubock, citizenship:

> designates a political status of individuals as well as a particular quality of a political system. As a normative concept citizenship is a set of rights, exercised by individuals who hold the rights, equal for all citizens, and universally distributed within a political community, as well as a corresponding set of institutions guaranteeing these rights. (Baubock, 1991, p. 28)

This definition of 'citizenship' warrants at least two rejoinders. First, while all citizens may enjoy equal citizenship rights within a *political community*, they will have unequal chances of realising, enjoying and experiencing these rights in practice. This is because citizenship 'provides capacities which may not be readily, fully and equally realised owing to interference from prevailing societal inequalities of condition and opportunity' (Close, 1995, p. 1), because of the intervening consequences of various social inequalities associated with social class, sex-gender, race-ethnicity, age-generation and so on.

Second, the accuracy of the claim that citizenship rights are *universally distributed within a political community* is questionable. As Gary Wickham has pointed out, citizenship is only 'extended to some individuals operating in any particular community and not to others', and 'different communities exclude, at different times, "women, children, slaves, resident aliens, and a variety of others" [Hindess, 1991, p. 178] from citizenship' (Wickham, 1993, p. 2). If so, then the issues arise of which communities exclude which individuals and why; and where and when children are excluded and why.

Baubock argues that 'citizenship has always been dependent on political struggles between collective actors' (Baubock, 1991, p. 29), where those seeking citizenship have couched their claims in terms of the *appeal of equality*, but where also, various *collective actors* have been denied citizenship on precisely the same grounds:

> the demand for equality was used as a justification for limiting universality, not only in the maintenance of external boundaries, but also in denying internal members full citizenship. The most common justification for excluding parts of society from (full) citizenship [was] that some populations were either dependent or undeserving. Dependent members of society had to be represented by those on whom they depended, or else equality would have been only a fiction and representation seriously distorted [see the chapter by Campiglio, this volume]. Equality could only exist between economically and politically independent individuals. Such was the basic argument for excluding women and the propertyless classes. A second category of persons was excluded for the reason of being not respectable and worthy of the honours of citizenship. This was true of slaves in ancient societies [....] and paupers in early industrial capitalism. (*ibid.*, pp. 29–30)

Formally, things have changed considerably for women, propertyless classes, slaves and paupers. Women have acquired equal citizenship rights and *citizenship*, just as they have acquired equal statutory rights in general, with men almost everywhere, and especially throughout modern societies. This has occurred in accordance with the *Convention on the Elimination of All Forms of Discrimination Against Women* (CEDAW), the UN human rights instrument that came into force on 3 September 1981. As of February 2009, 185 nation-states had ratified CEDAW; only eight UN Member States – Iran, Nauru, Niue, Palau, Qatar, Somalia, Sudan and Tonga – along with the Holy See (the sole UN-recognised independent, sovereign nation-state that was not a UN Member State), had neither ratified nor signed the treaty. One Member State had signed but not ratified, this being the United States (UN, 2009a).

It would seem that things have changed most for slaves, in that slavery has been formally abolished everywhere. Slavery 'is illegal in every country in the modern world' (BBC, 2007b; see also BBC, 2007c). The statutory outlawing of slavery at the global level – apart from symbolising the processes of globalisation, through which the world is becoming *a single global social (economic, political and cultural) space*[4] – has been achieved in compliance with prevailing UN human rights instruments and international law, including the UDHR and the ICCPR, which as of February 2009 had been ratified or signed by all but 20 of the UN's 192 Member States.

On the other hand, perhaps things have changed least for children, despite the UN's *Convention on the Rights of the Child* (CRC), which came into force on 2 September 1990, and which as of February 2009 had 193 States Parties: 192 UN Member States plus the Holy See. The only UN Member States, and indeed the only UN-recognised nation-states anywhere in the world, that had signed but not ratified the CRC were Somalia and the United States. According to the CRC, 'Bearing in mind that [...] "the child, by reason of his physical and mental immaturity, needs special safeguards and care, including appropriate legal protection, before as well as after birth"' (UN, 1990, Preamble), States Parties 'shall take all appropriate legislative, administrative, social and educational measures to protect the child from all forms of physical or mental violence, injury or abuse, neglect or negligent treatment, maltreatment or exploitation, including sexual abuse, while in the care of parent(s), legal guardian(s) or any other person who has the care of the child' (*ibid.*, Article 19).

However, contrary to the ideas, sentiments and principles enshrined in the CRC, children in modern societies are in practice relatively excluded vis-à-vis citizenship rights and, in particular, from the right to engage in employed (paid) labour, while being expected, required or indeed forced to engage in unpaid (productive) labour; in labour that is not rewarded as such by adults; and in labour, the product of which – in spite of its social importance and sociological significance – is not duly recognised, giving rise to the possibility of considerable, disturbing and damaging consequences for children's experiences, children's development towards adulthood, for adults and for society.

Children – in a similar way to non-nationals, or aliens (Close, 1995; Close & Askew, 2004a) – are excluded from (full) citizenship. However – referring back to Baubock's suggestion that the 'most common justification for excluding parts of society from (full) citizenship [was] that some populations were either dependent or undeserving' (Baubock, 1991, p. 29) – unlike aliens, women or slaves, children are excluded on the grounds that they are *both* dependent *and* undeserving. It is broadly assumed, as reflected in the CRC, that children are *naturally* dependent on adults and as a result do not constitute a deserving *collective actor* judged in terms of their social activities and contribution.

Against this, however, it is arguable that while the collective (adult) representation of children as 'dependent' may be in large part valid, the representation of children as 'undeserving' reflects an underlying misconception of children's social activities, contribution, importance and worth. This misconception is that children are 'undeserving' as an outcome of their (natural) dependence, when instead they are 'dependent' largely due to the way in which they are regarded as 'undeserving', or, in the first instance, of the way in which their social activities and contribution are considered to be 'unworthy'.

In so far as children are dependent, then their dependency – if mainly that of older children – will be largely socially constructed, rooted in the way their (productive) labour is not recognised and rewarded as such. This paradox, or contradiction, amounts to a major shaping feature of the shared condition and experience of children in modern society, being perhaps especially acute for older children. Children's social activities and contribution are judged not to warrant the kind of rewards – including the remuneration and citizenship rights – enjoyed and expected by adults and through which children's independence would be greatly enhanced. However, the misconception of children's social activities and contribution serves as a convenient cultural contrivance (or ideological fiction) through which children's collective dependency on adults, or adults' collective control over children, is augmented, sustained and secured.

DOMESTIC LABOUR

In popular, everyday discourses the labels 'labour' and 'productive labour' tend to be reserved for employed (paid) labour, which is then mainly the preserve of adults, to the point of being largely an adults-only activity, especially in principle and law (de jure), but also in practice (de facto). These labels tend not to be applied to children's activities, and especially not to children-only activities. They tend to be used interchangeably with, or as synonyms for, 'paid employment' to the exclusion of unpaid, non-employed activities such as those centred on leisure, pleasure and play, the home and the school.

But, this exclusive approach to 'labour' and 'productive labour' has been challenged in certain academic and activist discourses, as exemplified in the work of sociologists such as Daniel Bertaux, Catherine Delcroix, Janet Finch, Chris Harris and Paul Thompson, in the accounts of Marxists such as Wally Seccombe and in the arguments of feminists such as Bonnie Fox, Maxine Molyneux and Linda Muragroyd. These *critical discourses* are concerned with re-aligning the boundaries involved; with extending the 'labour' and 'productive' categories to include a range of unpaid, non-employed activities; with extending the sites where these activities are performed; and with embracing in particular the family, or domestic arena, the location of the performance of unpaid domestic labour.

Chris Harris argues that the 'family is the site of the reproduction of human-beings' (Harris, 1983, p. 181) and draws attention to the significance which this view of the family has for Marxists, 'those working in the tradition of historical materialism' (*ibid.*, p. 185). For Marxists, 'domestic labour [is performed] to the advantage of capital' (*ibid.* p.185), in that 'the domestic group under capitalism is not only the site of biological reproduction and of the production of subjectivities and ideologies, but [also] the site of the reproduction of labour power, both daily and inter-generationally' (*ibid.*, pp. 181–185).

For Marxists, the family, through the performance of domestic labour, is the site of the creation and recreation of a product, which is of fundamental importance to the operation of the capitalist mode of production (CMP), that of *labour power*. Through the production and reproduction of labour power, domestic labour and the family are 'functionally', productively and structurally connected in an intimate, beneficial and advantageous manner to the CMP.

The *historical materialist* notion of 'labour power' has been clarified by Marx himself:

> By labour-power or capacity for labour is to be understood the aggregate of those mental and physical capabilities existing in a human being, which he exercises whenever he produces a use-value of any description. (Marx, 1867)

Marx adds:

> Labour-power, however, becomes a reality only by its exercise; it sets itself in action only by working. But thereby a definite quantity of human muscle, nerve. brain, [etc.], is wasted, and these require to be restored. (*ibid.*, 1867)

For Marx, under capitalism, labour power is a commodity, and as with commodities in general, labour power is exchanged, sold and bought on the market. Uniquely, however, labour power is exchanged for wages. Labour power is a peculiar commodity in that as well as being produced by human beings, it is also embodied within – is also part of the constitution of – human beings themselves.

Labour power is sold on the market by workers and bought by capitalists, by whom it is then used, or consumed, for a (bought) period of time: labour time. During this period, workers actually labour (in conjunction with the means of production) to produce *use values*, or goods and services, which are in turn exchanged on the market by capitalists for revenues and profits. The difference between, on the one hand, the (value of the) wages that are received by workers in exchange for their labour power and, on the other hand, the value of the goods and services that workers produce is *surplus value*, the measure of their exploitation under capitalism by the capitalists.

After being exchanged on the market, put to work in the labour process and consumed in the production process, labour power needs to be replenished, restored, re-created or re-produced. The reproduction of labour power requires the consumption and purchase of goods and services, the value of which determines the exchange value of workers' labour power and wages.

Labour power has a *physical* (or health) component and a *moral historical* (or lifestyle) component, both of which are replenished during the workers' non-labour time. As Marx puts it:

> The maintenance and reproduction of the working-class is, and must ever be, a necessary condition to the reproduction of capital. But the capitalist may safely leave its fulfilment to the labourer's instincts of self-preservation and of propagation. All the capitalist cares

for, is to reduce the labourer's individual consumption as far as possible to what is strictly necessary [...]. (*ibid.*, 1867)

Following Marx, however, many Marxists, and especially Marxist feminists have re-assessed the relationship between the *reproduction of the working class*, or of labour power, and the *reproduction of capital* through the consumption of labour power. This was done within the *domestic labour debate* of the 1970s, the 'common underlying assumption' of which was that an investigation of housework, or domestic labour, 'can contribute to an understanding of women's subordination and to the formulation of a politics adequate to its supersession' (Molyneux, 1979). A central concern running through the debate was

> to show how the subordination of women [...] is, although often seen as 'extra-economic', in fact founded on a *material* basis and is linked into the political economy of capitalist society. [There was an attempt] to demonstrate housework's *economic* contribution to maintaining the capitalist system by providing labour necessary for the reproduction of labour power. It [...] raised the question of to what extent the development of capitalism has itself created the present domestic system and has, in particular, created 'housework'. This perspective [...] involved the attempt to apply to the sphere of housework concepts previously restricted to the analysis of the more general, conventional and public, features of the capitalist economy. (*ibid.*, 1979)

While for Marx, the reproduction of labour power is left to the *labourer*, contributors to the domestic labour debate argued that, more precisely, it is left to the *domestic labourer*, to those in the family, household or domestic unit who perform domestic labour, and therefore largely to women in their roles as wives and mothers. Moreover, women perform most domestic labour not so much because of their instincts, as because of their socially constructed sense of responsibility, obligation or duty (Finch, 1989). It is then this sense that drives women to perform domestic labour without pay, as a *free gift* to capitalists, whose wage costs are consequently less than they would be otherwise. That is, by virtue of being unpaid, women's domestic labour 'lowers the minimum cost of [wage] labour' (Harris, 1983, p. 185). In this way, (unpaid) domestic labour augments surplus value, profits and capital accumulation to the benefit of capitalists (Fox, 1980), and the family is productively, 'functionally' and structurally linked to the CMP. But, Chris Harris suggests,

> This argument [....] has two disadvantages. First, it is an essentially functionalist argument. If correct, it shows that the institution of domestic labour within the wider division of labour [is] functional for capital. But, it does not explain why that (has) happened or why it is that domestic labour [is] universally performed by women. Secondly, it poses certain difficulties for Marxist theory. According to the assumptions

of Marxist economics, the value of a commodity is determined by the labour time necessary for its production. Domestic labour contributes to the production of labour power and, hence, would seem to contribute to its value. But how much does it contribute to that value? Since domestic labour power is not sold and is not therefore a commodity, we cannot compare it directly with the labour power to whose [sic] production it contributes. (Harris, 1983, pp.185–186)

It is these difficulties with the Marxist argument that the family is productively linked to the CMP through the way domestic labour produces labour power, and in particular the way *women's unpaid domestic labour lowers the minimum cost of wage labour*, which has led to 'one of the few consensuses that seem to have emerged' from the domestic labour debate. This is that, after all:

domestic labour does not produce labour power. What it produces are use-values which are consumed within the household. It transforms commodities purchased out of wages received by the household into consumable form and provides services to other household members. The effect of the consumption it makes possible is the reproduction of labour power both daily and generationally, and the reproduction of the household to which the wage labourer belongs. The family, therefore, is located between two markets: the market for labour which it supplies, and the market for consumer goods ('wage goods') which it consumes. Hence, domestic labour mediates these two markets and brings them into relation. However, whereas household members sell labour power to capital, engage in social labour and consume wage goods produced by social labour, labour within the household is private labour. As [Wally] Seccombe puts it 'domestic labour contributes directly to the creation of the commodity labour power while having no direct relation with capital. It is this special duality which defines the character of domestic labour under capitalism' [Seccombe, 1974, p. 17]. It is exactly the duality that creates problems for further analysis. (Harris, 1983, p. 187)

The special duality of domestic labour under capitalism creates problems for, or limitations on, the Marxian (and subsequent Marxist) analysis of the relationship between domestic labour, the family and gender relationships, divisions and inequalities, on the one hand, and the CMP, on the other. In particular, the diminution of the productive status of domestic labour in relation to labour power and the CMP creates difficulties and impediments for feminists in accepting the analysis.

Remaining faithful to the Marxian inspired approach means discounting any contribution from domestic labour to the production of surplus value through the exchange (on the market) and consumption (at the point of capitalist production) of labour power, doing so on the grounds that domestic labour does not augment labour power's *exchange value* even though it contributes to the latter's *use value*. Under capitalism, domestic labour becomes private, unpaid labour, and therefore is marginalised in relation to the CMP, to the central activities and processes of modern society and to the main sources and agents of historical development. It follows that because the performance of domestic labour is highly gendered, women also become socially marginalised and historically sidelined. For many feminists, this implication reflects and reinforces collective (male-dominated) representations of women as found not only in popular (or patriarchal) culture but also in mainstream (or *malestream*) sociology (Murgatroyd, 1989), and so is unacceptable.

The implications, and in particular the limitations, of the Marxist approach to domestic labour and patriarchy led all sides at the close of the 1970s to move on (Molyneux, 1979) in search of alternative analytical approaches, frameworks and concepts, especially any which would centralise and pivotalise female-skewed activities and processes within gender relationships, divisions and inequalities. Contributions in this regard have come from, for instance, Margaret Stacey (1981), Linda Murgatroyd (1985, 1989) and Daniel Bertaux (1994; see also Bertaux & Delcroix, 2000; Bertaux & Thompson, 1997, 2006), around the use of fresh or revitalised concepts, including 'people work', 'people production' and 'the anthro-ponomic process'.

ANTHROPONOMIC PRODUCTION

Daniel Bertaux and Paul Thompson tell us:

> We conceive of families as units of production of their members' energies, or [...] of 'anthroponomic production'. Anthroponomic production, which for instance transforms infants into social adults, is very specific, and as every mother or teacher knows, demands great effort. Producing people implies both nurturing their physical growth and shaping their cultural and psychic energy. Its instruments [include] parental time and effort in caring for children, socializing and instructing them, and developing their specific abilities and character. (Bertaux & Thompson, 2006, pp. 19–20)

For Bertaux and Thompson, families are units of production, and more specifically of *anthroponomic production*; of that production, that is, in which people are produced and reproduced, in which *human beings* are created and recreated as *social beings*, and especially in which *human infants are transformed into social adults*. It is centered on building and sustaining people's energies, abilities and character, and especially of young people's during their transformation into adults.

Anthroponomic production demands *great effort*, especially *parental time and effort*, and therefore parental *energies*. As Daniel Bertaux and Catherine

Delcroix have put it, 'anthroponomic processes, the "production" (transformation) of children from mere flesh into fully socialised human beings mobolises immense energies and affects' on the part of parents and couples (Bertaux & Delcroix, 2000, pp. 78–79). It is as if the energies of one generation of adults is being transferred to those of the next generation through the way adults as parents and couples expend their energies in transforming their children *from mere physical (unsocialised) human beings into fully socialised human beings.*

Bertaux and Delcroix view 'the relation of filiation between parents and children as the core of the family phenomenon' and argue that 'the most encompassing way of looking at' anthroponomic production 'is to conceive of the relationship of filiation as characterised by the parents' [...] efforts at passing on/down their own resources and values to their children' so that the *'effort to transmit* is the key to deciphering what is taking place between parents and children' (*ibid.*, pp. 78–79).

At the same time, however, this transmission process is embedded in adult relationships that are *gendered.* For Bertaux and Delcroix:

> each family [is] primarily a unit of production, inasmuch as it is within it that, through a whole range of activities structured by the gender division of labour and summarised under the umbrella of 'domestic labour', the energies and energy orientations of its members get produced and reproduced anew. (*ibid.*, 2000, pp. 64–65)

Anthroponomic production is performed by adults as parents in a gender-skewed fashion, as an integral aspect of the prevailing, all-encompassing gender division of labour.

The differences between the domestic labour debate argument that domestic labour is productive and the more recent account by Daniel Bertaux and his co-writers that domestic labour is productive are obscure. While contributors to the domestic labour debate claim that domestic labour produces labour power and the latter claim that it produces 'people', what Marxists mean by 'labour power' seems to be similar to or covered by what is produced through the anthroponomic process, this being people's energies, abilities and character, especially during their transformation from mere physical human beings (children) into fully socialised human beings (adults). Perhaps, in effect, the domestic labour debate argument and Bertaux's account are more alike than they are different. Certainly, apart from any other ways in which they are similar, both approaches share a highly adult-oriented, or biased, view of the production of labour power and/or people and as a result are perhaps equally flawed.

ADULTERATED SOCIOLOGY

Linda Murgatroyd called her contribution to David Held and John Thompson's 1989 *Social Theory of Modern Societies* 'Only Half the Story: Some Blinkering Effects of "Malestream" Sociology' (Murgatroyd, 1989). But likewise, it seems to me, what might be called *adulterated sociology* has taken a blinkered view of the production and reproduction of people and their embodied labour power, telling only half the story. Sociology has tended to mask children's participation in and contribution to this process, doing so in a way that replicates popular approaches, compounds the everyday injustices experienced by children, and hinders the general progress of sociology.

Just as Marxist theory can be criticised for underestimating and marginalising domestic labour and so women (reflecting and reinforcing male-dominated collective representations of women), so Marxist theory, feminist theory and sociological theory can be criticised for doing something similar in the case of children, children's activities, labour and production, and childhood. These analytical frameworks can be taken to task for neglecting children's contribution to social production, in particular, by way of their participation in the creation and recreation of their embodied labour power.

In this regard, it is instructive to note how, in their sociological account of *Youth, Family and Citizenship*, Gill Jones and Claire Wallace argue,

> The sociology of family life, while it claims to have opened up the 'black box' of the family, imposed by 'structuralist' theories which saw the family as a unit in its relations with the external world, has barely focused on the relations between young people and their parents, and the economic roles of young people in households. It has instead concentrated on spouse relations, or the parenting of young children. [The] part that older children play in the family economy has been neglected as a research topic [...]. Children are regarded as dependents and therefore not intrinsically important in economic terms. (Jones & Wallace, 1992, p. 14)

While Jones and Wallace may be making a valid and valuable sociological point here, they are not referring to children's participation in the production of people and labour power, and more specifically, they do not have in mind children's contribution to the production of their own labour power.

Similarly, while Chris Harris draws attention to how the domestic arena is a site of the production and reproduction of labour power, he typically assumes that the productive labour involved is monopolised by women, including that labour the product of which is the labour power embodied in children. What about, it might be asked, the contributions made both by men, as husbands and fathers, and by children themselves? What about the part played by children in the 'family economy' and in the wider economy through the work, and more precisely the (productive) labour, they perform in creating their own labour power?

At the same time, however, answering this question would not complete the story given that, after all, the family is not the only site of the production and reproduction of people and labour power. Here, we can recall Daniel Bertaux's point that the transformation of *infants into social adults* demands great effort 'as every mother or teacher knows' (Bertaux & Thompson, 2006, pp. 19–20). Bertaux is alluding to a site of the production of people and labour power, which lies outside the family, to a site beyond that where the anthroponomic process occurs through domestic labour; to, that is, *the school.*

In school, *teacher knows best,* even though, it can be argued, *at school* teachers are far from being the only ones who work, who labour and who produce. Just as *the home* is a site of the production of people and labour power, so is *the school,* and, just as women perform most domestic labour, so children probably perform most *scholastic labour.* The latter is that kind of labour through which participants – both paid and unpaid – within systems of formal education contribute to the creation and recreation of children's labour power during their (children's) transformation from unsocialised, non-social human beings into fully socialised, social adults.

Nonetheless, as Jones and Wallace put it, 'school work, helping in the home, even part-time paid work, are not recognized as work in our society and do not carry any rights (such as National Insurance, trade union membership, or employment protection)' (Jones & Wallace, 1992, p. 21). Neither children's domestic work nor schoolwork are recognised as (productive) labour in popular discourses, and, concomitantly, children's contribution to the production of people and labour power whether at home or at school is not rewarded in the same way as adults' contribution, remuneratively or otherwise. This, of course, comes on top of, complements and compounds how, at the same time, children are denied the (full) right to exchange their 'own', embodied, largely self-created labour power on the market for wages.

SLAVE LABOUR

In the United Kingdom, in a similar way to the situation in all modern societies, while children – especially those under 13 – do not share (equally) with adults the statutory right to engage in paid (employed) labour, they at least share with adults the right not to be *forced* to do this kind of labour. Apart from anything else, this is in conformity with Article 4 of the UDHR, according to which no one shall be held in slavery or servitude, and with Article 8 of the ICCPR, according to which no one shall be held in slavery, slavery and the slave trade in all their forms shall be prohibited and no one shall be required to perform forced or compulsory labour.

Still, this does not mean that children also share with adults the statutory right not to be forced at all to do labour. In all modern societies, adults cannot be forced to perform labour, just as they cannot be enslaved. In contrast, however, there are grounds for arguing that in all modern societies, children are excluded from this right, are forced to perform (productive) labour, if not quite as slaves, at least not in the strictest sense.

After all, throughout the United Kingdom for instance, all children between certain ages are forced to participate in formal education, to engage in schoolwork, and, indeed, are forced to do so *full-time*. In England, full-time formal education is compulsory for everyone from 5 years to 16 years inclusive, after which anyone has the (conditional) right to remain in full-time education for two more years. Conversely, no one is compulsorily required to remain in full-time education after 16, at least currently. Under the *Education and Skills Act 2008*, the compulsory leaving age is being raised, starting in 2013, to 18 (Office of Public Sector Information, 2009).

Given this, we might recall Michael Simmons' point that *many school-aged children are forced to work*, by which he means to perform employed (paid) labour, especially but not exclusively in poorer countries (Simmons, 1998). But, it might be asked, what about the many school-aged children in the United Kingdom, for instance, who are not just *allowed to work* (and labour) within the system of formal education – including before 7 am and after 7 pm (see Caborn, 1998, above) – but also compulsorily required to do so? Given the compulsion entailed, what about regarding *children's work* (schoolwork) within the system of formal education as *forced labour*?

Of course, children's schoolwork is not generally viewed as forced labour, either in popular, everyday discourses or in scholarly – such as sociological – accounts. Viewing children's schoolwork as forced labour would not sit well with modern approaches to children and childhood, characterised as these are by emphases on children's *natural dependency* and vulnerability, and the provision of appropriate care and protection.

However, the way in which children in the UK are statutorily required to engage in full-time formal education is consistent both with legal provisions across all modern societies and with the element of compulsion enshrined in human rights instruments in relation to children, most notably the CRC. On the one hand, as noted above, the CRC urges States Parties to 'take all appropriate legislative, administrative, social and educational measures to protect the child from all forms of physical or mental violence, injury or abuse, neglect or negligent treatment, maltreatment or exploitation' (UN, 1990, Article 19), while, on the other hand, urging them to 'recognize the right of the child to education, and with a view to achieving this right progressively and on the basis of equal opportunity, [make] primary education compulsory and available free to all' (*ibid.*, Article 28).

That is, the human right to formal education as specified in the CRC is a *compulsory right*, and as such is peculiar in that it is the only right of this kind throughout all of the UN's human rights instruments. Furthermore, it is anomalous in that it seems to be inconsistent with both the spirit and the letter of the *International Bill of Human Rights*, which consists of the UDHR, ICESCR and ICCPR (OHCHR, 2009), as reflected in Article 1 of the UDHR, where it states that all human beings are born free and equal in dignity and rights, and is paradoxical, or contradictory, in that while the term 'right' (in the context of human rights) connotes an entitlement to be free, or at liberty, to do something (such as paid labour) or to be free from something (such as slave labour), the term 'compulsory' carries the opposite, contrary connotation.

The universal *compulsory right* of children to education, while being peculiar, anomalous and paradoxical, seems to be consistent with and to spring from what the CRC makes clear are underlying assumptions about children's *natural* condition, *immaturity* and vulnerability, and children's consequential special *needs* and *safeguards, care* and *protection* (*ibid.*, Preamble). According to the CRC, States Parties 'recognize the right of the child to be protected from economic exploitation and from performing any work that is likely to be hazardous or to interfere with the child's education, or to be harmful to the child's health or physical, mental, spiritual, moral or social development' (*ibid.*, Article 32), which is then interpreted to mean – given the assumed natural condition and special needs of children – denying (with exceptions) children the right to engage in paid labour, while compulsorily requiring them to engage in that unpaid (productive) labour that is centred on their social development, in particular within (formal systems of) education.

As noted above, formally, slavery has been abolished everywhere in compliance with prevailing UN human rights instruments and international law, in particular, the 1948 UDHR and ICCPR. The *Rome Statute of the International Criminal Court* (UN, 2009b) has characterised '"enslavement" as a crime against humanity falling within the jurisdiction of the Court and describes "enslavement" as "the exercise of any or all of the powers attaching to the right of ownership"' (BBC, 2007a), an approach to the notion of 'enslavement' which echoes with the definition of 'slavery' in the *Convention to Suppress the Slave Trade and Slavery* (or the *Slavery Convention*) of 1926, according to which slavery is 'the status or condition of a person over whom any or all of the powers attaching to the right of ownership are exercised' (Article 1).

As *The Abolition Project* has pointed out that 'form of slavery [...] in which the slave is treated as a piece of property, belonging to his or her owner, and has no rights' is *chattel slavery* (Abolition Project, 2007). Chattel slavery – in which 'slaves can be bought and sold just like cattle (from which the word chattel comes)' (*ibid.*) – is 'the obvious form', or 'the narrowest definition', of slavery (BBC, 2007b). Other 'practices that amount to slavery' include bonded labour or debt bondage, serfdom, 'other forms of forced labour' as well as 'child slavery'. The latter covers, for instance, the 'transfer of a young person (under 18) to another person so that the young person can be exploited' and 'forcing children to become soldiers' (*ibid.*). *The Abolition Project* otherwise defines slavery as 'keeping people as property, and requiring them to work under the domination of others' (Abolition Project, 2007), and the ILO uses the terms 'slavery' and 'forced labour' interchangeably – as synonyms – where the latter means 'all work or service which is exacted from any person under the menace of any penalty and for which the said person has not offered himself [or herself] voluntarily' (ILO, 2005). According to the ILO:

> at least 12.3 million people around the world are trapped in forced labour [...]. Forced labour takes different forms, including debt bondage, trafficking and other forms of modern slavery. The victims are the most vulnerable – women and girls forced into prostitution, migrants trapped in debt bondage, and sweatshop or farm workers kept there by clearly illegal tactics and paid little or nothing. (ILO, 2009b)

In some estimates, the number of slaves in the world is at least twice that of the ILO's estimate. The BBC has claimed that while 'slavery, slave-related practices, and forced labour are now regarded as [a] common international crime when committed against any person' (BBC, 2007a), and

> although slavery is illegal in every country in the modern world, it still exists, and even on the narrowest definition of slavery it's likely that there are far more slaves now than there were victims of the Atlantic slave trade. The last country to abolish slavery was the African state of Mauritania, where a 1981 presidential decree abolished the practice; however, no criminal laws were passed to enforce the ban. In August 2007 Mauritania's

parliament passed legislation making the practice of slavery punishable by up to 10 years in prison. Richard Re, writing in 2002, stated:

> Conservative estimates indicate that at least 27 million people, in places as diverse as Nigeria, Indonesia, and Brazil, live in conditions of forced bondage. Some sources believe the actual figures are 10 times as large.
>
> – BBC (2007a) and Re (2002)

Of course, the number of slaves, of those who suffer 'practices that amount to slavery' and of those who suffer 'other forms of forced labour', depends on the notions and definitions involved. As with the definition of 'childhood', while there cannot be correct definitions of 'slave', 'slavery' and 'enslavement', there may be best definitions, in particular, for sociological purposes. However, guided by the approach of the ILO and the Abolition Project to these notions, it is difficult to avoid the conclusion that 'slavery, slave-related practices, and forced labour' (BBC, 2007a) are far more common than even the highest of the above figures suggest.

CONCLUSION

If 'slavery' is *keeping people as property and requiring them to work under the domination of others* (Abolition Project, 2007) and 'forced labour' is 'all work or service which is exacted from any person under the menace of any penalty and for which the said person has not offered himself [or herself] voluntarily' (ILO, 2005), then it might be concluded that in modern societies, children are *enslaved*, or at least subjected to *slave-related practices*, in particular to forced (productive) labour. Children, after all, are compulsorily required (*under the menace of penalty*) to *work under the domination of others* and most obviously of teachers within systems of formal education or schooling.

In response, it might be argued that in modern societies, first, children are not *property*; second, many if not all children participate in schooling voluntarily; third, children benefit from and need schooling; but fourth, due to their age and immaturity, children are not always aware of how they benefit from and need schooling, and consequently do not always voluntarily participate, as a result of which they are and should be compulsorily required to participate. It might be argued, in other words, that the compulsion involved is *benign*, reflecting the CRC dictum that 'the child, by reason of his physical and mental immaturity, needs special safeguards and care' (UN, 1990, Preamble).

Nonetheless, it may be retorted, the compulsion involved remains *compulsion*. Quite simply, children can be and are often forced, under threat, to participate in schooling against their preferences, their (free) will. Indeed, in effect, all children, whether or not they willingly participate, are compelled to do so. No exceptions, escapes or options are allowed. All children are compulsorily required to perform schoolwork, participate in formal education and engage in that (productive) labour through which their embodied labour power is created and recreated. Essentially, it is difficult to avoid coming to the conclusion that all children are subjected to *forced labour* and *slave-related*, or *slave-like*, practices, notwithstanding the way in which the compulsion involved is explained and excused in terms of things such as children's dependency, immaturity and special needs.

Accounting for children's forced (unpaid) labour on these grounds both echoes how children's exclusion (albeit with exceptions) from the right to engage in employment along with a raft of other citizenship rights is rationalised and resembles how the similar treatment of women, propertyless classes, paupers and slaves has been legitimated (Baubock, 1991; Close, 1995; Wickham, 1993). In spite of similar cases, however, in modern societies, the approach to children's labour and rights is exclusive to children and brings to mind a number of specifically child-focused questions, including 'what are the actual needs of children?'; 'what is the relationship between children's actual needs and their assumed, or purported, needs?'; 'what is the relationship between children's dependency, immaturity and needs, on the one hand, and how children and their labour are represented and rewarded by adults?' and 'to what extent can children's needs, immaturity, dependency, experience and development be understood in terms of how children (like adults) perform (productive) labour, but at the same time (unlike adults) are forced to engage in unpaid labour while being denied the right to engage in paid labour?'.

In that children in modern societies are forced to engage in labour, in particular unpaid labour, they are subjected to slave-related practices. In that children are denied the rights, rewards and remuneration, which would give them the kind of control over their lives which is enjoyed by adults instead of having their lives decisively controlled by adults, they are in a property-like relationship with adults. In that children are forced to engage in unpaid labour while not being allowed to engage in paid labour, they are alienated from their labour and the product of their labour, their embodied labour power. Or, that is, there is a sense in which children's 'own' embodied labour power is not as such their own, in the sense of being (fully) owned by them. Their labour power is, instead, owned by others, adults.

There is a sense in which children's embodied 'capacity for labour', or 'the aggregate of [their] mental and physical capabilities' (Marx, 1867), is the property of adults, even though they themselves are just about spared this fate.

The approach taken in this chapter to making sense of child labour in modern society amounts to an invitation to sociologists to see through and look beyond those popular discourses that depict schooling in modern societies as simply a unidirectional 'free gift' to children and to recognise and take into account how children – in a similar way to women through unpaid domestic labour – through schooling especially, greatly contribute to social production and thereby in a fundamental manner to society and social change. This is not to ignore the strides that have already been made in this regard by some (Qvortrup, 1995), but instead to appeal for the same kind of progress to be made by all.

NOTES

1. The focus of this chapter is the 'modern societies' of the IMF's 34 'developed countries' group.

2. See Chris Jenks (1982, 1996, 2005a), and James, Jenks, and Prout (1998).

3. For me, 'the family' is that area of social life covering kinship and marriage within which a wide range of relatively discreet units, collectivities and groups including 'families', domestic units, households and homes can be observed (see Close & Collins, 1985; see also Close, 1989, 1992).

4. See Close (2008b); see also Close (2008a), Close and Askew (2004a), Close and Askew (2004b), Close, Askew, and Xu (2007), and Close and Ohki-Close (1999).

REFERENCES

Abolition Project. (2007). Chattel slavery. *Glossary, East of England Broadband Network*. Available at http://abolition.e2bn.org. Accessed on 12 February 2009.

Barbalet, J. M. (1988). *Citizenship rights, struggle and class inequality*. Milton Keynes: Open University Press.

Baubock, R. (1991). Migration and citizenship. *New Community, 18*(1), 27–48.

BBC. (2007a). The law against slavery. *Religion and ethics*, 30 January. London: BBC. Available online at http://www.bbc.co.uk/ethics/. Accessed on 11 February 2009.

BBC. (2007b). Modern slavery. *Religion and ethics*, 30 January. London: BBC. Available online at: http://www.bbc.co.uk/religion/. Accessed on 12 February 2009.

BBC. (2007c). *Religion and ethics*, 30 January. London: BBC. Available online at http://www.bbc.co.uk/ethics/slavery/. Accessed on 13 February 2009.

Bertaux, D. (1994). The anthroponomic revolution: First sketch of a worldwide process. *Annals of the International Institute of Sociology, IV*, 177–192.

Bertaux, D., & Delcroix, C. (2000). Case histories of families and social processes. In: P. Chamberlayne, J. Bornat & T. Wengraf (Eds), *The turn to biographical methods in social science* (pp. 71–89). London: Routledge.

Bertaux, D., & Thompson, P. (1997). *Pathways to social class.* Oxford: Clarendon Press.

Bertaux, D., & Thompson, P. (2006). *Pathways to social class* (Rev. ed.). Edison, NJ: Transaction Publishers.

Caborn, A. (1998). Save your child from Saturday slavery. *The Observer*, 31 May.

Close, P. (1989). Toward a framework for the analysis of family divisions and inequalities in modern society. In: P. Close (Ed.), *Family divisions and inequalities in modern society.* Basingstoke: Macmillan.

Close, P. (1992). State care, control and contradictions. In: P. Close (Ed.), *The state and caring.* Basingstoke: Macmillan.

Close, P. (1995). *Citizenship, Europe and change.* Basingstoke: Macmillan.

Close, P. (2008a). Regional integration the East Asian way, December. *Newsletter of the Center for Southeast Asian Studies* (CSEAS), Kyoto University, No. 59.

Close, P. (2008b). Regional integration the East Asian way: Towards an analytical framework, November. *The EU and East Asia within an Evolving Global Order*, EU-NESCA (Network of European Studies Centres in Asia) Conference, l'Institut d'Etudes Européennes (IEE), Université Libre de Bruxelles (ULB), Belgian Ministry of Foreign Affairs, Egmont Palace, Brussels.

Close, P., & Askew, D. (2004a). *Asia pacific and human rights: A global political economy perspective.* Aldershot: Ashgate.

Close, P., & Askew, D. (2004b). Globalisation and football in East Asia. In: W. Manzenreiter & J. Horne (Eds), *Football goes east: Business, culture and the people's game in China, Japan and South Korea* (pp. 243–256). London: Routledge.

Close, P., Askew, D., & Xin, X. (2007). *The Beijing Olympiad: The political economy of a sporting mega-event.* London: Routledge.

Close, P., & Collins, R. (Eds). (1985). *Family and economy in modern society.* Basingstoke: Macmillan.

Close, P., & Ohki-Close, E. (1999). *Supranationalism and the new world order.* Basingstoke: Macmillan.

DeGregori, T. (2002). *Child labor or child prostitution?* Washington DC: Cato Institute.

Finch, J. (1989). *Family obligations and social change.* Cambridge: Polity Press.

Fox, B. (1980). *Hidden in the household: Women's domestic labour under capitalism.* London: Women's Press.

Frønes, I. (2005). Modern childhood. In: C. Jenks (Ed.), *Childhood: Critical concepts in sociology* (pp. 325–340). London: Taylor and Francis.

Harris, C. (1983). *The family and industrial society.* London: George Allen and Unwin.

Held, D., & Thompson, J. (Eds). (1989). *Social theory of modern societies: Anthony Giddens and his critics.* Cambridge: Cambridge Univerisity Press.

Hindess, B. (1991). Imaginary presuppositions of democracy. *Economy and Society, 20*(2), 173–195.

ILO – International Labour Organization. (2005). Forced labour. *ILO Thesaurus 2005*. Geneva: International Labour Organization (ILO). Available online at http://www.ilo.org/public/libdoc/ILO-Thesaurus/english/index.htm. Accessed on 26 March 2009.

ILO. (2006). *The end of child labour: Within reach.* Geneva: International Labour Organization.

ILO. (2009a). *Convention concerning the prohibition and immediate action for elimination of the worst forms of child labour*, 27 February. Geneva: International Labour Organization, Available online at http://www.un.org/children/. Accessed on 27 February 2009.

ILO. (2009b). *Forced labour*, 13 February. Geneva, International Labour Organization. Available online at http://www.ilo.org/. Accessed on 13 February 2009.

James, A., Jenks, C., & Prout, A. (1998). *Theorizing childhood.* Cambridge: Polity Press.

Jenks, C. (1982). *The sociology of childhood: Essential readings.* London: Batsford Academic and Educational.

Jenks, C. (1996). *Childhood.* London: Routledge.

Jenks, C. (Ed.) (2005a). *Childhood: Critical concepts in sociology.* London: Taylor and Francis.

Jenks, C. (2005b). Summary. In: C. Jenks (Ed.), *Childhood: Critical concepts in sociology.* London: Taylor and Francis.

Jones, G., & Wallace, C. (1992). *Youth family and citizenship.* Milton Keynes: Open University.

Marshall, T. H. (1950). *Citizenship and social class and other essays.* Cambridge: Cambridge University Press.

Marx K. (1867). *Capital, volume one: The process of production of capital.* Moscow: Progress Publishers. Available at http://www.marxists.org/archive/marx/works/1867-c1/index.htm. Accessed on 1 February 2009.

Molyneux, M. (1979). Beyond the domestic labour debate. *New Left Review* (July–August), 3–28.

Murgatroyd, L. (1985). The production of people and domestic labour revisited. In: P. Close & R. Collins (Eds), *Family and economy in modern society* (pp. 49–62). London: Macmillan.

Murgatroyd, L., & Thompson, J. (1989). Only half the story: Some blinkering effects of "Malestream" sociology. In: D. Held & J. Thompson (Eds), *Social theory of modern societies: Anthony Giddens and his critics* (ch. 7, pp. 147–161). Cambridge: Cambridge University Press.

New World Encyclopedia. (2009). Child labor. *New World Encyclopedia.* Available at http://www.newworldencyclopedia.org/. Accessed on 9 February 2009.

Office of Public Sector Information. (2009). *Education and skills act.* London: Office of Public Sector Information. Available at http://www.opsi.gov.uk. Accessed on 27 February 2009.

OHCHR – Office of the United Nations High Commisioner for Human Rights. (2009). *International law*, 14 March. Geneva: OHCHR. Available at http://www2.ohchr.org/. Accessed on 14 March 2009.

Qvortrup, J. (1995). From useful to useful: The historical continuity of children's constructive participation. In: A.-M. Ambert (Ed.), *Theory and linkages between theory and research on children/childhood* (pp. 49–76). Greenwich, CT: JAI Press.

Re, R. (2002). *A persisting evil: The global problem of slavery.* Cambridge, MA: Harvard International Review.

Seccombe, W. (1974). The housewife and her labour under capitalism. *New Left Review, 83*, 3–24.

Simmons, M. (1998). End child labour, say 30,000. *Guardian* (6 May).

Stacey, M. (1981). The division of labour revisited: Or overcoming the two Adams. In: P. Abrams (Ed.), *Development and diversity: British sociology 1950–1980.* London: George Allen and Unwin.

Tuttle, C. (2001). Child labor during the British industrial revolution. In: R. Whaples (Ed.), *EH.Net Encyclopedia.* Available at http://eh.net/encyclopedia/. Accessed on 20 February 2009.

UN – United Nations. (1948). *Universal Declaration of Human Rights (UDHR).* Available at http://www.unhchr.ch/udhr/index.htm. Accessed on 26 March 2009.

UN. (1976a). *International Covenant on Economic, Social and Cultural Rights (ICESCR)*, 3 January. Available at http://www2.ohchr.org/english/law/cescr.htm. Accessed on 14 March 2009.

UN. (1976b). *International Covenant on Civil and Political Rights (ICCPR)*, 23 March. New York: United Nations. Available at http://www2.ohchr.org/english/law/ccpr.htm. Accessed on 21 February 2009.

UN. (1990). *Convention on the Rights of the Child (CRC)*, 2 September. New York: United Nations. Available at http://www.unhchr.ch/html/menu3/b/k2crc.htm. Accessed on 21 February 2009.

UN. (2009a). *Treaty collection*, 25 February. New York: United Nations. Available at http://treaties.un.org. Accessed on 25 February 2009.

UN. (2009b). *Rome statute of the international criminal court*, 27 February. New York: United Nations. Available at http://treaties.un.org. Accessed on 27 February 2009.

Wickham, G. (1993). Citizenship, governance and the consumption of sport. *International Conference on the Sociology of Consumption*, University of Helsinki.

THE VALUE OF CHILDREN – FERTILITY, PERSONAL CHOICES AND PUBLIC NEEDS

An-Magritt Jensen

Only individuals can bring a child into the world, and family, parenthood and childbearing are pillars of personal lives. But the production of new individuals for the nation also fills a public need. Present concerns over low fertility mirror the value of children to the nation. Although emphasised in rich countries, people all over the world are making the same choice to have fewer children, and populations are ageing. Despite its personal nature, childbearing is amazingly structured. Fertility is fascinating in how it links structural and individual perspectives. In this chapter, I discuss the value of children at the interface of the personal and the public. My topic is personal choices in conflict with public need.

   In Europe, fertility is reaching a historical low point. Demographer Wolfgang Lutz (1999) was already asking 'Will Europe Be Short of Children?' at the end of the 1990s.[1] Since then, the reluctance to have children has become manifest. Fertility has dropped below the replacement level in an increasing number of countries (Lutz, O'Neill, & Scherbov, 2003). Lutz and his colleagues argue that a 'low-fertility trap' is unfolding. Self-reinforcing mechanisms will lead to ever lower fertility. The situation calls for immediate action, they argue, 'by making children a part of normal life again' (Lutz,

Structural, Historical, and Comparative Perspectives
Sociological Studies of Children and Youth, Volume 12, 195–220
Copyright © 2009 by Emerald Group Publishing Limited
ISSN: 1537-4661/doi:10.1108/S1537-4661(2009)0000012013

Skirbekk, & Testa, 2006, p.188). In every European country, young people are giving birth to fewer children than their parents did. In the next 20 years, a German newspaper informs us, 'twice as many people will leave the labour market as those entering it'. The detrimental impact of low fertility is juxtaposed to the present-day 'Spekulationskapitalismus'.[2] The trend is world-wide. 'Over the last three decades', Lutz and his colleagues state, 'birth rates have been on decline in virtually all countries of the world' (*ibid.*, p. 168). What is driving this development? Even though most will agree that there is something 'out there' which makes people limit their childbearing, disagreement prevails on exactly what social forces are at play. The 'smoking gun' has been hard to find, but, as Caldwell and Schindlmayr (2003, p. 257) suggest, 'there must be a common deeper explanation' and, they continue, 'that explanation at its broadest must be the creation of a world economic system where children are of no immediate economic value to their parents'. The reluctance to have children is a result, these demographers tell us, of social structures undermining their own survival.

FERTILITY AND THE SOCIAL STRUCTURE

Structural factors are central to demographic theories in trying to explain the ups and downs in fertility. In scientific debates two perspectives have often been confronted, one in which the economy is seen as the driving force of change, the other in which culture and new ideas are emphasised. Whether changes in the value of children are driven by economic or cultural factors can be difficult to disentangle. The theory of the demographic transition is a starting point.

The sharp fertility decline in many western countries by the turn to the twentieth century was initially described by Frank Notestein (1976[1945]). He saw declining mortality as a condition for reducing fertility, which was a priority focus of the time. As more children were surviving, fewer had to be born. He called this a demographic transition, the essence of which was a shift from high levels of mortality and fertility to low ones. Behind the transition were broad social changes which were both economic and cultural. In Notestein's words, 'it is only when rising levels of living, improved health, increasing education and rising hope for the future give new value and dignity to the individual life that old customs break and fertility comes under control' (p. 57). Notestein saw increased welfare and increased hopes for future as fertility-reducing factors. However, high child mortality is also interpreted in the opposite direction, as resulting from too many children. Where children are born in too high numbers, child neglect (leading to more deaths) becomes a way of birth control. This, Knodel (1978) maintains, is why child mortality was so high in Europe historically. The 'excess' children, that is, those born beyond economic utility, were a cause of high child mortality. The relationship between fertility and mortality is central to both perspectives, but they differ in terms of what are the causal factors. van de Walle and van de Walle (1989, p. 154) propose that there is a mutual influence between child mortality and the value of the individual child, 'that interest in infants was low because the probability of death was high; and that mortality was high because there was little interest [in the individual child] and, possibly, infanticide'. They point to cultural changes as driving forces: changing power structures in the family, the 'modern invention' of love and the progress made in the medical sciences were important in transforming perceptions of children. Paediatrics appeared as a new science in 1872. Increasingly child health became a public concern, whereas 'it is only when death can be perceived as possibly avoidable that people will try to mobilize knowledge and technology to control the hazards of nature' (p. 163).

Life and death unfold in social circumstances. Both having children and losing them differ under conditions of economic wealth and poverty. If death is outside human control, neglect of weak children may also be a response in poor countries today. Among poor Brazilian mothers, Scheper-Hughes (1992) found that neglect of weak children increased the life chances of the healthy siblings. A lack of emotional attachment to weak children, she found, is used as a survival strategy. High fertility is broadly taken as an indicator of children's economic value to their parents, but the number of children that are needed differ according to circumstances. The value of children's lives depends on the structure of their society, its economic development and affluence, and how people adapt their lives in interactions with structural changes. How can we distinguish between societies with differences in fertility regimes?

A plethora of distinctions between societies has been used: modern and traditional, rich and poor, industrialised and agricultural, developed and developing and so on.[3] Goody (1976) used the term 'power bank' and distinguished between two kinds: one in which capital is the primary power bank, and the other in which land is. In Africa, land was crucial to the power bank, and wealth is determined by 'the strength of the arms or the number of sons' (p. 109). Children are valued by their number. By contrast, the power bank in Europe historically was private ownership and transmission of capital from one generation to the next. Fertility was kept at lower levels through the imposition of strong social norms on marriage. A high number of children could counteract the accumulation of wealth. The economic structure, be it based in land or capital, determines the optimal number of children. Child mortality is a threat where a sufficient number of surviving children are hard to get. But the deaths of children may be a solution if there is an oversupply.

The theory of the first demographic transition did not raise issues of the value of children, but from the 1970s demographers expanded their focus from fertility to children and started to ask why children were born in high numbers in poor regions of the world, and in low numbers in rich ones. The Value of Children study (later named the VOC study) is one prominent example of this approach, whereas the Australian demographer John Caldwell represents another. His 'wealth flow theory', indicating a positive flow from children to adults in the family, used fertility as an indicator of children's economic value. Outside the demographic realm, social scientists explored historical changes in the value of children in Europe and the USA as a part of mental history. Phillipe Ariès and Viviana Zelizer are important examples to whom I shall return.

FROM SOCIAL ORDER TO A PRIVATE CONCERN

The VOC study took place in the 1970s. It explored parents' perceptions of children in rich and poor countries[4] (see Fawcett, 1983) and was the first project to compare the value of children across world regions. More than 20,000 women and men were interviewed. Three groups of child values were studied: economic, emotional and social. A main finding in countries where birth rates were high (typically poor countries) was that parents associated economic and security advantages with having children. They expected children to provide financial and practical help, and to assist them in old age. By contrast, where birth rates were low (rich countries), parents rather perceived emotional advantages from having children, like companionship and love. Interestingly, emotional values included feelings of 'being tied down', and the results suggested that childrearing was associated with restrictions on personal freedom.

Caldwell (1982) has analysed the meaning of children's economic value in poor countries. He identified a society's 'mode of production' – its economic structure – as decisive. In short, in agricultural societies with family-based production children were valued for their economic utility, whereas in industrial societies with their market production children became an economic cost to their parents. Broadly in line with the VOC studies, he asked first, within which economic structures are children valued for their economic utility, and second, what is their impact on fertility.

Caldwell sees the value of children as a product of a family-based rather than a market-based economy. This distinction runs close to Goody's between land and capital as the sources of a society's power bank. At the heart of both theories is whether production is located in the family or in society at large. In farming societies, children are fed from and contribute to the family's production. The rationale for having many children goes beyond their direct utility: children are the only form of capital that poor people can produce. In countries lacking welfare institutions or well-functioning banking and insurance systems, a 'safety-first' rule of having many children is at work (see also Cain, 1981). The economic value of children cannot be separated from their social value, and children are plentiful where they underpin social standing. But the economic value of children is not gender-neutral. Caldwell finds that men favour many children where they contribute to the power bank. In such societies men gain respectability and influence from having many children. Women are suppliers of a resource wanted by men and strengthen their position in the family through having many children. Childless women, by contrast, are faced with a less favourable destiny. This is an economic system where men control production and reproduction, and where the latter is a means to strengthen the former.

Caldwell's 'wealth flow theory' was formulated from his studies of poor farming societies. The wealth flow is the stream of resources that runs between generations in a family, and the direction of the flow is crucial. Children's economic value is signified by an upward generational 'wealth flow': adults gain from children. The system is based on an unequal sharing of resources, and men have the 'situational benefit'. Children (and women) are not expected to receive a fair share. If the wealth flow shifts direction, running from the older to the younger, children become an economic and social burden. As a result, fertility declines. Caldwell argues: 'If children's chief advantage was the relative small amount that had to be spent on them, this could be just as easily achieved by reducing their number' (1982, p. 236). Under the rule of economic utility, children live with harsh realities. Economic value has few implications for a good life for the individual child, nor does it mean that parents make 'rational choices' before having each new child. Rather, childbearing results from an omnipresent economic consciousness with little motivation for reducing it. Social norms and economic benefits work together. Having many children is routine behaviour (a point I will come back to). Marriage is the central institution through which men can control fertility, and children are part of a larger social order. This system was altered with social changes that turned children into a private concern, a shift for which the mass schooling of children was crucial.

Schooling, Caldwell declared, impacts on the economic benefits parents obtain from children. As children spent their time at school rather than at the family farm, their costs increased. Parents lost their children's work capacity and had to pay for schooling in addition (fees, uniforms, contributions to teachers and school buildings and so on). But schooling also impacted on cultural understandings. Children were exposed to new and more costly tastes (such as for food and clothes) and life orientation (such as a hidden curriculum of white-collar work as superior to farm work). Traditional authority structures in the family were undermined as the younger generations received an education the older generations had not. The unequal sharing of family resources was challenged. Over time mothers acquired education themselves. They learned about hygiene and child care, and dared to break conventional norms.

The VOC study traced a systematic relationship between low birth rates and the emotional value of children. But changes in perceptions of children had been going on for a long time. In *Centuries of Childhood*, Ariès (1962) maintains that 'childhood' is a concept that arose in the upper classes in the sixteenth and seventeenth centuries, as children were perceived as different from adults and a concern for children's health appeared (see also van de Walle & van de Walle, 1989). Ariès saw schooling as essential to this development. This new awareness of children eventually diffused to all social classes. He explained the growth in 'affectivity' centred on children and the family as part of the mental history of a 'child-oriented' society. To Ariès, however, new perceptions of children were linked to cultural rather than economic forces.

Zelizer, in her book *Pricing the Priceless Child* (1985), takes an approach similar to that of Ariès. She provides an influential insight into the changing social value of children in the USA. Between the 1870s and the 1930s, the early period of industrialism, she observed that children's economic and emotional values became mutually incompatible. Childhood was 'sacralised'. The 'economically useful' child who could still be found in mines and factories was gradually replaced by the child at school. Laws banning child labour and introducing compulsory schooling completed the shift from economic to emotional values as 'lower-class children joined their middle-class counterparts in the new non-productive world of childhood ...' (1985, p. 6). Zelizer's work was innovative in illustrating the changing value of children. She demonstrates how sacralisation made economic arguments for compensating the loss of a child provocative, whereas ironically children's emotional value increased their monetary value. Zelizer is not concerned with demographic changes, but she provides important insights into the period of the first demographic transition. As with Ariès, her concern is with cultural changes in perceptions of children. Changes in economic, occupational and family structures are mentioned, but their impacts are not central to her argument.

The shift in perceptions of children in rich countries can be traced in science and literature through manifold sources. From etymology we learn that the Latin term 'proletarian' originally meant 'those who contributed to the state only through their offspring'.[5] Karl Marx redefined 'proletarian' to mean a person with no other contribution than their working capacity. Children (offspring) ceased to be counted as a contribution to society in the early phase of capitalism. Since then children have been replaced by manpower as the sole resource that poor people could contribute. At the end of the nineteenth century, the economic transformation of society was completed, children were put into school, and over just one generation fertility was reduced to replacement level. The linkage between economy and fertility, the historian Sogner and colleagues claim, is not difficult to see (Sogner, Randsborg, & Fure, 1984). They are in good company. Ariès, Zelizer and Caldwell all see mass schooling as a driving force of cultural change. But unlike Ariès and Zelizer, to Caldwell schooling is an integrated feature of an industrialized economy in which the 'strength of the arms or the number of sons' is no longer what matters. In the process, the attention given to the individual child increased.

Thus the position of children shifted from being an aspect of the social order to being a private concern. A major change following on from this shift is traced in the justification of marriage. Marriage regulated fertility through social norms. Since it was the only acceptable institution for childbearing, the age of marriage was a major reason why fertility in Europe was kept at lower levels before modern forms of contraception became available. However, as children ceased to be seen as part of the social order, marriage no longer mattered.

THE DEINSTITUTIONALISATION OF MARRIAGE

In the majority of rich countries, there has been a strong increase in extramarital births since the 1970s (Sardon, 2006), and in some countries having children outside marriage is as common as having them within it.

This was not always culturally accepted. In some countries, Norway being a case in point, creating families outside marriage was illegal and regulated in the penal code. Violation could lead to three months of imprisonment, and the law was not repealed until the early 1970s. The value of a child born outside marriage was very different than of one born within it. More of them died, their mothers were doomed to a life of poverty, and the children were socially disgraced by being called 'bastard' and 'illegitimate'. A widespread hospital practice at the birth of a child, still in force in the 1970s, was to mark the fever chart at the foot of the bed with the word 'spurious' if the mother was unmarried. Only a few decades later, more children are being born outside than within marriage, a feature Norway shares with the other Nordic countries. In just a few decades, breaking the marriage 'rule' became majority behaviour, a trend that is increasing in strength in most rich countries. Marriage was no longer central for childbearing.

Why Men no Longer Need Marriage

Why was marriage important for childbearing in one historical period, and why did it lose its importance in another? The declining importance of marriage goes hand in hand with the shift from the economic to the emotional valuing of children.

The focal point of marriage, O'Brien (1981) suggests, was the need for a social substitute for men's biological uncertainty: 'Obviously, the most persistent and successful form is marriage' (p. 56). It was through marriage, Foucault (1984) argues, that descendants (children) could be legitimated. Marriage implied 'handing down a name, instituting heirs, organising a system of alliances and joining futures' (p. 74). Marriage confirmed, as Therborn (2004) expresses it, 'The rule of the father and the rule of the husband, in that order' (p. 13). To O'Brien, it was through marriage that 'the rights of husbands to the exclusive sexual use of women's bodies and the right to the title of father of a particular woman's children' were ensured (1981, p. 55). Gillis (2000) describes pre-modern Europe as a society in which the father's position as a family head was a basis on which property, power and prestige rested. Fatherhood was a social necessity: bachelors had no social position. A man without a household of his own was excluded from central positions in society. By contrast, in modern societies, O'Brien observes, 'True potency appears only in the marketplace' (1981, p. 160).

During the twentieth century the family was democratized, and men's benefits from it declined. The need to legitimize their children through marriage had lost its economic foundation. Men could no longer expect, although some continued to, to have the dinner on the table and for their children to be quiet during their afternoon nap. 'Existing differentials in advantages by age and sex came under attack by the same forces that brought changes in the nineteenth-century Europe: education of children, relative rise in the position of females, and the lure of household consumption goods' (Caldwell, 1982, p. 177). Privileges previously taken for granted were no longer culturally acceptable. The ruler of the family became an anachronism as women's need for them as providers faded.

It was through marriage that men were able to obtain rights to a resource they desired. Why did men give up this right, with no traces of resistance? Because, I suggest, the change in children's value impacted on men's interests in children more than women's. The change surfaced through new behaviour among women and was tacitly accepted by men. Respect and social standing were no longer obtained from being the father of a family. Economic and social benefits were derived from a labour market with limitless demands on those who wanted to succeed. Having a large family was a distraction from putting one's full energy into one's working life. However, with rising demands on participating fatherhood, men (as well as women) also risked entering a conflictual minefield if they gave too much priority to work rather than children. Avoiding family and children could avert such conflicts. Social conventions kept marriage alive as a support system for several decades after the first demographic transition, but when women found they could manage without them, men were ready to accept the fact.

Why Women no Longer Need Marriage

During World War II, women joined the labour force to replace men fighting at the front. A famous American poster shows a determined-looking woman, in her working clothes, lifting her right arm, fist clenched, claiming: 'We can do it!' The process of taking women out of the home and into the work places was irreversible. When Betty Friedan published her *Feminist Mystique* in 1963, women grasped her message with both hands. Increasingly they earned their own money and acquired new life aspirations. They encountered a labour market that not only welcomed their work power, but also had limited tolerance for heavy caring obligations. The introduction of modern contraception was welcomed by both women and their employers. As Caldwell argued, capitalism needed individuals, not families (1982, p. 237).

There is broad agreement that the advance of female education and employment had implications for the weakening of marriage, all of which are associated with lower fertility. The arguments go like this: with education, women's life aspirations changed; through employment, their dependence on marriage was reduced and with increasing consumerism, the costs of children rose. All indicators suggest that women were a driving force in the post-war fertility decline, as they no longer needed marriage. But why did the original meaning of marriage change? The original meaning, as O'Brien, Foucault and Therborn suggest, was not the breadwinner function, but to secure men's right to children.

Over time, marriage in rich countries has changed from a fertility-producing to a fertility-reducing factor. This is best seen by comparing countries where childbearing and marriage remain closely tied with those where marriage no longer matters. The higher fertility is found in the latter countries. These are also countries where more mothers are working (Berlin Institute, 2008). Why? Perhaps because, where marriage matters less, women are able to have children without entering into lengthy negotiations with a reluctant man. By contrast, where marriage remains central to childbearing men have a greater say, and they are more likely to use this to suppress fertility. Billari and Kohler (2002) illustrate this mechanism in the cases of northern Italy and southern Germany, two areas where fertility is confined to marriage, where fatherhood is an inescapable result of marriage and marriage is forever. They find that it is men rather than women who postpone marriage, as a result of which fertility is delayed and reduced. Men, once in need of marriage to legitimize their children, now hesitate to marry in order to limit childbearing. Nonmarital childbearing favours higher fertility, but child responsibilities rest more heavily on mothers.

EMOTIONALLY VALUED CHILDREN –
AT WHAT COST?

The emotional value of children is associated with economic development. As production is capitalised, people move to urban areas and education becomes important. Each child demands resources from the family budget. Feeding and clothing children, and providing housing and transport, are heavy burdens on the household economy. Can the intrinsic joy of children balance the costs? Schultz (1973, p. 4) introduced the concept of 'human capital' as crucial to 'the economics of fertility'. Four sorts of consideration are important for childbearing: investments in human capital (education), allocations of human time, household production, and consumer choices. Parents respond to economic conditions in weighing the satisfaction and sacrifices of having children. Schultz, using the case of the USA, is concerned with the rise in expenditure to children (education, constrained labour market opportunities for women), on the one hand, and the decline in the costs of limiting childbearing through easy access to modern contraceptives, on the other. He builds on the early work of Becker, in particular his 1965 theory that the allocation of human time is relevant in understanding reproductive behaviour among women.

From Quantity to Quality Children

Becker (1993), who was awarded the Nobel Prize for Economics in 1992, was a pioneer in the New Home Economics. He also finds the explanation for the changing value of children in the economy: 'As societies have become more urbanized and developed over time, families have greatly reduced their demand for "quantity" of children and greatly raised their demands for education, health, and other aspects of the "quality" of children' (p. 95). He points to the 'opportunity costs' of having children, as the mother's income is reduced when having and raising children. With women in the labour market, the opportunity costs of having children increase. His argument is that children have to fit with other forms of satisfaction for adults, such as employment, a house, consumption and leisure. The economic approach is criticized for exaggerating rationality. Having children, it is claimed, falls outside economic rationality. People do not make calculations before having children: they go on having them, despite their costs, because children are a part of adult life, even a natural drive. However, proponents looking for cultural, rather than economic, forces also find that children are competing with other life satisfactions of adults. Once again Ariès was an important voice.

From King-Child to King-Pair

In 1980, Ariès published a short article which turned out to be very influential. He pointed to birth and death rates as the invisible signs of social changes 'below the surface' (Ariès, 1980). The reason why young people limited their childbearing, first around the beginning and then in the latter part of the twentieth century, was 'a cultural climate that, for over a century, had favoured a low birth rate' (p. 645). The process started with new family ideals among the upper classes. By the second decline, new ways of thinking had surfaced. The two declines had similar results (fewer children) but different causes (p. 649). While the first decline was motivated by the improvement in the life chances of children, the second decline 'is provoked by the opposite attitude. The days of the child-king are over'. In the new epoch, 'the child occupies a smaller place, to say the least' (p. 649). Ariès found that children were no longer the central focus of people's life plans: other options were available. He concludes: 'Thus the child's role in the family's plans, and his affective role within the family, changed between the end of the Middle Ages and the eighteenth century. His role expanded. In like manner, his role is changing today, before our very eyes. It is diminishing' (p. 650). Ariès disregards the impact of the economy: his concern is with how people view children as less important to their lives, thus reducing fertility. Though the decline in fertility at the beginning of the century was 'child-centred', towards the end it was 'adult-centred'. The emotional value of children could no longer compete with alternative life plans among adults. The first and the second fertility declines were both driven by cultural changes.

Ariès' argument was central to the initial formulation of the theory of the Second Demographic Transition (van de Kaa, 1987). van de Kaa pointed to the rise of cohabitation, parental break-ups, the pluralisation of family forms and expectations of a self-fulfilling life as forces behind the fertility decline. Following Ariès, he saw these changes as reflecting a reduced importance of children to adults: the King-Child was substituted by, in van de Kaa's words, the King-Pair. In the subsequent development of the theory, Lesthaeghe (1995) centred on the role of women. Since then, the value of children appears as a piecemeal perspective in demographic theories, and few have adopted this as a main approach. One example of research which incorporates the value of children, although not as a main perspective, is Thomson et al. (2000). They made an effort to specify the kinds of emotional values that children may have for couples in modern societies. They point to three key values. First, children are symbols of the commitment of their parents' own relationship. Second, children give adults status as parents. Thirdly, a second (plus) child gives older children the status of a sibling. The question is whether these values are important in rich countries today. Thomson and her colleagues tried to test their hypothesis in an analysis across European countries, but no uniform picture emerged. Maybe, as one of the authors has suggested in another article, the lack of clear results confirms that it is no longer children, but marriage, that now signals commitment of a union (Toulemon, 1995, p. 183). Children and the status of parent do not come through as important values to adult people. Nevertheless, new forms of children's values have attracted attention in recent years.

Children as Social Capital

Theories of fertility have been criticized for their focus on decline. They do not inform us, critics point out, why people continue to have children despite perceptions of their uselessness? A new kind of value is children's ability to create social capital. Social capital is a rather loosely defined concept used with different meanings. Some define it in terms of people's voluntary involvement in social and civic organizations. Others focus on the role of networks in the family, education and work. Schoen, Kim, Nathason, Fields, and Astone (1997) maintained that theories of fertility decline overlook the continued critical importance of kinship in modern societies too: 'We believe that having children is an important way in which people create social capital for themselves' (p. 339). They define social capital as 'a resource of individuals that emerges from their social ties' (p. 338). This value is not expected to lead to a high number of children, as it may work as well through having just a few children. But having children, even if just a few, is important for adults' social ties. Their analysis gave strong support to the expectation that children's ability to create social capital for their parents was 'a prime motivator for childbearing in low-fertility populations' (p. 349). They conclude on the optimistic side by claiming that: 'We find that children are not seen as consumer durables; they are seen as the threads from which the tapestry of life is woven' (p. 350). Since this article was published, much attention has been given to the social capital of children. However, in terms of fertility this value does not seem to be important and their conclusions are not supported in other research.

One relevant study is a follow-up to the early VOC study. As already mentioned, the first study revealed that the emotional values of having children can also be felt as a burden. Young people felt 'tied down' by having children, a matter increasingly in conflict with societies that have come to appreciate the freedom of mobility (Bauman, 2000). The VOC study has now been repeated and includes rich and poor countries, though partly different ones than the first round[6] (Nauck, 2007). The basic assumption is the same as in the first: people will have children if they see them as beneficial to themselves. Nauck focused on four aspects of child value. First, a measurement of 'comfort' was created which included children's potential contribution to family income, their work utility and social insurance. Second, 'stimulation and affect' measure the fun and pleasure of having children. Third, 'social esteem' includes children's ability to provide their parents with the social recognition of others. Fourth, a measurement of 'costs', defined as economic, social and personal, was included. Basically the project confirmed the original relationships from the VOC study. Only economic utility (comfort) is associated with having more children. The two emotional values (stimulation/affect and social esteem) do not have any impact and, to the researcher's surprise, 'child costs have practically no additional effect' (p. 623). People have more children if they expect some utility in either the short or the long term. The aspect of this study that is closest to social capital is defined as 'social esteem', and this did not turn out to have any impact.

Emotionally Valued – a Better Life?

Where children are valued for their economic contributions to the family, poverty prevails and living conditions are hard. As discussed, many children do not survive their childhood, and parents cannot afford to give much attention to the individual child. In pre-transitional countries, child mortality was high and physical punishment widespread. Children had no say. Did children fare better as their emotional value gained in importance? During the first period after the western fertility decline, children were not given much space. Schoolwork, obedience and good manners were the ideals of upbringing. Children should be seen and not heard. Fathers were expected to ensure discipline and authority when needed, whereas mothers provided care. By the 1960s, children were expected to conform (expressed as children having good manners, being neat and clean, and acting in accordance with sex-role expectations). In the following decades, a strong change in parents' expectations regarding their children took place. By 1980 parents were promoting autonomy and self-direction (Alwin, 1989). Both the initial ideals of children's obedience and later expectations regarding their autonomy accord with social structures.

Through the first half of the twentieth century, children were a means for the family to climb socially, Ariès tells us: 'seeing that one's children got ahead in a climate of social mobility was the deep motivation behind birth control' (1980, p. 647). In this situation, it is no wonder that parents give emphasis to obedience and schoolwork in their children's upbringing. As mothers joined fathers in the labour force, the idea of a self-managed child accorded with children coping without a parent (the mother) ever present in the home. Ariès sees progress in children's life conditions in the first period, and a decline in the attention given to children in the later period. Caldwell (1982) sees the protection of adult interests throughout: 'Real children's liberation movement have not proved to be possible, although the speed of fertility decline can undoubtedly be explained by ever more successful demands by children for a more equal share in family consumption and pleasure and to do less work in household production' (p. 254). For Caldwell, fertility was always governed by adults' interests: 'with the emotional flow directed towards them, a large number often become an emotional burden too' (p. 230).

Ariès' argument that the days of the 'King-Child' are over has been contested. Many will argue that children today are at the heart of their parents' concerns. They take part in family negotiations and are listened to. Physical punishment has been outlawed in an increasing number of countries.[7] It is widely acknowledged that the position of children has changed, and it is not uncommon to state that the child is the ruler of the family. Children are acquiring increasing attentions as individuals, but as Gillis notes, it is the idea of the Child rather than the actual living child who has won our awareness. The physical child, needing two parent's care and time, conflicts with other needs that parents – as adults – have in relation to an ever more demanding working life, leisure and even love life: 'contemporary society remains obsessed with childhood, even as it neglects and abuses real children'. Gillis (2003) also finds that 'maintaining children as icons has been costly, particularly to children themselves' (p. 161). Children occupy a limited space in adults' lives. A longer period of an adult lifespan elapses before he or she has children, and a shorter period is dedicated to raising fewer children, whereas children themselves spend more time in day-to-day life outside the home. With an increasing proportion of children having parents who live apart, the time spent with both parents is substantially reduced. More disturbing, some would argue, is that, even under conditions of very low fertility and parents spending more time on employment outside the family: 'The proportion of children living in poverty has risen in a majority of the world's developed economies' (UNICEF, 2005). Poverty depends heavily on family composition and employment. Children with only one income earner in the family are at risk of poverty, especially if they live with a lone mother, as more and more children are doing. A mother's employment is not only a matter of personal preferences, but also a matter of keeping poverty at bay. Even in rich countries, in the EU about one in five children are estimated to be living in poverty (see the chapters by Campiglio, Johansen, and Hernandez et al., this volume). As a strategy to improve the life chances of 'quality' children, reducing the number of children is only partially successful.

Nauck's study found that in most cases fertility is a matter of 'routine solutions'. People do what other people do. This goes for having many children, as well as for having fewer. Individual choices to break conventional behaviour will primarily take place at times of rapid social change. Lutz et al (2006) draw attention to the long time that passes until young people enter parenthood. In many countries, young people struggle to complete an education, find a job and create a household. Over extended periods, they become accustomed to networks in which many of their age mates are living without children. Delays, reductions and avoidance in having children gain momentum where such patterns become widespread. This is what may have been happening recently. The 'tapestry of life', as Schoen et al. (1997) call it, is increasingly being woven from other kinds of threads than children.

FREE CHOICE – SAME CHOICE

The 'child choice' has become a major issue. The question is whether, when and how many children to have. Great value is given to the planned, chosen child, the child who must fit into an array of life circumstances. Freedom of choice is assumed to be a marker of modern societies, and it is a widespread perception that people can create their own biographies. Beck and Beck-Gernsheim (2002) call this the 'elective biography' or the 'do-it-yourself' biography. The obligatory life-course events of marriage and children are replaced by individual and limitless choices. In the name of individuality, one would expect that this should lead to a broad array of choices. One choice, however, has acquired universality: the choice to delay, limit or avoid having children.

Why, in countries where freedom of choice is crucial, do young people act in a uniform way in reproductive matters? The magnitude of child avoidance points to some common forces to which there is a dominant response. This is not necessarily perceived as 'compulsory' since people make the choice themselves. By observing the everyday lives of those who have children too early or too many of them, people are informed of the consequences of a 'wrong choice', among which the risk of poverty is pronounced. Fears of having one's life transformed if a child is handicapped may increase despite a decline in the actual likelihood of such events happening. It is the 'hidden hand' of a social structure in which having children is subjected to a set of unfavourable circumstances. I have so far discussed theories that consider whether children are a benefit or a liability to their parents. However, a rising proportion of young people are not entering parenthood, in particular among men.

Childless People: The New Turn

At the turn to the twenty-first century, childlessness in Europe is rising. Every fourth woman born in 1975 is expected to remain childless (Sobotka, 2004). There is some variation between countries, but, in general, childlessness is increasing even more among men than women. Norway is an example where childlessness is low but gender gaps are rising. In 1980, 10 percent of all women were childless at the age of 40 compared to 15 percent of all men. By 2007, childlessness among women had stabilised at 12 percent whereas a steady growth had resulted in 24 percent of childless men (Statistics Norway, 2008). Consequently, one in four men had not (yet) become a father at an age well into adulthood. Even at the age of 50, one in five men remains childless, which is also a strong increase since 1980. Denmark reveals the same gender pattern: 24.5 percent of all men born in 1960 remained childless in 2002, compared to 12 percent of women (Tanturri & Mencarini, 2008). Other European studies confirm the picture, such as in the UK, where the proportion of childless men is higher than among women at all ages (Burghes, Clarke, & Cronin, 1997, p. 17). Fewer men than women also live with children, whether from childlessness or as a result of family structure. The gender difference in relation to who lives with children cuts across European countries (Jensen, 1998).

Surveys indicate that a major factor behind this trend is the low desire to have children. A study of fertility intentions among women and men who have not yet started a family in Norway finds that, while 77 percent of the men expect to have a child, 90 percent of the women do (Lyngstad & Noack, 2005). Similar observations are found in a study from Sweden: fewer men than women regard having children as the meaning of life, and more give a higher priority to work and leisure. Young men envisage a future life with good earnings, whereas women emphasise how work and family can be combined (Bernhardt, 2000). These findings are in line with European countries in general. Sobotka and Testa (2008) have compared intentions regarding having children in 14 countries. The proportion of all men (aged 18–39) replying that they intend to have no children, or are uncertain if they want any, is higher than the proportion of women in every country. In some countries, both men and women have very low child intentions. One example is West-Germany, where 40 percent of all men and 23 percent of women give this answer. Focusing only at those who have not yet had a child, 60 percent of the men and 46 percent of the women have no child intention or are uncertain. In Austria one-third of young men consider it an ideal not to have any children (Lutz et al., 2006). The pattern is also found in rich societies outside Europe. A recent Australian study found that men want fewer children at the start of their reproductive life, and over time their desires for children are revised downwards (Qu & Weston, 2004/2005). For Japan, Bumpass, Rindfuss, Choe, and Tsuya (2008) arrive at the same conclusion. A substantial proportion of both young women and men do not want, or are uncertain, if they want children. But again men are more reluctant than women. More than every third man under 35, compared to every fourth woman, has no clear intention of having children.

A study from the Netherlands has explored the mechanisms behind this pattern among couples. It concludes that it is men rather than women who are the 'blocking power' to fertility (Kalle, Lambrechts, & Cuyvers, 2000). They find a difference in terms of the timing of children and their number. The critical points are when to have the first child, and whether or not the couple should have a third child. Though men agree with women that they want a child, they tend to say 'not yet'. Agreement prevails concerning child number two, whereas a new problem surfaces when a third child is at issue. The researchers call this 'the Porsche option', since the costs of having a new child are similar to the costs of having an expensive car like a Porsche. More men prefer an expensive car; more women want a third child.

It is astonishing how little attention is given to men's fertility patterns. Most demographic theories focus on women only. The theory of the Second Demographic Transition is one example. Lesthaeghe (1995) emphasised cultural changes, such as the increased importance of consumption, materialism and individualism. Caldwell (2004) opposed this approach. To him morality (or cultural changes) is produced by economics: 'What is most disconcerting about this thesis is the implication that these attitudinal and behavioural changes were the fundamental driving forces behind fertility decline' (Caldwell, 2004, p. 311). Caldwell is consistent in his economic approach to fertility, but he also leaves many questions in his own theory unanswered.

First, Caldwell has argued that men (fathers) in agricultural societies obtain a situational benefit from having many children. But he does not ask whether the loss of such benefits in industrial societies has turned men into blocking powers, as Kalle and his colleagues indicate. Furthermore,

Caldwell, in line with others, claims that mass schooling is a main factor reducing the economic value of children to the family. But he does not ask whether this value is relocated from the family to society. This is Qvortrup's argument that children remain economically useful, but that their usefulness is transferred to society and is no longer of benefit to the parents.

CHILDREN OF THE NATION

Qvortrup (1995) rejected the idea that, through schooling, children had joined 'the new non-productive world of childhood ...' (Zelizer, 1985, p. 6). By contrast, schooling was how children acquired an economic value to society. Schooling was what modern societies needed from children. By transferring children's economic value from parents to society, a cleavage arose between those producing the children (parents), on the one hand, and those benefitting from them (society), on the other. The social value of children, however, was largely ignored, as children remained a private concern. An immediate reaction was falling fertility.

Ariès argued that the first fertility decline was 'child-oriented', motivated by improving the life chances of fewer children. There is wide agreement that children acquired emotional values along with the fertility decline, as they also increased their parent's social esteem by climbing the educational ladder. To Caldwell this is not 'child orientation' since children remain instrumental to adults' need and, in Caldwell and Schindlmayr's words, 'the strategy of enabling their children to rise was a way of making gains in a kind of class war' (2003, p. 244). But children's economic usefulness did not disappear, Qvortrup argued: it was transferred to societies that expected to benefit from children's contributions as adults, leaving the costs to their parents.

The long-term fertility decline suggests that in ever fewer countries are children valued for their economic contributions to their parents. In rich nations, worries for the future consequences are growing. These include a concern over a halt to the rate of economic growth, shrinking markets, a lack of people in the work force, depopulation of the land and declining geopolitical influence. Europe, inhabited by 22 percent of the world's population in 1950, is projected to be down to 7 percent in 2050 (Wattenberg, 2004). It is not the emotional values of children that are central in present population debates but their economic values to the nation. Children do count, but individuals do not have children to serve the nation. With more people without children, nations have more people without childbearing responsibilities (see the chapter by Qvortrup, this volume). As Folbre (1994, p. 86) argues: 'Individuals who devote relatively little time or energy to child-rearing are free-riding on parental labor'.

Public turmoil over the issue is becoming apparent. Newspapers bring out articles, books are written, conferences and meetings are held, research programmes into the low birth rate are launched, and policy-makers are looking for solutions. The EU advocates policies to reconcile work and childbearing. Modern nations are lacking in children, and the predicted consequences are detrimental. The bottom line of the concern is the public value of children. However, the response in different countries is hesitant. An array of measures has been suggested, but their scope is limited and their impact on those who are expected to produce children is hard to trace. Public transfers to children have fallen far below actual costs and are likely to decline further with an ageing population. In many cases the political efforts are just lip service, since having children is deeply rooted as a private matter and responsibility. Nations need more children, but the means seem out of political reach as reproductive 'free riders' are productive winners: men more than women, and those with high levels of education more than those with lower levels. As children become ready for the labour market, thus paying taxes, providing services and producing economic growth, parents and non-parents will benefit alike. In Folbre's words, 'as children become increasingly public goods, parenting becomes an increasingly public service' (*ibid.*). But parenting is largely women's responsibility. Women have always been the 'biological reproducers of the collectivity', as Yuval-Davis (1997) has expressed it. The number of children that women are allowed to bear, and sometimes forced to, has been subjected to thorough controls. But one measure is difficult to regulate: through education, women have gained more power over their own bodies and have been able to join men in a search for benefits that count more. It has been an expectation that children would be 'delivered' for free because people just want them. But the natural drive is not sufficient any longer. Altruism does not solve the matter. We are left with the question of why we are witnessing, as Therborn argues, 'a unique historical turn to deliberate, peacetime below-reproduction fertility among the world's leading countries' (2004, p. 294).

GLOBAL CHILD AVOIDANCE

Despite 'individualization' and freedom of choice, fewer children are being born to families in one world region after another. There is some variation in timing, pace and magnitude, and still in the level of fertility. But the downward trend is uniform. It is more pronounced in rich countries, but poor countries are joining the trend. At the turn of the millennium, populations had already started to decline in many countries.

Having a child is a personal choice, and yet the systematic variation in the willingness to have children across both historical periods and world regions demonstrates that choices are structured. The recent falls in fertility cut across world regions, economic development, cultures and religions. The decline is particularly strong in Arab and Muslim countries. Though women would typically have given birth to six or seven children or even more a few decades ago, they are now rapidly approaching replacement level (2.1). Iran is just one example. At the time of the 'Islamic Revolution' in 1979, Iranian women were giving birth to close to seven children on average. Despite the strong religious hold over the population, and over women, in particular, fertility is now slightly under replacement level. '[E]verywhere, even in Africa, the world is running out of children', Longeman (2004) wrote.[8] In Watterberg's words: 'Never have birth rates and fertility rates fallen so far, so fast, so low, for so long, in so many places, so surprisingly' (2004, p. 149). Internet debates under headlines like: 'Baby Bust!' referring to the 'world panicking' and 'demographic disaster' are frequent.[9]

No matter what economic, cultural and religious divides, fewer children are being born. For a global trend in fertility, we need to ask what global force has gained in strength over the last decade. Many point to the acceleration of neo-liberal economics and the rising power of the market as symbols of our time (Connell, 2007). In the same vein, Bauman (2000) contends that mastery over mobility is the foundation of the most important social divisions. Stability and rootedness are core aspects of family life, but in conflict with the market economy, where Sennett (2006, p. 149) notes that, 'Movement and incompleteness equally energize the imagination; fixity and that solidity equally deaden it'.

Managing everyday life in this economy is not easily combined with having children. Children have to be delivered and fetched at fixed hours at day care and schooling. The mechanisms of market forces accord with people's desire not to be 'tied down', as the VOC study noted already in the 1970s. The winners in the global economy are free to move at very short notice; losers are not, Bauman tells. Goody's argument regarding the power bank may not be such a bad idea for understanding the changing values of children. With the advance of a neo-liberal economy ('Spekulationskapitalismus', as *Die Zeit* called it), being tied down by children is detrimental to the power bank, and 'the strength of the arms or the number of sons' become deficits rather than capital. Global economic development is also the biggest source of uncertainty for ordinary people. As Caldwell and Schindlmayr (2003, p. 257) conclude, many people feel the 'cold blasts of liberal economics ... to award economic growth a higher priority than demographic growth'. The impact of this economy is spreading to the distant corners of the world as 'a near-global political system makes people in poorer countries yearn for the same possessions, especially motor cars, often giving the desire for such possessions priority over children' (*ibid.*).

All over the world, more and more people are living in large cities. More are trying to manage in marginal settings. Labour markets are become less secure, housing expenses are rising, and families' livelihoods are becoming less stable. Who are most likely to bear and raise children in this situation? Folbre (1997) argues that in every society there will be a tendency among those in power to distribute costs to those with less power. Capitalists tend to distribute costs to workers by keeping salaries low; adults tend to distribute the costs of having children to the family, as men transfer most of the raising of children to women. Leaving the costs of children to the more powerless involves economic gains for those in power since 'somebody else is raising the kids who will support me in my old age' (p. 650). Childless women can manage on a par with men, and to manoeuvre in the economic game, minimizing child-raising obligations is essential to both genders. Policy-makers may try to convince us that children are 'a source of intrinsic, non-substitutable pleasure' (Schoen et al., 1997, p. 335), but individuals are now managing with too few of them.

I have addressed an increasingly vital issue: why are children being born in ever lower numbers, and what does this tell us about the marginalisation of children as a public value? Population, however, is not the only concern of our times. Unstable stock markets, risky hedge funds and aggressive investments are major indicators of a global economy. The financial crisis is unfolding alongside the environmental one. It is tempting to suggest that the decline in fertility is linked to these broader issues, and thus to point to a deep structural riddle affecting finance, the environment and fertility simultaneously. If this is the case, we are faced with a three-fold melt-down. The global baby-burst, the focus of this chapter, is part of larger structural forces and signifies an economic system which has turned against itself. The reluctance to bring children into the world is one factor in the global crisis and is likely to continue as long as the economic system continues to disregard the value of children to society. With the present breakdown of 'Spekulationskapitalismus', a further decline is possible as insecurity increases. However, the crisis might also raise awareness of humans as the basic resource in any society's power bank.

NOTES

1. On average the fertility rate is 1.5, well below the replacement level at 2.1 and in several countries fertility is down to 1.2 and 1.3.
2. *Die Zeit*, 19.02.2009.
3. In general Europe, North America, Australia and Japan are counted among the first group of countries, while the latter includes Africa, Asia and Latin America. For the sake of simplicity, I shall mostly speak of rich and poor countries. See http://esa.un.org/unpp/index.asp?panel=2, accessed 07.01.09.
4. Poor countries were Asian. The USA, Germany and Japan represented rich countries.
5. Online Etymology Dictionary (http://www.etymonline.com/).
6. The new study also includes African countries.
7. Although this has met with much resistance, and a country like the UK still has no legislation banning the parents' right to punish their children physically.
8. *New Statesman*, 31 May 2004. See also 'Empty Cradles', 2004.
9. Examples are 'Reason on the baby bust' and 'Baby Bust! The world is panicking over birthrates. Again'. Accessed 19.12.08.

REFERENCES

Alwin, D. F. (1989). Changes in qualities valued in children in the United States, 1964 to 1984. *Social Science Research: A Quarterly Journal of Social Science Methodology and Quantitative Research, 18*, 195–236.

Ariès, P. (1962). *Centuries of childhood. A social history of family life.* New York: Vintage Books.

Ariès, P. (1980). Two successive motivations for declining birth rate in the West. *Population and Development Review, 6*(4), 645–650.

Bauman, Z. (2000). *Liquid modernity.* Cambridge: Polity Press.

Beck, U., & Beck-Gernsheim, E. (2002). *Individualization.* London: Sage Publications.

Becker, G. S. (1993). *A treatise on the family* (Enlarged edition). Cambridge: Harvard University Press.

Berlin Institute for Population and Development. (2008). *Europe's demographic future: Growing imbalances.* Berlin: Berlin Institute for Population and Development.

Bernhardt, E. (2000). *Unga vuxnas syn på familj och arbete: Rapport från en enkätundersökning. [Young Adults Perspectives on Family and Work: a survey report].* Stockholm: Centrum för kvinnoforskning.

Billari, F. C., & Kohler, H.-P. (2002). The impact of union formation dynamics on first births in West Germany and Italy: are there signs of convergence? In: E. Klijzing and M. Corijn, (Eds.), *Dynamics of Fertility and Partnership in Europe: Insights and Lessons from Comparative Research,* edited by United Nations Economic Commission for Europe (Vol. 2, pp. 43–58). Geneva: United Nations.

Bumpass, L., Rindfuss, R., Choe, M.K., & N. Tsuya (2008). The institutional context of low fertility: The case of Japan. Paper presented at the International Conference on Low Fertility and Reproductive Health in East and Southeast Asia, Nihon University Population Institute, Tokyo, 12–14 November.

Burghes, L., Clarke, L., & Cronin, N. (1997). *Fathers and fatherhood in Britain*. London: Family Policy Studies Centre.

Cain, M. T. (1981). Risk and insurance: Perspectives on fertility and agrarian change in India and Bangladesh. *Population and Development Review*, 7(3), 435–474.

Caldwell, J. C. (1982). *Theory of fertility decline*. London: Academic Press.

Caldwell, J. C. (2004). Demographic theory: A long view. *Population and Development Review*, 30(2), 297–316.

Caldwell, J. C., & Schindlmayr, T. (2003). Explanations of the fertility crisis in modern societies: A search for communalities. *Population Studies*, 57(3), 241–263.

Connell, R. (2007). *Southern theory: The global dynamics of knowledge in social science*. Cambridge, UK: Polity.

Fawcett, J. T. (1983). Perceptions of the value of children: Satisfaction and costs. In: R. A. Bulatao & R. D. Lee (Eds), *Determinants of fertility in developing countries. Fertility rand institutional influences*, (Vol. 2, pp. 429–457).

Folbre, N. (1994). Children as public goods. *American Economic Review*, 84(2), 86–90.

Folbre, N. (1997). The future of the elephant-bird. *Population and Development Review*, 23(3), 647–654.

Foucault, M. (1984). *The history of sexuality, Vol III: The care of self*. London: Penguin Books.

Gillis, J. R. (2000). Marginalization of fatherhood in Western countries. *Childhood*, 7(2), 225–238.

Gillis, J. R. (2003). Childhood and family time: A changing historical relationship. In: A.-M. Jensen & L. McKee (Eds), *Children and the changing family: Between transformation and negotiation* (pp. 149–162). London: Routledge Falmer.

Goody, J. (1976). *Production and reproduction: A comparative study of the domestic domain*. Cambridge: Cambridge University Press.

Jensen, A.-M. (1998). Partnership and parenthood in contemporary Europe: A review of recent findings. *European Journal of Population*, 14(1), 89–99.

Kalle, P., Lambrechts, E., & Cuyvers, P. (2000). *Partner interaction: Partner interaction, demography and equal opportunities as future labour supply factors*. European Commission SOC 98 101387-05E01. Netherlands Family Council.

Knodel, J. (1978). European populations in the past: Family-level relations. In: S. H. Preston (Ed.), *The effects of infant and child mortality on fertility* (pp. 21–45). New York: Academic Press.

Lesthaeghe, R. (1995). The second demographic transition in Western countries: An interpretation. In: K. Oppenheim Mason & A.-M. Jensen (Eds), *Gender and family change in industrialized countries* (pp. 17–62). Oxford: Clarendon Press.

Longeman, P. (2004). *The empty cradle: How falling birth rates threaten world prosperity and what to do about it*. New York: Basic Books.

Lutz, W. (1999). Will Europe be short of children? In: *Family observer* (pp. 8–16). Brussels: European Commission.

Lutz, W., O'Neill, B. C., & Scherbov, S. (2003). Europe's population at a turning point. *Science*, 299(5615), 1991–1992.

Lutz, W., Skirbekk, V., & Testa, M. R. (2006). The low fertility trap hypothesis: Forces that may lead to further postponement and fewer births in Europe. *Vienna Yearbook of Population Research, 5*, 167–192.

Lyngstad, T., & Noack, T. (2005). Vil de velge bort familien? En analyse av unge nordmenns ekteskaps- og fruktbarhetsintensjoner' [Are they choosing family away?]. *Tidsskrift for Velferdsforskning, 8*(3), 120–134.

Nauck, B. (2007). Value of children and the framing of fertility: Results from a cross-cultural comparative Survey in 10 societies. *European Sociological Review, 23*(5), 615–629.

Notestein, F. W. (1976 [1945]). Population: The long view. In: T. W. Schultz (Ed.), *Food for the world* (pp. 36–57). New York: Arno Press.

O'Brien, M. (1981). *The politics of reproduction.* London: Routledge & Kegan Paul.

Qu, L., & Weston, R. (2004/2005). Family size: Men's and women's aspirations over the years. *Family Matters* (69), 18–23.

Qvortrup, J. (1995). From useful to useful: The historical continuity in children's constructive participation. In: A.-M. Ambert (Ed.), *Theory and linkages between theory and research on children: Special volume of sociological studies of children* (pp. 49–76). Greenwich, CT: JAI Press.

Sardon, J.-P. (2006). Demographic trends in the developed countries. *Population.* English Edition, *61*(3), 198–266.

Scheper-Hughes, N. (1992). *Death without weeping: The violence of everyday life in Brazil.* Berkeley: University of California Press.

Schoen, R., Kim, Y. J., Nathason, C. A., Fields, J., & Astone, N. M. (1997). Why do Americans want children? *Population and Development Review, 23*(2), 333–358.

Schultz, T. W. (1973). The value of children: An economic perspective. *Journal of Political Economy, 81*(2)Part 2: New Economic Approaches to Fertility, 2–13.

Sennett, R. (2006). *The culture of the new capitalism.* New Haven: Yale University Press.

Sobotka, T., (2004). *Postponement of childbearing and low fertility in Europe.* Doctoral Thesis, University of Groningen, Dutch University Press, Amsterdam.

Sobotka, T., & Testa, M. R. (2008). Attitudes and intentions toward childlessness in Europe. In: C. Höhn, A. Dragana & I. A. Kotowska (Eds), *People, population change and policies*, in the series. *European studies of population*, (Vol. 16/1, pp. 177–193).

Sogner, S., Randsborg, H. B., & Fure, E. (1984). *Fra stua full til tobarnskull* [From full house to two-child-families], Oslo: Universitetsforlaget.

Statistics Norway. (2008). Befolkningsstatistikk. Fødte 2007. [Population Statistics. Births 2007]. Available at http://www.ssb.no/emner/02/02/10/fodte/tab-2008-04-09-08.html. Retrieved on 08 February 2009.

Tanturri, M. L., & Mencarini, L. (2008). Childless or childfree? Paths to voluntary childlessness in Italy. *Population and Development Review, 34*(1), 51–78.

Therborn, G. (2004). *Between sex and power: Family in the world, 1900–2000.* London: Routledge.

Thomson, E., Hoem, J. M., Vikat, A., Prskawetz, A., Buber, I., Toulemon, L., & Henz, U. (2000). Union commitment, parental status and sibling relationships as sources of stepfamily fertility in Austria, France and West-Germany. Paper at Fertility and Family Surveys Flagship Conference, Brussels.

Toulemon, L. (1995). The place of children in the history of couples. *Population: An English Selection, 21*(4), 303–316.

UNICEF (2005). *Child poverty in rich countries 2005*. Report Card No 6, Innocenti Research
    Centre, Florence.
van de Kaa, D. J. (1987). Europe's second demographic transition. *Population Bulletin*,
    42(1)Washington: Population Reference Bureau, Inc.
van de Walle, E., & F. van de Walle (1989). The private and the public child. In: J. Caldwell,
    S. Findley, P. Caldwell, G. Santow, W. Cosford, J. Braid & D. Broers-Freeman (Eds.),
    *What we know about Health Transition: the cultural, social and behavioral determinants of
    health*. The Proceedings of an International Workshop, Canberra (Vol. 1, pp. 150–164).
Wattenberg, B. J. (2004). *Fewer: How the new demography of depopulation will shape our future*.
    Chicago: Ivan R. Dee.
Yuval-Davis, N. (1997). *Gender and nation*. London: Sage Publication.
Zelizer, V. A. (1985). *Pricing the priceless child: The changing social value of children*. New York:
    Basic Books, Inc.

CHILDREN'S RIGHT TO VOTE: THE MISSING LINK IN MODERN DEMOCRACIES

Luigi Campiglio

> Rulers and ruling classes are under a necessity of considering the interests and wishes of those who have the suffrage; but of those who are excluded, it is in their option whether they will do so or not; and however honestly disposed, they are in general too fully occupied with things they *must* attend to, to have much room in their thoughts for anything which they can with impunity disregard.
>
> – John Stuart Mill (1861) (italics in the original)

> The difficulty lies, not in the new ideas, but in escaping from the old ones, which ramify, for those brought up as most of us have been, into every corner of our minds.
>
> – John Maynard Keynes (1936)

INTRODUCTION

The aim of this chapter is twofold. First, we want to show how children and minors are fundamental in any consideration of the major issues and goals of economics and politics, especially with regard to the relationship between democracy, well-being and economic development. Children's well-being is a valuable goal in itself, and given that minors represent the long-distant future, it is also a measure of the economic potential of each country and the world. Despite its inherent value and economic importance, children's

Structural, Historical, and Comparative Perspectives
Sociological Studies of Children and Youth, Volume 12, 221–247
Copyright © 2009 by Emerald Group Publishing Limited
All rights of reproduction in any form reserved
ISSN: 1537-4661/doi:10.1108/S1537-4661(2009)0000012014

well-being is an issue largely overlooked by politicians, and the main theme
of this chapter is that this is inevitable because there is no political incentive
for politicians to address it. As a consequence, the second aim of this
chapter is to argue that granting children the right to vote would provide the
best political incentive, as well as the missing link in modern democracies.
We propose some reasons as to why extending the right to vote to minors
represents the full achievement of universal suffrage for a mature society,
rendering democracy absolute and improving its economic potential.
Parents, who already represent their children's interests in everyday
decisions, should naturally be entitled to represent them in the polling
booth as well, qualifying their participation in the functioning of democracy
through their role as parents. We argue that this change in electoral rules
would force politicians to consider children, pushing minors' well-being to
the top of all political parties' agendas and prompting the market and
politics to ensure a better allocation of resources between generations.

The chapter is organized as follows. In Sections "Children, missing
endowments, family decisions and the market mechanism" and "Children,
missing interests and democracy," we lay the theoretical economic and
political foundations for our arguments, pointing to the consequences of the
missing vote for children and their unheard voice in the decision-making
processes of democracy. Sections "Intergenerational resource allocation and
child poverty" and "History matters: Irreversibility and efficiency of early
childhood investments" analyze the two main issues concerning children's
well-being: the question of intergenerational equality (see also the chapter
by Johansen, this volume) and the crucial importance of well-being during
early childhood for later achievement as a youth and adult. Section
"Equality of opportunity from birth, incentive and 'good' consequences"
further analyzes the issue of the moment of birth as the starting point for
pursuing real political equality of opportunity, putting the relationship
between merits and rewards into a clearer context. Section "The economic
risk of childbearing and the fertility rate: Private virtues and social vices"
further analyzes intergenerational equality from the point of view of the risk
of childbearing and its consequences on the fertility rate. Section "Do
suffrage and political 'sympathy' matter for the achievement of social
outcomes?" asks the question of whether changing the rules of the political
game also implies a change in political decisions and the related allocation
of resources, and brings together recent studies which indeed confirm this
relationship. Sections "Who should represent the economic interest of
minors politically?" and "Parents represent their children's interests in
everyday life: Why not in politics too?" ask who should represent the

economic interests of minors politically, and we give reasons as to why their parents would be the most natural answer. Extending the right to vote to children would complete the democratic process, with potential social and economic advantages.

CHILDREN, MISSING ENDOWMENTS, FAMILY DECISIONS AND THE MARKET MECHANISM

The theory of competitive markets assumes the existence of two agents, the household and the firm (Arrow & Hahn, 1971); although the "black box" inside the firm has been explored over the past thirty years, its counterpart within the household still requires closer investigation, especially with regard to internal decision-making processes. The theory of market mechanisms assumes that households have preferences and an initial endowment of goods and a potential labor supply as exogenously given; the inclusion of children in this framework raises some new and interesting questions, as regards both preferences and initial endowment.

The assumption of a positive initial endowment is necessary because it is essential for exchanges in the markets, and therefore for their efficiency. Household members will go to the market and exchange goods or labor services with a positive value there, for other goods or services in such a way as to maximize the household's utility according to their given preferences. If and how children have a special role in this process has still to be investigated. It would seem obvious that the initial endowment cannot include child labor for physical reasons (see the chapters by Close and Qvortrup, this volume); this is certainly true while they are still babies or toddlers, but it is a sad historical fact that during the early stages of the industrial revolution, the exploitation of child labor was common, to the point that the abolition of child factory labor, together with free education, was proposed by Karl Marx and Friedrich Engels (1848) as one of their required changes for a new society in their *Manifesto*. A succession of factory acts gradually extended the protection of children in economically advanced countries, but the problem still exists and is widespread in less-developed countries. The exploitation of child labor is normally driven by the fight for survival, the accomplishment of the latter usually being taken as an assumption in theoretical analysis. However, the adoption of a "survival assumption" is a weakness because it takes as given what should instead be proven, that is the market mechanism can achieve efficiency while allowing children to survive.

Thomas Payne was clearly aware that initial endowment was a problem when, in 1796, he proposed that out of a national fund "there shall be paid to every person, when arrived at the age of twenty-one years, the sum of fifteen pounds sterling, as a compensation, in part, for the loss for his or her natural inheritance" (quoted from van Parijs, 1997, p. 45). This proposal, which has received attention from scholars and politicians in more recent years, suffers from a crucial flaw in that at the age of twenty-one inequalities and disadvantage are already established: if the initial endowment is intended to compensate for social and natural inheritance inequalities, it should be granted at least partially from birth, possibly diluting its distribution until the age of majority.

With regard to households' preferences, children are valuable in the marketplace as far as their needs have a market value, as expressed on their behalf by their parents; we must note a crucial distinction between family and markets, because markets are supposed to reward agents according to their merits, whereas inside the family resources are usually allocated according to needs rather than merits, which is obvious in the case of early childhood. If families with children are financially constrained, the satisfaction of the children's needs will also inevitably be constrained, in some cases to the bare minimum, whereas a socially desirable goal would be that children should be the least constrained. To the question of whether the market mechanism can achieve this socially desirable goal through the working of a competitive price system, the answer is no, because the children's needs that society would want to satisfy (almost) without economic constraints cannot be fully included in a low-income household's effective demand at the given prices. To achieve this socially desirable goal for children, the efficiency of the market mechanism would have to be supported by an appropriate reallocation of resources (possibly with a larger share for unconstrained in-kind programs). This is known as the Second Theorem of Welfare Economics (Varian, 1992).

The presence of children implies a generalization of the concept of incentive compatibility, originally introduced by Hurwicz (1972, 2006): the basic idea is that to achieve a socially desirable goal, such as the aggregation of decentralized decisions of firms and households in the marketplace, we need rules and institutions that give these actors the incentive to reveal their true preferences. A well-known example is Vickrey's auction mechanism, which is ingeniously designed so as to give the bidder the incentive to reveal his true willingness to pay: he submits his offer in a sealed-bid auction, with the known rule that if his bid is the highest, he will pay the second-highest price. It is intuitively clear that he will respond to the incentive to reveal his true willingness to pay given that he will not have to pay this amount, while he would like to avoid being outbid. The question is whether we can conceive of an analogous mechanism by which children's preferences and their long-term interests can be transmitted to the market through a political mechanism, to achieve their needs with the minimum amount of constraints, as a socially desirable goal.

CHILDREN, MISSING INTERESTS AND DEMOCRACY

Although prices are the main factor in the market mechanism, votes are the main factor in the political mechanism. Votes can be considered as the equivalent of a voice, as proposed by Hirschman (1970). The analogy of competition for sales between firms and competition for votes between political parties follows Schumpeter (1942) and his widely accepted concept of democracy, defined as the "institutional arrangement for arriving at political decisions in which individuals acquire the power to decide by means of a competitive struggle for the people's vote" (p. 269). According to this view, competition is the driving force in both the market and the political arena; there are however major differences. It is politics, through parliament and the government, which chooses the most suitable mechanism for achieving the desired goal, and as a consequence the institutional organization and market rules which are implied. Moreover, a relevant share of Gross Domestic Product (GDP) is allocated following political, rather than market, rules: public expenditures represent approximately 30% of the GDP in the United States and Japan and approximately 45% in Europe.

The principal–agent framework is useful for explaining the conflict of interest in all the economic relationships where the outcome desired by the principal, for example a patient, can only be achieved through the decision of an agent, for example a physician; the problem is the potential conflict of interest if the physician's utility function is not the same as the patient's. The principal–agent relationship is also a useful framework for analyzing the political relationship between citizens and politicians: the voting citizen is the principal, whereas the politician and his political party are the agent acting in his interest. The politician seeks election and political clout, competing with other politicians for citizens' votes, whereas his party seeks parliamentary majority. In striving to achieve electoral success, the politician or his party try to discover, aggregate and satisfy citizens' preferences, according to the equality principle implied by the rule of "one man one vote." The crucial point here is that minors, a substantial share of the population, are missing from the political competition, and, as a consequence, their economic and social interests are largely overlooked: according to UN statistics in 2006, the percentage of the population less than 15 years old was 28% worldwide (1,846 million out of a total population of 6,593 million), 41.2% in Africa, 29.5% in Latin America and the Caribbean, 20.3% in Northern America, 27.6% in Asia, 15.7% in Europe and 24.7% in Oceania (United Nation, 2008, p. 52). The close relationship between interests and political representation was clear to John Stuart Mill (1861) who neatly understood that

> rulers and ruling classes are under a necessity of considering the interests and wishes of those who have the suffrage; but of those who are excluded, it is in their option whether they will do so or not; and however honestly disposed, they are in general too fully occupied with things they *must* attend to, to have much room in their thoughts for anything which they can with impunity disregard. (italics in the original)

Children's interests are missing in the competition for votes to win the elections, thus inevitably distorting attempts to achieve justice, welfare and liberty, to which all modern constitutions are committed; this issue, despite its numerical and political relevance, has received only scanty attention from scholars and social scientists.

Robert Dahl has perhaps provided the most compelling political argument against the inclusion of children in the political process: he provides an extensive discussion of different views on the concept of citizenship, and considering too narrow and only procedural Schumpeter's concept, he proposes a view of democracy and political equality, which applies only to adults "because the only defensible ground on which to exclude children from the demos is that they are not fully qualified [to govern] ... [and as a consequence] any assertion of a universal right of all persons to membership in a demos cannot be sustained" (Dahl, 1989, p. 127). He also proposes exclusion from the class of adult members of transients and persons judged to be mentally defective. Admittedly Dahl's arguments rationalize a view that is nowadays commonly accepted, as it was commonly accepted until a century ago that women were not qualified to vote. Oddly enough he does not raise the question of whether the aims of democracy such as effective equality of opportunities could be seriously undermined by the fact that the interests of a significant share of the population (approximately 20% of the European population is less than 18 years old) are denied political representation. In fact, as Dahl (1989, p. 129) himself concedes, democracy is an instrument for achieving common desired goals, but "an exclusive demos is unlikely to protect the interests of those who are excluded. 'Universal teaching must precede universal enfranchisement', Mill wrote. But it was not until *after* the extension of the suffrage in 1868 that Parliament passed the first act establishing public elementary schools. The historical record since then has demonstrated even more fully that when a large class of adults is excluded from citizenship their interests will almost certainly not be given equal consideration. Perhaps the most convincing evidence is provided by the exclusion of southern blacks from political life in the United States until the late 1960s."

Democracy is a social institution, a mechanism like the market, and what matters is how the goals that a society wants to realize are really achieved; these goals are in turn the result of the common and shared values of a community, ranging from the family to the whole of human society. In fact, the election of a United States President of African origin would have not been conceivable fifty years ago, but on closer investigation this is in fact the outcome of new rules and institutions.

INTERGENERATIONAL RESOURCE ALLOCATION AND CHILD POVERTY

All official sources show clearly the existence of a serious inequality problem regarding intergenerational resource allocation according to age, which substantially penalizes minors and children; recent significant results include the following.

A new OECD Report (2008, p. 191) for the main advanced countries shows clearly that minors experience the heaviest burden of material deprivation, as measured by situations such as inadequate heating, restricted food choices, overcrowding, poor environmental conditions, arrears in paying utilities, arrears in mortgage or rents and inability to make ends meet. This result is very important because it points directly to the outcome of not having a monetary measure of the level of subsistence, which we now analyze.

Another report by the European Commission entitled Child Poverty in the EU (2008) shows that although in 2005 the population aged 0–17 in the EU-27 was 97.5 million, 10 million less than that in 1995, "yet, in 2005, 19 million children lived under the poverty threshold in the EU-27, meaning that 19% of children were at risk of poverty, against 16% for the total population" (*ibid.*, p. 13). In all European countries, the risk-of-poverty rates for children increase with the size of the family and are highest for single parents (*ibid.*, Table A1). The report explains differing child poverty rates with three main factors: whether both parents are working, their work "intensity" (ranging from joblessness to full-time job) and government social transfers. The first two factors are market-related, whereas social transfer is instead policy-determined; in this regard the report shows "a strong relationship between the amount spent on social protection (excluding pensions) and the impact of social transfers measured as the percentage of reduction in the poverty rate once social benefits other than pensions are taken into account" (*ibid.*, p. 39). The report provides much new information on child poverty but it is, perhaps inevitably, rather non-specific when it comes to policy proposals.

UNICEF and Innocenti Research Centre (2007) have recently addressed the broader issue of child well-being from a wider perspective, ranking the more advanced countries on the basis of six criteria, which include, beyond material well-being and poverty, aspects such as education, family and peer relationships, behavior and risks, subjective well-being. One of the main findings of the report is that "no country features in the top third for all six dimensions of child well-being (though the Netherlands and Sweden come close to doing so)." Although these results show that no country is without problems, perhaps the main contribution of the report is the endeavor to break down the major aspects of child well-being, many of which have a direct political implication and afford a richer notion of democracy. A step forward is the effort to address the issue in absolute terms, rather than in the form of rankings, indicating an absolute level of well-being for children, which an advanced democratic society cannot fall short of understandably a difficult undertaking.

To better assess the impact of social transfers – clearly the result of a policy decision – on poverty rates, we take as a specific measure of their efficiency the decrease in the population at risk of poverty after social transfer in the EU-27 countries, as officially measured by Eurostat in 2006. We run a simple Ordinary Least Squares (OLS) regression, taking the efficiency of social transfers (excluding pensions) as a dependent variable, measured by the decrease from ex-ante to ex-post risk-of-poverty rates (DEC), and two specific items within all the social transfer programs as explanatory variables, namely transfers for family and children (FAM) and transfers for disability (DIS), as a percentage of GDP. Regression estimates (Table 1) show that the efficiency of social transfer improves with increasing resource allocation to families, children and the disabled; this is a clear

Table 1. Efficiency of Social Protection Expenditures.

Variable	Coefficient	Standard Error	*t*-Statistic	Probability
C	0.772236	1.366521	0.565111	0.5772
DIS	2.479314	0.694015	3.572422	0.0015
FAM	2.138589	0.780091	2.741461	0.0114
R-squared	0.686504	Mean dependent variable		9.777778
Adjusted *R*-squared	0.660379	S.D. dependent variable		4.651992
S.E. of regression	2.711040	Akaike info criterion		4.936981
Sum squared resid	176.3938	Schwarz criterion		5.080963
Log likelihood	−63.64925	*F*-statistic		26.27800
Durbin–Watson stat	2.604266	Prob(*F*-statistic)		0.000001

Notes: Dependent variable: DEC; method: least squares; sample: 1 27; included observations: 27. DEC = decrease: ex-ante risk-of-poverty-rate − ex-post risk-of-poverty rate; C = constant; DIS = transfers for disability as a percentage of GDP; FAM = transfers for family and children as a percentage of GDP.

indication that in many countries political decisions are clearly wide of the mark with regard to child poverty. The missing original endowment for children, as measured in monetary or multidimensional terms, is therefore the other side of the coin of their missing representation: the missing political representation of children is not only an issue concerning equality but also a matter for concern as regards efficiency.

HISTORY MATTERS: IRREVERSIBILITY AND EFFICIENCY OF EARLY CHILDHOOD INVESTMENTS

A growing body of research shows that what happens in early childhood, in terms of quality of health and nutrition, material deprivation and poverty, lack of parental care and presence, poor emotional environment, has a profound and enduring influence on educational and economic achievements later in a child's life, while still young and then in adulthood. Cumulative effects, so common in social sciences, are clearly present in early childhood, and as a consequence any deprivation suffered by a child is likely to have consequences for the rest of his or her life, worsening rather than improving. The history of early childhood determines the path (dependence) of the adult, and when children reach the age of 18, they are already endowed with character, personal traits and values, education, income and peer relationships; most of what really matters for their future has already happened. The crucial political implication is that the goal of ensuring equal opportunities, central to all modern democracies, is meaningless unless it is pursued as of birth. The economic implication is also crucial, in that public and private resources devoted to early childhood are much more in the nature of irreversible investment than current expenditures.

When the initial conditions of a dynamic process, such as a child's birth and early childhood, heavily influence the direction of its further evolution, we are in a situation where "history matters," and because of the influence of the initial conditions, this evolution is called "path dependent" (David, 2007). As Arrow (2004) states, there is path dependence if the limit of an evolving system depends on the initial conditions, as in the case of a drop of rain falling on a hill and which will eventually go into a valley, but which valley depends on the point of initial contact with the ground; his crucial suggestion is that the root of path dependence lies in the irreversibility of investments. He concludes that the aspect common to all the examples of path dependence is the durability of the capital, to be taken in a broad sense, such as the irreversibility of human capital investment.

Overcoming the empirical problems of collecting long-term panel data, in recent years, a growing body of economic research has confirmed how crucial early childhood investments are for the future outcome of the ensuing adult, as well as for overall economic efficiency. Feinstein (2003) shows the existence of a strong relationship between the socio-economic status (SES) of children at their birth and the subsequent development of their cognitive abilities. The gap between high and low SES is self-reinforcing over time and further polarizing, because children whose initial abilities are low are less compensated than those of the families with a high SES. He argues that "family background clearly plays a tremendously important role in determining the continued development of ability of UK children."

Recent works by James Heckman have further extended our knowledge of the relevance of early childhood on the subsequent economic performance of the adults and the economy. His insight, again, concerns the crucial importance of early intervention, because skills beget skills, and learning begets learning according to a cumulative process that influences the quality of the labor force and, through this channel, output and productivity growth too (Heckman & Masterov, 2007). Moreover, there are also substantial social benefits associated with less crimes and social deviance. Heckman (2008) estimates that about half of the inequality in the present value of lifetime earnings is due to factors determined by the age of 18, whereas the family plays a powerful but not adequately recognized role in shaping adult outcomes.

The traditional concept of human capital is becoming richer, to include not only formal education, i.e. cognitive ability, but also values and behavioral traits such as motivation, tenacity and discipline in pursuing a goal, which seem to have an economic value in the marketplace and which are known as non-cognitive abilities. Recent literature has tried to identify which personal traits are more relevant, and there is at present a consensus on a group of five, the so-called big five, which are Openness to experiences, Conscientiousness, Extraversion, Agreeableness and Neuroticism (emotional stability) (summarized by the acronym OCEAN). The policy implication is also relevant: although schools and universities play the major role in cognitive development, for values and personal traits the major role is played by the family, especially during childhood.

EQUALITY OF OPPORTUNITY FROM BIRTH, INCENTIVE AND "GOOD" CONSEQUENCES

The principle of equal opportunity, central to all notions of democracy, is compatible with that of meritocracy to the extent to which each individual can be taken as fully responsible for his efforts and choices. On the contrary, the incentive argument behind the relationship between efforts and choices is constrained by equality considerations if equal opportunity is not fully feasible. We can represent this fundamental trilemma in Fig. 1.

Adult rewards and merits are fully deserved as long as they are the result of effort and choice, if there is equality of opportunities; otherwise, inequality of opportunity puts a constraint, either mild or strong, on merits and rewards. The choice of whether to give equality from the moment of birth is aptly summarized by Romer (2000, p. 18) who argues that "there is

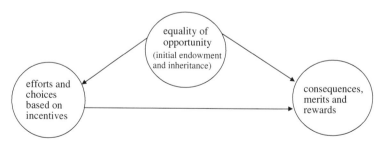

Fig. 1.   The Social Trilemma.

in the notion of equality of opportunity a 'before' and an 'after': before the competition starts opportunities must be equalized, by social intervention if need be, but after it begins individuals are on their own. The different views of equal opportunity can be categorized according to where they place the starting gate that marks the point after which they are on their own". In our view there is in fact a road, with an initial and a final gate: the initial gate is the moment of birth, whereas the final gate is the conventional age for adulthood; this view seems to be coherent with Heckman's empirical results, quoted earlier, but at the same time we have to recognize that the trilemma is the symbol of an intrinsic tension between political values and economic incentives, even if both point to same goal of efficiency and meritocracy.

The word "meritocracy" was introduced by Young (1958), whose formulation of merit as the sum of intelligence and effort ($M = I + E$) is still quoted, although inappropriately, because he also underlined how much education builds on initial mental endowment. In other words, genetic and cultural endowments are closely intertwined. Moreover, as Sen (2000) argues merit and rewards are indeed instrumental with respect to the consequences of the actions taken on their basis; "good" consequences need to be evaluated with reference to a notion of a "good" and just society, of which distributional concerns should be part, as happens with payments to top executives. Rawls' (1971, p. 101) theory of justice is in this respect rather radical because he regards "the distribution of natural talents as a common asset" whose benefits are to be commonly shared, a view which is questioned by Arrow (1973, p. 99) who points to the economic and ethical tension between equality of opportunity and rewards, because of the conflict with the "productivity principle" whereby individuals are entitled to the results of their efforts.

Rawls' approach does however have a solid rationale: he argues that "no one deserves his place in the distribution of native endowments, any more than one deserves one's initial starting place in society." He goes even further, arguing that "the assertion that a man deserves the superior character that enables him to make the effort to cultivate his abilities is equally problematic; for his character depends in large part upon fortunate family and social circumstances for which he can claim no credit. The notion of desert seems not to apply to these cases" (Rawls, 1971, p. 104). In fact, we need to generalize Rawls' intuition and address the generally neglected question about meritocracy, i.e. the fundamental issue of inheritance. Inherited economic wealth, both real and financial, as well as parents' values and human wealth, define how wide the field of opportunities open to each child is. The issue of initial endowment is fundamental for any economic policy striving to achieve effective equality of opportunity.

The perspective proposed here allows us to draw some general indications: first, the goal of equal opportunity for each child has to be put properly in the context of his family, as growing empirical research confirms. More specifically, the problem of initial endowment, or wealth inherited, is fundamental, although really difficult to tackle; however, the ideal of equality of opportunity is meaningless without efforts to achieve more equality of initial wealth. Second, the crucial importance of non-cognitive abilities and personal traits acquired in very early childhood stress the role and responsibility of the family; the concept of human capital needs to be enlarged and enriched accordingly. Third, distributional issues implied by assuring equal opportunity from birth to each child in a "good" society can be empirically tested against the degree of social mobility measurable in a society. In this regard, it is worth noting the persistency of intergenerational correlation in socio-economic conditions and adverse trends in social mobility, as evidenced by research in many advanced countries, including the United States, which have always seen themselves as the "land of opportunity." Despite this common belief, the intergenerational elasticity of permanent income remains high (0.6) and one in two of the children born into a household in the lowest income decile will not rise further than the lowest third. Fourth, it is always worth remembering that equality of opportunity does not imply equality of results, outcomes, income distribution, health or SES: equality in one domain such as the life opportunity inevitably implies inequality in other domains. Even at a theoretical level, ex-ante equality does almost always imply ex-post inequality, in a world of uncertainty (Hammond, 1981). The real issue is therefore determining the levels of ex-post income and social inequality, of income and (even more so) of wealth, that a society is willing to accept and, in addition, the safety net to be provided should this level not be reached.

THE ECONOMIC RISK OF CHILDBEARING AND THE FERTILITY RATE: PRIVATE VIRTUES AND SOCIAL VICES

There are major issues, ranging from the environment to the public debt, for which politicians ask citizens to make sacrifices for the sake of the future, embodied by our children; there is obvious incongruity in calling for these sacrifices while denying the children any weight as citizens. Although they do indeed represent our common future, or better our main common good, in contrast with other kinds of public goods, family and households are required to bear most of the cost of childbearing and child raising. A steady population requires a fertility rate of 2.1, but in the EU countries only France has recently come very close to this value, while for many years Germany, Italy and Spain have been recording a much lower value, which is now around 1.3, despite the contribution of new immigrants. The dramatic change in age structure of the declining population in many European countries has already had a distinct and slowing impact on potential economic growth and productivity, whose more serious and immediate consequences imply serious imbalances for the pension system and the labor market. Children are the common good of our future, but their cost is mostly a private family concern, and as a consequence an economic risk too often borne privately rather than socially. The private cost of childbearing is too high, and the common good of the future embodied by our children is therefore under provided for. The following analysis provides new empirical evidence for this claim.

Family/household size has a direct impact on the welfare of the children and the decision to have the first or a further child; the crucial point is that the risk-of-poverty rates for children increase with the number of children. For the EU-25, the child poverty rate is 19% on average: it increases from 12% for couples with one child to 14% for couples with two children and to 25% for couples with three children or more. The pattern is common to the majority of the EU countries, with the exception of Finland, Denmark and Germany (European Commission, 2008, Table A1); however, there are no exceptions for couples with three or more children, whose poverty rate is uniformly higher than that of the couples with two children. The decision to have one more child is economically risky in many countries for couples who already have one child and is much more risky in all countries for the couples with three children or more. We have to remember that the fertility rate compatible with a steady-state population is in fact the average of a statistical distribution representing the most private and decentralized family decision, the trade-off between actual and desired number of children, given economic and social constraints.

To gain a deeper understanding of the economic and social variables that influence a family's decision to have a child or one more child, we draw on a wide survey carried out by the Eurobarometer program, with regard to "Childbearing and Family Issues in Europe" (Eurobarometer Special, 2006).

The data available are for 29 European countries in 2006, on which we run two OLS cross-sections; the dependent variable is the fertility rate, whereas as independent variables we take:

a) the percentage of women aged 15–39 who when responding to the question "Generally speaking, what do you think is the ideal number of children for a family?" answered three children or more (THREE). The percentages range from a high of 46% for Sweden, 45% for Finland, France and Ireland and 41% for Denmark to a low of 7% for Romania, 8% for Austria, 16% for Portugal and Malta, 18% for Germany and 19% for Italy (*ibid.*, Table 5). This measure is intended to capture the cultural dimension of families' fertility decisions, but it is also a critical value for a stable population, given the distribution of fertility rates around the value of 2.1 children;

b) the percentage of males 15–39 who when responding to the question "According to you, how important is each of the following in the decision on whether to have or not to have a/another child?" answered referring to the working situation of the father and the working situation of the mother (*ibid.*, Table 21). The importance of the father's work (MWMALE), as viewed by the males, ranges from a high of 87% for Greece and 83% for Bulgaria to a low of 36% for Finland and 28% for Denmark. The importance of the mother's work (MWFEMALE), as viewed by the males, ranges from a high of 58% for Portugal, 55% for Turkey and 54% for Spain to a low of 17% for Denmark and Finland and 15% for France. This measure is intended to capture the family's economic constraints from the man's viewpoint;

c) the percentage of females 15–39 who when responding to the question "According to you, how important is each of the following in the decision on whether to have or not to have a/another child?" answered the working situation of the father and the working situation of the mother (*ibid.*, Table 21). The importance of the father's work (FWMALE) ranges from a high of 90% for Greece and 85% for Turkey to a low of 24% for Denmark and 34% for Finland. The importance of the mother's work (FWFEMALE) ranges from a high of 68% for Portugal and 63% for Spain to a low of 11% for Finland and 25% for France. This measure is intended to capture the family's financial constraints from the woman's point of view.

The estimates of the regressions (Table 2) show that according to the interpretation given to the dependent variables, cultural and economic

Table 2. Fertility Rates.

Variable	Coefficient	Standard Error	*t*-Statistic	Probability
C	1.860747	0.154197	12.06737	0.0000
THREE	0.006417	0.002170	2.956571	0.0069
MWMALE	−0.006522	0.002227	−2.928674	0.0073
MWFEMALE	−0.003582	0.002826	−1.267427	0.2172
R-squared	0.733470	Mean dependent variable		1.485000
Adjusted *R*-squared	0.700154	S.D. dependent variable		0.219435
S.E. of regression	0.120159	Akaike info criterion		−1.268442
Sum squared resid	0.346515	Schwarz criterion		−1.078127
Log likelihood	21.75819	*F*-statistic		22.01542
Durbin–Watson stat	2.198427	Prob(*F*-statistic)		0.000000
C	1.752875	0.145817	12.02106	0.0000
THREE	0.007203	0.002130	3.382057	0.0025
FWMALE	−0.003469	0.002315	−1.498266	0.1471
FWFEMALE	−0.005225	0.002482	−2.105105	0.0459
R-squared	0.729370	Mean dependent variable		1.485000
Adjusted *R*-squared	0.695541	S.D. dependent variable		0.219435
S.E. of regression	0.121080	Akaike info criterion		−1.253175
Sum squared resid	0.351846	Schwarz criterion		−1.062860
Log likelihood	21.54445	*F*-statistic		21.56066
Durbin–Watson stat	2.265366	Prob(*F*-statistic)		0.000001

Notes: Dependent variable: FER; method: least squares; sample: 1 28; included observations: 28. FER = fertility rates; C = constant; THREE = percentage of women who consider "ideal" a family with three children; MWMALE = percentage of males who consider the work situation of the male important; MWFEMALE = percentage of males who consider the work situation of the female important; FWMALE = percentage of women who consider the work situation of the male important; FWFEMALE = percentage of women who consider the work situation of the female important.

factors influence simultaneously a family's decision to have the first child or more children. The estimates suggest at least two interpretations:

a) the critical number of three children can, indeed, be interpreted as a cultural and social value interacting with the fathers' and mothers' financial situation, which is statistically significant from both the male and the female points of view. In others words, the fertility rate is positively influenced when three children are considered an ideal "normal" family size, as in Sweden and France, while taking into account the interaction with the family's financial situation; this appears to be a fundamental condition for achieving a stable level of population and a well-balanced age structure;

b) the work situation of the family members represents an economic constraint (negative sign) on the couple's decision to have the first or more children; estimates show that the work situation is relatively more important for the males, from their perspective, as it is relatively more important for the females, from their perspective. It is however true that in absolute terms, the importance of the male's work, from the male perspective, is uniformly higher than the importance of female's work, from the female perspective.

As is revealed quite clearly by the cases of France and Sweden, having one or more children is therefore less risky in the countries where the ideal family size of three children can be considered "normal," given a distribution of fertility rates around this value and institutions which support this common and shared knowledge in financial terms; in the European countries, financial constraints are revealed as being crucial for the planning of offspring. As a consequence, the ex-ante number of desired children does not materialize as the ex-post actual number, and although the mean ideal number of children is above 2.1 for males and females in all countries, with an average of 2.25 for EU-15 and EU-25, the fertility rate is well below this value for many countries such as Germany, Italy and Spain, and with the exception of a few countries such as France and Sweden. Along with cultural values, there are financial and other interacting constraints, and our estimates are compatible with this empirical evidence. According to the survey, financial constraints may be relaxed with work income, more so for the male, together with a policy of income transfers, as shown previously. A policy for improving job opportunities and family income stability for men and women is crucial for the relaxation of financial constraints, as are policies for improving the reconciliation of work with family life; together with a comprehensive policy for social transfers to the family, this policy can help to reduce the financial risk of having more children.

Private costs interact at the intergenerational level with some of the most pressing social macroeconomic issues in European economies, particularly for the labor market and even more so for the pension system, which is basically a problem of transferring goods, services, assets and purchasing power over time for each generational cohort, from youth to old age. The proper working of a pension system implies that society will have a future in the long run and a balanced age population structure; this is not the present situation. The old-age-dependency ratio, that is the percentage ratio between the total number of persons aged 65 or over and the number of persons of working age, 15–64, was highest in Germany and Italy (30.4) and lowest for countries such as France (25.0) and the Czech Republic (20.5) (Eurostat, 2008). The average for the EU-27, which will be 25.9 in 2010, is projected to reach the ratio of 31.05 in 2020, 38.04 in 2030, 45.36 in 2040 and 50.42 in 2050. Addressing the financial imbalance of the pension system implies dealing with the consequences of the problem rather than its original cause, which is the gap between the actual and desired number of children. Children are a common good, whose costs are born mostly privately while their wider benefits are commonly shared; this is an example of the private virtue of the family corresponding to a public vice in the political system. In fact, despite its importance, economic policy regarding the family and children is in general rather meager, and the extent to which politicians are willing to listen to children becomes a basic issue concerning both economic efficiency and social justice. The question arises as to whether we can create channels and incentives that can implement the social goals of children's well-being, with a view to the future of democratic societies.

DO SUFFRAGE AND POLITICAL "SYMPATHY" MATTER FOR THE ACHIEVEMENT OF SOCIAL OUTCOMES?

We ask therefore whether a change in suffrage, namely its extension, or a more "sympathetic" parliamentary assembly (to be defined later) could modify the outcome of political decisions. Changes in the eligibility to vote at political elections span at least two centuries of history, following a pattern of a gradual extension of male suffrage until universal suffrage for male adults is reached, and a subsequent extension of the suffrage to woman, then a gradual lowering of the minimum age to vote; the pattern has been that of diffusion, with one country starting and the others following suit.

The first country to introduce universal adult male suffrage was France as of 1792, with no property or tax restrictions for eligibility; it is however in the period 1848–1918 that the diffusion of universal male suffrage reached its highest momentum. The democratic upsurge for universal suffrage in Europe was accompanied by the diffusion of social reforms, with the German Reich taking the lead "for the foundations of a much praised and widely imitated policy of social insurance ... [and] also the roots of an effective policy of workers' protection and of a socially conceived labor legislation" (Hentschel, 1989, p. 755). For that period Rimlinger (1989, p. 599) notes that

> there is a general pattern in the emergence of social security programs. The right to compensation for industrial injuries regardless of fault almost everywhere preceded any other form of income protection. Most European countries guaranteed this right before 1914. The next program introduced was usually sickness or pensions in case of disability or old age.

With regard to women's universal suffrage, the first example was Wyoming in 1869, spreading from there to the United States as a whole and Europe, where Finland was the first country, in 1904, which extended the right to vote to women. Again the pattern of diffusion is repeated with Germany, Austria and Russia following suit in 1918, but it took many decades to reach Switzerland (1971), Portugal (1976), Lichtenstein (1984), Kazakhstan and Moldavia (1993) (Bard, 2001, p. 459). The possible relationship between the extension of universal suffrage and the birth of the twentieth-century welfare state is worthy of further analysis.

Some recent academic works have put this insight on firmer ground, taking advantage of the availability of more detailed data and some significant "historical experiments." Husted and Kenny (1997) draw on the social and behavioral break brought about in the United States by two voting rights acts: the first, in 1965, asserted the non-constitutionality of poll-taxes (implementing the Twenty-Fourth Amendment to the US Constitution, prohibiting poll taxes), whereas the 1965–1970 Voting Rights Act prohibited literacy tests, which were known to lower voter turnout, to the disadvantage of lower income voters. The authors' econometric estimates show that poll taxes and, to a minor extent, literacy tests do indeed have an impact on welfare spending: their central result is that welfare spending increases as the pivotal voter becomes poorer. They conclude that "welfare spending rises as political power shifts from a state's richer citizens to its poorer citizens. The elimination of poll taxes, a fall in the income of voters relative to that of population, and a shift from Republican to Democratic control all lead to higher welfare spending." Using a similar approach, Abrams and Settle (1999) consider the case of Switzerland, where the female franchise was granted recently (in 1971), showing that the extension of eligibility brought about an increase in social welfare spending, as well as of the overall size of the Swiss government.

Lott and Kenny (1999) take advantage of the fact that granting the right to vote to women took place across the United States over many years, both during and after World War I, allowing them to pinpoint with more accuracy the effect on turnout, spending and revenues. On the basis of their estimates, granting women the right to vote increased the turnout and an immediate rise in public expenditure (14%), which further increased to 28% over 45 years. Education, sanitation and hospitals seem to be the main expenditure items influenced by the extension of women's suffrage. Women's electoral impact is clearly significant and large, especially in terms of the gender gap, but still requires a convincing explanation. A further qualification is suggested by Campiglio (2005), who points to the significant correlation for European countries between the percentage of women appointed to ministerial positions and the percentage of GDP devoted to public expenditure for children and the family.

To explain why the extension of the suffrage to women has this effect, we can draw on the concept of sympathy to which Adam Smith devotes the first chapter of his "Theory of Moral Sentiments." Following Smith (1761),

> As we have no immediate experience of what other men feel, we can form no idea of the manner in which they are affected, but by conceiving what we ourselves should feel in the like situation ... sympathy, though its meaning was, perhaps, originally the same, may now, however, without much impropriety, be made use of to denote our fellow-feeling with any passion whatever ... sympathy, therefore, does not arise so much from the view of the passion, as from that of the situation which excites it ... [and, as an example, Smith asks] What are the pangs of a mother, when she hears the moaning of her infant that during the agony of disease cannot express what it feels?

This seems a convincing explanation of why women and poor people would favor with their vote an extension of welfare expenditure, either for their personal needs or out of their (Smithian) sympathy for how other people live. This line of argument is consistent with recent results that show how even political decision-making can be influenced by the "sympathy" of the legislator for her or his own family (Washington, 2008).

On the basis of historical and empirical evidence, we conclude that the extension of suffrage is very important for achieving a given social goal such as a wider and better welfare system. In Europe, the welfare system would have been shaped differently under different suffrage rules; in the United States, the welfare system would probably be different and wider were there a much higher turnout at the political elections. Eligibility rules and women make a difference in achieving the goal of a better life for children.

WHO SHOULD REPRESENT THE ECONOMIC INTEREST OF MINORS POLITICALLY?

Democracy is an instrument that should enable citizens to achieve participation in the political process and represent their interests; according to the prevailing view, participation is not a value in itself but rather a way for each individual to express his or her own good or interests, to be counted equally in a social decision-making process through which a social goal, deemed "good," is chosen by a community. As shown earlier, eligibility rules are crucial in defining and achieving a given social outcome, and therefore, it seems odd to exclude children from the count. Indeed, we suggested that the problem of the "missing children" dramatically distorts resource allocation, worsening their well-being and undermining any reasonable notion of equal opportunity, central to all democracies. We may take the view that democracy is a process of participation by competent adults, but even so the difference in position between parents of children and individuals without any offspring should be acknowledged, and the former weighted according to the number of children they have.

The question of children's political representation therefore calls for an urgent solution, without which generations of young people will continue to be excluded from democracy – which itself cannot be considered fully realized. The problem of children's political representation is deep-rooted in the conventional wisdom of past history, but nonetheless is indirectly coming to public attention; in this regard Austria's recent decision to lower the voting age to 16 (as of 2008) represents a turning point, as do the reasons for which the decision was taken by the Austrian Parliament, with a large majority. Austria's Chancellor Alfred Gusenbauer advocated the measure "as a means to react to the population aging and caring for the youth"; the decision took other European countries by surprise, and as in the past, other countries are likely to follow suit sooner or later. The crucial point is that the decision reflects uneasiness regarding tackling the deeper question of how to represent children's interests politically.

At the same time, we have to record a historically significant official declaration by the European Parliament whose general acceptance of the idea is a sign, which should not overlooked, even though it is without practical consequences. The Castex Report (European Parliament, 2008) on the demographic future of Europe, approved by a large majority as the European Parliament's Resolution of 21 February 2008 declares (art. 102) that it "considers that the crucial issue in an ageing society is that of the political representation of minors, who represent the common future (and hence the political future) of the community, yet currently have no voice and exert no influence in decision-making." In the same session, it was acknowledged as an Opinion of the Committee on Civil Liberties, Justice and Home Affairs, that (art.3) "an increase in the birth rate is a priority; it is emphasized that this priority can be pursued through efficient family and social policies fighting the poverty of certain families, reducing the number of children at risk of poverty and promoting equal opportunities."

If we assume that the Parliament is expressing some socially desirable goals, the question arises of which mechanism, and therefore which kind of political rules and incentives, can be used to ensure their achievement. One could argue that some European countries are much closer to achieving these goals without introducing any new mechanisms, as in the case of France and Scandinavian countries. It is arguable that in the Scandinavian countries concern about keeping the economy growing, in the face of the risk of a smaller and declining population, is probably the main drive behind a deliberate policy in favor of a higher fertility rate, even though the level of children's well-being is not yet satisfactory. It would still be the case that political competition arising from children's political representation would improve public efforts to promote their equality of opportunities, especially with regard to inequalities arising from the economic conditions of their childhood.

The case of France is in many ways subtler: as Pedersen (1993) convincingly shows, France, with its renowned favorable approach to family and children, is in fact the unintended outcome of quite different and less worthy motivations, such as the view of children as future soldiers. Pedersen's conclusion is that "children should be seen in part as a collective charge ... a greater recognition of the claims of children form a necessary pillar to any modern welfare state" (Pedersen, 1993, p. 426); the same approach is argued by Gosta Esping-Andersen (2002, p. 26). The policy problem is how the new child-centered welfare state he convincingly sustains could be implemented. Counting on politicians' benevolence or their farsightedness is bound to lead to disappointment for the reason so well anticipated by Stuart Mill, whereas (Smithian) sympathy, exercised by women in parliament, would be a step forward but still a modest second-best.

PARENTS REPRESENT THEIR CHILDREN'S INTERESTS IN EVERYDAY LIFE: WHY NOT IN POLITICS TOO?

The idea that parents could represent their children politically goes back, as far as we know, to Antonio Rosmini, who in Proposition 8 of his constitutional project of 1848 proposed that a man could cast his vote as the representative of his children and wife: it took about century to complete women's universal suffrage while, it has to be admitted, the push was not equally strong for attributing the right to vote to parents as representatives of their children. There have been some attempts in France, documented and analyzed by Van Parijs (1998), and more recently in Germany, but without sufficient strength and conviction to achieve the necessary political support.

Indeed the very notion that parents could cast a vote in the name and interest of their children seems bewildering to those who, erroneously, assume that a child has a political opinion that could be represented by the parents; parents represent their children's interest in everyday life, sometimes on matters of life and death, and it is hard to understand why they should be barred from representing them at elections too. In many countries, parents, already vote for their children in elections for class representatives in school councils. Parents represent their children's interest according to the principle of "one man, one vote": if a parent has two children in different classes at the same school he/she will vote twice. Democracy in schools means allowing the parents to participate in the name and interest of their children through their elected representatives in the school decision-making processes. Allowing parents to choose political representatives in the name of their children follows the same idea.

The crucial point that needs to be grasped is that the driving force for a mechanism of complete universal suffrage is *not* how parents can represent the political preferences of their offspring, which is obviously meaningless especially when children are very young, but rather how their needs and votes, proxied by their parents, could become a vital issue on the agenda of each party and indeed politician, who would try to win an election by taking the demands of the enlarged constituency into account. The driving force would be political competition, and we know that franchise rules make a difference in determining socially desirable goals; universal suffrage extended to each newborn child is a system which would, at last, reconcile the long-term view of society with the short-term view of the political process. Moreover, the view of democracy as participation and dialogue would achieve completeness, granting parents a right on the same ground to those with no children.

Children's voting rights, exercised on their behalf by their parents, is now a missing link in the social chain which brings together all the member of a given community; a democracy that leaves its future to the short-sighted political process is bound to fail, sooner or later. Moreover, minors' exclusion from the status of citizen is a form of age discrimination which it is hard to defend. This missing link is the cause of embarrassment and puzzle on many critical issues: for example Bennet (2003) points to the problem of defining the size of the population on which to fix constituency boundaries for elections. The inclusion or exclusion of minors can make a big difference and for this reason the matter has been the subject of two judicial sentences by the US Supreme Court. Moreover, if one applied the old dictum "no taxation without representation," there is no doubt that children, as members of a family taking financial decisions, do indirectly pay taxes, without being represented.

The growing generational imbalances we are trying to tackle are probably the reason why a number of scholars from different cultural backgrounds have recently made the same proposal of extending the franchise to children; they include Campiglio (1997), Schmitter (2000) and Bennet (2003), all of whom have made the same proposal independently from the point of view respectively of the economist, the political scientist and the scholar of law. The system by which to assign to each parent the right to vote on behalf of their children is still a matter of debate: Campiglio (2005) favors giving the vote to the mother, because she usually better understands the child's needs, especially at an early age, and furthermore ,this is a simpler eligibility rule that could favor better political competition, given the low number of women appointed as ministers in national parliaments. Other scholars prefer different schemes such as splitting delegation according to the age of the children, for example the mother until the age of 9 and the father from 10 to 18, or alternating the delegation of voting between the mother and the father; still other schemes can be conceived, but we think this represents a secondary task upon which agreement would be easy to achieve. The main task is to convince scholars, politicians and the people to recognize the problem as such, asking them to find a better solution. As Keynes aptly wrote in 1936, at the end of the introduction to "The General Theory of Employment, Interest and Money": "The difficulty lies, not in the new ideas, but in escaping from the old ones, which ramify, for those brought up as most of us have been, into every corner of our minds."

CONCLUSIONS

We have shown how economic inefficiency and generational injustice is the inevitable consequence, in the market as well as in the political process, of the lack of child representation and the consequent lack of information about children's interests. Intergenerational equality is a fundamental problem, to the disadvantage of the young and especially the very young; we draw attention to the importance of enriching the concept of human capital to include values and personal traits, which are mainly acquired through the family in early childhood. Private and public expenditure during this early period of a child's life is more in the nature of an irreversible investment rather than an expenditure. We provide empirical estimates showing that social security expenditures for the family, children and the disabled are especially effective in reducing the number of children at risk of poverty; we provide further empirical results concerning the impact of economic and work constraints on the decision to have one or more children, as well as the interacting notion of what the ideal size of a normal family is. We show that changing the extent of suffrage has a significant impact on political decisions, both directly through political competition and indirectly through female sympathy. We discuss the merit of extending universal suffrage to minors as of birth, with delegation to their parents while the offspring are under age, and we underline the importance of focusing on political competition as the main driving force for achieving the desired goal. Children's well-being will rank very highly on the political agenda of parties and politicians if their needs become decisive for winning elections. Children are not imagined as having political preferences which parents should translate in votes; rather parents are only required to seek their children's interest, as they hopefully do in everyday life. Competition between parties and politicians trying to win elections is the mechanism on which we can really count to achieve the desired social goal of improved well-being for children.

REFERENCES

Abrams, B. A., & Settle, R. (1999). Women's suffrage and the growth of the welfare state. *Public Choice*, *100*, 289–300.

Arrow, K. (1973). Some ordinalist-utilitarian notes on Rawls's theory of justice. *Journal of Philosophy*, *70*, 245–263. Reprinted in Collected Papers of Kenneth Arrow, *Social Choice and Justice*. The Belknap Press of Harvard University Press, 1983.

Arrow, K. (2004). Path dependence and competitive equilibrium. In: T. W. Guinnane, W. A. Sundstrom & W. Whatley (Eds), *History matters: Essays on economic growth, technology, demographic change* (pp. 23–35). Stanford: Stanford University Press.

Arrow, K., & Hahn, F. (1971). *General competitive analysis*. Amsterdam: North Holland.

Bard, C. (2001). Femmes (droit de vote des). In: P. Perrinau & D. Mouchard (Eds), *Dictionnaire du vote*. Paris: Presses Universitaire de France.

Bennet, R. W. (2003). *Talking it through. Puzzles of American democracy*. Ithaca, NY: Cornell University Press.

Campiglio, L. (1997). Political participation, voting and economic policy: Three problems of modern democracies. In: A. Breton, G. Galeotti, P. Salmon & R. Wintrobe (Eds), *Understanding democracy. Economic and political perspectives* (pp. 196–208). Cambridge: Cambridge University Press.

Campiglio, L. (2005). *Prima le donne e i bambini. Chi rappresenta i minorenni?* Bologna: Il Mulino.

Dahl, R. A. (1989). *Democracy and its critics*. New Haven and London: Yale University Press.

David, P. (2007). Path dependence: A foundational concept for historical science. *Cliometrica*, *1*, 91–114.

Esping-Andersen, G. (2002). A child-centered social investment strategy. In: G. Esping-Andersen, D. Gallie, A. Hemerijk & J. Myers (Eds), *Why we need a new welfare state*. Oxford: Oxford University Press.

Eurobarometer Special. (2006). *Childbearing preferences and family issues in Europe*. European Commission, October.

European Commission. (2008). *Child poverty and well-being in the EU*. European Commission.

European Parliament. (2008). *Report on the demographic future of Europe*. A6-0024/2008, Rapporteur: Francois Castex, 30 January 2008.

Eurostat. (2008). Old-age – dependency ratio-%, 2008, Dataset, Code TSDDE510, last update 20.05.2009; Projected old-age – dependency ratio, Dataset, Code TSDDE511, last update 14.05.2008.

Feinstein, L. (2003). Inequality in the early cognitive development of British children in the 1970 cohort. *Economica*, *70*(277), 73–97.

Hammond, P. J. (1981). Ex-ante and ex-post welfare optimality under uncertainty. *Economica*, *48*(191), 235–250.

Heckman, J. J. (2008). Schools, skills, and synapses. *Economic Inquiry*, *46*(3), 289–324.

Heckman, J. J., & Masterov, D. V. (2007). *The productivity argument for investing in young children*. NBER Working Paper Series, Working Paper 13016, April.

Hentschel, V. (1989). German economic and social policy, 1815–1939. In: *The Cambridge Economic History of Europe. VIII. The industrial economies: The development of economic and social policies*. Cambridge: Cambridge University Press.

Hirschman, A. O. (1970). *Exit, voice and loyalty*. Cambridge, MA: Harvard University Press.

Hurwicz, L. (1972). On informationally decentralized systems. In: C. B. McGuire & R. Radner (Eds), *Decision and organization: A volume in honor of Jacob Marshack* (pp. 297–336). North-Holland: Amsterdam.

Hurwicz, L. (2006). *Designing economic mechanism*. Cambridge: Cambridge University Press.

Husted, T., & Kenny, L. (1997). The effect of the expansion of the voting franchise on the size of government. *The Journal of Political Economy*, *105*(1), 54–82.

Keynes, J. (1936). *The general theory of employment interest and money*. New York: Macmillan St Martin's Press.

Lott, J., & Kenny, L. (1999). Did women's suffrage change the size and scope of government? *The Journal of Political Economy*, *107*(6), 1163–1198.

Marx, K., & Engels, F. (1848). *Manifest der Kommunistischen Partei*. Italian translation Manifesto del partito comunista, Editori Riuniti, 2001.

Mill, J. S. (1861). Consideration on representative government. In: J. S. Mill (Ed.), *On liberty and other essays*. New York: Oxford University Press.

OECD. (2008). *Growing unequal? Income distribution and poverty in OECD countries.* Paris: OECD.

Pedersen, S. (1993). *Family, dependence, and the origins of the welfare state. Britain and France 1914–1945.* Cambridge: Cambridge University Press.

Rawls, J. (1971). *A theory of justice.* Oxford: Oxford University Press.

Rimlinger, G. S. (1989). Labour and the state on the continent, 1800–1939. In: *The Cambridge economic history of Europe. VIII. The industrial economies: The development of economic and social policies.* Cambridge: Cambridge University Press.

Romer, J. (2000). Equality of opportunity. In: K. Arrow, S. Bowles & S. Durlauf (Eds), *Meritocracy and economic inequality.* New Jersey: Princeton University Press.

Schmitter, P. C. (2000). *How to democratize the European union – and why bother?* Lanham, MD: Rowman & Littlefield.

Schumpeter, J. A. (1942). *Capitalism, socialism and democracy* (Oxford University Press: Oxford, 1998). Harper & Row Publishers: New York.

Sen, A. (2000). Merit and justice. In: K. Arrow, S. Bowles & S. Durlauf (Eds), *Meritocracy and economic inequality.* New Jersey: Princeton University Press.

Smith, A. (1761). *The theory of moral sentiments* (1976.). Oxford: Oxford University Press.

UNICEF and Innocenti Research Centre. (2007). *Child poverty in perspective: An overview of child-well being in rich countries. Innocenti Report Card* 7, 2007. UNICEF Innocenti Research Centre: Florence.

United Nation. (2008). *Demographic yearbook 2006.* New York.

Van Parijs, P. (1997). *Real freedom.* Oxford: Oxford University Press.

Van Parijs, P. (1998). The disfranchisement of the elderly, and other attempts to secure intergenerational justice. *Philosophy and Public Affairs, 27*(4), 292–333.

Varian, H. (1992). *Microeconomic analysis.* New York: W. W. Norton & Company.

Washington, E. L. (2008). Female socialization: How daughters affect their legislator fathers' voting on women's issues. *American Economic Review, 98*(1), 311–332.

Young, M. (1958). *The rise of the meritocracy, 1870–2033.* London: Thames and Hudson.

TOO MANY CHILDREN LEFT BEHIND: THE INADEQUACY OF INTERNATIONAL HUMAN RIGHTS LAW VIS-À-VIS THE CHILD

Alison M. S. Watson

On January 8, 2002, President George W. Bush signed into law, amidst significant publicity, the No Child Left Behind Act (NCLB), a piece of legislation designed to ensure that all American children would have access to high quality education. The Act was seen by commentators as potentially 'the most important piece of federal education legislation' in four decades (Rudalevige, 2003, p. 23) and came hard on the heels of other US government initiatives to address the status of childhood in America in the twenty-first century, covering areas as diverse as childhood obesity, youth crime and the challenges posed to childhood by the increase in new technologies such as computer gaming and the Internet. At the same time, however, as such concerns regarding the conditions of contemporary American childhood continued, and continue, to grow, the United States remains the furthest away from ratification of the United Nations Convention on the Rights of the Child (UNCRC), something which arguably carries undesirable consequences in terms of the credibility of the rights regime as it relates to the child, not only in the United States but also in the wider global arena (Almog & Bendor, 2004, p. 284). Moreover, such difficulties are intensified when considered within a wider international

Structural, Historical, and Comparative Perspectives
Sociological Studies of Children and Youth, Volume 12, 249–271
Copyright © 2009 by Emerald Group Publishing Limited
All rights of reproduction in any form reserved
ISSN: 1537-4661/doi:10.1108/S1537-4661(2009)0000012015

human rights regime where 'problems of agreement, interpretation, and enforcement inhere even in the most minimalist formulations of human rights' (Gutman, 2001, p. xii).

This chapter will examine these issues within the context of an analysis of the structures of international human rights law as they relate to the child. More than ever before, the state of childhood, as this volume suggests, is impacted by economic, political, social, cultural and technological factors that together inform the way in which the international policy regime addresses the nature of childhood itself. I would argue, however, that within this, the nature of children themselves has changed very little. Rather it is our expectations of them, and the way in which adults construct these, that continue to impact upon the framing of childhood, of children's everyday lives and, crucially, upon their ability to acquire agency within the contemporary global system. After the first section that analyses the nature of human rights and children's rights in general, this chapter will move on to examine some of the major policy issues surrounding international childhood as it exists today – conflict and radicalization, agency and activism, and disease and development. It will demonstrate that we are not so much witnessing the crisis of the child, as the crisis of the adult, because it is in the very nature of the boundary between adult and child, and the interpretation of such boundaries in international discourse, that the future place of 'children' lies.

HUMAN RIGHTS AND CHILD RIGHTS

The roots of the present human rights regime vis-a-vis children go back to the aftermath of World War I, when Eglantyne Jebb – cofounder of the Save the Children Fund – drafted, as part of her work with refugee children in the Balkans, a Children's Charter. In this document, she argued that there were certain rights for children that should be claimed and universally recognized and indeed that it was the duty of the international community to put such rights to the very forefront of their planning decisions: '[i]t is our children' Jebb argued 'who pay the heaviest price for our shortsighted economic policies, our political blunders, our wars' (Hammarberg, 1990, p. 98). What Jebb in fact created was a practical document later used as the basis for the Geneva Declaration of the Rights of the Child that was adopted by the League of Nations in September 1924 and that set out five precepts governing the 'duties' that mankind had, 'beyond and above all considerations of race, nationality or creed'. These included allowing the child to be first in receiving relief in times of distress and providing all manner of support to the 'needy' child (defined at the time as being those suffering hunger and sickness, orphans and those who were 'backward' or 'delinquent'). The language of the Declaration may have moved on, but it remains a landmark document in that it set the tone for many of the child's rights initiatives that followed, in particular, in terms of the 'children first' ethos that was to become a fundamental element in later child rights campaigns (Hammarberg, 1990, p. 98). Indeed, the 1924 Declaration has been widely depicted as a turning point for international political efforts relating to the child, and too for the advocacy movement that surrounds them, providing inspiration for many of the efforts on their behalf that were to follow. Like many of these subsequent efforts towards putting children first, however, political events overtook political will, and the attempt to improve children's lives at this time stalled as the world moved once again towards war. It would therefore be much later – in the aftermath of World War II, and following the 1948 approval by the UN General Assembly of the Universal Declaration – before the international community turned its attention once more to the welfare of the child, and it is in the work that was done during this time that the roots of the current international legal regime governing children can perhaps most clearly be recognised.

Even before the Universal Declaration was drafted, a feeling existed – within non-governmental organisations (NGOs) in particular – that a separate document specifically examining the rights of the child was justified. As early as 1946, and during its first session, the UN Social Commission (the predecessor to today's Commission for Social Development) had expressed its view that the terms of the 1924 Declaration on the Rights of the Child should be as binding on the people's of the world in 1946 as they were in 1924. This may seem an odd statement to make – particularly given that it had never actually achieved a legally binding status – however, the 1924 Declaration was arguably seen by the Social Commission as a *morally* binding document, and therefore, the international community should feel as morally bound to it as it had appeared to be over twenty years previously (Alston, 1994, p. 1). The problem with this of course, as with any discussion of human rights legislation, is that there is an assumption of a moral universalism that signals consensus, where in actuality, as Ignatieff (2001, pp. 21–2) has noted:

[h]uman rights is nothing other than a politics, one that must reconcile moral ends to concrete situations and must be prepared to make painful compromises not only between ends and means, but between ends themselves.

Nevertheless, the Social Commission's position was the first step towards getting something more concrete onto the international agenda. This was followed by the 1948 Universal Declaration (which specifically mentions children in two places – Articles 25 and 26(3)) and two years later by the adoption of a Draft Declaration on the Rights of the Child, which was subsequently, at the request of the Council, scheduled for consideration in 1951, by the Commission on Human Rights (Alston, 1994). Once again, however, political events external to the process took over. The Commission on Human Rights was preoccupied at the time with both the drafting of the International Human Rights Covenants and the arrival of the Cold War, and as a result, the Commission did not even hold a preliminary discussion of the Draft Declaration until 1957 and did not turn to any serious drafting until it met in March, 1959. The result was the adoption by the UN General Assembly, in November of that same year, of the second Declaration on the Rights of the Child, a document that remains highly significant, for a number of reasons. First, there was the Declaration's statement that '[t]he child shall enjoy special protection' (Principle 2), effectively separating children from adults as a category under international law.[1] Second, and perhaps its major contribution, was in the fact that it gave broad consent to the concept of children's rights per se. At the time, none of the major international human rights instruments, including the Universal Declaration of Human Rights and the two International Human Rights Covenants (which were then only in draft form), used the term 'children's rights' or 'rights of the child'. Instead, it appears to be that what was assumed was that since the overall corpus of human rights applied to children in the same way as to all other groups, there was no need to give any particular recognition to children. The second Declaration, on the contrary, emphasised children's emotional well-being, with the latter being seen as important not only for the welfare of any individual child, but also because of the 'social capital' that such well-being might help to engender, and the concomitant impact that this might have on the wider community. Additionally, the Declaration emphasised the need for children to have access to emergency assistance, an emphasis that has become increasingly important given the fact that the changing nature of conflict – and the impact on civilians of the so-called new wars (Kaldor, 2006) – was meant that children are more likely than ever today to become victims of war and political violence.

Despite the fact that its contemporary relevance demonstrates the efficacy of the 1959 Declaration – at least in terms of its significance as an initial step towards a coherent child rights regime – the principles did not have a strong legal basis. As a Declaration, it remained merely a statement of the standards that the international community hoped would be achieved, rather than a document that was binding upon the UN member states (Hammarberg, 1990, p. 98). It also had several shortcomings, the most striking of which was the relative absence of a wider discussion on civil and political rights (Alston, 1994). Efforts aimed at formulating a more precise set of standards were thus required to continue, and during the 1970s, discussions began with regard to the possibility of formulating a UNCRC that, unlike previous efforts, would be binding under international law and would more clearly define the obligations that states had towards their children. This would also allow the international community to bring those measures that already existed together into one comprehensive law, thus addressing the differences in standards that existed between the member states in interpreting the prevailing legislation. By this time too, there was an altered view of children and their capacities compared to when the declarations of 1924 and 1959 had been instituted, with much more of an awareness of children as social actors in their own right (Alston, 1994). As Hammarberg (1990, p. 98) notes:

> [a]mong the rights of children should not only be those related to protection and material welfare but also the rights to influence one's own situation and to take part in decisionmaking.

Thus, twenty years after the 1959 Declaration, and during the International Year of the Child, Poland submitted a proposal for a Convention on the Rights of the Child to the General Assembly, which was in turn submitted to the United Nations Commission on Human Rights. Several bodies, alongside the working group of the Commission, contributed to the drafting of the Convention – including governments, UN agencies and NGOs, who made appropriate written and oral interventions (Cohen, 1990, p. 138), and the resulting document was adopted by the General Assembly in November 1989.

The UNCRC is a wide-ranging document, providing a 'gold standard' that encourages its signatories to seek to improve children's lives, whilst acknowledging the fact that under international law every child has certain basic rights that should be upheld. These include the right for a child to have his/her own identity and to have a home and an education. The Convention also raises certain obligations that the state and the parents have to act in the best interests of the child, as well as acknowledging that children have the right to express their own opinions, and to have these opinions taken into consideration where appropriate (the now famous Article 12).

Moreover, since its inception, the UNCRC has been further enhanced to include two Optional Protocols adopted by the General Assembly in May 2000: the Optional Protocol on the Involvement of Children in Armed Conflict and the Optional Protocol on the Sale of Children, Child Prostitution and Child Pornography. These additional protocols are significant in that they address elements of children's welfare that were seen as only weakly covered in the UNCRC. For example, as Hammarberg (1990, p. 101) notes, the article that addressed the issue of children in armed conflicts:

> was weakened during the drafting process ... The reason for the setback was pressure from the US delegation. A formulation that 'no child' should take a direct part in hostilities was adopted twice with consensus, with the US delegation included. But suddenly in November/December 1988 that decision was no longer acceptable. The US delegation requested a formulation that only those below fifteen should be protected against war service. As the commission worked in the spirit of consensus the others accepted; the most conservative voice played the tune.

What is ironic, of course, is that the United States has yet to ratify the UNCRC despite the fact that the original document was in some ways weakened to attempt to ensure their agreement. That they have not yet done so is indicative not only to the contested nature of childhood itself but of the way in which the place of the child within society remains a matter for debate. Arguably childhood, as much as it is a social construct, is also a social stereotype and thus subject to all of the power dynamics that such stereotyping engenders, that is, not just in terms of the power of economic exploitation and of physical coercion but also of broader cultural or symbolic power, including the power to represent someone or something in a certain way within what Hall (1997, p. 259) has termed certain 'regimes of representation'. For children, such regimes have resulted in contrasting characterisations and often 'paradoxical features' that must be taken into account in any analysis of the boundary between adult and child (Oldman, 1994, p. 44). The result, as Wyness (1999, p. 1) has persuasively argued is that,

> a recurring set of dominant ideas within political and academic domains ... draws a generational boundary between adults and children, in the process restricting children to subordinate and protected social roles.

It is to an examination of these roles, specifically within the key policy areas of conflict, activism and development, that this chapter will now turn.

CONFLICT AND RADICALIZATION

Children have always been affected by war either directly, because they themselves are caught in the crossfire or, indeed, because they choose to take part in war as combatants, or indirectly, because they form part of the untold numbers that feel the impact of the often war-related conditions of famine, disease and economic degradation. To attempt to address these issues requires some notion of the size of the problem; however, acquiring accurate statistics is problematic. In terms of the indirect impact of war, there is little data regarding how many people are actually impacted by such conditions, and what does exist is often methodologically flawed.[2] In direct terms, there are a number of legal mechanisms in force, some of which relate to those children who actually participate in armed conflict, in whatever form, whilst others relate to the protection of civilian victims. None, however, are unproblematic. Thus, for example, Protocol No. 1 to the 1949 Geneva Conventions, which entered into force on 7 December 1979, relates to the Protection of Victims of International Armed Conflicts, making it for the first time illegal for the parties to a conflict to allow the direct participation of children under fifteen years in hostilities. After much consideration, and intense lobbying from NGOs, the drafters of the UNCRC set the same age for child recruitment, adding that the oldest children should be selected first, whilst in February 2002, a protocol to the Convention came into force, which raised the age at which governments may send soldiers into battle to eighteen. However, the age of fifteen still remains significant. With the establishment of the International Criminal Court (ICC), Article 8 of the ICC statute defines the conscription, enlistment or use in hostilities of children under the age of fifteen years. This statute also included other important measures to protect children in armed conflict, for example, special arrangements for children as victims and witnesses, and the exemption of children below the age of eighteen from prosecution by the court.[3] This does not mean, however, that the provisions for the protection of children are adequate. The inability to monitor the participation of children in armed conflict leaves the ICC statute potentially ineffective (Millard, 2001, p. 189). In the majority of situations, a government will deny involvement in an internal armed conflict (as classified by the 1949 Geneva Conventions or the 1977 Additional Protocols) believing that such a denial will place it outside the scope of bodies such as the International Committee of the Red Cross, thus making the monitoring of governmental activity more difficult (Purohit, 1995). For non-state actors, the process of monitoring is even more problematic, and therefore, the recruitment of children, by both state and non-state actors, continues with little international observation.

Even if the presence of child combatants in an internal armed conflict has been recognised, however, difficulties may still arise. Specifically, if the presence of child combatants is denied by the parties to the conflict, then it is often the case that no organization or government is willing to put at risk an often fragile peace to ensure that the children who participated receive the most appropriate post-war attention. This was the case in Mozambique, where the use of children was effectively overlooked as part of the official peace process, despite knowledge of children's involvement. Under such conditions, the issue of child combatants may be talked of behind closed doors, but not openly confronted. They are usually ignored in cease-fire negotiations and often excluded from the process of what, in UN parlance, is termed as DDR, that is, Disarmament (the collection of weapons within conflict zones and the safe storage or disposal of these weapons), Demobilisation (the formal registration and release of combatants from duty, providing assistance to help them meet immediate needs and transport back to their home communities) and Reintegration (the process of helping former combatants return to civilian life and readjust both socially and economically) (Millard, 2001, p. 191). However, once a conflict has ended, it is important that children are given the opportunity to recover and to deal with whatever range of experiences that situation has thrown at them. Indeed, the UNCRC guarantees that children should be provided with psychosocial recovery and social reintegration following such experiences (Machel, 2001). Sierra Leone's 1999 Peace Agreement, for example, though flawed, was the first to recognise the needs of child soldiers and to plan for their demobilisation and reintegration into community life. Another difficulty in the existing legal framework is that there is a conflict between the provisions of the UNCRC and the provisions of the ICC. The upholding and enforcement of the provisions of the Convention on the Rights of the Child depend on the good will of parties to it. However, in the case of child combatants, the notion of good will has been countered by the 1998 Statute of the ICC, which outlines, in Article 8, that the use of child combatants will be regarded as a crime of war. Admitting the use of child combatants is thus tantamount to admitting that a war crime has taken place. Moreover, although the UNCRC, on the whole, does not limit its applicability to governments, neither does it make its applicability to non-state parties explicit in Article 38, such that non-state actors can argue that they are not bound by its terms (Millard, 2001, p. 189). Thus, despite the international legal framework that exists to protect children and the international legal framework designed to protect human rights, the protection of the child under such measures remains inadequate – children continue to take part in conflict, and those conflicts may prove more intransigent as a result. Yet, what if this is related not only to the victimization of children in such conflict-ridden societies but also to our own adult Western notions of what we expect children to be. How, for example, can we say that children under the age of fifteen should not be recruited, or under eighteen should not fight, when we may be dealing with a society where accurate birth records do not exist and indeed where chronological age may not be something that defines the end of childhood in that particular culture. How too does the international community deal with those children who, despite the existing international legal structure, are still determined to fight? These days the criticism of the young martyrs of war are held up as a prime example of the ways in which young people are abused by adults in conflict societies, their sacrifice mythologised whilst the western liberal critique argues about their ability to demonstrate agency. Standard liberal western discourse would suggest that children do not actually want to fight and are coerced into it, but this is ascribing to them a lack of agency that is unhelpful and indeed is not borne out by the history of conflict even in the west where the bravery of youth in conflict has itself been mythologised. During World War I, for example, a large number of boys falsified their birth dates in order that they could join up, and as a result, many were younger than the official minimum age of nineteen, including some as young as fourteen. Is there any real difference between these children, and children today, or is it our own adult expectation of the nature of childhood that has altered, and indeed, how does our view of the child and their abilities change with the context in which the childhood is taking place? For example, on 22 November 2008, it was widely reported in the British news media that a thirteen-year-old girl had won the right to refuse treatment after a hospital ended its bid to force her to have a heart transplant. John Jenkins, a paediatrician and chairman of the Standards and Ethics Committee of the UK's General Medical Council (GMC), said doctors can face 'real dilemmas' in such cases (Triggle, 2008):

> We say to doctors that you have to make a judgement about whether they have the ability and maturity to weigh up the risks and understand what is happening ... What we find is that children, when they have been having treatment for many years, are often experts in their own condition.

This very brave child was correctly recognized as being able to demonstrate the agency necessary to make a very difficult, and some would say, 'adult' decision. On that very same day, it was also reported in the UK news media that a thirteen-year-old Iraqi girl had became one of the youngest ever suicide bombers, killing five Iraqi guards in Baquba, a town that has become notorious for attacks by women bombers. Reports went on to say that (Hider, 2008),

In the past militants have exploited women and youngsters for use as suicide bombers ... This callous deployment of youngsters has helped to fuel a backlash against groups such as al-Qaeda within the Sunni community.

Two girls, both aged thirteen, both making decisions about their lives – why is it assumed that the thirteen-year-old Iraqi girl must have been coerced?; why is it not the case that she has weighed up the costs and benefits and decided that killing herself in the name of her cause is the sensible thing for her to do? We do not think this, because as adults we feel that we cannot. We feel that we must always assume that the child who takes part in such a heinous act has been radicalised into doing so – and indeed to an extent they may have been, but it must also be recognised, as indeed the UN has, that their decisions are rational ones that 'may be driven by the desire to connect, be engaged, identify others who share similar interests, seek excitement and feel empowered'[4] – desires that may also be characterised as 'adult'.

This issue of whether a child volunteers to take direct part or is coerced remains problematic, but it is important for two reasons (Brett & Sprecht, 2004, p. 105). First, given that the voluntary decision to fight may have been made in response to a particular set of societal circumstances, if there has been no change in those circumstances, then there is no guarantee that they will not return to military service even if they have been successfully demobilised. Second, there is the issue of how the international legal and rights framework deals with such children. For state armies, the issue may be less complex because by definition, the state's actions will be covered by the international rules of war (thus allowing seventeen-year-olds in the United Kingdom to go into conflict zones as long as they do not pick up a gun), but for non-state groups, the legal position is entirely ambiguous. Because children cannot be seen to have actually volunteered, they are not therefore criminally accountable, which is a positive in terms of the rights of the child, but may be negative in terms of post-conflict reconstruction processes. Those who have been impacted by the crimes of the child soldier may feel that this situation is wholly inadequate and thus that there can be no real reconciliation until some form of justice has been achieved. Moreover, the irony of the way in which we currently view the child in the international system is that we will never have the structures necessary to protect the child until we recognise the level of agency that they may potentially demonstrate. As Brett and Sprecht (2004, p. 117) note,

[i]nsofar as the young people themselves are concerned, if they consider that they volunteered, this has to be taken seriously in identifying the reasons why they joined and in planning how to address them whether as a preventative or a remedial measure.

Recognition of the agency of the child thus involves recognition that they may choose to act in ways that may not be commensurate with our stereotype of what a child is and of what their childhood entails. Of course, in the post-conflict environment, this may not only be concerned with the child who has fought. For children who find themselves in a post-conflict environment that is without parental involvement, their need to guarantee their rights may be fundamental to their survival and indeed to the survival of any siblings that are in their care. For example, following the genocide in Rwanda, some orphaned children taken in by foster families found themselves the victims of land theft, something that government officials did little about (Human Rights Watch, 2003). Yet, in a similar vein to the land rights issues of women, land rights for children need to be recognised as a way of achieving human security. The problem is, of course, that for this to be the case, the concept of human security itself needs to be reimagined. Human security changes the focus such that the person – either individual or in collective – becomes the referent of security (Newman, 2001, p. 239). However, the notion of 'human security' itself has become institutionalised such that it has sometimes become just another symbol of liberal democratic stricture as opposed to a real opportunity for dialogue on the issues that lead to the continuation of conflict. Thus, the 'jury remains out', regarding whether 'human security' is a term filled with 'empty rhetoric' or whether it has indeed, as its supporters suggest, become a 'rallying cry [that] has chalked up significant accomplishments, including the signing of an anti-personnel land mines convention and the … creation of the criminal court' (Paris, 2001, p. 87). Whatever the outcome, it is fair to say that the liberal democratic model, for all its emphasis on the individual, remains an essentially top-down approach to governance, requiring no fundamental change in the notion that the state system is the optimal guardian of human rights. Thus, for children, the question remains how best to address their marginalization in such systems. Considering children as part of a 'circle of responsibility', rather than in terms of the binary opposition between adult and child, moves us beyond the zero-sum game of dealing with children as victims in conflict and post-conflict settings – to be viewed either as innocents or demons – to instead lead us to some way to deal with the agency that they may potentially claim. If they are not seen clearly as either adult or child, then their roles are not defined by the labels that are attached to them, and they can more clearly assume a place in society that is equal to others. Their acquiral of agency in turn becomes less problematic and threatening to the existing societal order, given that the impact that they may potentially have is not seen as something that takes power or authority away from others.

AGENCY AND ACTIVISM

Within the childhood studies literature, in particular, the question of children's 'agency' has become a significant site of negotiation between those who interpret children as fully competent social actors, able to make legitimate claims for the realisation of their rights, and those who advocate a univalent theory of rights that interprets 'the passage from infant to adult as a transition from object to person' (Lomasky, 1987, p. 157), their claims for rights only realised by adult actors on their behalf (Hughes, 1989). As this volume demonstrates, however, whichever view is taken, the significance of the structures that surround childhood is crucial to the realisation of their agency. Those who advocate for the significance of the UNCRC argue that it provides a positive structure within which 'active citizenry for children' can take place (Stasilius, 2002, p. 507). It does this, however, within an atmosphere where childhood is 'fetishized' (*ibid.*) as something 'other'. Indeed, this otherness is something Jones (2001, p. 173) highlights as needing acknowledgement and respect 'within the various, welcome attempts in social science study, and society more widely, to somehow bring children into various practices, to listen to their voices and to see things through their eyes'. The problem remains, however, that there is a reluctance on the part of adult decision makers to allow children into the policy process, particularly, given the current 'anti-democratic cast of neo-liberal governance' (Stasilius, 2002, p. 507). One area where this reluctance has been noticeable is in children's attempts to take an active political role in the area of child labour. Article 32 of the UNCRC states that children should not be employed in activities that are hazardous or that interfere with their education or that are harmful to their health. The International Labour Organisation (ILO) monitors child labour at an international level with, for example, ILO Convention 182 having the objective that the worst forms of child labour be eliminated by 2016. Countries that ratify these conventions commit to having in place the legal frameworks that will enforce these provisions. Too often, however, the legal frameworks that are in place are weak or indeed are unenforceable. Moreover, there remains debate concerning the extent to which children themselves are active in campaigns for labour rights. Such involvement is not new – one famous historical example is the Chicago newsboys strike of 1912 (Bekken, 2000, p. 49) – but since the creation of the UNCRC, it has become more pertinent. In particular, it demonstrates the ambivalence with which the UNCRC actually views the acquisition of labour rights and indeed of the right to work itself. As Invernizzi and Milne (2002, p. 404) note,

> On the one hand, there will be some children who will be allowed and encouraged to use their participatory rights *as long as they conform* [their emphasis] to the controls that are now subtly being imposed on them. On the other hand, those children who are attempting to claim their rights through the channel of social action that conforms to the pertinent articles of the CRC will be chastised for so doing since they are speaking out for children *who work illegally* [their emphasis].

Once again, the message appears to be that children be given the right to participate, but that the nature of that participation should conform to our (Western liberal) opinion of what it is that is appropriate for children to do. It follows that for children labouring in the developed countries in particular, their use is seen as exploitative. Nieuwenhuys argues that this creates a paradox in that by morally condemning child labour, the assumption is being made that children's place in modern society must be one of dependency and passivity. Such a denial of their capacity to legitimately act upon their environment by undertaking work that is of economic value then makes children dependent on entitlements that are guaranteed by the state (Nieuwenhuys 1996, p. 237). By denying children's labour agency, in other words, we may actually make it more likely that they will be dependant. Moreover, this constrained liberal viewpoint itself masks the reality of children's lives in the industrial north. As Invernizzi and Milne (2002, p. 406) again note,

> It is ... the impact of the lives of the 'other' rather than ourselves on which the worldwide effort to end child labour depends. An extremely good example of the kind of document on which public opinion is built has been the series of *By the Sweat & Toil of Children* reports prepared by the US Department of Labor. They are graphically well written documentations of working children in poor nations, but very carefully pass over the opportunity to look at the USA itself more than fleetingly. Studies of the USA show that numbers of children are as significant as in many other countries and that exploitation of those children is no less by any degrees. Much [the same] can be said for most other so-called advanced capitalist nations.

Much of the way in which child rights activism takes place requires the agency of interested adults to be utilized. In the contemporary international environment, there are a number of different categories of NGO, both northern and southern based, that provide advocacy for the child. First, there are those international NGOs that promote children's rights under the banner of a larger scale rights organisation or as part of an ongoing campaign in various regions. These include Human Rights Watch (HRW), which identifies children's rights as one of its issues of global concern; Amnesty International, which campaigns to uphold the rights of children and young people (see, e.g., its current campaign on child soldiers);[5] and the ILO (see, e.g., their recent economic study on the costs and benefits of eliminating child labour).[6] Second, there are international NGOs that have children as their primary campaign focus, either in terms of promoting their rights in general or within specific issue areas such as Save the Children or War Child. Defence for children international was set up during the International Year of the Child (1979) to ensure on-going, practical, systematic and concerted international action specially directed towards promoting and protecting the rights of the child.[7] Third, there are regionally based organisations, such as Casa Alianza (which works particularly to promote the rights of street children in Central America), and domestically based organisations (northern and southern) that work to improve children's welfare within a particular country or area.[8] Finally, there are also a number of umbrella organisations that represent a coalition of networks and organisations that campaign for the interests and rights of the children that they represent. Examples include Euronet, the European Children's Network, whose members share a common concern that children as a group are 'invisible' within the European Union, and the Coalition to Stop the Use of Child Soldiers (CSC), founded in 1998, which unites national, regional and international organisations and networks in Africa, Asia, Europe, Latin America and the Middle East.[9] There are, then, many experiences of child advocacy, and mechanisms for incorporating the child into international and domestic policy, and a variety of different frameworks within which it can be viewed, and policy responses that may be taken. Taken together, these experiences point to a new social movement, 'tamed' within the structures of NGOs (Kaldor, 2003, p. 86) and organised around the rights of the child, that is, arguably, of increasing significance to the public, professional and political communities.[10] Yet, children remain, in many ways, marginal to these processes. NGOs argue for the primacy of the child, but in reality, theirs is the world of adult policymakers speaking the language of other adult policymakers, when what is required is possibly an altogether different scenario, one in which the child is engaged more fully as an actor in their own right.

DEVELOPMENT AND GLOBALISATION

The World Bank recognises publicly in statements on its website:[11]

> that child labor is one of the most devastating consequences of persistent poverty and has adopted a clear position to help reduce harmful child labor through its ongoing poverty reduction efforts and new initiatives ... Since its establishment, the Global Child Labor Program (GCLP) has functioned as the Bank's focal point for child labor activities, training, capacity building and policy ...

> The overarching objectives of GCLP are to enhance the effectiveness and to increase the impact of the World Bank's work on children's issues especially in the area of translating analysis into the development of programs and projects to address child labour at the Bank's operational level. Partnerships have been and continue to be essential to achieving these objectives.

Despite such recognition, however, the World Bank has been criticised for being increasingly out of touch with development needs in the face of global economic change. Until comparatively, recently, the World Bank seemed to have accepted that social development and social equity were important elements of national development. More recently, however, this seems to have given way to a reliance on the forces of growth and, increasingly, a 'trickle down' approach (Dollar & Kraay, 2000), despite the fact that the World Bank has declared 'social capital' the 'missing link' in international development and a significant part of the framework constituted by international development discourses (Harriss, 2002). The place of children within this, despite the rhetoric, has, for the most part, been inadequate. It is either ignored or relegated to secondary status (Bradshaw, 1993, p. 134). The significance of children to development was recognised at the Millennium Summit of 2000 with the Millennium Declaration calling on the world's governments to reaffirm their duty 'to all the world's people – especially the most vulnerable, and in particular, the children of the world, to whom the future belongs'. Yet, progress towards achieving the Millennium Development goals remains patchy for reasons that are 'rooted in inequality and injustice', with major efforts in particular required if the goals related to children are going to be achieved by the designated date.[12] This is one side of the impact of the global system on children – children as passive receivers of the vagaries of international financial mismanagement.

On the contrary, the social and economic dimensions of global markets are significant for other reasons, impacting upon children's culture with the very much related notion of childhood being somehow 'lost' as a result of the exposure that children now have to what are perceived to be adult cultures. Thus, when children are targeted by multinational companies because they see them as a large market with significant purchasing power, this leads to advertising and marketing campaigns that are targeted directly at them. This in turn has led to significant concern over the effect that this has on children with concerns that this is teaching them to be consumers, conscious of material things, at the expense of social development (Smithers, 2003, p. 5). As is the case with much of that which relates to the study of childhood, there are differences in national and cultural norms that result in a heterogeneity in policy response. Even in the European Union, where it would be expected that there would be a degree of cohesion given their common legal frameworks, there remain wide differences. Thus, in Sweden, advertising that is targeted specifically at children is considered unacceptable and is therefore banned for children under twelve. On the contrary, in France, there remains a feeling that advertisements are part of the preparation of children for a future life in a consumer society, and thus, they are perceived as being far more acceptable.[13] In the United Kingdom, despite a comparatively lax advertising policy, concerns are also surfacing such that the government recently launched an inquiry into the possible harmful effects of advertising on children, in particular, whether commercial pressure had a 'negative impact'.[14] Moreover, the widespread use of the Internet by children raises concerns about their safety and, indeed, about the nature of childhood itself. Recent research finds that children's often superior abilities in using the Internet in comparison to that of their parents have the potential to result in 'a lasting reversal of the generation gap' as a result of 'young people's willingness to experiment' (Livingstone, Bober, & Helsper, 2005). Meanwhile, there is an argument that the Internet provides the potential for an alternative public sphere in which children, and other marginalized groups, can assume a wider public role. Online, children can state their political opinions, whether through comment or online votes, join pressure groups and politically debate in ways that they would be unable to do through the normal course of public political action. In reality, we have no real idea as to the extent to which children participate in this way, but by doing so, they are able to 'use the internet as a transnational public sphere' and therefore may potentially already be contributing to the invention of 'new forms of citizenship, community and political practices' (Bernal, 2006, p. 161).

This may be a form of existing political participation that governments have been slower to recognize, but others have been keen to exploit the desire for enfranchisement for negative political ends such that, for example, 'much of the propaganda posted on ... terrorist sites is focussed on Islamic youth' (Wagner, 2008, p. 22). Such sites are viewed by governments as exploitative, and they undoubtedly are, but they may also be an example of children's enfranchisement that we are unwilling to recognize, and about which there remains little real knowledge, in terms of either its impact or its extent (Hinton, 2008, p. 296).

This issue of enfranchisement raises the much larger question of the citizenship of the child, and the implications that it might have for membership of a political community. In T. H. Marshall's classic view, citizenship resulted from a collection of civil, political and social rights that taken together determine whether or not a particular individual may be recognized as a member of a political community. Such recognition, for Marshall, was fundamentally dependant on the boundaries drawn up and regulated by the nation-state; boundaries that themselves resulted in patterns of inclusion and exclusion that critical citizenship theorists would argue create 'differential opportunities for, and constraints upon, the exercise of agency' (quoted in Lister, 2003, p. 44).

In theoretical terms, the question of children and their citizenship is a significant one. If age is a reason to exclude 'citizens' from franchise, then questioning this could potentially have an impact on the rights and duties of all citizens within a given society (Ennew, 2000), at the same time challenging the overarching assumptions that continue to exist regarding who is rational, or irrational, in citizenship terms. Yet, the international community appears unready to truly examine the nature of citizenship as it pertains to the child (Bloomberg, 2000). The European Union is a case in point: as Atkinson notes, '[c]hildren are a constituency who are pan-European, but who are largely invisible in the public debate about Europe' (Atkinson, 1998, p. 2).

If children are largely absent from active participation in public debate, it may be useful to consider the question of their rights within the context of the private domain, in particular, in terms of their relationships to others. This is in keeping with a shift, now becoming apparent in the literature, 'from children per se to children in relation to others', including an increasing emphasis in the development literature 'on rationality and the significance of relationships' (Hinton, 2008, p. 289). That the family is an important consideration in examining the rights of the child is obvious. Moreover, the role of the child as citizen is particularly important in the context of the economic significance of childhood, especially the economic responsibilities of families in bringing up their children. The latter has an economic impact on society as a whole that may be significant, and therefore is often the focus of state policies of income maintenance. As Sgritta (1997, p. 393) powerfully notes,

> Not to do so [i.e. to recognise and compensate], as still happens in many countries, is the equivalent of relegating children to a position of inferiority; the equivalent of not considering children as a part of society with the right to participate in the conditions of life and well-being of the whole community; it means, after all, not considering the child as 'citizen.

Lomasky (1987, p. 165) has written of the significance of the family as the 'the major protectors of children', whilst the United States stance on the UNCRC is informed by the notion of the primacy of the family, in particular, the role of the parents. The concern, particularly on the part of conservative Christian groups, is that the UNCRC in some way undermines parental rights and authority (Kilbourne, 1999, p. 27), the implication being 'that power rests either with children or with adults, as though it is a zero-sum game' (Hinton, 2008, p. 287). There is therefore a fundamental dichotomy at the heart of the UNCRC in that, whilst it advocates for the increased participation of the child,

> international norms concerning the life of the family call on the state to protect the institution of the family and enshrine the rights of the privacy of the family. Both the duty to protect the family and privacy rights discourage direct state intervention in the life of the family. (Sullivan, 1995, p. 127)

Thus, the UNCRC effectively requires others – whether family members or NGOs – to ensure that the rights of the child are realised, thus begging the question: do children really have rights at all?, or is child participation actually a myth that has become, as Hart (2008, p. 410) suggests,

> a means, intended or otherwise, to produce compliant subjects of the state and producers/consumers within the global market. Thus, far from promoting active citizenship capable of challenging inequities and social injustice, participation may be a means of co-option and silencing.

CONCLUSION

This chapter began with an overview of the position of the United States, and a recognition that the United States, as the most powerful Western economy, leads by example: that their position on the UNCRC is lax impacts upon the rest of the international system. However, in actuality, the place of the child in the international rights regime is affected by far more that the institutional apparatus of the UNCRC and whether or not a state has signed up to it. Until we realize that it is adult perceptions of the child, and the structures that these engender that truly create the conditions of childhood, nothing for children will significantly change. Just as the discourse on gender is impacted by our own personal views of gender construction, and their impact on our own lives, so our views as adults on the place of the child in the international rights regime are impacted by our own childhoods and how we ourselves 'became'. This is no reason not to push for change, but it is a plea for recognition that our own views – negative and positive – may be limiting our narrative regarding what children today may offer us in terms of agency, activism and true social change. The question remains, of course, of what an alternative narrative might potentially include – and for this, there are a few immediate answers. First of all, it would have to include an examination of children as complete, as opposed to partial, political actors. Currently, there is a temptation to think of children as only being relevant when policies that appear to directly affect them are discussed. Thus, they are confined to discussions of issues of education, child health and, when things go wrong, youth violence. Yet to create a stable political regime requires all actors to feel enfranchised by the political environment, and continually allowing children to speak only when they are spoken to does nothing to help in the creation of vibrant democracies – the current problems with youth and political engagement in western liberal democracies are testament to this. Second, there must be the realization that the liberal call for an active civil society actually requires liberal policymakers to put their money where their mouths are and give civil society real political clout. Only by fully using the knowledge and abilities that civil society has will it be able to have the impact that their existence appears to so clearly promise. Third, the dominant policy discourse appears to favour the dominant academic discourse – policy-makers thus largely use the expertise of those who tell them what they want to hear. This is in many ways understandable, because to do otherwise entails a sometimes radical shift in the political agenda, and does not offer the short-term solutions that political expediency so clearly requires. Yet, continuing to plough in the same furrow means that there is no hope of political change. It also begs the question of whether the current policy regime actually is designed for change or whether there is more to gain for those with vested interests from the maintenance of traditional power relationships. Only by examining the significance of such vested interests, and exploring how they may be overcome, will there ever really be a notion of the true potential of childhood – and of its significance to the maintenance of human rights norms in the international system.

NOTES

1. As Näsman (1994, pp. 172–73) notes, related to this separation is 'the extent to which children are identified and made visible as individuals in public statistics, a powerful force in the political process ... a huge part of the body of public statistics and administrative registers of public agencies hides children as individual citizens and obscures the summarized life conditions of children as a social category'.
2. Deadly Connections: The War/Disease Nexus Workshop Report Vancouver, March 22–23, 2004, Human Security Centre, page 1.
3. http://www.hrw.org/children/icc.htm
4. Implementing the UN General Assembly's Counter-Terrorism Strategy: Addressing Youth Radicalisation in the Mediterranean Region. Lessons Learned, Best Practices and Recommendations, 11–12 July 2007, Rome, Italy, Co-Chairmen's Report.
5. http://web.amnesty.org/pages/childsoldiers-index-eng
6. http://www.ilo.org/public/english/standards/ipec/publ/download/2003_12_investing child.pdf
7. http://www.defence-for-children.org/
8. These could include the work of the Children's Rights Centre in South Africa and the Zimbabwe Council for the Welfare of Children.
9. The founding organisations of the CSC are Amnesty International, Defence for Children International, Human Rights Watch, International Federation Terre des Hommes, International Save the Children Alliance, Jesuit Refugee Service, the Quaker United Nations Office, Geneva, and World Vision International. In addition, the CSC maintains active links with UNICEF, the International Red Cross and Red Crescent Movement, and the Special Representative of the Secretary General for Children and Armed Conflict.
10. James R. Tompkins, Benjamin L. Brooks and Timothy J. Tompkins, Child Advocacy, History Theory and Practice, (Carolina Academic Press, 1998), p. 5.
11. http://web.worldbank.org/WBSITE/EXTERNAL/TOPICS/EXTSOCIAL PROTECTION/EXTCL/0,,menuPK:390559~pagePK:149018~piPK:149093~the SitePK:390553,00.html
12. One other issue to mention is how the face of development itself is impacted by the place of the child in the global political economy. Portraying the child as a Southern victim of the developed North impacts upon not only the perception of the child in the international system but also an infantilised perception of the South.
13. http://www.ppu.org.uk/chidren/advertising_toys_eu.html
14. http://news.bbc.co.uk/1/hi/education/7134943.stm

REFERENCES

Almog, S., & Bendor, A. L. (2004). The UN convention on the rights of the child meets the American institution: Towards a supreme law of the world. *The International Journal of Children's Rights, 11*(3), 273–289.

Alston, P. (Ed.) (1994). *The best interests of the child: Reconciling culture and human rights.* Gloucestershire: Clarendon Press.

Atkinson, A. B. (1998). EMU, macroeconomics and children. Innocenti Occasional Papers, Economic and Social Series, No. 68, Florence.

Bekken, J. (2000). 'Crumbs from the publishers' golden tables: The plight of the Chicago newsboy. *Media History, 6*(1), 45–57.

Bernal, V. (2006). Diaspora, cyberspace and political imagination: The Eritrean diaspora online. *Global Networks, 6*(2), 161–179.

Bloomberg, D. (2000). Nearly citizens? Child citizenship and the perspectives of 16–18 year olds in an Israeli 'Children's Village'. *The International Journal of Urban Labour and Leisure, 2*(2). Available at http://www.ijull.co.uk/vol2/2/000014.htm

Bradshaw, Y. W. (1993). New directions in international development research: A focus on children. *Childhood, 1*, 134–142.

Brett, R., & Sprecht, I. (2004). *Young soldiers, Why they choose to fight.* Boulder: Lynne Reinner Press.

Cohen, C. P. (1990). *Children's rights in America: United Nations convention on rights of the child compared with United States Law.* Chicago: American Bar Association.

Dollar, D., & Kraay, A. (2000). *Growth is good for the poor in Policy Research Working Paper.* World Bank.

Ennew, J. (2000). *How can we define citizenship in childhood?* in *Harvard Center for Population and Development Studies*, Working Paper Series Volume 10 No. 12.

Gutman, A. (2001). Introduction. In: M. Ignatieff (Ed.), *Human rights as politics and idolatry.* Princeton: Princeton University Press.

Hall, S. (1997). *Representation: Cultural representations and signifying practices.* Culture Media and Identities Series. London: Sage.

Hammarberg, T. (1990). The UN convention on the rights of the child and how to make it work. *Human Rights Quarterly, 12*(1), 97–105.

Harriss, J. (2002). *Depoliticizing development: The World Bank and social capital.* London: Anthem Press.

Hart, J. (2008). Children's participation and international development; Attending to the political. *International Journal of Children's Rights, 16*(3), 407–418.

Hider, J. (2008). Girl of 13 becomes youngest suicide bomber in day of carnage. *The Times Online*November 11, Available at http://www.timesonline.co.uk/tol/news/world/middle_east/article5126873.ece

Hinton, R. (2008). Children's participation and good governance: Limitations of the theoretical literature. *International Journal of Children's Rights, 16*(3), 285–300.

Hughes, J. (1989). Thinking about children. In: G. Scarre (Ed.), *Children, parents and politics* (pp. 36–51). Cambridge: Cambridge University Press.

Human Rights Watch (2003). Lasting wounds. *Human Rights Watch*, April 2.

Ignatieff, M. (2001). *Human rights as politics and idolatry.* Princeton: Princeton University Press.

Invernizzi, A., & Milne, B. (2002). Are children entitled to contribute to international policy making? A critical view of children's participation in the international campaign for the elimination of child labour. *International Journal of Children's Rights, 10*(4), 403–431.

Jones, O. (2001). 'Before the dark of reason': Some ethical and epistemological considerations on the otherness of children. *Ethics, Place and Environment, 4*(2), 173–178.

Kaldor, M. (2003). *Global civil society. An answer to war.* Cambridge: Polity Press.

Kaldor, M. (2006). *New and old wars: Organized violence in a global era.* Cambridge: Polity Press.

Kilbourne, S. (1999). Placing the convention on the rights of the child in an American context. *Human Rights Magazine, 28*(2), 22–27.

Lister, R. (2003). *Citizenship: Feminist perspectives.* New York: New York University Press.

Livingstone, S., Bober, M., & Helsper, E. (2005). *Inequalities and the digital divide in children and young people's internet use. Findings from the UK Children Go Online Project.* London: London School of Economics and Political Science.

Lomasky, L. E. (1987). *Persons, rights and the moral community.* Oxford: Oxford University Press.

Machel, G. (2001). *The impact of war on children: A review of progress since the 1996 United Nations report on the impact of armed conflict on children.* Washington: University of Washington Press.

Millard, A. S. (2001). Children in armed conflicts: Transcending legal responses. *Security Dialogue, 32*(2), 178–200.

Näsman, E (1994). Individualisation and insititutionalisation of childhood in today's Europe. In: J. Qvortrup, M. Bardy, G. B. Sgritta & H. Wintersberger (Eds), *Childhood matters. Social theory, practice and policy* (pp. 165–187). Aldershot: Avebury.

Newman, E. (2001). Human security and constructivism. *International Studies Perspectives, 2*(3), 243–248.

Nieuwenhuys, O. (1996). The paradox of child labour and anthropology. *Annual Review of Anthropology, 25,* 237–251.

Oldman, D. (1994). Adult-child relations as class relations. In: J. Qvortrup, M. Bardy, G. B. Sgritta & H. Wintersberger (Eds), *Childhood matters, social theory, practice and policy* (pp. 43–58). Aldershot: Avebury.

Paris, R. (2001). Human security: Paradigm shift or hot air. *International Security, 26*(2), 87–102.

Purohit, R. (1995). Child soldiers: An analysis of the violations of the rights of the child. *Human Rights Brief, 5*(2), 51ff.

Rudalevige, A. (2003). No child left behind: Forging a congressional compromise. In: P. E. Peterson & M. R. West (Eds), *No child left behind? The politics and practice of school accountability* (pp. 63–70). Washington, DC: Brookings Institution Press.

Sgritta, G. (1997). Inconsistencies, childhood on the economic and political agenda. *Childhood, 4*(4), 375–404.

Smithers, R. (2003). On your marks. *Guardian Education, 29*(April).

Stasilius, D. (2002). Introduction: Reconfiguring Canadian citizenship. *Citizenship Studies, 6*(4), 365–375.

Sullivan, D. (1995). The public/private distinction in international human rights law. In: J. Peters & A. Wolper (Eds), *Women's rights, human rights: International feminist perspectives* (pp. 126–134). London: Routledge.

Triggle, N. (2008). Why children have a say over care. *BBC News*, 11 November. Available at http://news.bbc.co.uk/1/hi/health/7721630.stm

Wagner, B. (2008). Electronic jihad: Experts downplay the imminent threat of cyberterrorism. *National Defense*, 1(July).

Wyness, M. G. (1999). *Contesting childhood*. London: Routledge.

CHILDREN AS BEARERS
OF THE DREAM ☆

Richard H. de Lone[†]

> Poverty, the poverty of civilized man, which is everywhere coexistent with unbounded
> wealth and luxury, is always ugly, repellent and terrible either to see or to experience; but
> when it assails the cradle, it assumes its most hideous form.
>   – John Spargo, The Bitter Cry of the Children (1906)

Americans have not ignored the facts of social and economic inequality in
our society. Inequality often troubles the American imagination, and for
well over a century the nation has periodically tried to do something about
it. Myriad programs, private and public, have been devised to deal with
aspects of poverty – to help relieve the suffering of its victims and to improve
their prospects for good health, an adequate education, and economic
opportunity. To a considerable extent, these programs have focused on
children. It is also true that public policy in the United States, when it
addresses the needs of children, has typically focused special attention on
children who live in poverty[1].

An explicit connection between children and equality in the formation of
public policy was first made 150 years ago at the birth of free and universal

☆This chapter is reprinted from Small Futures: Children, Inequality, and the Limits of Liberal
Reform by Richard H. de Lone for the Carnegie Council on Children, pp. 20–34. Harcourt
Brace Jovanovich, New York and London. The chapter is reprinted with kind permission from
Carnegie Corporation of New York. References in this chapter to other chapters pertain to the
book from which the reprint has been made.

Structural, Historical, and Comparative Perspectives
Sociological Studies of Children and Youth, Volume 12, 273–286
2009 Published by Emerald Group Publishing Limited
ISSN: 1537-4661/doi:10.1108/S1537-4661(2009)0000012016

public education in Massachusetts, which its proponent, Horace Mann, proclaimed would end poverty. The same equation was made at the turn of the century, when every city saw the creation of settlement houses in part to improve family life, when the progressives undertook to reform the public schools, and when the first White House Conference on Children was convened in 1909. Recently the same connection between a concern for equality and a concern for children can be seen in programs such as Project Head Start, compensatory education, and a host of programs for children's health and nutrition, all components of the War on Poverty in the 1960s.

CHILDREN AND EQUAL OPPORTUNITY: TYING THE KNOT

These public programs have typically been advanced on the grounds that social and economic inequality is at least partly the result of a vicious cycle that can best be broken by intervening in the victim's childhood – that poor children have poor parents who will rear them poorly to lead poor lives unless society steps in to "help." It has been generally assumed that programs of individual assistance to children caught in this cycle can enhance their social and intellectual development and therefore improve their life chances – that is, the likelihood that they will capitalize on opportunity to achieve secure, comfortable, or even rich status as adults. These are claims that programs to help individual children will help equalize opportunity for them, making the odds facing Bobby and Jimmy faker. Whether or not programs of assistance to individuals can do this is a matter of debate (and is discussed at some length in Chapter 3). But the interesting point is how quickly the hopes for more equal opportunity for all have been confused with the presumption that making opportunity more equal will reduce the overall extent of poverty or economic inequality in the society. For 150 years this has been a recurrent claim of public policy concerning children and concerning inequality.

It is quite remarkable that the marriage of children's policy and egalitarian policy has lasted so long, for the facts suggest that it has served neither children nor equality well. Sometimes the laws and programs issuing from this marriage have had benefits for some particular children and their families, but at other times they have been so warped in practice that they actually damage their intended beneficiaries. And when we look at the results in broad perspective, the record shows a repeated failure to achieve more than minimal progress toward social and economic equality in the United States, a record particularly limited in the past third of a century.

Since World War II neither the heroic efforts of the civil rights movement nor the billions of dollars spent in domestic antipoverty programs have dislodged our solid structure of inequality. In these 30-odd years the distribution of income and wealth has been virtually frozen[2]; the historic differentials separating blacks and whites in earnings and unemployment have endured.[3] Despite affirmative action and the women's movement, women's salaries for comparable work remain substantially lower than men's.[4] Despite cycles of educational reform under the banners of "basic skills" in the post-sputnik 1950s, "the open classroom" in the 1960s, or "back-to-the-basics" in the 1970s, the correlation between the socioeconomic status of a child's family and the child's school performance and attainment (years of education) seems unshakable.[5] The extent of inequality – the gap between those at the top and those at the bottom – has not diminished.

Faced with these facts, some observers urge that we simply accept the biblical maxim "The poor ye shall have always with ye." Others argue that policies and programs aimed at eliminating poverty have been either badly designed or ineptly implemented. Yet the first proposition need not be true, and the partial truth of the second misses a deeper point. America's failure over 150 years to create a genuinely egalitarian society and to eliminate the hardships and lifelong denial of opportunity that inequality means for some children can be attributed to a tangle of misconceptions almost inevitable when egalitarian policy and children's policy are bound so closely together. That the misconceptions have held firm through so many failures is testimony to how deeply rooted they are in our culture. These misconceptions – perhaps better characterized as half-truths – are the beliefs that:

– Poverty is an absolute state that one escapes by achieving a certain level of material well-being.

This misconception, enshrined in the federal government's poverty line, misses the essentially relative nature of poverty: in a given society, one is poor primarily in relationship to others and the standard of living in that society. The idea that poverty is an absolute obscures the key issue – namely, distribution, or how great the income spread is between the richest and the poorest fifths of the population.

– The cause of poverty lies in individuals and the way they develop. Specifically:

First, it is widely believed that individual inadequacies are what determine who ends up poor. Anyone who wants to succeed can do so, says the myth.

Therefore, those who do not succeed must somehow be choosing not to or must not have what it takes.

Second, it is generally assumed that if someone is inadequate, he either was born that way or suffered the wrong influences in childhood. American psychological and social thought widely subscribe to the idea that, as Wordsworth wrote, "the child is father of the man."

Third, it is widely believed that whenever inadequacy can be traced to environment rather than to genes, the probable environmental factors are no wider than the family or, at most, the neighborhood or school.

Together, these misconceptions naturally lead to assumptions that poverty can be treated by itself, without relationship to the rest of the society, that the way to treat it is to "improve" the individuals who suffer from it, and that the most fruitful time to intervene in individuals' lives is during childhood.

These beliefs, and elaborations on them, have shaped American social policy in era after era, producing programs of assistance to individual children at earlier and earlier ages, either directly or through their families. The reasoning is that such assistance will give poor children a decent chance to become competitive, economically self-sufficient, successful adults. Unfortunately, when the state and the powerful members of society undertake to "help" poor children, they often cross the fine line between enhancing development and stamping out deviance, between assisting individuals and trying to control them. When this happens, egalitarian efforts stand on their heads and become means of reinforcing inequality.

Egalitarian children's policy has also been plagued by a deep cultural ambiguity about the concept of equality itself. Equality has long been a powerful ideal, but it is also an elusive concept that makes many people uncomfortable.

Americans have sometimes agreed that beyond one-man, one-vote and equal treatment before the law, things are not "as equal" as they should be. But it is always easier to argue that position than to answer the question "How equal should they be?" Some people maintain that we should pursue absolute equality for all, or equality of condition, but the only clear standard here is the empty concept of mathematical sameness. The more popular and enduring answer has been that society should provide equality of opportunity, specifically that no individual should be denied opportunity by virtue of race, creed, sex, national origin, or other such arbitrary characteristic. But without reference to the end results (which we know to be about as unequal as they ever were in this century), it is no easy task to decide whether equality of opportunity in the competition for social prizes and economic rewards is being achieved. Finally, it is important to remember that "equal opportunity" tells us nothing about equality of condition. To use a simple example: if society consisted of a rich king and 900,000 impoverished subjects, and the king were chosen by lottery, there would be perfect equal opportunity, but little equality to cheer about.

CHANGING STRUCTURE, NOT INDIVIDUALS

The ideal that makes sense to us is that no child should face systematic hardship in the present or systematic inequalities in life chances, as many children have faced for years in this society. At his desk in the second-grade classroom, Jimmy should have as good a chance as Bobby for living a rewarding and productive life. So should every child in the classroom, boy or girl, white or nonwhite, well-off or poor. It is the purpose of this book to argue that progress toward this goal will require that social policy eschew the half-truths and directly attack the issue of social and economic inequality.

A first step in our argument is to demonstrate that the beliefs we have called half-truths are indeed just that; next, to understand their source; beyond that, to appreciate how deeply the half-truths have conditioned our view of childhood and how deeply they are rooted in our culture and its dominant institutions.

The first necessity in this analysis is a reconsideration of the historic marriage between children's policy and egalitarian policy. Unless the conceptual framework binding children's policy and egalitarian policy is considerably altered, it is hard to be optimistic about the future prospects of either. If we Americans wish children to reap the equality of opportunity that is so honored a goal of our society, we must address an issue that has, ironically, been obscured by our focus on equality of opportunity; we must attempt to create greater equality of social condition directly, not indirectly through children.

To back up this sweeping statement, this book will veer away from children per se to a consideration of the tradition of American liberalism, which has provided the matrix for thinking about children, child and family policy, and equality. We will try to demonstrate the connections between liberal social policy and the way Americans think about children and their development, arguing that many aspects of children's policy in this country have been more an effort to use children to resolve deep-seated tensions and contradictions in adult society than a genuine effort to help children themselves. By and large, the effort has failed on both fronts.

THE ORIGINS OF OUR LIBERAL IDEOLOGY

Far beyond inspiring and sustaining the half-truths that plague children's policy and egalitarian policy alike, American liberalism has provided a continuum of political institutions and public values unmatched in any other industrial nation. "Liberalism" in this context does not mean the views of liberal Democrats, but a tradition of thought – a set of axioms about man and society – that emerged in late seventeenth- and eighteenth-century European thought and became embedded in Western culture, perhaps above all in American culture.[6] Since this book argues that contradictions in the liberal tradition are exactly what cause the repeated failure of many of our best-intentioned public programs, it is worth sketching in outline what the contradictions are and where they came from.

Three ideas dominate classic liberalism: one, that a rational natural law governs the universe; two, that this natural law can be deciphered and mapped by the operations of human reason, specifically the operations of the empirical mind (this idea attended the birth of modern science); and three, that individual well-being is the ultimate point of society, as opposed, for instance, to promotion of the church, the state, or any other institution as an end in itself. This third concept, the primacy of the individual, is directly derived from the first two; natural law, the philosophers of the Enlightenment argued, conferred on man certain "inalienable rights" which were the foundation of individual freedom, and through the development and exercise of reason the individual not only gained an understanding of those rights but became, in effect, their custodian. Liberal political theory, stressing the rights of individuals rather than inherited rights, gave birth to modern democracy. Similarly, the emerging economic order of the Industrial Revolution, also endorsed and sustained by liberal ideology, was built on the prerogatives of individuals to retain the rewards of their labor, not to work for the greater glory and profit of the local baron.

The peculiar irrationality of liberalism is not that it dismisses the existence of a dark, emotional, or irrational side of human nature, but that it believes that through a particular set of political arrangements called democracy and a particular set of economic arrangements called private enterprise or the free market, an ideal and eminently rational equilibrium will be achieved in the individual and in the society at large, and thus we will have "the best of all possible worlds."

An eloquent expression of this belief is Alexander Pope's poem "An Essay on Man," a pure piece of eighteenth-century liberal theory that builds to the famous conclusion that "everything that is, is right."

> Two Principles in human nature reign;
> Self-love, to urge, and Reason, to restrain;
> Nor this a good, nor that a bad we call,
> Each works its end, to move or govern all;
> … Self-love and reason to one end aspire,
> Pain their aversion, pleasure their desire;
> But greedy that, its object would devour,
> This taste the honey, and not wound the flow'r.

Liberal theory, as Pope's lines so deftly demonstrate, is at root a psychological theory ("Two Principles in human nature reign"). In liberalism, as it was developed in the Enlightenment, both political theory and economic theory reflect this individually focused psychological underpinning.

In the political theory of democracy, best exemplified by the second of John Locke's Two Treatises of Government, the origins of government were seen as a social contract formed among reasoning individuals who consent to a duly constituted form of government to preserve their own self-interest, including the protection of their natural rights. The opening paragraphs of the Declaration of Independence are often construed as an expression of Lockean social-contract theory.[7] "Natural law" gives individuals the right to withdraw from a government that no longer preserves their "inalienable" individual rights to "life, liberty and the pursuit of happiness." Governments derive their just powers from the consent of the governed, and "all men are created equal"; each has a vote, no greater in power or influence than any other's.

In liberal economic theory, epitomized by Adam Smith's Wealth of Nations, we can see the same combination of self-love and reason, and again the individual has primacy. The pursuit of self-interest, enlightened by rational choices in a marketplace governed by the laws of supply and demand (the economic equivalent of natural law), results, in theory, in a perfect equilibrium in which production is optimally efficient and the "unseen hand" of the market (the cumulative choices and decisions, based on self-interest, of rational individuals) determines which goods are produced. Quite literally the theory of free markets claims that when markets are free, "everything that Is, is right." The implication is that in a free market all outcomes are fair, because every individual has been as free as any other to capitalize on his talents to the best of his ability. In such a situation, obviously, those who come out on top must be those who have the ability.

POLITICAL EQUALITY VS. ECONOMIC INEQUALITY: WHO WINS?

There is, as many writers have observed, a deep tension in liberal thought between the political and the economic traditions. The political tradition emphasizes the equal rights of all individuals, rights conferred by the natural law from which human reason draws its strength. The economic tradition emphasizes not so much the rights as the prerogatives of individuals in the pursuit of self-interest, for example, the accumulation of property and wealth. Rights and prerogatives often clash. The political tradition of rights embraces equality whereas the economic tradition of prerogatives leads to inequality. Perhaps this would not be troublesome if the political and economic domains were separate and distinct, but of course they are not. Economic monopolies have been widely acknowledged, from Adam Smith on, as being as potentially tyrannous as political totalitarianism, and economic power is regularly converted into political power.

The tension between the political and economic sides of the liberal tradition becomes a full-blown contradiction when history is considered. For although political rights are theoretically conferred anew as each individual reaches adulthood, economic privileges, capital, power, and opportunity can be, and are, passed on from one generation to the next. Being born rich (or poor) does not guarantee that one will stay that way, but it does make it much more likely. And liberalism, with its emphasis on the individual as maker of his or her own fate, has difficulty coming to grips with inequalities that are ordained at birth. In idealizing the individual, liberalism discounts the importance of historical forces beyond the control of the individual.

Liberal theory not only takes the individual out of time but also obscures the importance of social context. The political order is viewed as the product of individual "signatures" to the social contract, symbolized by the vote. The liberal economy is pictured as the result of individual choices, in both production and consumption. Though it is obvious that, in fact, the society as a whole – its culture, classes, and institutions – influences the way individuals think, act, develop, and choose and that the society as a whole shapes the opportunities and options available to individuals, liberal theory per se is at a loss to account for how. The "feedback" loop is generally missing: liberalism views the whole society as the product of its individual parts, and it frequently ignores the impact of the whole over time on the development of those parts. American psychology, for one highly influential example, has a propensity to focus almost exclusively on the individual and frequently fails to consider, except in a limited sense, the impact of social structure on individual development. This issue is discussed at length in Chapter 4; here, suffice it to say that while psychologists of various schools have focused on the interaction of the child and the child's environment, their definition of environment has been quite narrow, effectively limited in many studies to "Mom."

PSYCHOLOGY IN THE LIBERAL TRADITION

The thought of John Locke was seminal in forming a binding connection between liberal social theory and modern psychology. His essay Concerning Human Understanding bears much the same relationship to modern psychology as his writings on government do to modern political theory. In it he probed the nature of the individual who was elsewhere central to his social thought, arguing that there were no innate ideas – only senses that were the doorway to experience, which shaped the child's thought and, in turn, were shaped to coherence by the logical mind. In Locke's view, the child was both the object of experience and, to use a contemporary term, the processor of experience.[8]

Lockean psychology and, more generally, the psychology of the Enlightenment more or less originated the idea of development as we understand it today. The individual, acted on by experience and acting, through reason, on that experience, passes through a distinct stage of life called childhood. The child stands outside the social contract, and childhood, the time of development, is critical to the formation of the faculties that enable the individual to be party to the social contract. Proper shaping of the child, accordingly, was a way to shape a more perfect society. We can trace the influence of Locke, whose essay Some Thoughts Concerning Education wrestled with the best way to shape the experience of children, on much of pedagogic thought since the seventeenth century. It is reflected in the nineteenth-century pedagogies of Pestalozzi and Froebel and other Europeans, which in turn were the source for the pedagogic ideas of Americans from Mann through Dewey;[9] In the current stress on the importance of early childhood education; and in such apparently competing schools of educational thought as the open classroom and behaviorism, both of which share an underlying assumption about the importance of childhood experience in shaping adult patterns of thought or behavior.

The competing psychological theories from which educational theory is derived are likewise yoked together in the broad spectrum of liberal thought. Our psychologies, with only minor exceptions, are first and foremost psychologies of the individual. In Freudian theory, the pleasure and pain principles are as fundamental as they were to Pope, albeit differently treated, and both flow from experience acting on the individual. Piagetian psychology, with its emphasis on the formative influence of experience on cognition, mediated by the innate cognitive capacity of the child, can be seen as a subtle and sophisticated reworking of the Lockean dualism. The rewards and punishments of the behaviorists (whom many Freudians regard as their polar opposites) are themselves a reworking of the pleasure–pain dichotomy.

At this point, it is possible to begin to draw together some of the threads that have constituted the fabric of liberal social policy over time and to begin to understand the centrality of the child to that fabric. What liberalism provided was a remarkably complete set of basic ideas.

No system of thought – in the West, at any rate – has since arisen to displace it. The ideas of science, progress, democracy, classical economics, and human nature – as it is formally studied by psychology – are all part of the same bundle, the same broad, encompassing view of human nature, and society. This is not to suggest that liberalism is as simplistic as such a capsule treatment makes it sound or that all thought since has been a simple repetition of Locke. Quite simply, it is to suggest that the uses that liberal social policy has made of children are intrinsic, not incidental, to liberalism's basic precepts. In a nation that embraced those precepts with a "charming innocence,"[10] trying to achieve social reform by returning to the original precepts results in a powerful and peculiar conservatism. Reforms billed as "new eras" turn out to be replays of old efforts, with the same tragic flaws. This twist is particularly apparent when the logic of reform is applied to the salvation of children.

AMERICAN REFORM MOVEMENTS

The continued power of the basic liberal misperceptions in shaping American views of children and social policy can be understood by reviewing the record of liberal reform in three crucial eras – the Jacksonian period (roughly 1828–1848), when the rudimentary precepts of equal opportunity ideology took shape; the Progressive era (ca. 1895–1914), when these precepts became professionalized, bureaucratized, and deeply rooted in institutions and disciplines that are strikingly similar to those of the present; and the years from the inception of the Great Society era to the present. For while these periods differ in many important ways, and while each was characterized by internal disagreement about what to reform and how, there are striking continuities in the dominant theory and practice of reform in all three. The common concern with inequality and its handmaiden, poverty, helped produce in each era social reform movements that were expected to ameliorate social and economic inequalities. And in each era, the reformers' script was, in broad outline, a rewrite of the same play. The synopsis goes something like this:

> Social protest is triggered or accompanied by shifting economic conditions, which always produce social dislocation that disturbs the patterns of all classes. The have-nots demand change, using protest, polemics, and sometimes violence to call attention to inequalities. The threat of disorder, together with genuine moral alarm, bestirs the more affluent and influential members of the society, who gradually reach a consensus on programs to restore social harmony.

In theory, two different strategies for ameliorating inequality are always possible. One is to make profound direct changes in the means of distributing wealth and privilege in the society, changing the ground rules, the focus of decision making, the means of decision making, and the nature of decisions in both the economic and the political spheres. Some such changes happened in each era. In the Jacksonian period, the structure of banking was changed; in the Progressive era antitrust laws were established; and the income tax was instituted just thereafter; and the Great Society promoted affirmative action and briefly supported community action. But the primary emphasis of reform each time has been not on structural change, but on the second strategy – assistance to individuals.

This strategy has several familiar elements. First, instead of emphasizing redistribution of income as the means to achieve greater equality, reformers look to economic growth to make the pie larger and give everyone a bigger piece. The reformers put their faith in free-market economic theories, which argue that the market's distribution of goods, resulting from individual efforts and individual choices, is the best possible distribution. It then follows that the focus on stimulating economic growth will be subtly transmuted into a focus on stimulating individual development. (It is more than semantic coincidence that growth and development are key words in both psychology and economics, for liberalism's emphasis on the primacy of the individual suggests that growth in these two realms is intertwined.) The three periods of liberal reform each saw great emphasis placed on individual growth and development, primarily through education. In each, individual development was perceived as both the strategy for enhancing equality and a means to enhance economic growth.

It is at this point that the concept of equal opportunity comes into play and with it the emphasis on children. The economy has developed inequalities, rooted in economic status but inevitably accompanied by political and social inequalities as well. The reformers' chosen strategy for reducing inequality is, first, to stimulate economic growth so that opportunity in general will be increased; second, to make sure that anyone who has ability and exercises effort can capitalize on that opportunity (e.g., by the passage of antidiscrimination laws); and third, to provide various kinds of compensating assistance to people whose backgrounds handicap them in the race to seize opportunity. Here, liberal social theory and liberal psychology meet in policy and programs to help children, for long before child developmentalists began arguing the importance of early years, liberal society had begun to operate on the assumption that adulthood is too late to do much to influence development. So the reform eras whose histories we will review have seen the birth of common schools, of settlement houses and social work aimed at improving family life, of juvenile courts given great power over family life in the name of promoting the best interests of the child, of early childhood health programs and education programs, of parent education, and, part and parcel of all these, the growth of psychological and educational professions armed with theories that are themselves profoundly shaped by liberal precepts.

What does the effort to manage individual development do equality? Very little of benefit to children, if we can believe the data. But it does do something peculiar, even perverse, to people's perception of the issue of equality. For as professional-class reformers assume the management of individual development, their standards become the standards against which development is measured, and the child's task, as it were, becomes measuring up to these standards; the helper as manager has a substantial power over individuals. This may seem to conflict with liberalism's emphasis on "inalienable rights," but in our legal tradition, inalienable rights do not by and large apply to children.

In the liberal tradition, the emphasis on individual assistance has an ironic footnote when individuals fail to profit from the "help" they receive, the blame may be laid on the individual, not on the helper or the program. "Blaming the victim," as one writer has called it,[11] has been a pervasive habit in the history of liberal reform. At its most vicious, this practice takes the form of racism, proclaiming that the poor – especially members of a minority group who are predominantly poor – are genetically debased. Indeed, resurrection of the genetic hypothesis is often the final stage of reform. As the cycle completes itself, liberalism's emphasis on the individual proves to serve equally well as the rallying cry for social action and as the rallying cry for racism, individual blame, and reaction.

In a certain sense, the individualistic emphasis of liberal reform has been highly successful. Under the banner of equalizing opportunity, it has been possible to promote economic growth and preserve social harmony while holding out the promise of a millennium – the promise that, in the next generation, children will fulfill the dreams of their parents. As that peculiarly American admonition of parent to child, "Better yourself," suggests, the mission of childhood in this country has been defined to a considerable extent by the promise of equal opportunity.

NOTES

1. Mann's view of schooling as the "great equalizer" that prevents poverty is discussed in Chapter 2 [of from *Small Futures: Children, Inequality, and the Limits of Liberal Reform*, by Richard H. de Lone for the Carnegie Council on Children, pp. 20–34, Copyright ©1979 by Carnegie Corporation of New York].

2. See the discussion of these distributions in the Introduction [of from *Small Futures: Children, Inequality, and the Limits of Liberal Reform*, by Richard H. de Lone for the Carnegie Council on Children, pp. 20–34, Copyright ©1979 by Carnegie Corporation of New York].

3. Stanley M. Lebergott, The American Economy: Income, Wealth and Want (Princeton, NJ, 1976), concludes that the median income of black families has been between 52 and 64 percent that of white families since 1900. Occasionally, this ratio has dipped up or down a few points and in recent years there has been a dip up from 56 percent in 1965 to 64 percent in 1970; but in the 1970s this trend toward racial equality of family income has mildly reversed itself. (See Bernard E. Anderson, James R. Dimpson, et al., The State of Black America, 1978, National Urban League, p. 6). Since World War Iithe unemployment rate for black males has averaged about twice that of white males, with only modest fluctuations from this ratio, as many reviews of Bureau of Labor Statistics figures show.

4. See Manpower Report of the President (Washington, DC, April 1975) or other reviews of Bureau of Labor Statistics data discussed in the Introduction [of from *Small Futures: Children, Inequality, and the Limits of Liberal Reform*, by Richard H. de Lone for the Carnegie Council on Children, pp. 20–34, Copyright ©1979 by Carnegie Corporation of New York].

5. This well-known correlation characterizes dozens of studies, some of which are discussed in Chapter 3 [of from *Small Futures: Children, Inequality, and the Limits of Liberal Reform*, by Richard H.de Lone for the Carnegie Council on Children, pp. 20–34, Copyright ©1979 by Carnegie Corporation of New York].

6. Discussions of liberalism in this chapter and throughout this book draw generally on a large body of political theorists, with a special debt to Louis Hartz, The Liberal Tradition in America (New York, 1955).

7. A contrasting view has been voiced by Garry Wills, *Inventing America* (New York, 1978).

8. Although, Locke rejects the Cartesian concept of innate ideas and is popularly remembered for portraying the human mind as a tabula rasa, or blank slate, on which experience leaves its imprint through the senses, there did remain in his thought an implicit dualism, a belief that certain faculties of reason and judgment which operate on experience are innate, a dualism that subsequent radical empiricists tried to eliminate (see Ernst Cassirer, *The Philosophy of the Enlightenment* [Princeton, NJ, 1951], especially Chapter 3, for a discussion of these issues). The basic elements of this tension of ideas still reverberate in psychological theory.

9. On the development of American pedagogic theory in the nineteenth century, see Lawrence A. Cremin, *The American Common School: An Historic Conception* (New York, 1951), or Merle Curti, *The Social Ideas of American Educators* (Paterson, NJ, 1959). In addition to the ideas of Locke, the educational ideas of Rousseau, who represents the more radical and egalitarian path of development from liberal theory (in politics and in education), played, of course, a significant role in shaping these concepts.

10. The phrase is Louis Hartz's.

11. William Ryan, *Blaming the Victim* (New York, 1976).

CHILDHOOD: NORMALIZATION AND PROJECT[☆]

Giovanni B. Sgritta

The discovery of childhood, the delimitation of this age among the many ages of man, and the recognition of the needs specific to the social education of the child, meant the child's rescue, culturally and materially, from the "anonymity and indifference of times past, instead to become the most precious of creatures, full of promise and pregnant with a future" (Ariès, 1979, p. 551). This new status, with its host of external identifying characteristics – for example, in clothing, in play, in the style and practices of pedagogy, in the relations of everyday life, in the rules of child-raising, in hygiene, and in child welfare – was matched by an affirmation of the family as the sphere of intimacy and private life where the individual may enjoy relative autonomy from social constraints, as a locus of psychological emancipation evolving and taking root in close attunement with the political and economic emancipation attendant on the rise of bourgeois society. This was a process of a slow but progressive spread of cultural uniformity, drawing first the upper classes (the traditional nobility and the court and mercantile bourgeoisie) and then later the popular classes (Stone, 1983; Ariès, 1968) into its ambit. In measure as the family progressively embraced

[☆]This chapter is reprinted from *International Journal of Sociology*, Fall 1987, Vol. 17, No. 3, pp. 38–57. It is reprinted with permission from M.E. Sharpe, Inc. Armonk, NY, USA.

Author's extract from his Normalizzazione e progretto nella socializzazione dell'infanzia. In *Regale e socializzazione*, edited by G. B. Sgritta et al. Torino: Loescher, 1984.

Structural, Historical, and Comparative Perspectives
Sociological Studies of Children and Youth, Volume 12, 287–304
2009 Published by Emerald Group Publishing Limited
ISSN: 1537-4661/doi:10.1108/S1537-4661(2009)0000012017

more and more of the private sphere, encapsulating it progressively into the intimacy of the household, and as parents were invested with the unaccustomed responsibilities of child-raising, a specific socializing function came to be ascribed to women.

Interpretations of this phenomenon diverge widely. On the one hand, there is the view that there has been a progressive evolution of a more liberal attitude toward children, marked by a new respect for the child, an attitude that finds expression in a concerned and caring effort to comprehend the needs qualitatively peculiar to childhood (Shorter, 1978; deMause, 1976; Stone, 1983; Degler, 1980). Then, to this view is counterposed a view of a process of liberation stressing just as emphatically the limitations that such an affirmation placed on the autonomy of childhood and on its expression within the family and publicly (Ariès, 1968; Donzelot, 1977; Lasch, 1977; Rutschky, 1977; Hengst, 1981).

These contrasting views clearly stem from the very nature of the problem, its singular complexity, and from the sheer fact that as it has evolved the problem has assumed various and diverse aspects and moments susceptible of quite different interpretations. But even while acknowledging the concomitant existence of such strongly contrasting tendencies in the way society today has come to construe childhood and the sense of family, we must also keep in sight the need to understand how such manifestations may be interlinked with one another, as well as being inextricably intermeshed with changes, that is, with the emergence of other no less important processes of change that give the complex life of society its substance and forge stable and enduring links between the most intimate recesses of private life and the public world without. We must go deeper, therefore, behind the outward appearances of this new identity acquired by childhood and private life, to uncover the complex signs of a historicosocial transformation that has brought about a profound change in the whole of reality, setting new goals and imposing new tasks on the evolution of knowledge and how it is acquired in this and other broader spheres of social life.

It is surely not possible, for example, to disregard the fact that the institutionalization of childhood involved, in addition to those manifestations aforementioned, the parallel emergence of a set of expectations, demands, commands, and repressions, which in forms and modes different from the past have perdured as specific expressions of the new condition. Nor can it be ignored that the discovery of childhood also involved the imposition of a set of explicit rules on how this age of man was to be shaped, on the behavior of those encharged with doing so, on the child's physical and moral development, and on the rational definition of the phases and contexts of the learning process, to say nothing of the vast, almost overwhelming, multitude of prescriptions and controls on the spatial and temporal parameters of a child's life.

How society construes childhood, that is, that specific period in which the individual learns and is molded into a social being, is determined by the same needs that characterize the social setting as a whole. Hence, within the specific constitutive and defining context, childhood unfolds by virtue of the constitution, organization, and imposition of a set of cognitive models and basic rules to govern the activity of socialization by legitimizing the diverse practical measures required, depending on the social context. Indeed, the needs of society – that is, the needs attendant on the reproduction of social labor in determinate forms and on the relations of which society is constituted – and the mind sets and the cultural forms reflecting them, could very well come into contradiction with the "idea of education as an end in itself" (Habermas, 1971, p. 651).

CHILDHOOD: ITS AFFIRMATION AND SOCIAL CONTROL

To derive reductively "the prime driving force of change ... from *psychogenic* mutations in the personality and character structure brought about by the interaction between parents and children over the course of generations" (deMause, 1976) neglects the whole set of circumstances and relations that have accompanied the affirmation of childhood as a social space peculiar to modern society. This, in turn, means to overlook the fact that the imposition of technically elaborated forms for defining norms and for social control began at a given point in time to spread to other adjacent spheres of social life as well: not only to familial relations as regards the social condition of women, to the institutionalized segregation of madness and differentness, to the repression and prohibition of sexuality, but also to the affective level of the mechanisms of education and care, and the institutional apparatus for the punishment and control of deviance (Foucault, 1963, 1976; Donzelot, 1977).

All these domains of social practice must therefore be examined and catalogued insofar as they are collateral to and provide the context for our argument. The perspective and scope of our analysis must be modified if we wish to undertake to define the functions of a process of change which, although seem to take place in a more restricted dimension compared with the past (in the intimacy of private relations and in the orientation toward childhood) in reality extends much more broadly throughout the body social. The institutionalization of childhood and of the socializing strategem necessary to it involved the imposition of a whole new set of rules. Childhood and socialization, therefore, should be examined as they relate to the general needs of a modern economic society: namely, as part of an overall strategy for restructuring society in ways capable of making it more systematic, more effective, more constant, and more predictable in its functioning. To comprehend the sense of this change and of the organic connection between the relations of everyday life and the complex structures of society we need to know more than merely the effects inferable from our observations of life as it goes on.

At this more general level, it is the rationalizing discourse of science and technology rather than the norms dictated by tradition that give form and meaning to this transformation. The old traditional paradigm in which childhood had been framed, anchored in the harsh school of existence and authoritarian, sometimes violent practices, has also had to submit to the logic of scientificity, which to varying degrees is gradually encroaching on the different spheres of the body social, and so has emerged much more defined, more intangible, and more intricate; more indirect than direct, yet definitely more rigidly authoritarian and efficacious.

Thus does "an entire set of problems assume definition: the problem of the architecture of a system ... designed ... to permit an internal, articulate, and detailed control"; the problem of the hospital as a structure that "has gradually become an instrument of medical action"; the problem of the school, which also must obey the imperatives of control over and discipline of the learning process and of social education in the broad sense; or the problem of the huge factories and plants that have radically altered the modes of surveillance and supervision compared with the old domestic overseeing of the master and, as integral parts of the process of production and reproduction of society, must reproduce the new mode of organization of society from A to Z (Foucault, 1976, pp. 188–911).

But as Foucault observed elsewhere, the problem is not to conduct a deductive analysis of this process in terms of the traditional categories of domination, from the center or from above, by society's upper classes. Rather, we must examine the way these mechanisms are structured "to perceive that these phenomena ... have had their instruments and their logic at work at the affective level of the family, the immediate environment, the elementary units and lowest levels of society, and have responded to certain needs; we must show that, namely, the immediate environment, the family, parents, doctors, etc., have indeed been the real agents of these phenomena and processes" (Foucault, 1977, pp. 186–187).

In the system of control and surveillance that evolved with modern society, a whole set of personages emerged to take their respective places in the social panorama, in part complementing, supplanting, and making use of the traditional figures (parents, master, teacher, tutor, priest, etc.), according to the case, the socioeconomic context, and the conditions of need that call for and justify intervention. This was especially evident in the family, which in the event acquired its definition as the locus where a private space was defined and structured through the alliance established between the figure of the mother and an intricate network of professional figures: doctors, criminologists, and alienists who in the next century would be joined by social workers, psychiatrists, child development specialists, pediatricians, marriage counsellors, juvenile court judges, etc.; where the peculiar notion, centered on a cult of domesticity which, punctuated by an outward show of emancipation from the bondage of patriarchal tradition, assigned to the mother new and more burdensome chores and responsibilities in the exercise of a function growing steadily in its social importance, was necessarily accompanied by the pervasive imposition of stifling controls on the part of recognized overseers of society's more general need of rationalization; and where, finally, the rationalization of all the minute activities of family life, and of child-raising and socialization, now informed by the precepts of scientific knowledge and mediated by an ever-broader network of professional roles, required the forging of a crucial alliance between the mother and a humanitarian philanthropy that set itself the task of "reconciling the interests of the family with the interests of the state, and *pax familiorum* with the imposition of moral standards on individual behavior" (Donzelot, 1977, p. 28).

Thus there is a mutual overseeing, based on a reciprocity of interests that family figures and public authorities perceive in the exchange, although it is a reciprocity that varies depending on the circumstances and social conditions. In the bourgeois family this mutual reciprocity takes the form of a *protected liberation* [libération protegée] "within which the child's material and psychological development is encouraged, placing all the accomplishments of educational psychology at its services, even as it is discreetly watched over"; in the families of the common people, this reciprocity is based on an educational model of *supervised freedom* [liberté surveillée], the aim of which is to surround the child with increasingly hermetic and effective controls against the temptations and perils of the outside world (Donzelot, 1977, p. 48). Yet the overall result is the same, namely, that of reducing the private and social horizon of the family to the

functions of reproduction under supervision and necessarily restricting
the care of childhood to a delegated, dependent institution subordinated to
the acquisition of and a respect for uniformity and the norm, in forms and
modes that will vary depending on the family situation.

It is indeed necessary to distinguish the principal components of the
process even at the risk of annoying the reader with a seemingly rambling
list of facts or an impression of overhasty generalization, where we should
rather be attentive to the complex intricacies of the real world, to differences
among different countries and local settings, to the contradictions inherent
in affirming that there is one predominant model, thereby implicitly
imposing a typology that can be but an arbitrary and oversimplified
abstraction. But, however arbitrary such a procedure may seem, and
however justified it may indeed be here, if only because it is necessary to at
least distinguish the general trends in the transformation of attitudes toward
childhood and socializing institutions, the uniformity of the change and the
similarity of the outcomes recorded over the course of time in spheres and
countries differing so greatly among themselves remain a fact, and, as such,
a sufficient basis for asserting the validity of our argument.

To return, then, to our problem, it is a relatively uniform process that
seems to have entrenched itself at a specific period both in the family and in
the school (Chamboredon & Prévot, 1979; Donzelot, 1977) in institutions of
social services (Donzelot, 1977), in the judiciary sphere (Foucault, 1976;
Donzelot, 1977; Lasch, 1977; Riedmüller, 1981), in psychiatric aid and in
medicine (Foucault, 1963, 1969; Castel, 1980): we see a steady, progressive,
point-by-point extension of the disciplinary mechanisms lying at the basis of
the social order and its equilibrium; these are the mechanisms that enable it
to function smoothly at the most elementary levels of social life, and presume
a connection between a preeminently therapeutic need of social control, the
emergence of social pathology as a profession, and the replacement of familial control by a type of control that overarches the family, delegating to it
the discharge of necessary social functions at key points and in key contexts
within the social fabric.

PROTECTION AND CONTROL

Can we find an affirmation of childhood in modern society, an affirmation of
a child-centered cultural vision anchored in the autonomy of the private as
opposed to the public sphere; has there taken place a *libération* of the
spontaneous element of childhood, thus enabling the harmonious growth of

the child, disencumbered of the material and cultural necessities and tasks of adult society? Has there been a relaxation of disciplinary practice or, rather, a transformation of procedures, rendering them better fit for much more complex and intricate needs attendant on the dual aim of establishing norms for individual conduct and of simplifying the work of control that has been entrusted to the tacit alliance between the family and the manifold constellation of the new custodians of rule who, as Donzelot has picture-squely described, "se font mutuellement plaisir dans le mythe de la protection" [administer mutually to one another's pleasure in the myth of protection] (Donzelot, 1977, p. 134). And has an autonomous isolation of family life become a precondition for the unqualified expression of affectivity and the free play of emotions, or rather has the family been cautiously identi-fied as the social locus affording the most reliable response to the delegation of social tasks while at the same time being most receptive to conventional rules?

It is difficult to give an answer, inasmuch as it is perfectly possible for both states to be present at the same time, representing an inseparable mix of contrary processes and tendencies. But if we take the preceding observations as external signs of a long cycle, the ultimate effects of which can be readily discerned in the present condition of childhood, it is certainly possible to pinpoint the *institutionalization of childhood* as the moment that signaled the entry of the child into the symbolic universe of rules and disciplines identified with the logic and practices of technical-scientific knowledge. Similarly, the material and emotional emancipation of the private sphere, and the broader individuality and autonomy acquired by women relative to their traditional relations of dependence, and of children vis-à-vis their parents, may be seen as tangible evidence of the existence of a double regime of protection and control. These are the premonitory signs of a tendency toward a society of *normalization*, the locus of a growing power to define what is appropriate behavior, or a power to constrain, under the guise of scientific objectivity; a growing power to adapt to a projected conformity, or to rules that are to be respected: an external authority, impersonal and suprapersonal, which legitimates the possible paths and admissible solutions for achieving socially preordained goals.

These are the markings of a society of normalization which, through new mechanisms of power, seems capable of replacing the "old principle of *violence and rapine* that reigned in an economy based on power ... by the principle of *gentility, production, and profit* so as to bring the multitude of men and the abundance of production systems into line with one another (in this context, production is understood to mean not only production in the strict sense but also the production of knowledge and of attitudes in the educational system, the production of health in the hospitals, and the production of destructive might in the armed forces)" (Foucault, 1976, pp. 238–239).

THE LIQUIDATION OF CHILDHOOD:
A HYPOTHESIS

This and this only then is the vantage point from which one may grasp the connections established between the characteristic features of this transformation, so deeply entrenched at the levels of symbol and feeling, and the subsequent developments in socialization and the evolution of the cultural system into its present configuration. It is thus that we may understand the socially necessary, logical connections established among a multitude of institutional facts and behavioral strategies; the dissemination of well-defined value orientations; how childhood is affirmed at the institutional and symbolic levels; and the "discovery" of childhood as a specific and discrete age of man, as an object of pedagogical interest, and as a market and a focus for professional effort. It is thus, finally, that we can come to understand how these facts flow together in a "systematic structuring of institutions, rules, frames of reference, and instruments for defining childhood that steadily systemizes more aspects of the child" (Chamboredon & Prévot, 1979, p. 158), embracing all its respective spheres and roles in an ever more differentiated and specialized noose of tutelage and control.

Only from this vantage point, for example, with regard to relations between the generations, can we understand the subdivision of childhood into different ages and the social definition of the capacities and performances expected of each of these ages. It is worth mentioning in this context, in particular, the apparently paradoxical fact that the line marking the boundary between those ages that need to be cared for primarily at the physiological level and those ages that call for attention to cultural needs (Chamboredon & Prévot, 1979, p. 151) has been moving more and more toward the age of early childhood, effacing the differences in behavioral experiences among the different ages. These ages of childhood, in traditional societies characterized by a complex system of rigidly codified rites and ceremonies of initiation and symbolic assimilation of adult roles (Lapassade, 1971, pp. 88ff.) are today becoming increasingly compressed and unified into an undifferentiated scenario of models and types tending toward the ultimate inclusion of the entire age pyramid of the population.

A book recently published in German, *Die Liquidierung der Kindheit als objektive Tendenz*, claims that childhood "is being liquidated because today society is invading all those areas in which formerly children had been trained to meet the qualitatively different demands of adulthood. The gap between the generations is narrowing because important segments of reality either have come largely to coincide (as in leisure-time activities), or different spheres of experience (such as school and job) are similarly structured and call forth comparable appropriation processes and 'survival strategies'" (Hengst, 1981, p. 65).

Here too evidence in support of this hypothesis must necessarily be presumptive, but the presumption that such a tendency does in fact exist is not at all undermined by one quite important fact, namely, that modern childhood directly experiences its distance as regards the resolute absence of everything having to do with the world of work, its distance from the childhood of the past, as well as from the present stages of adulthood (Pancera, 1979). Indeed one can encounter this tendency in the ever-greater concern over the ends of pedagogical practice with regard to the child; in the behavior and choices that invest in various ways the child's school and preschool experience; in the invasion by the rhetoric of achievement of the domain of play and recreational activities (Lasch, 1981; Livolsi, De Lillo, & Schizzerotto, 1980); in the degeneration of the true ludic nature of sports, both notionally and substantively, into a drive to excel and into embattled competition (Köhler, 1981); in the irreversible subjugation of the world of childhood to the technological apparatus of commodity production (from the first objects with which learning begins to games for entertainment; from the instruments of leisure time activity to children's literature and the messages of the mass media, etc.); and it is to be found in the ever-growing similarity between the styles and fashions in children's clothing and the models used in adult fashions; or finally in the diminishing generational differences as regards the manifold activities of a social and material nature which, surprisingly, show parallels, if only formal, with the situation in the premodern era, described by Ariès.

To sum up, it is in the totality, or singularity, of these manifestations that we will find confirmation, direct or indirect, of a consolidated movement blurring the differences between the ages of man, and leveling the needs ascribed culturally to the different generational groups, of, in a word, a movement bent on the acculturation, colonization no less, of childhood, using models, guidelines, and frames of reference tailored to a notional image, an ideal type, of needs and experiences proper to adults. Nor is this the only sphere in which one may perceive the connections sketched out earlier. The changes that have taken place in the maternal role, and hence in family strategies of child-raising and socialization, may be explained in similar fashion, if with minor qualitative differences among the social strata. The institutionalization of childhood, and the extension of guidelines and evaluative criteria taken from science, has brought about a "professiona-lization" of the figures traditionally encharged with socialization; and it has brought about their progressive subjugation to a multitude of behavioral rules and models for utilizing social resources and social opportunities to optimize the social success of the "socialized product."

The obverse side of this change is too well known for us to need to dwell further on it here. But the same sequence of events that has produced this result has also brought about a parallel, seemingly paradoxical deterioration of the capacities and competences traditionally ascribed to those encharged with socializing the young. The permanent ambiguity and uncertainty surrounding the outcome and consequences of socialization within a complex and rapidly changing society has in fact resulted in a chronic paralysis of judgment as regards the validity of the projects and choices of socializing agents. And hence the ultimate consequence, identifiable in the form of two interdependent processes, is: the *intensification* of family life, a more attentive concentration, on the part of the family and society, on the minimal details of child-raising and on adult–child relations, on the one hand, and on the other, a *shift away* from the internal family sphere to the external social sphere, that is, a growing dependence of the family and its members on a complex constellation of external agencies of control and resocialization, a tangible sign of the functional importance to which the family has been reduced [*impuissantisation* functionelle de la famille] (Donzelot, 1977, pp. 202–204).

The relative autonomy of the family and the imputation to it of specific responsibilities in the social education of the child; the transformation of maternal activities of child-caring and child-raising into learned socializing skills; and however, the manifold invasion, the stripping of social figures of their competences; the vulgar "laicization" of the traditional agencies of socialization; the devalorization of the spontaneous – all these things together represent the two-pronged expression of the more general tendency, discussed earlier, namely the logical and practical concatenation of the two parallel processes of protection and control of childhood and family life.

Paradoxically, it was society's recognition of the importance of primary socialization within the home, and so a collective awareness of the links between the modes in which this task is carried out and its social results, which were the factors responsible for the appearance and spread of a network of "service professions of aid and assistance (Lasch, 1981, p. 250) dedicated to the control of the social risks attendant on the malfunctioning of the family and other social agencies. But the affirmation of a social and therapeutic professionalism and the extension of the jurisdiction of social experts over domestic life has not been to the detriment of patriarchal authority alone; the authority formerly exercised by women over childbirth and child-raising, and over the domestic economy has also been undermined; at the same time the potential culpability and responsibility of women have grown considerably. In alliance with the helping professions "women improved their position in the family only to fall into a new kind of dependence, the dependence of the consumer on the market and on the providers of expert services, not only for the satisfaction of her needs, but for the very definition of her needs" (Lasch, 1981, p. 27).

And so relations between parents and children are commandeered into a technical sphere operating under the general surveillance of the state and steered by an intricate system of institutions providing educational, health, and legal services. Finally, it is at this level that the more specific connections between the institutionalization of childhood and the restructuring of the institutional apparatus of society can be apprehended. It is in the profound ambiguity of this process (Baudrillard, 1976, p. 246) that the social fabric reveals in filigree the dual import of the private sphere's sham concern, on the one hand, and of the invasion of that sphere by the tutelary apparatus of the state and its service institutions, on the other. This means that the entire economics of affect and the reproduction of norms is delegated to the family, whereas at the same time it represents the "lieu névralgique de la soumission sociale de l'impossibilité d'autonomie individuelle ..." [sore spot of social subjugation, and the impossibility of individual autonomy] (Donzelot, 1977, p. 205). The traditional side of practice in dealing with childhood was shaped and drew its strength mainly from a continual rehearsal of a consistent and unchanging nucleus of elementary rules, deeply rooted in the material necessities of survival; but with the emergence of professional apparatuses and the subsumption of socializing practice under an ever-increasing number of scientific paradigms, norms themselves came to be "legitimate norms, *scientifically* founded," and so became technical knowledge in contrast to, and indeed alien to, the competence of the layman.

As Chamboredon and Prévot noted, "a deep rupture was thus affected into the relationship to childhood.... The social definition of the ages that are normal for specific functions tends to become a *scientific* definition instead of the traditional and personal definition it had been in the past. The inversion is analogous to the movement from practical to theoretical morality. The spread of such a definition is promoted by the institutionalization of psychology as the practice of caring for childhood, or at least by the institutionalization of psychology in the treatment of deviant cases – something that contributes notably, by way of constrast, to the propagation of a norm. Furthermore, the existence of a *vulgate* of child psychology and family psychology... supplants the normal conception of functions seen as discrete, disconnected behaviors unrelated to one another, by the definition of a set of consistent and cohesive behaviors. On the one hand, the separation of the various stages of childhood was so discrete that childhood came to exist in a field apart, which was considered to have no major influence on future behavior ... yet, on the other hand, the spread of psychological knowledge and of the techniques of guidance and control based on psychology ... has at the very least had the effect of tending to convince people of the great value of predicting children's behavior ..." (Chamboredon & Prévot, 1979, pp. 166–167).

The affirmation of a *defined set of disciplines* presupposes, at one and the same time, the disintegration of the personal aptitudes of the traditional socializing agents, as well as an exaggerated estimation of the importance of the intervention of the family, using the self-same techniques, into the first stages of child upbringing. In measure as the responsibility for these tasks devolves more and more on parents, the power of these formal disciplines, and of their official representatives, extends ever more broadly into the system of public and private services. The professionalization of roles traditionally delegated to parents implies, in other words, the technical delegation of these tasks to a specialized sector, whether its function be that of spreading information about techniques regarded as correct, or that of intervening where the existence of a need, or the necessity of preventing such a need, is presumed.

But the entrenchment of such a set of formal rules for the evaluation and care of children acquires a critical importance, more because of its potential indirect affects than because of the actual spread of the practices of direct therapeutic intervention. The latter are, of course, by no means of negligible importance, and the lowering of the tolerance threshold with regard to abnormality has indeed helped to broaden the forms of therapeutic intervention and control (Castel, 1982; McKnight, 1977). But the important point is that the professionalization, direct or indirect, of the activities attendant on the socializing process in effect assumes the child's psychosocial development to be "normative, or reducible to norms, so that it becomes possible for all the psychopedagogical disciplines to consider developmental states and stages and to ascribe a pathological etiology to any deviation from the norm" (Wambach, 1981, p. 220). The implication is that the erection of an edifice of scientific and technical norms for the child and for society's conception of childhood constitutes, in turn, the precondition for the continuous production of increasingly more specific and detailed rules of conduct and, hence, as a corollary, for the detection of corresponding anomalies in the behavioral practices of both the socializing agent and the socialized subject.

THE AMBIVALENCE OF THE
SOCIALIZING PROCESS

There are, of course, numerous aspects and problems which remain outside the scope of this chapter and which, if they were considered, would certainly provide a much more uneven and erratic picture of the processes of socialization and control in present-day society, in all their variegated characteristics and forms (thereby at the same time documenting the inherent complexity of the body social in this domain and perhaps also the futility of trying to force the kaleidoscopic diversity of its manifestations into a single coherent framework); it seems legitimate, nonetheless, bearing in mind these reservations, to endeavor to improvise a rough, tentative balance sheet from this analysis. To continue, then, there seems to be a general tendency discernible from the beginning with the emergence of modern society, toward a progressive expansion of a *disciplinary apparatus* which, by grafting itself onto the traditional core of parent–child relations, and from there extending beyond it into a multiplicity of nonfamilial contexts, has imposed on social life a growing normative regulation of socializing behaviors and techniques. A very specific image of childhood has thus been fashioned through this use of socializing techniques to regiment social conduct. And it has provided categories and criteria for classifying and evaluating the child and the different aptitudes presumed to correspond to the different periods of child development, and for assessing the extent to which the different phases in the formative process conform to, and are in consonance with, the ends of socialization. Intent on establishing the normative conditions of a child's social upbringing, this tendency has in fact projected a general code onto the entire cultural superstructure and institutional apparatus – a code that sees the child mainly as the instrument and a symptom, the vehicle and the expression, respectively, of the normative institutionalization of the social order and its chronically precarious condition, in short, of its successes and of its failures. And as a consequence it has deprived the child and our conception of childhood of those qualities that alone can be conducive to the constitution of a new social existence, a new "social birth," qualities that are perceivable in abstraction in the possibility of affirming a set of *countervalues* in opposition to a whole list, also abstractly determinable, of social *values* that have become *dysfunctional*; in the hypothetical prospect of a reversal of the traditional direction of learning (from childhood to adulthood rather than vice versa); in the affirmation of a multiplicity of discrete personal projects or in the view that sees childhood as the expression and reliable measure (because it is extraneous to entrenched social interests) of a model of social development characterized by a more tangible awareness and appreciation of the quality of life; in the affirmation, finally, of those qualities that would permit the symbolic use of childhood not only as the vehicle of the *continuity* of social reproduction but also as the modality and social locus for *arresting* social processes and social patterns that, though collectively experienced as negative or undesirable, nonetheless tend tenaciously to persist or even spread.

However, alongside of this indubitable progression of the normcreating apparatuses and institutions, held together and sustained by the extension of the functions of protection, care, and assistance to the spheres of pedagogy, psychology, medicine, and social work, in general, there is another process equally patent, namely, the spread of an unprecedented solicitude and understanding of childhood, for example, an almost neurotic attention to the health and general well-being of the child on the part of the parents, or the erection of a wall of privacy between the family and the outside world, sometimes even opposing the former to the latter or viewing it as a *habitus* which, by encouraging the child to "make himself seen, and to demonstrate the uniqueness of his being," has brought about a significant change in the socializing climate: "notions of children's time replace notions of adult time; notions of a space for children replace adult space; facilitation replaces command, and accommodation replaces domination," as Bernstein fittingly put it (Bernstein, 1979, pp. 196, 200). These phenomena are above all evident in the middle and upper classes, but are spreading steadily into the less-advantaged classes through the mediation of preschool institutions of secondary socialization.

And so it is this *dual* dimension that defines the problem of childhood and socialization in modern society, and it is the *ambivalence* of the socializing activities of institutions encharged with this task that defines the peculiarity of the symbolic condition of childhood in present-day society. As Donati observed, "The dilemma that exists today in particularly acute form" is reflected in the fact that faced with the "need for security, which demands the elimination of the risks of childhood, more and more mechanisms of public control are forged; but at the same time these mechanisms obstruct the processes that give meaning to relations between children and adults, producing perverse effects that show up in the form of greater dependence, increased passivity, and the alienation of childhood itself" (Donati, 1981, pp. 118–119).

A refusal at least to consider the existence of this ambivalence, which punctuates the autonomy and the dependence of the condition of childhood, would be effectively to bar the way to an understanding of the reality of the phenomenon of socialization, in particular, and of social phenomena, in general.

STANDARDIZATION AND A POSSIBLE FUTURE

The problem thus shifts into another domain, and the question becomes that of assessing the ultimate direction of the tendencies at work, endeavoring to determine the net effect of the contingent settings of such dissimilar processes and events. The foregoing reflections seem in large measure to incline toward a somewhat pessimistic conclusion with regard to any real possibility of affirming a project of social change that would do justice to the needs of childhood for growth and self-expression, and, moreover, adequately defend the right to a full and rich existence. For instance, such an analysis would certainly call attention to a largely unopposed progression of events and interventions that are working together to further restrict the space in which normality is defined socially and symbolically, and hence at the same time to increase estrangement and aberrancy from an institutionalized image of conformity to established rules. The chain reaction that this situation could bring about has been described well by Moscovici; namely, an increment in social dependence and interpersonal pressure, a broadening of social control and uniformity, and thus a diminution in the trend toward autonomy and an increasing conformity (Moscovici, 1981, p. 35). If such a situation should prevail – and there is enough evidence to suggest that it will – there is hardly any doubt that the "liquidation of childhood" will turn out to be an accurate sociological prognosis rather than merely an effective literary metaphor.

However, the possibility of resisting the tendency toward the standardization and "normalization" of childhood as well as of other social categories presumes the availability of a "project," a coordinated strategy, worked out collectively, at the political, economic, social, and cultural levels. But to be effective, such a project, expressing a multitude of criteria for transforming and updating what already exists, must necessarily engage and guide collective feelings toward a realizable end, whereas at the same time avoiding succumbing to the defeatist illusion of impotence within a permanent and irreversible present, or the opposite illusion of a futile, theatrical, and fanciful utopia.

In this case as well, the substance of politics amounts to the conflict over realistically pursuable ends on the part of the group, yet at the same time over the areas where uncertainty with regard to the ways of achieving those ends is inevitable. But the choice is by no means between a reformist gradualism with its inherent risk of permitting existing errors to grow and multiply, and however, a sterile revolutionary illusion nourished by trivial, episodically appearing alternative experiences that do not always dispose over adequate consciousness and means for addressing the broader, more articulate needs of society as a whole.

To be effective, a project must be able to provide first and foremost a tentative critical clarification of the present social system: it must provide a general awareness of the illiberal, authoritarian, and antihuman results of the predominance, even at the symbolic level, of the logic of exchange, the rules of the market, productivity, and self-fulfillment within these relations as ends in themselves. Further, such a project should be able to provide a social proposal that counterposes to the symbolic inefficacy of the values related to childhood in the present society's ethical system, the affirmation of a different way of life that calls for production tailored to the needs of the whole person in place of the present system, which basically produces a subject as a social object.

But however important creativity and social imagination may be for the realization of such a project, we must also be aware that such a project never begins from zero, but must operate always within a framework of very limiting conditions, characterized by inertia and opposition. Offe once observed that in modern society the representation of general social interests, such as those presumably borne by the agencies responsible for childhood, possesses limited powers of organization since these interests are not "linked to well-definable groups of functions or statuses, are not capable of generating conflicts as they have no functional importance, or are unable to reject collectively or to threaten in any credible way to renounce a function essential for the system" (Offe, 1977, pp. 45–46). If, then, these interests do not have essential prerequisites for compelling the collectivity to recognize their needs, then clearly substantial doubts must be entertained concerning the realizability of a project that does not bear upon or implicate, across a broad front, the quality and organization of social life.

The real affirmation of the needs of childhood in this sense will always transcend the historical limits of the present social system. It manifests itself directly as a problem calling for a substantial change in an illimitable number of spheres and circumstances of collective life; and it is manifested as a radical conflict over the modes of social organization and the rules for governing society.

What is special about the question of childhood – as of many other social subjects and categories that exist in a state of dependence and social impotence and have neither the capacity nor legitimacy to impose rules or to oppose those that already exist – is precisely that it cannot be posed as a special problem. It is especially fitting in regard to this point to recall Barrington Moore's words in his *Reflections on the Causes of Human Misery*: "The inevitable hardships of one historical epoch can become deliberate cruelty if they are allowed to continue into the following epoch" (Moore, 1974)

REFERENCES

Ariès, P. (1968). *Padri e figli nell'Europa medievale e moderna (Italian Trans.)*. Bari: Laterza.

Ariès, P. (1979). Infanzia. In: *Enciclopedia* (Vol. 7, pp. 431–442). Turin: Einaudi.

Baudrillard, J. (1976). *La società dei consumi (Italian Trans.)*. Bologna: Il Mulino.

Bernstein, B. (1979). Classe e pedagogie: visibili e invisibili (Italian Trans.). In: B. Becchi (Ed.), *Il bambino sociale. Introduzione* (pp. 192–224). Milano: Feltrinelli.

Castel, R. (1980). *L'ordine psichiatrico (Italian Trans.)*. Milan: Feltrinelli.

Castel, R. (1982). *Verso una società relazionale (Italian Trans.)*. Milan: Feltrinelli.

Chamboredon, J.-C., & Prévot, J. (1979). Il mestiere di bambino. Verso una sociologia dello spontaneo (Italian Trans.). In: E. Becchi (Ed.), *Il bambino sociale. Introduzione* (pp. 150–191). Milano: Feltrinelli.

Degler, C. N. (1980). *At odds: Women and the family in America from the revolution to the present*. Oxford: Oxford University Press.

deMause, L. (Ed.) (1976). *The history of childhood*. London: Souvenir Press.

Donati, P. (1981). La politica dell'infanzia. In: P. Donati (Ed.), *Famiglia e politiche sociali* (pp. 83–127). Milano: Angeli.

Donzelot, J. (1977). *La police des familles*. Paris: Minuit.

Foucault, M. (1963). *Storia della follia (Italian Trans.)*. Milan: Rizzoli.

Foucault, M. (1969). *Nascita della clinica (Italian Trans.)*. Turin: Einaudi.

Foucault, M. (1976). *Sorvegliare e punire (Italian Trans.)*. Turin: Einaudi.

Foucault, M. (1977). *Microfisica del potere (Italian Trans.)*. Turin: Einaudi.

Habermas, J. (1971). *Storia e critica dell'opinione pubblica (Italian Trans.)*. Bari: Laterza.

Hengst, H. (1981). Tendezen der Liquidierung von Kindheit. In: H. Hengst, M. Koehler, B. Riedmueller & M. M. Wambach (Eds), *Kindheit als Fiktion* (pp. 11–72). Frankfurt: Suhrkamp.

Köhler, M. (1981). Unterhaltung als Botschaft und Kauf als Erfahrung: Die Equipierung der Kindheit. In: H. Hengst, M. Koehler, B. Riedmueller & M. M. Wambach (Eds), *Kindheit als Fiktion* (pp. 93–131). Frankfurt: Suhrkamp.

Lapassade, G. (1971). *Il mito dell'adulto (Italian Trans.)*. Bologna: Guaraldi.

Lasch, C. (1977). *Haven in a heartless world*. New York: Basic Books.

Lasch, C. (1981). *La cultura dcl narcisismo (Italian Trans.)*. Milan: Bompiani.

Livolsi, M., De Lillo, A., & Schizzerotto, A. (1980). *Bambini non si nasce. Una ricerca sulla condizione infantile*. Milan: Angeli.

McKnight, J. (1977). Professionalized service and disabling help. In: I. Illich, I. K. Zola, J. McKnight, J. Caplan & H. Shaiken (Eds), *Disabling professions*. London: Boyards.

Moore, B. (1974). *Reflections on the causes of human misery (Italian Trans.)*. Milan: Comunità.

Moscovici, S. (1981). *Psicologia della minoranze attive (Italian Trans.)*. Turin: Boringhieri.

Offe, C. (1977). *La stato nel capitalismo maturo (Italian Trans.)*. Milan: Etas.

Pancera, C. (1979). L'infanzia laboriosa. Il rapporto mastro-apprendista. In: E. Becchi (Ed.), *Il bambino sociale, Introduzione* (pp. 77–113). Milano: Feltrinelli.

Riedmüller, B. (1981). Hilfe, Schutz und Kontrolle. Zur Verrechtlichung der Kindheit. In: H. Hengst, M. Koehler, B. Riedmueller & M. M. Wambach (Eds), *Kindheit als Fiktion* (pp. 132–190). Frankfurt: Suhrkamp.

Rutschky, K. (Ed.) (1977). *Schwarze Paedagogik. Quellen zur Naturgeschichte der bürgerlichen Erziehung*. Frankfurt: Suhrkamp.

Shorter, E. (1978). *Famiglia e civiltà (Italian Trans.)*. Milan: Rizzoli.

Stone, L. (1983). *Famiglia, sesso e matrimonio in Inghilterra tra Cinquecento e Ottocento (Italian Trans.)* (English version 1977: The family, sex and marriage in England 1500–1800. Abridged and revised edition. Harmondsworth: Penguin). Turin: Einaudi.

Wambach, M. M. (1981). Kinder als Gefahr und Risiko. Zur Therapeutisierung von Kindheit. In: H. Hengst, M. Koehler, B. Riedmueller & M. M. Wambach (Eds), *Kindheit als Fiktion* (pp. 191–241). Frankfurt: Suhrkamp.